THE GRID OF THE GODS

The Aftermath of the Cosmic War and the Physics of the Pyramid Peoples

Other Books by Joseph P. Farrell:

LBJ and the Conspiracy to Kill Kennedy
Roswell and the Reich
Nazi International
Reich of the Black Sun
The S.S. Brotherhood of the Bell
Secrets of the Unified Field
The Cosmic War
The Giza Death Star
The Giza Death Star Deployed
The Giza Death Star Destroyed

THE GRID
OF THE
GODS

**Joseph P. Farrell
with Scott D. de Hart**

Adventures Unlimited Press

The Grid of the Gods

Copyright 2011
by Joseph P. Farrell and Scott D. de Hart

ISBN: 978-1-935487-39-5

Published by:
Adventures Unlimited Press
One Adventure Place
Kempton, Illinois 60946 USA
auphq@frontiernet.net

www.adventuresunlimitedpress.com

Cover by Joe Boyer

10 9 8 7 6 5 4 3

Above all, to
Scott Douglas de Hart:
A true master, adept, and poet of deep mysteries, who crossed the Rubicon with me:
Anything I could say, any gratitude I could express, are simply inadequate for you;

You are a true

Thank you seems so completely inadequate.

To George Ann Hughes:
Dear and good friend:
You are a constant encouragement; thank you, but again, it seems so inadequate.

And to
Tracy S. Fisher:
You are, and will always be, sorely missed;

"This is meant to be only an essay. It is a first reconnaissance of a realm well-nigh unexplored and uncharted. From whichever way one enters it, one is caught in the same bewildering circular complexity, as in a labyrinth, for it has no deductive order in the abstract sense, but instead, resembles an organism tightly closed in itself, or even better, a monumental 'Art of the Fugue.'"
Giorgio de Santillana and Hertha von Dechend,
Hamlet's Mill: An Essay on Myth and the Frame of Time, p. 1.

"...we are speaking about an intelligent geometric pattern into which, theoretically, the Earth and its energies are organized – and possibly in which the ubiquitous ancient megalithic sites are also positioned."
David Hatcher Childress,
Anti-Gravity and the World Grid, p. 5.

"Thus, while the mute creation downward bend
Their sight, and to their earthly mother tend,
Man looks aloft; and with erected eyes
Beholds his own hereditary skies."
Ovid,
Metamorphoses, Book I,
trans. John Dryden, Alexander Pope, Joseph Addison, William Congreve, et al., p. 6.

TABLE OF CONTENTS

ACKNOWLEDGEMENTS

It would be impossible for me to thank all the people who have made this book possible, for it would include the many readers who have so graciously contributed donations to my website, donations that made the assembly of much of the research presented herein possible. Without them, this book simply would not exist. To them, I can only say an inadequate "thank you," with the hope that they know it is accompanied by heartfelt prayers and good wishes for them, in every thing and circumstance.

I also owe thanks to my publisher, David Hatcher Childress, for taking a chance on this book – sight unseen! – and for so generously affording me the advance and the time to do it. Indeed, without his own personal explorations and publications on the mysteries of ancient technology and the world grid, this book – again – would not have seen the light of day.

Thanks must also go to my friend, Richard C. Hoagland, who many years ago shared his knowledge of one source utilized herein – H.S.M. Coxeter's *Regular Polytopes* – in a lecture given at the United Nations. Without his willingness to share and discuss ideas others deem to be taboo, again, this book would not have seen the light of day.

But always and above all, my deepest gratitude goes to my co-author on this book, my friend and brother of so many, many years, Dr. Scott D. de Hart, in deep thanks for all the years of many stimulating conversations, many of whose contents and subjects of discussion are reflected here, and for his undying friendship and persistent and consistent brotherhood and encouragement:

Thank you, thrice over, my friend.

Joseph P. Farrell
2011

FOREWORD

BY

SCOTT D. DE HART, PH.D.

Why are we here? How did we get here? Who put us here? These questions have occupied the minds of the greatest philosophers and theologians through the ages, but they have also echoed in the minds of the most simple man or woman born. One can safely arrive at the conclusion that if the answer had ever been infallibly set forward, the question would cease to be asked. Surely, it is not that answers have not been produced, nor that some of the answers did not attract commanding audiences, but the question remains because each person born must ask the question again and find an answer that is personally acceptable. According to the sixteenth century French Reformer, John Calvin, "our wisdom, in so far as it ought to be deemed true and solid wisdom, consists almost entirely of two parts: the knowledge of God and of ourselves."[1] Consequently, if it is a personal knowledge that is to be deemed true knowledge, (or at least a fraction of true knowledge) the question will be asked over and over with the birth of each person. But where is one to turn for an answer?

It might be thought absurd to suggest that a finite being can ever reach an infallible answer concerning a question of this magnitude but this barrier of human limitation has never hindered the best efforts of men to strive for it. The most apparent relic from this search for an answer is found in religious practice and belief. These two giants stand as twin pillars in a temple of wisdom erected by previous generations of *knowers*. They have a voice, a message – it is not breathing though it is living and memorialized in stone, symbols, writings, and perpetually acted out within the sacred temples scattered across the earth.

This urge to *know* has long been associated with pilgrimages to sacred sites, the study of sacred texts, meditation or prayer in the hallowed space. Such a pilgrimage is exactly what led me to Chichen Itza, a Mayan ruin in the Yucatan Peninsula. On a dark and rainy day I stood in the shadow of that pyramid and literally felt a pulse of the universe passing through my body, an eerie and foreboding energy

---

[1] John Calvin, *Institutes of the Christian Religion*, Book 1, Chapter 1.

i

flooded over me as I beheld the serpents and skulls staring at me, judging me, calling me to acknowledge their presence. Within the Great Ball Court with its circular stones and the winding serpent tails surrounding it, I heard my own voice echoing across the open field, a mingling of voices from the past making a haunting chorus and opening up a portal that is difficult to describe. My inability to put this experience into words is the purpose of this book by Dr. Farrell.

What is the Temple but an earthly copy of a higher idea? What is the ritual of that temple but the best human effort to cross over, to unite, consummate, die, and be reborn? It is the story told in the arrangement of the furniture; the placement of the altar; the ascent of the steps; even the very geographic and directional positioning. Heavenly alignments are mirrored on earth and ritualistically carried out by those who inherited fragments of the answers to those eternally nagging questions. Could there have been "architects of the gods"? Is it possible that the placement, patterns, symbols and rituals, are not earthly constructions but rather sacred *re-constructions* that unlock the door that mankind has been knocking at for thousands and thousands of years? Is it also possible that a tradition exists of those *"in the know"* who built, symbolized, ritualized, and initiated chosen disciples to carry on the message and pass along the sacred inheritance? The answer presented herein is a resounding yes! What happens on earth is not necessarily earthly and the rituals of times past or present are more than re-enactments, they are portals to understanding.

This book is not about experience, *per se*, but through carefully documented research and detailed scholarly analysis, it will provide answers for the pilgrim and the student alike, and will raise new questions. For those familiar with Joseph Farrell's previous works, this volume fits in as one more piece in an intricate puzzle that few would be capable of writing. His background in history, theology, physics, mathematics, classical music theory, and ancient languages, tested in the cauldron of the oldest English speaking university in the world (the University of Oxford) is a resume par excellence for such a work, but it is his intuitive sense of science and spirituality that sets this volume apart as a must read.

Scott D. de Hart, Ph.D.
2011

INTRODUCTION

"There is beauty, simplicity and power in this early technology and modern enthusiasts have mistaken the knowledge and sensitivity to natural forces intrinsic to this technology as indicative of a positive force at work."
Michael A. Hoffman II[1]

A. A Curious Activity

Modern science is but a technique of the imagination to bring into reality the operations of the magical intellect and the mythologies of the ancients, with consistent and predictable regularity. This implies, therefore, that the magical intellect encountered so often in ancient texts, myths, and monuments is, in fact, the product of a decayed science, but a science nonetheless. Much of modern physics may be viewed as but Hermetic metaphysics with "topological" equations,[2] and by a similar process of examination, much of modern genetics may be viewed as but the myths of Sumer, Babylon, and even the Mayans, given flesh by the techniques of genetic engineering.[3]

That said, this book is a mirror image of *The Philosophers' Stone: Alchemy and the Secret Research for Exotic Matter*, in that the previous book began with an excursion through *ancient* and mediaeval alchemy in order to remain focused on a trinity of *modern* pursuits for an "alchemical physics." In this book, we begin with yet another alchemical trinity in *modern* times, in order to pry open the mysteries and secrets of an agenda and activity of two surviving post-Cosmic War elites in *ancient* times: the building of enormous temples, structures, and pyramids, all precisely located at various points all over the Earth's surface, and in many different cultures. The question is *why*? Why did they do this? What is the real explanation? And why are so many of these structures either *pyramids* of one form or another, or great circles of massive stones?

---

[1] Michael A. Hoffmann II, *Secret Societies and Psychological Warfare* (Coeur D'Alene, Idaho: Independent History and Research, 2001), p. 21.

[2] See my *The Giza Death Star Destroyed* (Adventures Unlimited Press, 2005), pp. 222-245, and my *The Philosophers' Stone* (Feral House, 2009), pp. 42-48.

[3] See my *Genes, Giants, Monsters, and Men* (Feral House, 2011), ch. 3.

The real explanation, as this book will argue, is that this activity constitutes the coordinated effort of those post-Cosmic War elites, and that the ultimate purpose lies in the preservation *and eventual recovery* of a physics and a worldview that would otherwise have been lost without such memorialization in these monuments. This book accordingly lives in that strange world where a hidden physics interfaces with human history and with human myths, and where each conceptual substance within this disciplinary trinity illuminates the other in a kind of esoteric circumincession.

For that reason this book is inherently and unavoidably technical and speculative. The reader is thrown, at the outset in chapter one, into the deep end of a very technical discussion that opens the door to some of the activities of these post-Cosmic War elites and their modern heirs, and to the deep physics upon which they were based. Fortunately, the technicality diminishes rather quickly once the point of illuminating history is revealed! So for the less-technically inclined reader, he is encouraged to bear patiently through the technical details, for oftentimes the physics and history devil can only be made completely clear by details that seemingly have nothing to do with the subject of this book, and this is particularly true in the first chapter.

In any case, it is, by anyone's lights, a *peculiar* activity: the placement of certain types of megalithic monuments at certain places on the surface of the earth, an activity that upon close examination transcends the cultures to whom such activities are normally attributed. It is perforce an activity that also required enormous effort and expenditure of human labor and treasure, and, as will be seen, in some cases also implies the use of some rather extraordinary technology.

The transcendence of this activity across times and disparate cultures thus only emphasizes its peculiar nature. Like it or not, we are in the presence of a unified religio-scientific "sub-culture" propping up the more tangible cultures that allegedly produced these structures. This implies a measure of coordination and contact, of unified purpose and activity, that transcended these cultures, and points to the hidden problems with the modern academic assumptions of diffusionism and the evolution of civilizations.

It is one thing to maintain, for example, that certain sites in Great Britain — Stonehenge, Silbury Hill, the Avebury circles, the Rollright circle of Oxfordshire, and so on — are situated according to a discernible and definite pattern or grid upon the topography of that country. But it is quite another thing when that activity is also being done by Mesoamerican Mayans, or South American "Incas," or ancient Egyptians, or primitive Teutons, or Modern Freemasons laying out Washington, D.C. or Chinese geomancers following the precepts of *feng shui* and at virtually all times in their history. The activity spans all times and transcends cultures, and yet, it is being done according to the same basic principles, and it all appears to have been done according to a "grid" pattern of amazing complexity and global extent. Any attempt at plumbing the depths of the entire phenomenon is therefore beyond the capabilities of any one researcher, or any one book.

It is nonetheless the commonality of activity across so many cultures, over such a long span of time, which begs for explanation. And standard academic theories, here as elsewhere, fall short, because this common activity itself reflects a common purpose, a purpose transcending times and cultures, and pointing to hidden players, to the activities of hidden elites, guiding the constructions for their own purposes, purposes that can only be discovered by noting *where* such structures are located, by noting *what* the structures are, by noting the mythological traditions about them and the cultures that built them, and by taking into consideration the modern measurements of these sites and structures. As will be discovered, part of the motivation for such a vast undertaking is clearly alchemical.

However, this activity is but one activity — albeit a major, if not *the* major, one — of those post-Cosmic War elites. Accordingly, it will perhaps be helpful to the reader to review here the model I have assumed concerning these elites, and their *other* post-Cosmic War activities.

B. *The Wider Context of the Activity*

I assume, in the first instance, that there were essentially *two* surviving elites from that very ancient interplanetary warfare that I call "The Cosmic War," a "good" elite, wishing to restore to humanity in its entirety the benefits of the civilization destroyed in that War, a long and arduous process. There was also a "bad" elite, wishing to restore all the technological instruments of its own hegemony, and essentially to enslave the rest of mankind by means of them, perhaps for the purposes of once again marching out into space in an orgy of conquest.[4]

In any case, these two elites, like the surviving Nazi and Anglo-American elites after World War Two, were thrust together in an uneasy post-war detente, for mutual cooperation was essential if either were to survive.[5] Due to this circumstance, when examining the traces of the putative activities of these elites in ancient times, it more often than not is difficult to determine which group is most active in a given region, if one considers only textual evidence, but as will be seen in this book, there is one profound clue that emerges from a consideration of the Gird: human sacrifice.

In the second place within this model I assume that both elites understood the very-long term nature of their goals and commitments, and thus set into place structures and institutions to ensure their survival and activities over a prolonged period of time. I thus assume that they *endured* throughout the millennia down to our own times. It is these two elites which are, in my opinion, the origin within esoteric and occult tradition of the idea of two "brotherhoods" and two paths: (1) the "white" brotherhood, emphasizing the right-hand path of love, peace, harmony, "white magic," virtue, and tolerance, and (2) the "black" brotherhood, pursuing the left-hand path of violence, chaos, "black magic," social engineering, and the "occult" in the standard sense, inclusive of blood sacrifices as we shall discover.

Concomitant with this model is the implication that both elites know that at some point in history this detente is destined to break down, and open struggle between them will resume. While this book is not the place to pursue *that* discussion, I believe that there are distinctive signs in the last ten to twenty years that this is taking place.

In this light then, a view of some of their other post-Cosmic War activities is in order, with a view to place the grid-building activity that is the subject of *this* book into its proper and wider context. In

---

[4] These ideas constitute some of the major themes of my books *The Giza Death Star Destroyed* and *Babylon's Banksters.*

[5] See my *Babylon's Banksters: The Alchemy of Deep Physics, High Finance, and Ancient Religion* (Port Townsend, Washington: Feral House, 2010), chapter 1.

previous works, I have outlined and explored three other interrelated activities of these elites:

1) In the aftermath of such a devastating Cosmic War, if there was to be a revival of a genuinely global civilization, there had to be a revival of commerce, carried out at great distances and between the emerging cultures of the Earth. This could only be facilitated by an accurate system of weights and measures capable of reproduction anywhere on Earth. This in turn could only be achieved via the relatively stable measures provided by geodetic and astronomical measurement itself. Thus, the first task of these elites was to establish the methods for acquiring such measures and then to propagate them as widely and quickly as possible;[6]

2) Crucial to the re-creation of a genuinely global civilization was the restoration of social cohesion. Here there were two problems faced by the post-Cosmic War elites:

   a) In the aftermath of the war, their population was most likely devastated and depleted. It was accordingly necessary to expand the population base as quickly as possible and to create a work-force capable of carrying out the necessary projects and constructions. It is here, I believe, that we have a partial rationalization for the genetic engineering experiments and indications within ancient Mesopotamian (and Mayan!) texts that modern humanity is a chimerical engineered creation, part "god" and partly whatever pre-existent "hominid" as was available. Those texts make it clear that mankind was created precisely as a worker-serf for the "gods," a *slave*. The difficulty was, these new creations had too much of the "gods" in them, and thought too independently. Some method of cohesion was therefore necessary to maintain order;

   b) At this juncture I have suggested that one mechanism and technique for the engineering of social cohesion was the

---

[6] See my *Genes, Giants, Monsters, and Men: The Surviving Elites of the Cosmic War and Their Hidden Agendas* (Port Townsend, Washington: Feral House, 2011), chapter 2.

introduction of religion, and in particular, monotheistic religion requiring absolute unquestioning obedience.[7] This certainly has profound implications for standard religious apologetics, and it is best to allow professional theologians and apologists to deal with them, but nonetheless, it is a clear implication of this type of reading of ancient texts. Religion, on this view, becomes the principal technique of social engineering, and, read a certain way, parallels the institutionalized terrorism of the great revolutions in modern times, demanding unquestioned obedience to theocratic authority on pain of death. While I have not pursued extensive commentary on the subject, I have also suggested as well that the institution of human sacrifice was a component not only of this program, but also a kind of "collateralization" of humanity to certain types of monetary policy that began to emerge in ancient times, and that this in some cases was a component of social engineering via religion.[8] As we shall see here in this book, however, there is yet another reason for such brutal practices, and that lies within certain conceptions the ancients held of the physical medium itself. In other words, some aspects of religious social engineering arises out of the nature of the physics itself;

3) The most telltale sign, I believe, of the activities and orientations of these two post-war elites arises in connection with ancient monetary policy and financial structures. If the goal was to jump start civilization as quickly as possible, not only was commerce necessary, and therewith an accurate and reproducible system of geodetically-based weights and measures, but a medium of exchange was also necessary to facilitate it. Here as in modern times, two philosophies of money arose, each backed by their respective elite:

a) Money was a receipt on the surplus goods and services, that is to say, on the gross domestic product, of the state

---

[7] See my *Genes, Giants, Monsters, and Men*, (Feral House, 2011), chapter 3.

[8] See my interview on The Byte Show: "The Philosophers' Stone and the Magic of Social Engineering, Part 4." www.thebyteshow.com.

itself, and thus was issued by the state debt-free as an instrument of exchange. In my opinion, this activity and philosophy represented the policies of the "good" elite, seeking to democratize the benefits of civilization as widely and quickly as possible. It is a policy mirror in some cases — as we shall see — by a peculiar attitude of some of the "gods" to the idea of sacrifice;

b) Money was monetized debt, i.e., an instrument of exchange *loaned* into circulation at interest by private monopolies, thus creating a closed economic system where there is never enough "money" in circulation to pay the interest on the principle. This creates scarcity, and led to the most useful tool of social engineering and private profiteering: war. In my opinion, this financial policy and activity reflects the interests and agenda of the "bad" elite,[9] for as will also be seen, the notion of blood sacrifices and debt are also deeply entangled.

In my opinion, it is against this wider context that the grid-building activity should be viewed.

C. The Chronological Context and Layers

But there is another context in which it must be viewed, and that has already been implied: the chronological one.

If one examines the various megalithic and pyramidal sites across the globe, one is immediately struck by a curious fact: the more *ancient* the structure — such as the Great Pyramid, or the remains at Lake Tiahuanaco and Puma Punkhu in Bolivia — the more highly engineered, and the more obvious a product of a sophisticated engineering technology, it is. As one moves forward in history closer to present times, the less skilful these structures become. Thus, situating these structures within time and cultures is very difficult, because this phenomenon raises difficult questions for standard academic theories and histories: did the ancient Egyptians *really* build the Great Pyramid? And did they *really* achieve its near perfect alignments and optical precision using ramps, logs, scaffolds, pulleys

---

[9] See my *Babylon's Banksters*, pp. 187-207.

and thousands of slaves? Did the ancient Incas *really* build the remains in Latin America attributed to them, walls with gigantic granite rocks with irregular cuts placed so precisely, and without mortar, that a sheet of paper cannot be slipped into the joints? (And again, did they do this with ropes, logs, pulleys, and copper saws?) Did the Olmecs and Mayans *really* have a role in the construction of Teotihuacan in Mexico? We are fairly certain they had a role in the construction of places such as Chichen Itza or Tikal, but Teotihuacan? But if it was not them, then who did?

A closer look at these chronological layers is even more revealing of the complexity of these questions, and is, additionally, necessary, for these layers will form the basic organizational model and methodology of this essay, as we push our way back from modern times to increasingly more ancient ones.

For purposes of this book, I distinguish between three broad layers of development:

1) The oldest layer, which I term "megalithic" in a very broad sense, meaning structures and sites and pre-date the rise of the ancient classical civilizations of Egypt, Sumer, the Indus Valley, and so on. Here we are dealing with sites of great antiquity, older than 7,000 BC. For our purposes here, this means that sites such as Pumu Punkhu at Lake Titicaca in Bolivia, some of the megalithic stone circles in Britain, continental Europe, and Egypt, including the Sphinx, temples, and the two great Pyramids of Giza, are understood to be older than the civilizations that eventually came to occupy these sites. The reasons for this view will be advanced in the main text;

2) the classical layer, where structures — such as the other Egyptian pyramids, or the Mayan pyramids of Mesoamerica — are the products of the civilizations themselves; and,

3) a modern era, where sites are situated according to older grid locations, an activity clearly evident in the Middle Ages with

the placement of Christian churches on or near older pagan "sacred sites".[10]

This broad classification is not, of course, a hard and fast rule, for as we shall see, considerable mystery surrounds some of the sites and just who really built them, such as Teotihuacan outside of Mexico City.

D. *The Activity of the Elite and the Meaning of the Term "Grid" in this Work*

One need only glance at these chronological layers and at certain ancient texts — and to take those texts seriously — to see the activity of these elites at work behind the scenes, manipulating social policy and culture at the minimum, and, as we shall discover, attempting to manipulate the physical medium itself by means of their surviving technologies and techniques.

The activity may be glimpsed at the following account from the Aztec *Codex Chimalpopoca:*

> Well, it is told and related that many times during the life of Queztlcoatl, *sorcerers tried to ridicule him into making the human payment, into taking human lives.* But he always refused. He did not consent, because he greatly loved his subjects, who were Toltecs. Snakes, birds, and butterflies that he killed were what his sacrifices always were.
>
> And it is told and related that with this he wore out the sorcerers' patience. So it was then that they started to ridicule him and make fun of him, *the sorcerers saying they wanted to torment Quetzlcoatl and make him run away.*
>
> And it became true. It happened.
>
> ....
>
> Then they tell how Quetzlcoatl departed. It was when he refused to obey the sorcerers about making the human payment, about sacrificing humans. Then the sorcerers deliberated among

---

[10] This tripartite classification of basic chronological periods of building activity in ancient times is that of Alan Alford. See my *The Giza Death Star Deployed* (Adventures Unlimited Press, 2003), pp. 25-36.

themselves, they whose names were Tezatlipoca, Ihuimecatl, and Toltecatl. They said, "*He must leave his city. We shall live there.*"[11]

Leaving commentary on the relationship between human sacrifice and the physics of the pyramid peoples to the main text, note what we have in this passage:

1) A "god-king," in this case Quetzlcoatl, who refuses to institute a certain policy demanded by
2) an "elite," in this case, "sorcerers," who then determine to
3) depose the king and drive him from the capital, and take possession of it and of the symbols of authority in order to institute its social policy.

In other words, taken at face value, the "god-king" Quetzlcoatl represents the public face of a more hidden elite, and when the policies of the two come into conflict, he must be deposed. Notably, this suggests that Quetzlcoatl represents one elite, the "white" brotherhood, while the "sorcerers" represent the other. Were it just the Aztecs saying such things, one could perhaps summarily dismiss them, save for the fact that one encounters very similar ideas in Egypt at various points in its mythology and history, and in the Mayan legends, and even in a famous mediaeval Christian theologian, as we shall discover in the main text.

A final word is necessary on what the term "grid" means in the pages that now follow, though again, we shall defer detailed commentary on these points to the main text. The "grid," as we shall eventually discover, embodies at least three distinct types of numerical encoding:

1) A "grid" based on latitude and longitude positions of ancient sites, using as a prime meridian the line running from the north to the south pole through the apex of the Great Pyramid at Giza;

---

[11] John Bierhorst, trans. and ed., *History and Mythology of the Aztecs: The Codex Chimalpopoca* (Tuscon: The University of Arizona Press, 1992), p. 31, emphasis added.

2) Within many if not most of these structure, there is present another "grid" of encoding the numbers of "sacred geometry," a science that has persisted in the designs of cities and public places down to our own times, as exemplified in the layout of Washington D.C., and other cities;[12] and,

3) A final "grid" directly encoding a *physics* that incorporates two distinct aspects:

   a) An astronomical-astrological "celestial grid" encoding the physics of the very large, according to the alchemical and hermetic axiom "as above, so below;" and,

   b) a much less-well-known encoding, within certain megalithic structures, of the actual coefficients of the constants of quantum mechanics, encoding the physics of the very small.

This book is thus very different than previous books on the world grid system, which tend to focus on only one of these three aspects (and as we shall see, only two of them focused on the last aspect concerning quantum mechanics). This book will attempt to integrate all three forms of the grid and the structures upon them, and where possible, the myths and legends of the cultures surrounding them, in order to argue speculative possibilities on what all this means about the physics of the pyramid peoples and the activities of the elites that created them.

With this in mind, I also mean the term "pyramid peoples" to be taken rather loosely and broadly, for while pyramid building was a major activity of these post-Cosmic War elites, it is not their only building activity, as the inclusion of Pumu Punkhu and other sites mentioned in this study would suggest. The term simply designates the building activities of all those peoples associated with these sites, activity that including pyramid building to be sure, but also the construction of numerous Stonehenge-like structures and other megalithic constructions.

---

[12] While this book will not go into any detailed discussion of the modern principles of this alchemical geomancy and architecture, particularly in the case of Washington, D.C., it is worth noting that there have been studies of these subjects, most notably David Ovason's *The Secret Architecture of Our Nation's Capital* (Perennial Books, 2000).

A final word is necessary. This book is to be understood as yet another essay standing in the series of books that began in *The Cosmic War: Interplanetary Warfare, Modern Physics, and Ancient Texts,* continuing through *The Philosophers' Stone: Alchemy and the Secret Research for Exotic Matter, Babylon's Banksters: the Alchemy of High Finance, Deep Physics, and Ancient Religions,* and *Genes, Giants, Monsters and Men: The Surviving Elites of the Cosmic War and Their Hidden Agendas.*

Like all my books on ancient topics, this is a highly speculative work, though I do my best to argue the case put forward here, namely, that when one considers the three various kinds of encodings taking place in these structures, a complex and very advanced physics comes into view, and with it, the likelihood that one is dealing with the elites that were legacies of a Very High and "paleoancient" Civilization. Nonetheless, it remains a speculative case.

Joseph P. Farrell
2011

PART ONE:
THEURGY, GEOMANCY, ALCHEMY, GOVERNMENTS, AND THE GRID

"Meanwhile in the 20th century, because of numerous aircraft crashes in the Lake Ontario Earth Grid area... the Canadian national Research Council and U.S. Navy began Project Magnet *in 1950 to investigate the area's magnetic anomalies and possible magnetic utility. This has been the **only known official governmental** research program into the Earth Grid system."*
Richard Lefors Clark, PhD.
Diamagnetic Gravity Vortexes, cited in
Anti-Gravity and The World Grid, pp. 53-54.

(...and that, strictly speaking, isn't *exactly* true.)

1

THERMONUCLEAR THEURGY:
OR, A FUNNY THING HAPPENED AT GROUND ZERO

*"In the case of time, **there also exists a variable property which can be called the density of intensity of time.** In a case of low density it is difficult for time to influence the material systems, and there is required an intensive emphasis of the causal-resultant relationship in order that the force caused by the time pattern would appear."*
Dr Nikolai Kozyrev[1]

Their names were "Mike," "Shrimp," and "Runt." They were a true alchemical trinity — genuine alchemical works — for when each was fired, for a brief moment, all the elements of the universe were recapitulated in a starburst. "Mike" was the world's first "thermonuclear device," a reassuring euphemism for the world's first hydrogen bomb, for "Mike" was, for all intents and purposes, an artificial man-made sun, the fire of the ancient star-gods brought down to earth by an act of thermonuclear theurgy. "Mike" was a star that for a brief and terrifying moment would fire and light up the sky, outshining the sun itself, until he consumed himself and his fuel in a deafening roar of destruction, rising as a pillar of fire and smoke into the stratosphere. Every precaution had therefore been taken; calculations of his yield were checked and re-checked. Calm statements from Pentagon leaders reassured the American people, and indeed, the world population, that "Mike" would not ignite the hydrogen in the atmosphere and turn the entire planet into a funeral pyre. Newsreels of calm, confident pipe-smoking military men were prepared to announce to the world that mankind had entered a new age, the "thermonuclear" age, an age that made the short-lived "atomic" age seem a mere kindergarten by comparison. "Shrimp" and "Runt" were also "devices," only in this case the euphemism was for actual deliverable weapons, but we'll get back to them. First, we must deal with "Mike."

---

[1] Dr Nikolai Kozyrev, "Possibility of the Experimental Study of the Properties of Time," www.abyme.net, pp. 10-11, emphasis in the original.

Behind the scenes, the military was not, of course, being entirely truthful, and in that deception was bound all the insanity of the "thermonuclear age". The committee that had overseen "Mike's" development, the Panda committee, had "estimated that the Mike device would yield one to ten megatons, with the remote possibility that it might go as high as fifty to ninety megatons. The likeliest yield estimated was five megatons, the equivalent of ten billion pounds of TNT."[2] Of course, a certain amount of latitude should perhaps be accorded this wild margin of error; after all, mankind was firing his first "thermonuclear device" and no one knew for certain how well and efficiently it would work, or even if it *would* work, until it was actually detonated.

Those estimates should nevertheless give one pause, for the military was throwing the thermonuclear dice. There is a great deal of difference between an explosion of one megaton, or a "mere" two billion pounds of TNT, and one of ten megatons — twenty billion pounds of TNT — not to mention the "outside" possibility of *ninety* megatons which would amount to a whopping *one hundred and eighty billion pounds* of TNT. The point is an important one, for the military would, of course, station observation ships and aircraft around the test site in the Pacific to monitor and witness the test; how far away from the "event" would they have to be stationed? How many local natives would have to be evacuated from their homes? And to what distance? The military decided on the likeliest yield — five megatons — and stationed the observation ships and aircraft, and evacuated the natives, accordingly.

The reason for this decision lay in "Mike's" design itself.

A. The Design of "Mike" and the Actual Test: The First "Woops!"

"Mike," like most hydrogen bombs ever since, was a "staged device," that is, it was actually three bombs in one: (1) a standard "atom splitting" or fission bomb which was used to ignite (2) the second stage of the actual "atom fusion" reaction, not *splitting* atoms *apart*, but actually fusing them *together*, and (3) a third stage, another fission bomb to boost the yield even more. It is important to

---

[2] Richard Rhodes, *Dark Sun: The Making of the Hydrogen Bomb* (New York: Touchstone, Simon and Schuster, 1996), pp. 493-494.

understand that the first two stages are *essential* to a working hydrogen bomb, as the atom bomb is required as the "fuse" to achieve the enormous heat and pressures required to fuse atoms together. Thus, *all* hydrogen bombs are "staged devices" possessing at least the first two stages, the fission bomb (stage one) that sets off the fusion bomb (stage two), and most hydrogen bombs are three staged fission-fusion-fission bombs simply as a matter of efficiency, since the third stage provides the extra "kick" to make the reaction burn efficiently and to boost the yield of such devices.

"Mike" was part of a two-test series codenamed "Ivy," with the second shot being the test of a pure but high yield uranium atom bomb codenamed "King" with an expected yield from four to six hundred kilotons.[3] The second test was thought to be necessary in case the "Mike" test, for whatever reason, failed. The design of "Mike" was simplicity itself.

Imagine a long cylinder several feet tall, as shown in the following photograph of the actual "Mike" device. Note the man sitting in the lower right of the picture for a comparison of scale.

Photo of the "Mike" Device During Construction. The Actual Device is the vertical cylindrical structure on the left. The horizontal pipes leading from the device to the right are the pipes for measuring radiation emissions that would allow scientists and engineers to determine if each stage fired, and if so, how efficient the reaction was.

---

[3] Richard Rhodes, *Dark Sun*, p. 487.

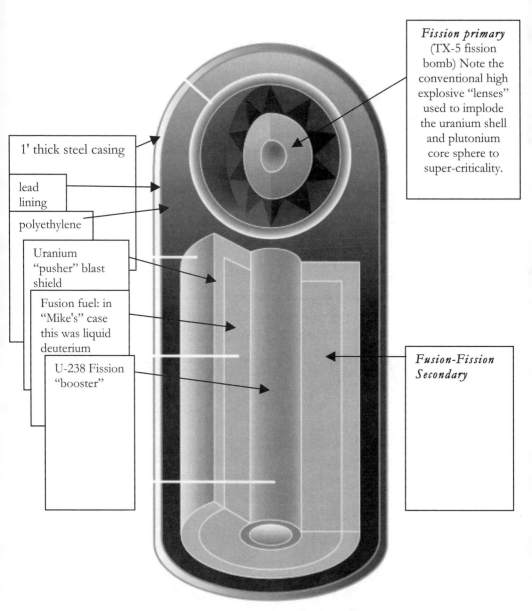

Fission primary
(TX-5 fission bomb) Note the conventional high explosive "lenses" used to implode the uranium shell and plutonium core sphere to super-criticality.

1' thick steel casing

lead lining

polyethylene

Uranium "pusher" blast shield

Fusion fuel: in "Mike's" case this was liquid deuterium

U-238 Fission "booster"

Fusion-Fission Secondary

Simplified Schematic of a Three Stage Fission-Fusion-Fission Hydrogen Bomb first tested in the "Mike"

In order to understand this simple schematic of a hydrogen bomb, we will go through each of the steps of how this device actually functioned when "Mike" was fired, describing what happened in the witch's brew of the thermonuclear mechanics of the device. The essential thing to understand about hydrogen bombs is that the fusion reaction itself is triggered by the use of *radiation itself* to drive a massive shockwave inwards around the secondary core containing the fusion fuel — in this case cryogenically cooled liquid deuterium[4] — literally squeezing and compressing it to fusion temperatures and pressures.

This reveals the secret of the design on the facing page, for scientists very early recognized that the pressure of soft X-rays generated by the explosion of the primary atom bomb would not be sufficient to achieve the needed pressures to do this.[5] So "Mike's" designers first decided to surround the entire device with a foot of steel casing, which would act as a reflector for the radiation for just the briefest fraction of a second. In addition to this, they lined the inside of this thick steel casing with a liner of lead, over which was layered a further lining of polyethylene plastic. This polyethylene, in the instant of the detonation of the primary atom bomb initiating the whole process, would act as a plasma generator since its atoms would be instantly turned into an ionized gas.

So, while referring to the diagram on the facing page, let us now describe what happened when "Mike" was fired, and how the design of the device itself engineered a sequence of events that all occurred within a few millionths of a second:

1) 92 detonators[6] around the "high explosive lenses" surrounding the spherical fission fuel (uranium-235 and plutonium-239) represented as a ball at the top of the diagram on the left, of the primary atom bomb are fired;

---

[4] Deuterium is simply the most common heavy isotope of ordinary hydrogen, with an extra neutron in the nucleus. Ordinary hydrogen's nucleus contains only one proton. Tritium, the next most abundant heavy isotope of hydrogen, has two neutrons in the nucleus, in addition to the proton.

[5] Richard Rhodes, *Dark Sun*, p. 492.

[6] Ibid., p. 505.

5

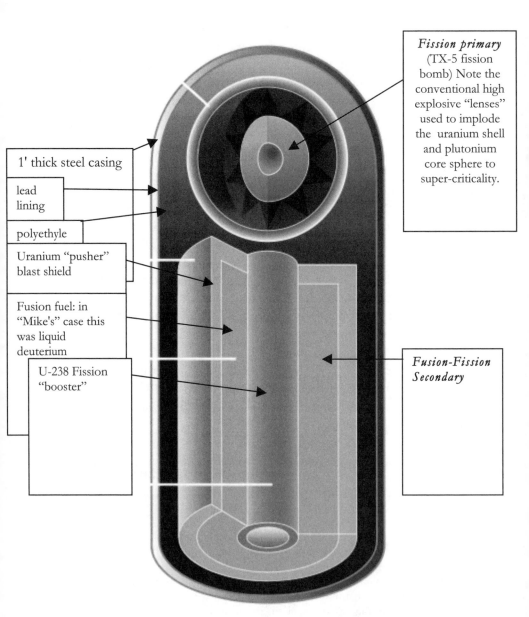

Fission primary
(TX-5 fission bomb) Note the conventional high explosive "lenses" used to implode the uranium shell and plutonium core sphere to super-criticality.

1' thick steel casing

lead lining

polyethyle

Uranium "pusher" blast shield

Fusion fuel: in "Mike's" case this was liquid deuterium

U-238 Fission "booster"

Fusion-Fission Secondary

Simplified Schematic of a Three Stage Fission-Fusion-Fission Hydrogen Bomb first tested in the "Mike"

2) Each section of exploding high explosive is detonated within a fraction of a microsecond of every other detonation, and each drives a shockwave forward, merging with the shockwaves from all the other detonators, creating a shockwave "front" which presses forward to the aluminum casing surrounding the uranium and plutonium core of the primary;[7]

3) The aluminum is instantly vaporized by this compressing shockwave, which passes through it and on to the surrounding U-235 shell of the core, liquifying it and pushing it across a small gap between it and the plutonium 239 core. It is important to note that in the very center of this plutonium core there was a device called an "urchin," a small ball of the metals beryllium and polonium which, under intense stress (such as being symmetrically imploded by an explosion!) will spit out a lot of "thermal" or "fast" neutrons, the "bullets" used to split the nucleus of atoms;[8]

4) At this point, the polonium ejects alpha particles into the beryllium, which in turn spits out approximately a half a dozen thermal neutrons for each impacting alpha particle, which are slammed into the supercritical, i.e., superdense, mass of uranium 235 and plutonium 239. As these neutrons slam into the nuclei of U-235 and Pu-239, the atoms split, spit out more fast neutrons which collide with more U-235 and Pu-239 nuclei, and the chain reaction has begun, with each generation of fissioning atoms growing in number, like compound interest;

5) A mere eighty generations of fissioning atoms after this — which has all occurred in a "few millionths of a second"[9] — X-rays from the fission fireball at the center of the primary(hotter than the center of the Sun!) have escaped beyond the assembled mass at the speed of light, and have traveled down the cylinder around the secondary and also shown over the entire interior surface of the casing. These x-rays caused the polyethylene lining to instantly heat to a

---

[7] Richard Rhodes, *Dark Sun*, p. 505.
[8] Ibid.
[9] Ibid.

plasma, which *reflected* the x-rays *back on to the uranium casing of the secondary*, which,

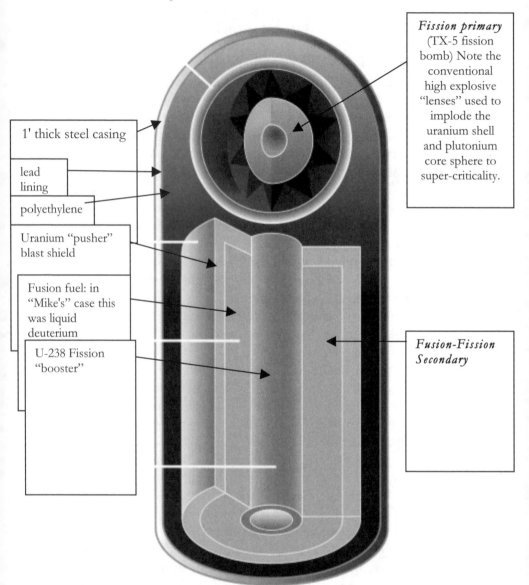

Fission primary (TX-5 fission bomb) Note the conventional high explosive "lenses" used to implode the uranium shell and plutonium core sphere to super-criticality.

1' thick steel casing

lead lining

polyethylene

Uranium "pusher" blast shield

Fusion fuel: in "Mike's" case this was liquid deuterium

U-238 Fission "booster"

Fusion-Fission Secondary

Simplified Schematic of a Three Stage Fission-Fusion-Fission Hydrogen Bomb first tested in the "Mike"

course, liquified and vaporized the uranium as it was being driven inward by the sheer pressure of x-ray radiation;[10]

6) As this liquifying and vaporizing uranium is being crushed and relentlessly compressed around the cylinder of cryogenically cooled liquid deuterium, that deuterium itself begins to be intensely pressurized as its temperature rises within microseconds to fusion energies;[11]

7) All this extremely hot witches' brew then further compresses around the uranium-238 fission booster, which, under the extreme pressures and radiations of x-rays and thermal neutrons, also fissions, spitting even more x-rays and neutrons into the whole recipe. These x-rays further heat the compressing deuterium, pushing its nuclei past the barriers of electrostatic repulsion and causing them to fuse together;[12]

8) At this juncture, according to hydrogen bomb historian Richard Rhodes, three different kinds of fusion reaction occurred, and here, we begin to observe the beginnings of a "problem":

   a) According to Rhodes, some of these deuterium nuclei "fused to form a helium nucleus — an alpha particle — with the release of a neutron, the alpha and the neutron sharing an energy of 3.27 MeV."[13] This neutron then shoots "through the mass of fusing deuterons"[14] and escapes, while the positively charged alpha particle adds its own energy to the mass of heating deuterons, further heating it;[15]

   b) But there is another reaction that occurs. Some deuterons fuse to form a tritium nucleus — that is, a hydrogen isotope's nucleus consisting of one proton and *two* neutrons — releasing a free proton which in turn dumps its energy into the heating mass of deuterons, with "the triton and the proton sharing 4.03 MeV;"[16]

---

[10] Rhodes, *Dark Sun*, pp. 505, 507.
[11] Ibid., p. 507.
[12] Ibid.
[13] Ibid. MeV = mega-electron volts.
[14] Ibid.
[15] Ibid.
[16] Ibid.

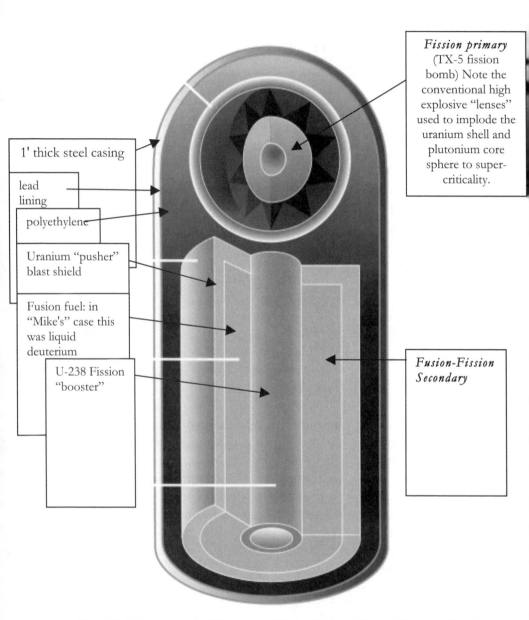

Fission primary
(TX-5 fission bomb) Note the conventional high explosive "lenses" used to implode the uranium shell and plutonium core sphere to super-criticality.

1' thick steel casing

lead lining

polyethylene

Uranium "pusher" blast shield

Fusion fuel: in "Mike's" case this was liquid deuterium

U-238 Fission "booster"

Fusion-Fission Secondary

Simplified Schematic of a Three Stage Fission-Fusion-Fission Hydrogen Bomb first tested in the "Mike"

c) The third reaction that can occur is when a tritium nucleus fuses with one of deuterium to form yet another alpha particle — a helium nucleus of two protons and two neutrons — plus a thermal neutron that, among them, share an energy of 17.59 MeV;[17]

(We will return to the "problem" posed by this account in a moment. For the present, it suffices to note simply that there may *be* a problem here.)

9) The thermal neutron from the tritium-deuterium reaction described in point 8)a) above has an energy of 14 MeV, and this neutron then escapes the compressing deuterium plasma and collides with the uranium-238 "fission booster" in the secondary, which then itself begins to fission under this intense thermal or high energy neutron bombardment, and this of course floods even more intense x-ray radiation into the deuterium plasma.[18] In effect, this means that the deuterium plasma is trapped "between two violent walls of heat and pressure."[19] This creates three further reactions:

a) As neutrons are banging around in this witches' brew, some of the deuterium nuclei will capture them, transforming from deuterium (with one proton and one neutron) into tritium (with one proton and two neutrons). This tritium then fuses with other tritium, which produces a helium nucleus or an alpha particle (two protons and two neutrons) plus two free thermal neutrons, all of which share an energy of 11.27 MeV;[20]

b) Some of this deuterium-created helium then in turn fuses with deuterium and creates heavy helium (a helium nucleus with an extra neutron) plus a "highly energetic proton;"[21]

c) Some of the fusing deuterons breed tritium plus a proton, with further release of energy in the form of more

---

[17] Rhodes, *Dark Sun*, p. 507.
[18] Ibid.
[19] Ibid.
[20] Ibid.
[21] Ibid.

radiation, and further fueling the force of "Mike's" explosion.[22]

All of this led to a colossal detonation, the largest at that point in time that had ever been seen on the Earth:

Momentarily, the huge Mike fireball created every element that the universe had ever assembled and bred artificial elements as well. "In nanoseconds," writes the physicist Philip Morrison, "uranium nuclei captured neutron upon neutron to form isotopes in measurable amounts all the way from ^{239}U up to mass number 255. Those quickly decayed, to produce a swath of transuranic species from uranium up to element 100, first isolated from that bomb debris and named Fermium."

Swirling and boiling, glowing purplish with gamma-ionized light, the expanding fireball began to rise, becoming a burning mushroom cloud balanced on a wide, dirty stem with a curtain of water around its base that slowly fell back into the sea. The wings of the B-36 orbiting fifteen miles from ground zero at forty thousand feet heated ninety-three degrees almost instantly. In a minute and a half, the enlarging fireball cloud reached 57,000 feet; in two and a half minutes... the cloud passed 100,000 feet. The shock wave announced itself with a sharp report followed by a long thunder of broken rumbling. After five minutes, the cloud splashed against the stratopause and began to spread out, its top cresting at twenty-seven miles, its stem eight miles across...

... The explosion vaporized and lifted into the air some eighty million *tons* of solid material that would fall out around the world... It stripped animals and vegetation from the surrounding islands and flashed birds to cinders in midair.[23]

That was not all:

Fireball measurements and subsequent radiochemistry put the Mike yield at 10.4 megatons —

---

[22] Rhodes, *Dark Sun*, p. 507.
[23] Ibid., p. 509, emphasis added.

This, of course, is our small "problem," for this, it will be recalled, was almost *double the most likely predicted yield for the "device;"* the scientific term for it would be: "Woops!"

> — the first megaton-yield thermonuclear explosion on earth. Its neutron density was ten million times greater than a supernova, Cowan remarks, making it "more impressive in that respect than a star." The Little Boy uranium gun that destroyed Hiroshima was a thousand times less powerful. Mike's fireball alone would have engulfed Manhattan; its blast would have obliterated all New York City's five boroughs. More than 75 percent of Mike's yield, about eight megatons, came from the fission of the big U238 pusher around the secondary; in that sense it was less a thermonuclear than a big, dirty fission bomb.[24]

Our "little" problem has now grown into a monster, for *where did all this extra energy —some four to six megatons over the predicted likely yield — come from?*

One answer came immediately: it came simply from the efficiency of the reaction burns themselves.

As we shall see, this does not really solve the problem, but rather, only amplifies it, for as we shall now see, the problem only became more acute in the next series of thermonuclear "miscalculations..."

B. The Designs of "Shrimp" and "Runt": The Second and Third "Woops!"

All this would not have been so bad, except for the fact that it happened again, and with a vengeance, during America's first test of an actual *deliverable* hydrogen bomb, the "Castle Bravo" test of March 1, 1954, and for yet a *third* time during the "Castle Romeo" test a few days later, on March 27, 1954. Once again, the bombs, when fired, ran far away from their predicted pre-test yields.

As we saw in our survey of the "Mike" test, the actual device used liquid cooled deuterium as the fusion fuel in its secondary, making the device not only large, but giving it a weight of 62 *tons*, making it simply impractical as a deliverable weapon of any sort. The actual reason for the test was simply to determine if the various stages for a hydrogen bomb could actually be engineered to *work* in

---

[24] Rhodes, *Dark Sun*, p. 510.

the sequence outlined in the previous pages. However, once the shot had proven that the basic design principles of staged reactions were sound — never mind that "little problem" that the actual yield almost doubled the likely predicted yield — design of a solid-fueled, deliverable weapon began in earnest, and the first of these, a device named "Shrimp" was detonated during the "Castle Bravo" test of March 1, 1954, the test that soon became infamous around the world.

The "Shrimp" device used a mixture of lithium-6 and deuterium — lithium deuteride — as the main fusion fuel in its secondary. Approximately 40 percent of the lithium in in this lithium deuteride was composed of the lithium-6 isotope, while the other 60 percent was composed of the more common and stable lithium-7. The problem was, the predicted yield for the device was about 6 megatons, plus or minus 2 megatons. In other words, the expected yield was 4-8 megatons. Yet, when it was actually detonated, the explosion quickly went out of control, and ran away to *15* megatons, almost 4 times the low end of the predicted yield, and almost double the high end![25]

The Castle Bravo Dry-Fueled Deliverable "Shrimp" Device, with a Human Silhouette Superimposed to show approximate size. Compare with the much larger "Mike" device on page 3.

---

[25] "Operation Castle," http://nuclearweaponarchive.org/Usa/Tests/Castle/ html, p. 11.

This "slight miscalculation" was not without its consequences and repercussions, for

The Bravo test created the worst radiological disaster in US history. Due to failures in forecasting and analyzing weather patterns, failure to postpone the test following unfavorable changes in the weather, and combined with the unexpectedly high yield and the failure to conduct pre-test evacuations as a precaution, the Marshallese Islanders on Rongelap, Ailinginae, and Utirik atolls were blanketed with the fallout plume, as were U.S. servicemen stationed on Rongerik.

Within 15 minutes after the test radiation levels began climbing on Eneu Island, site of the test control bunker, which was supposed to be upwind from the test and thus immune to fallout. An hour after the shot the level had reached 40 (Rads per hour), and personnel had to retreat from the control room to the most heavily shielded room of the bunker until they could be rescued 11 hours later.

An hour after the shot Navy ships 30 miles south of Bikini found themselves being dusted with fallout with deck radiation levels rising to 5 (Rads per hour). Navy personnel were forced to retreat below decks and the ships retreated farther from the atoll.

As the fallout drifted east U.S. evacuation efforts lagged behind the plume. At Rongerik, 133 (nautical miles) from ground zero, 28 U.S. personnel manning a weather station were evacuated on 2 March but not before receiving significant exposures. Evacuations of the 154 Marshallese Islanders only 100 (Nautical miles) from the shot did not begin until the morning of 3 March. Radiation safety personnel computed that the islanders received a whole-body radiation dose of 175 rad on Rongelap, 69 rad on Ailininae, and 14 rad on Utirik.[26]

But that was not the end of the fallout — pun intended — from the event.

The Japanese fishing vessel Daigo Fukuryu (Fifth Lucky Dragon) was also heavily contaminated, with the 23 crewmen receiving exposures of 300 R, one of whom later died — apparently from

---

[26] Ibid., pp. 2-3.

complications. This incident created an international uproar, and a diplomatic crisis with Japan.[27]

One cannot blame the Japanese government for being more than a little angry, because the "Castle Bravo" shot meant, in effect, that it was the *third* time America had nuked Japan, and this time, the two countries were not even at war and the victims were innocent fishermen trying to make a living!

After the dramatic and completely unexpected yield of "Castle Bravo," a yield at the minimum almost double of what was expected, the United States abandoned its fire control bunkers on Bikini atoll, opting in the future for distant remote control firing, and the exclusion zones around test areas was increased to 570,00 square *miles*, or a circle *850 miles* across![28]

The Castle Bravo Test From About Fifty Miles Away, approximately two and a half minutes after the explosion.

---

[27] Ibid., p. 3.
[28] Ibid.

The fireball of the "Castle Bravo" test "expanded to nearly four miles in diameter. It engulfed its 7,500 foot diagnostic pipe array all the way out to the earth-banked instrument bunker, which barely survived. It trapped people in experiment bunkers well outside the expected limits of its effects and menaced task force ships far out at sea."[29] To put it mildly, the "Shrimp" bomb was a runaway monster, and left the physicists and engineers dumbfounded, even as they were staring at their visible bones in their hands, even through their tightly-shut and goggled eyes.

While the U.S. military were scrambling to rescue the islanders and service personnel endangered by the test shot, a red-faced State Department was trying to explain the "curious results" to the angry governments of the region, not the least of which was Japan. How could such a drastic miscalculation have happened? What had gone wrong, or from the weapons designers' point of view, what had gone so incredibly *right?*

The crisis had barely abated, when on March 27, 1954, the United States once again rolled the thermonuclear dice in the "Castle Romeo" test, and once again achieved some rather unexpected results. Its original predicted yield, prior to the spectacular "Bravo" success (or, depending on how one wants to view it, failure), was for a yield of 4 megatons, with outside limits being 1.5 to 7 megatons.[30] In the wake of the "Bravo" test, however, scientists quickly revised their yield predictions, and now calculated a yield of between 1.5 to 15 megatons with the likely yield being 8 megatons![31] When fired, the "Castle Romeo" device, a bomb codenamed "Runt I" once again "ran away," yielding an explosion of 11 megatons. Of course, this fell well within the *revised* predicted yield, but *only* because the predicted yield was of such a wide margin of error, as compared with the pre-"Bravo" yield of 4 megatons with outer limits of 1.5-7 megatons!

Once again, our little problem has returned, the problem that began with "Mike," and continued with "Runt I": *where was all this extra energy coming from?*

---

[29] Rhodes, *Dark Sun*, p. 541.

[30] "Operation Castle," http://nuclearweaponarchive.org/Usa/Tests/Castle/html, p. 11.

[31] Ibid.

1. *An Interesting Story*

More light can be shed on that question by a glance at the tables for the pre- and post-Bravo predicted yields for the Castle series of nuclear tests, for these tables tell an interesting story.

The Castle series of tests was to have consisted of eight shots, designated Bravo, Union, Yankee, Echo, Nectar, Romeo, and Koon, respectively. The following table gives the names of the tests, the name of the device tested, and the pre-Bravo predicted yields expected for each:

Table of Pre-Bravo Predicted Yields for the Castle Series of Nuclear Tests[32]

Codename of Test	Codename of Device and Purpose of the Test	Pre-Bravo Predicted Yield
1. Bravo	SHRIMP TX-21 prototype	6 Mt (4-8 Mt)
2. Union	ALARM CLOCK Ec-14 Proof Test	3-4 Mt (1-6 Mt)
3. Yankee (I)	JUGHEAD EC-16 Proof Test	8 Mt(6-10 Mt)
4. Yankee (II)	RUNT II	No pre-Bravo prediction; test scheduled *after* the Bravo shot
5. Echo	RAMROD Cryogenic Experiment	125 Kt (65-275 Kt)
6. Nectar	ZOMBIE TX-15 Proof Test	1.8 Mt (1-2.5 Mt)
7. Romeo	RUNT I EC-17 Proof Test	4 Mt (1.5-7 Mt)
8. Koon	MORGENSTERN Solid-fuel experiment	1 Mt(1/3-2.5 Mt)

But in the wake of the "Bravo" success as a firing, and its failure as an international incident, the figures for all remaining tests were re-

---

[32] Table compiled from "Operation Castle," http://nuclearweaponarchive. org/Usa/Tests/Castle/html, p. 11.

calculated, and an explanation for its run-away success was found, but in that explanation, a new, and terrible, mystery surfaces, as we shall see.

2. The Standard Explanation for "Castle Bravo" and "Castle Romeo"

It will be recalled from our previous description of the "Bravo" test's "Shrimp" device that approximately 60 percent of the lithium mixture of the lithium deuteride was ordinary, stable, everyday common lithium-7. And therein lay the explanation (at least, as far as we have been told):

> The room-temperature Shrimp device used lithium enriched to 40 percent lithium 6; it weighed a relatively portable 23,500 pounds and had been designed to fit the bomb bay of a B-47 when it was weaponized. It was expected to yield about five megatons, but the group at Los Alamos that had measured lithium fusion cross sections had used a technique that missed an important fusion reaction in lithium 7, the other 60 percent of the Shrimp lithium fuel component. "They really didn't know," Harold Agnew explains, "that with lithium 7 there was an n, 2n reaction (i.e., one neutron entering a lithium nucleus knocked two neutrons out). They missed it entirely. That is why Shrimp went like gangbusters." Bravo exploded with a yield of fifteen megatons, the largest-yield thermonuclear device the US ever tested.[33]

Woops.

Certainly the lithium-7 reactions *do* explain *most* of the reason why such an inordinately high yield was achieved, and do so within acceptable margins of error.

Or do they?

Let us do a bit of detective work concerning this lithium-7 explanation. We first observe that the explanation of the extra energy achieved for those tests on the basis of the fusion of ordinary lithium-7 might be true in the cases of those tests, except for one important problem: the *original* H-bomb test, "Mike," was *not* fueled by lithium reactions at all, but solely by the fusion of *deuterium* reactions along with the fission reactions in the primary and

---

[33] Rhodes, *Dark Sun*, p. 541.

secondary. *Nowhere* in standard thermonuclear reactions is there a reaction that forms lithium-7 from various reactions of deuterium, either with itself or with other products within its family of reactions![34] So where did *"Mike's"* extra energy come from?

We are told that the lithium-7 reaction accounted for this extra "boost" in the reaction yield, but as we have already seen, in the overwhelming case of lithium-7 reactions, the resulting products will allow only one component, tritium, to continue fusion reactions, and those reactions form a comparatively *small* percentage of normal fusion reactions.

To put it bluntly, and succinctly, though it would appear that while the lithium-7 explanation accounts for *most* of the extra yield of these two devices, it is unlikely that it accounts for *all* of it. Why are we reasonably confident of this? Because, once again, the original hydrogen bomb, "Mike," contained no lithium-6 *or* lithium-7, and yet it too "ran away"! Its reactions would have been confined to reactions *not* involving lithium-7, and *these would have had to have burned very efficiently to achieve its actual yield.*

Some *other* energy source might therefore also have been in play in *all* these devices.

But if so, what was it?

A final and extremely important clue is afforded by careful study of the following table:

---

[34] Q.v. "Nuclear Fusion," Wikipedia, www. en.wikipedia.org/wiki/Nuclear_fusion, pp. 9-10.

Table of Post-Bravo Predicted Yields, Actual Yields, and Deviations from
Original Predictions for the Castle Series of Nuclear Tests[35]

Test Name	Device Name	Pre-Bravo Predicted Yield/Range	Post-Bravo Predicted Yield/Range	Actual Yield	Deviation from Original Prediction	Test Date
Bravo	Shrimp	6 Mt (4-8 Mt)	-NA-	15 Mt	+ 150%	1 March 1954
Romeo	Runt I	4 Mt (1.5 — 7 Mt)	8 Mt (1.5 — 15 Mt)	11 Mt	+ 175%	27 March 1954
Koon	Morgen-stern	1 Mt (0.33 — 2.5 Mt)	1.5 Mt (0.33 — 4 Mt)	110 Kt	- 89%	7 April 1954
Union	Alarm Clock	3-4 Mt (1 — 6 Mt)	5-10 Mt (1 — 18 Mt)	6.9 Mt	+73% to +130%	26 April 1954
Yankee I	Jughead	8 Mt (6 — 10 Mt)	Cancelled in the wake of Bravo	-NA-	-NA-	Cancell-ed in the wake of Bravo
Yankee II	Runt II	No Scheduled Second test of Runt Device before Bravo Test	9.5 Mt (7.5-15 Mt)	13.5 Mt	+42 % (post-Bravo prediction	5 May 1954
Echo	Ramrod	125 Kt (65-275 Kt)	Cancelled in the Wake of the Koon "fizzle"	-NA-	-NA-	Cancelled in the Wake of the Koon "fizzle"
Nectar	Zombie	1.8 Mt (1 — 2.5 Mt)	2 -3 Mt (1 — 5 Mt)	1.69 Mt	- 6.1%	14 May 1954

Note first of all the Castle Bravo, Romeo, and Union tests. In each of these cases, the deviation from the original predicted yields *at the minimum* exceeds 73 percent and goes as high as a 175 percent deviation!

But note also the significance of the "Castle Koon" test, the test of a device designed by Lawrence Livermore Laboratories under the

---

[35] Table compiled from "Operation Castle," http://nuclearweaponarchive. org/Usa/Tests/Castle/html, pp. 11-12.

direct supervision of Dr. Edward Teller.[36] Its revised yield was a comfortable 1.5 megatons, *but instead, the device "fizzled" and failed to achieve barely any fusion reactions at all, coming in at a mere 110 kilotons.*

We are told that of the fizzled yield, only 10 kilotons was accounted for by fusion reactions, or about 9 percent of the total yield. The other 91 percent of the yield was obtained from the fission reactions of the primary and secondary. The explanation for this "fizzle" (which nonetheless managed to carve out a crater 990 feet wide and 75 feet deep!) was "an unexpectedly long time delay between the primary firing and the secondary ignition. Reportedly this was due to a simple design flaw — the neutron flux from the primary had preheated the secondary leading to poor compression."[37]

Of course, in the thermonuclear kettle of these witches' brews, the slightest change of just a few nano-millimeters of the thickness of any solid state item within the device, the slightest change of positioning of various components, *can* — within the split-seconds' timing of the various stages of the reaction — alter its efficiency significantly, and either enhance, or impede, the overall reaction yield. So from one point of view, this explanation has merit.

But from another point of view, do *any* of these explanations really make sense? Are we really to believe that Los Alamos National Laboratory knew *absolutely nothing* about lithium-7 reactions before the "Castle Bravo" test, that it rolled the thermonuclear dice having missed one whole component of nuclear chemistry? Are we really to believe that those reactions burned *so efficiently* so as to account — after the fact! — for a runaway bomb? And are we really to believe that Lawrence Livermore Laboratory, under Dr. Edward Teller, the "father of the hydrogen bomb" himself, could not successfully design the very bomb he is credited with inventing?

And how, after all this, does the lithium-7 explanation really work in the final analysis, since it would account for none of the excess yield in the very first hydrogen bomb test, that of "Mike"?

To answer these questions we have to journey to the Soviet Union, where a famous Russian astrophysicist was having similar

---

[36] Operation Castle," http://nuclearweaponarchive.org/Usa/Tests/Castle/html, p. 7.
[37] Ibid.

difficulties with the *sun,* and from there, to Argentina, where a Nazi scientist knew about lithium-7 reactions *before* the Castle Bravo test...

C. The Soviet Union Encounters a "Little Problem" Too: Astrophysicist Nikolai Kozyrev, the "Tsar Bomba," and "a Little Problem" with the Sun

1. Dr. Nikolai Kozyrev's "Little Problem" with the Sun

Russian astrophysicist Dr. Nikolai Kozyrev (1908-1983) was unquestionably one of the twentieth century's unsung geniuses. But to appreciate why, one must understand his discovery of a problem within the conventional models of stellar thermonuclear fusion. Like America's hydrogen bomb engineers and scientists, what Dr. Kozyrev was noticing was a similar anomalous "yield" in the energy streaming from the sun and other stars:

> In short, when he compared "the observed data about luminance, masses, and sizes of stars," the observed luminance and radioactivity could *not* be adequately accounted for by the theory that stars are nothing but gigantic hydrogen bombs in a state of perpetual detonation; the theory of thermonuclear fusion alone was inadequate to account for the phenomenon of stars. Indeed, Kozyrev's analysis "brought him to a conclusion that the processes of thermonuclear synthesis cannot serve as a main source of stellar energy." In other words, the fusion-gravity geometry model of standard stellar processes — a geometric model inspired in large part by Einstein's General Relativity and extrapolations from it performed by other scientists — was simply not able to account for the enormous energy pouring out of stars. Some other mechanism altogether was at work.[38]

In other words, Kozyrev's stars and America's hydrogen bombs were doing the same thing: producing more energy than the standard models would allow. The only question was, why?

Dr. Lavrenty Shikhobalov explains Kozyrev's rather unorthodox answer in strikingly simple terms: Kozyrev "made a hypothesis that

---

[38] Joseph P. Farrell, *The Philosophers' Stone: Alchemy and the Secret Research for Exotic Matter* (Feral House, 2009), p. 155, citing Dr. Lavrenty S. Shikhobalov, "N.A. Kozyrev's Ideas Today, p. 291.

Time is a source of stellar energy."[39] As I concluded elsewhere, Kozyrev had hypothesized

> that the *geometry of local celestial space is a determinant in the energy output of fusion reactions, and that the latter, depending on that geometry, will 'gate' now more, now less, energy into the reaction itself as a function of that geometry.* Kozyrev had, in short, surmised why the Russians — who had no doubt encountered similar anomalous energy yields in their own hydrogen bomb tests — were getting such strange results, results that could *not* be explained on the standard theory and its methods of calculations of yields.[40]

But what, precisely was being "gated" by the sun from these celestial geometries?

2. His Explanation: Torsion

Kozyrev's answer forms one of the major themes of this book: torsion. If time was a source of stellar energy then, like all forms of energy, it had a definite shape or structure, a *pattern* as Kozryev put it, a pattern that was, moreover, spiral and rotating in nature.[41] This is exactly what torsion does to the fabric of space-time. It may be simply illustrated by an analogy that I often use to describe it. Imagine taking an empty aluminum soda can, and wringing it in both hands like a dishrag. This counter-rotating motion will spiral and fold and pleat the can, drawing its ends closer together. In this illustration, the can represents space-time itself and the spiraling is what torsion does to it.

The sun thus becomes, in Kozyrev's model, a massive torsion machine, for in the rotation of its hot thermonuclear plasma, it functions as a gate, transducing the energies of the geometry of local space, the very geometries caused by the variations in planetary positions. Another analogy will help in understanding what Kozyrev is hypothesizing. If we imagine each planet as representing one of our empty soda cans, each spiraling, folding, and pleating space-time in its own unique way, and giving off "spiraling waves" of this energy,

---

[39] Dr. Lavrenty S. Shikhobalov, N.A. Kozyrev's Ideas Today," p. 291.
[40] Joseph P. Farrell, *The Philosophers' Stone*, p. 155, emphasis in the original.
[41] Ibid., see the discussion on pp. 153-155.

eventually, these waves will overlap in ever-changing patterns, like rocks thrown into the surface of a calm pond. The effect of so many torsion systems overlapping each other is called dynamic torsion, though there is one important difference between it and our example of rocks thrown into a calm pond, and that is that the motions of planets are entirely predictable, and therefore, at least theoretically, the mutual influences of dynamic torsion can be predicted, *with experimental observation being conducted to formulate the laws that would allow such prediction.*

It was precisely such experimental observation that Kozyrev undertook in the 1950s in the former Soviet Union, work that in 1959 caused him to be publicly denounced in *Pravda*. But it was only revealed *after* the collapse of the Soviet Union that Kozyrev and his research had disappeared into the highest and most secret reaches of classification in the Communist state.

> One may reasonably and logically conclude, therefore, that the 1959 *Pravda* attack on Kozyrev was really a cover story to denounce his work, to *de-legitimize* it to anyone in the West who may have been paying attention to it, while Kozyrev, and his work, disappeared — as they did — into the highest reaches of classification within the Soviet Union, for his work provided the necessary key to understand why H-bombs were returning such anomalous yields, yields that, moreover, most likely varied with the time of their detonation. Kozyrev knew why: it was because the bomb itself became, for that brief brilliant nanosecond of the initial explosion, a dimensional gateway, a sluice-gate, opening the spillway to a hyper-dimensional cascade of torsion into the reaction itself.[42]

Just exactly *how* all that functioned will be revealed in a moment, but before considering those details, it is worth briefly mentioning what happened a mere two years after Kozryev's denunciation in *Pravda*, and the disappearance of his work into the extreme secrecy Soviet black projects.

---

[42] Joseph P Farrell, *The Philosophers' Stone*, p. 191.

3. The "Tsar Bomba": Khrushchev's Propaganda Triumph and Its Real Significance as an Engineering Breakthrough

To demonstrate their newly-acquired thermonuclear engineering prowess, Soviet Premier Nikita Khrushchev directed that the Red Air Force test the world's largest deliverable hydrogen bomb on the island of Novaya Zemlya near the Arctic Circle on October 30, 1961. While yield estimates for this gargantuan monster vary, most place it at approximately 57 megatons — the explosive power of a gigantic 114,000,000,000 pounds of TNT! — with estimated low and high ends of the yield being 50 megatons and 67 megatons respectively.

It is perhaps not surprising that this enormous weapon was developed and tested *after* Dr. Kozyrev's disappearance into the bowels of the black projects empire of the Soviet Union a mere two years after being publicly denounced in *Pravda*. From the purely engineering point of view, the Tsar Bomba was a triumph, but its enormous yield does raise the specter that perhaps the Soviet Union had learned to apply Dr. Kozyrev's results to its bomb-engineering, a point that we now more fully explore in connection with the little-known, and little-understood, work of a Nazi scientist working in a secret post-war project in Juan Perón's Argentina.

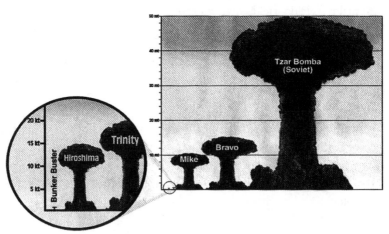

A Dramatic Comparison of Device Yields by Mushroom Clouds,

Note the Tiny Specks in the bottom left of the diagram, blown up in the circle, representing Hiroshima and the Trinity atom-bomb test in New Mexico of July, 1945.

D. The Lithium-7 Mystery, a Nazi Scientist in Argentina, and a Curious Coincidence

While Kozyrev may have been solving the yield-efficiency dilemma for the Soviets on the basis of torsion effects in rotating plasmas like the sun, a Nazi scientist in Argentina may have been giving the Americans specific clues about the lithium-7 reaction — and torsion effects in fusion reactions in rotating plasmas — discoveries he claimed to have made long before the Castle Bravo test, and here we are confronted with an even greater mystery.

That Nazi physicist's name was Dr. Ronald Richter, and he stunned the world when his ostensible boss, Argentine President Juan Domingo Perón, announced to the world that Argentina had successfully discovered the secret of the hydrogen bomb at a press conference on April 2, 1951. Perón went on to disclose that Argentina had achieved this feat after a mere nine months' research![43] Perón then introduced Dr. Ronald Richter, the Nazi scientist heading the project, to the assembled journalists, and Richter proceeded to inform them that he knew how to control thermonuclear reactions *precisely*. These assertions, if true, were highly problematical, since America had not even detonated "Mike" yet, nor would it, until the next year on November 1, 1952! Richter, and Argentina, had beaten America to the thermonuclear punch by over a year! Or so, at least, Juan Perón said.

Needless to say, the world press, and in particular, the American media, denounced the whole affair as a fraud and roundly condemned Richter for charlatanry, and for a very simple reason: as we have seen, it takes an atom bomb to create the heat and pressures necessary to set off a hydrogen bomb, and Argentina had tested no

---

[43] Joseph P. Farrell, *The Nazi International: The Nazis' Postwar Plan to Control Finance, Conflict, Physics and Space* (Kempton, Illinois: Adventures Unlimited Press, 2009), pp. 249-250.

such bomb. Therefore Richter's story — on the conventional analysis — *had* to be a case of pure fraud.

Confronted by this media outcry and denunciation, Perón became justifiably suspicious of his Nazi physicist and the project that was consuming vast amounts of money, and he appointed a special commission of Argentine scientists to investigate it and report its findings directly back to him. Heading this commission was the young Argentine nuclear physicist, Dr. Jose Balseiro.

It is when we consider Dr. Balseiro's findings that the lithium-7 explanation of the Castle Bravo test takes on a very new, and very sinister, significance, for lithium-7 reactions were the precise reactions upon which Dr. Richter was basing his claims!

> Balseiro begins his report by observing that "the basis upon which Dr. Richter's experiments rest are the two *known nuclear reactions*
>
> $$Li^7 + H = 2He^4 + Q, Q=17.28 \text{ MeV}$$
> $$H^2+H^2=H^3+Q+n, Q= 3.18 \text{ Mev}."$$
>
> That is, in the first case, the fusion of a lithium-7 atom with a hydrogen atom will produce two helium atoms plus an enormous quantity of electromagnetic energy (in the form of an x-ray and gamma ray burst) of 17.28 million electron volts of energy. In the second case, the fusion of two deuterium atoms (atoms of hydrogen with an extra neutron in the nucleus) will produce an atom of tritium (an atom of hydrogen with *two* extra nuetrons in the nucleus) plus a free neutron plus a burst of electromagnetic energy of 3.18 million electron volts.[44]

Before proceeding any further, it is important to pause here and note exactly what is being said, *well in advance of the Castle Bravo test and the lithium-7 explanation used to explain its runaway results, for this reaction was clearly known and understood by an Argentine physicist,* **and** *a Nazi physicist,* **before** *the test even took place. It is thus* **highly** *unlikely that we are being told*

---

[44] Joseph P Farrell, *The Nazi International*, pp. 259-260, citing Dr. José Balseiro, "Report About the Experiments of Dr. R. Richter, according to what was Witnessed by Me During the Visit made to the Atomic Energy plant at Isla Huemul, from 5 to 8 September 1952," www.ib.edu.ar/informes-huemul/reports-huemul-principal.html, p. 2, emphasis added.

the truth when we are told that our scientists and engineers did not even consider litrhium-7 reactions in their calculations of the Castle Bravo yield.

Thus, the standard lithium-7 reactions were known, making it unlikely America's thermonuclear "theurgists" were unaware of it. Some *other* reaction may therefore also have been involved, and once again, Dr. Richter in Argentina indicated that he knew what it was, for the *standard* physics models simply did not work. Indeed, for Dr. Balseiro, this was the whole problem posed by Dr. Richter. Richter was claiming to have achieved fusion reactions within a lithium-7 plasma at atmospheric pressures and under relatively "cool" conditions of pulsing it with electrical discharges. Dr. Balseiro puts the difficulty this way:

> For 1% of the nuclei to have enough energy to start the reaction, we need therefore, an initial temperature of at least 40 millions of degrees Kelvin. As a comparison, it is of relevance to recall that the temperature in the hottest zone of a voltaic discharge arc does not reach higher than 4,000 K and that the highest instantaneous temperatures reached in the laboratory by Kapitza are of the order of 100,000 K.[45]

But this was not the only problem, and Dr. Balseiro was honest enough to record what the real problem with Dr. Richter was:

> The analysis made above, shows the impossibility, according to present knowledge, of achieving in the laboratory this type of nuclear reactions (sic). **Dr. Richter, however, claims on this point to have discovered a set of phenomena that make invalid the type of reasoning exposed above. Furthermore, he insists these new phenomena discovered by him, constitute the basic secret of the process of thermonuclear reaction.**
> *It is not possible to foresee to what class of phenomena Dr. Richter refers to(sic), in particular because their existence cannot fail to contradict some of the basic knowledge which is accepted at present.* In the first place, if the (Lithium-Hydrogen reaction) would occur at temperatures

---

[45] Dr. José A. Balseiro, "Report About the Experiments of Dr. R. Righer, according to what was witnessed by Me During the Visit Made to the Atomic Energy plant at Isla Huemul, from 5 to 8 September 1952," www.ib.edu.ar/informes-huemul/reports-huemul-principal.html, p. 2, cited in my *The Nazi International* (Adventures Unlimited Press, 2009), p. 260.

substantially below 20 (thousand electron volts) this would imply a fundamental change in our present knowledge of nuclear structure and quantum mechanics.[46]

There it is: Richter claimed to have discovered a very different phenomenon, one allowing him to induce thermonuclear fusion reactions under conditions of stress and heat several orders of magnitude less extreme than that required by conventional theory.

The only question is, what was it?

Again, Dr. Balseiro is to be commended for his honest recording of Dr. Richter's assertions, and here, they are quite revealing:

> Dr. Richter has stated that the control device of the themonuclear device is based on *the resonance obtained between the Larmor precession frequency — which originates in the interaction of the magnetic field acting on the intrinsic magnetic moment of the (lithium-7) atom — and that of the oscillating magnetic field produced by a radio frequency generator.*[47]

Let us pause and note carefully what we have by comparing Dr. Balseiro with Dr. Richter's view.

Balseiro assumes the standard model of fusion reactions is true. That is, he assumes:

1) that fusion reactions can only occur under conditions of extreme heat and pressure, under temperatures in excess of 40 million degrees Kelvin; and that,
2) *nothing else* is involved in the reaction; and that,
3) Lithium-7, the very reaction allegedly overlooked by the American bomb engineers, was well known to the Argentine

---

[46] Ibid., p. 3,. cited in my *The Nazi International*, p. 261, boldface emphasis in the original, italicized emphasis added.

[47] Dr. José A. Balseiro, "Report About the Experiments of Dr. R. Righer, according to what was witnessed by Me During the Visit Made to the Atomic Energy plant at Isla Huemul, from 5 to 8 September 1952," www.ib.edu.ar/informes-huemul/reports-huemul-principal.html, p. 2, cited in my *The Nazi International* (Adventures Unlimited Press, 2009), p. 262, emphasis added. For a fuller discussion of the problems inherent in Dr. Richter's claims on the basis of the standard models, and Dr. Richter's highly anomalous behavior before the Argentine Commission, see pp. 262-274.

physicist who interviewed Richter fully two years before the Castle Bravo test.

But Dr. Richter is assuming something entirely *different* and upon close examination, much more comprehensive:

1) The mention of the Larmor precession simply means that Dr. Richter is thinking in terms of a *rotating* plasma, just as was Dr. Kozyrev;

2) Moreover, he is also taking into account that an oscillating magnetic field inside of a static one will contribute additional factors of stress to the plasma, making fusion reactions possible under conditions of stress in the plasma very *different* from those assumed in standard engineering, under heat and pressures several orders of magnitude *less* than those assumed to be necessary in the standard model; Richter is thinking of the *sun* as a model, with its rotating plasma, and its magnetic field. He is thinking in almost exactly the same terms as Dr. Kozyrev, and moreover, doing so *before* Dr. Kozyrev. Richter is thinking in terms of *torsion*.

It is after Richter was denounced by the Argentine commission and placed under house arrest by Perón that things began to get *really* interesting, for while the U.S.A. was busy publicly denouncing him, very quietly and it was sending Air Force officers to secretly interview him and analyze what he was saying, and this was being done *after the Castle Bravo tests and its anomalous yields.* Small wonder, for Richter explicitly stated that he was achieving fusion reactions in lithium-7 and at atmospheric pressures to boot!

But what Richter told his American interrogators must have stunned them. "We assume," he wrote for his American visitors,

that highly compressed electron gas (i.e., a plasma, ed.) *becomes a detector for energy exchange with what we call zero point energy...in a shock-wave-superimposed, turbulence-feed-back controlled plasma zone...(and that) on the basis of exchange coupling, it seems to be possible to 'extract' a compression-proportional amount of zero-point energy by means of a magnetic-field-controlled exchange fluctuation between the compressed electron gas and (a) sort of cell structure in space...*[48]

In other words, Richter is saying the *exact same thing as Kozyrev: a rotating plasma under conditions of magnetic stress and resonance will transduce energy from the local geometry of space-time itself, and that geometry includes the position of a thermonuclear detonation on the surface of the earth, and the time of the detonation, i.e., the relative position of the sun and planets.*

The reception of this comment by his American counterparts led to something of an impasse within American scientific circles; some continued to denounce Richter as a fraud and a montebank... but others were not so sure, and in fact, one Atomic Energy Commission scientist stated that Richer was "a mad genius working in the 1970s," decades ahead of his American counterparts.[49]

It is the *timing* of this assessment — in the mid-1950s — that suggests quite strongly that America's interest in Richter and his explanations of lithium-7 reactions was in response to the anomalous yields from the Mike and Castle Bravo H-bomb tests. Richter had told them that, yes, part of the reason was that lithium-7 had entered the chain fusion reactions, but he had also told them something else: the bombs were gating extra energy beyond the reactions themselves, energy coming into the reaction by dint of a coupled resonator effect between the reaction and the geometries of local space-time — what Richter is calling a "cell-like" structure or *grid* structure in local space — and all by dint of the *rotation* of the fusion plasma. Richter was telling them, like Kozyrev in the Soviet Union, that the bombs were "torsion machines," activating the energy of that global, and celestial, grid.

E. *Explanations and Transitions*

But why bring *rotating* plasmas into the description at all, since *nowhere* in the descriptions of the fusion reactions of "Mike"

---

[48] Joseph P Farrell, *The Nazi International*, p. 343, emphasis added, citing Richter's Paperclip file.

[49] Q.v. Joseph P Farrell, *The Nazi International*, pp. 314-342 for a fuller discussion of the Air Force attempts to assess Dr. Richter and its ultimately ambiguous conclusions.

examined previously is rotation ever mentioned, and for a very important reason: there was *absolutely nothing within the engineering of the Mike device that was designed to rotate the plasma inside a magnetic field.*

...or was there?

Might rotation in the plasma of that bomb have been accidentally introduced, and thus with it, hidden torsion effects?

The answer is a simple yes, and a closer look is in order.

Look once again at the atom bomb primary at the top of our diagram of a standard hydrogen bomb.

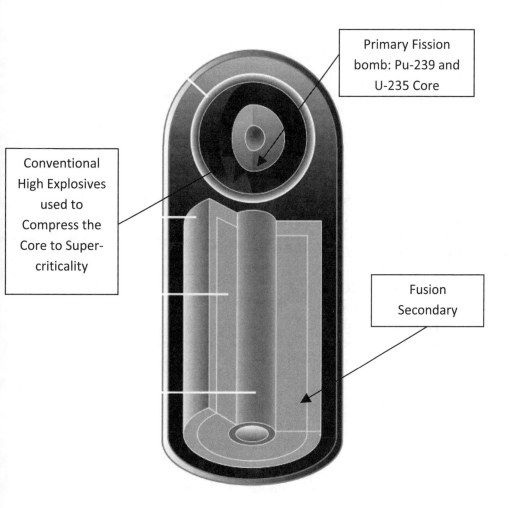

Primary Fission bomb: Pu-239 and U-235 Core

Conventional High Explosives used to Compress the Core to Super-criticality

Fusion Secondary

It is this atom bomb that sets all else in motion, for in order for a fission reaction to take place, the core must be symmetrically compressed in a matter of a few thousandths of a second. But the likelihood of all the conventional explosives firing at *exactly* the same instant to achieve such symmetrical compression is very small; there will be minute nanoseconds' of difference between the firing of one set of explosives versus another, and this means that *a slight asymmetry will be introduced into the shockwaves compressing the core. That asymmetry could conceivably induce vorticular, rotating structures in the core as it burns into a plasma, and those structures in turn may be strong enough to endure into the fusion reactions in the secondary.*

All this, let it be remembered, takes place inside yet *another* rotating system with a magnetic field: planet Earth, a system with its own natural standing waves and torsion effects.

Richter was telling the American scientists that more was involved in thermonuclear reactions than simply the particle-nucleus reactions and extreme heat; there were hidden factors at work: factors of rotation, of magnetic fields, and the placement of the device itself on the surface of the earth. These were *totally unaccounted for in standard physics models and in the standard engineering resulting from them.* For a brief moment, just as he stated, a strong fusion reaction acted as a resonator, tapping into the structure of space-time, a structure that would perforce include the bomb's placement on the planet itself. Vary the position, and time, of the detonation, and the yield will vary.[50] The reactions driving the awesome destructive power of hydrogen bombs were truly magical, alchemical acts, calling down the heavenly fire of the gods of old, the planets and the stars.

Torsion may thus also explain why the Soviets tested their massive "Tsar" Bomb so close to the Arctic Circle, for there, any torsion effects of the Earth's rotation would be smaller since the

---

[50] Richter's explanation also suggests that such devices establish longitudinal pulses in the physical medium itself, pulses which would be detectable to those having the physics and technology to do so. The coupling effect spoken of by Richter with the zero-point energy may rationalize why some UFOlogists maintain that "ET" started showing up in high numbers after the beginnings of human nuclear testing, i.e., such tests literally sent "hyper-dimensional" pulses of energy through the medium itself.

angular momentum of the planet at extreme northern latitudes is much less than that closer to the equator.[51]

In any case, in offering these explanations, Richter was really telling the American scientists that there was an ancient aspect to the engineering of such massive weapons, an aspect dependent upon *time and location*. Small wonder that this former Nazi scientist would say such a thing, for he also told his American interrogators that he made these discoveries in Nazi Germany in the year *1936!*[52] And little wonder, too, that in addition to investigating such torsion-based technologies of "thermonuclear theurgy", that Nazi Germany was also investigating the world grid system and pursuing its own geopolitical geomancy as well...

---

[51] There is a school of thought, to which this author does *not* subscribe, that suggests that thermonuclear weapons are space-time harmonics weapons to *such* a degree that they only can be set off at certain locations and times, or otherwise they will not work. This is total nonsense and is *not* representative of the theories of thinking of Drs Richter or Kozyrev.

[52] Joseph P Farrell, *The Nazi International*, p. 293.

Dr. Nikolai Kozyrev

Dr Ronald Richter

2

GEOPOLITICAL GEOMANCY:
NAZI TRANSMITTERS AND THE EARTH GRID

"There can be little coincidence in the observation that Nazi German radio and radar
stations were constructed on ancient mark-points in the land's sacred geometry."
Nigel Pennick[1]

Reichsführer SS Heinrich Himmler may justifiably be said to be the most powerful man ever to have attempted the resurrection of "Atlantis" and to have attempted to understand, and activate, the world grid system that was its legacy. This he did by establishing officially, on July 1, 1935, a department called the *Ahnenerbedienst*, the so-called "ancestral research bureau" to research ancient texts and sites and to establish their supposed Aryan patrimony. By 1940, it had been wholly absorbed by Himmler's other notorious creation, the SS. It was, as researcher Peter Levenda has quipped, "a humanities program. With guns."[2]

The *Ahnenerbe Forschungs und Lehrgemeinschaft* or "Ancestral Heritage Research and Teaching Society" was but the tip of a very large iceberg of all manner of projects involving occult methods and practice within the Third Reich. Dowsers using pendulums over maps were employed to successfully locate Benito Mussolini when he was being held prisoner in 1943 after the collapse of his government.[3] The German Navy employed a "research" institute that attempted to locate Allied ships using similar methods, including dowsers, astrologers, pendulum geomancers, naval charts, and a whole host of occult and magical techniques. According to Wilhelm Wulff, who was involved in these projects,

---

[1] Nigel Pennick, *Hitler's Secret Sciences: His Quest for the Hidden Knowledge of the Ancients*, (Suffolk: Neville Spearman, 1981), p. 171.

[2] Peter Levenda, *Unholy Alliance: A History of Nazi Involvement with the Occult* (New York: Avon Books, 1995), p. 152.

[3] Ibid., p. 212.

All intellectual, natural, and supernatural sources of power — from modern technology to mediaeval black magic, and from the teachings of Pythagoras to the Faustian pentagram incantation — were to be exploited in the interests of final victory.[4]

The Nazi Reich, in other words, was attempting literally to resurrect the ancient magic, the lost science of the gods, in some cases, quite literally by invoking them.

Concomitant with this all-encompassing philosophy, all manner of esoteric practice was pursed for its potential military application. Within the *Ahnenerbedienst* alone there were

> over fifty separate sections devoted to a wide range of scientific and pseudoscientific research... There was a Celtic studies group within the Ahnenerbe; a group to study the Teutonic cult center at Externsteine (near Wewelsberg), which... was believed to be the site of the famous World-Tree, Ydragsil or Yggdrasil; a group devoted to Icelandic research (as the Eddas were sacred to the Teuton myth...); a group that was formed around Ernst Schäffer and his Tibet expeditions; a runic studies group; a "World Ice Theory" division; an archaeological research group that scoured the earth for evidence of Aryan presence in lands as remote from Germany as the Far East and South America...[5]

In addition to this, one does not have to dig very long to see that part of this research also included serious effort to understand the "world grid," and if possible, to tap into whatever sources of power it represented, from geomancy to torsion.

A. The Grid and Hitler's East Prussia Headquarters

Hitler's East Prussia headquarters, the *Wolfsschanze* at Rastenburg, for example, has always been something of a mystery to military historians unaccustomed to examining the influence of esoteric systems of thought on Nazi practice. Why was it built *there*, "set as it was in the swampy woodlands of Die Görlitz among the Masurian

---

[4] Walter Schellenberg, *The Schellenberg Memoir* (London: Andre Deutsch, 1956), p. 75, cited in Peter Levenda, *Unholy Alliance*, p. 214.

[5] Peter Levenda, *Unholy Alliance*, p. 162.

Lakes of East Prussia"?[6] Why build a headquarters in a wooded swamp?

The answer, if one knew about the world grid and the Nazis' obsession with anything that could confer power, was simple:

> When Hitler's engineers laid out the fortress in 1940-41, they incorporated a civilian graveyard lying astride a ley line which ran from a high point west of Rastenburg, through a church in the town, the church and chapel at Karlshof near Krausendorf, a suburb of Rastenburg, through the site of the *Kurhaus* itself (a high point at *137 meters above sea level*), on through the graveyard to the island of Tautenburg and thence to the village of Schwiddern. Himmler's headquarters in East Prussia, Hochwald, was situated in another wood twelve miles away to the north east of the Wolfsschanze. It was linked to the *Kurhaus* by another ley line which ran from Hochwald via the *Kurhaus* to several high points (marked by triangulation markers) to the south-east and south-west of the town of Rastenburg itself. In *Ancient German Sanctuaries* Wilhelm Teudt had noted the coincidence of triangulation markers in his holy lines and it was borne in mind by Himmler's men when selecting the site of Hochwald.
>
> The occult function of the headquarters is obvious. Placing them in significant positions according to sacred geography enabled their rulers to transmit psychic power over the areas covered by the geomantic grid. Of these two lines, one ran almost due east-west, whilst the other, which linked the two sites, ran towards the north-east in the direction of Moscow.[7]

But there may have been something more than just Nazi obsession with geomancy and "psychic energies" in the placement of the two leaders' headquarters, for it should be noted that the number 137 forms a part of the coefficient of the fine structure constant of physics, with a value of 1/137.035999679. The constant was introduced into quantum mechanical theory by Arnold Sommerfeldt in 1916.[8]

---

[6] Nigel Pennick, *Hitler's Secret Sciences*, p. 172.

[7] Nigel Pennick, *Hitler's Secret Sciences*, pp. 172-173, emphasis added.

[8] Arnold Sommerfeldt's importance cannot be overestimated. See my *Secrets of the Unified Field: the Philadelphia Experiment, the Nazi Bell, and the Discarded Theory* (Adventures Unlimited Press, 2008), pp. 171-175. As for the importance of the fine

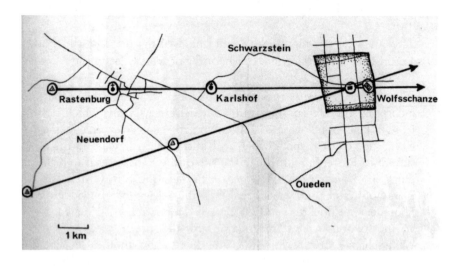

The Convergence of Ley Lines near Hitler's Wolfsschanze Headquarters near Rastenburg, East Prussia. Note the Placement of the Fortress on the East-West Line.[9]

B. Grid Geopolitical Geomancy

Might the Nazis have found (or at least *thought* they had found) the means to "activate" or even tap into the physics of the alleged energies of the global grid system?

The answer to this question is more disturbing.

Official and unofficial German interest in the occult in general and geomantic systems in particular goes back at least to the era of the Holy Roman Empire, when the secret imperial star chamber, the *Heilege Vehm* or "Holy Vehm's" initiates and executioners would often meet secretly at night at various sacred geomantic sites.[10] By the time of King Frederick the Great's Prussia, this esoteric interest had become fully fledged. Frederick founded the *Afrikanischen Bauherren,* or Order of Architects of Africa, centering it at his *Constantinople*

---

structure constant to modern theoretical physics and the anthropic cosmological principle, this is the subject of another book. It should be noted that 137, the basic coefficient of the constant, is the 33rd prime number.

[9] Nigel Pennick, *Hitler's Secret Sciences,* photo insert.

[10] Ibid., p. 7.

Lodge in Berlin. There, "its initiates studied hieroglyphics, the sciences, history and antiquities, and the Manichaean Mysteries."[11] This fascination with ancient mysteries, esotericism, and knowledge was accompanied by an interesting claim, for Frederick's Prussian Grand Lodge also asserted its continuity from another ancient society, the World Wise Men:

> This 'White Lodge' is the same group of hidden masters described by Madame Blavatsky's Theosophical Society and the German Thule Society from which many leading Nazis came. The Prussian Freemasons claimed that these World Wise Men were none other than the Carpocratians, a group of Christ's disciples to whom he communicated a secret science, transmitted afterwards to the Templars and thence via Scotland to the Swedish Rite Freemasons... They were also traditionally endowed with the mastery of a mysterious power drawn from the Earth — *Vril.*[12]

We note then that the idea of continuity with an ancient elite was very much a part of the Masonic tradition,[13] particularly in Prussia.

The peculiar connection with the Earth grid, however, is manifest in the fact that the Freemasons of Frederick the Great's Prussia claimed this hidden elite had the mastery of the *Vril* energy drawn from the Earth. These ideas of a continuity with an ancient elite, and of *Vril* or Earth energy force became cardinal principles of the ideology of the *Thulegesellschaft*, the Thule Society, one of the secret fraternities that helped to midwife the Nazi Party into existence.

> The Thule society believed that by harnessing this force they could raise Germany to an unassailable position of world domination. By 1919, the Thule Society (which had been founded in 1912) had become a rallying-point for Bavarian mystical anti-Semites. Anton Drexler, original leader of the German Workers' Party, was a

---

[11] Pennick, *Hitler's Secret Sciences,* p. 10.

[12] Ibid., pp. 10-11, emphasis original. Pennick also notes that Frederick the Great's personal librarian in Berlin "was a former Benedictine monk, Dom Antoine Joseph Pernetty, a man well versed in occult matters... Pernetty believed in the Philosopher's Stone, the Mysteries of the Qabalah, apparitions, Patagonian Witcheries and the Race of Giants."(p. 10).

[13] See my *Giza Death Star Destroyed* (Adventures Unlimited Press, 2005), pp. 84-94, and *The Philosophers' Stone* (Feral House, 2009), pp. 27-29.

member. So was Rudolf Hess, soon to become Hitler's right-hand man, as was Alfred Rosenberg, future philosopher of National Socialism. This society claimed to be the instrument of the legendary 'Secret Chiefs' of Tibet — descendants of the survivors of Atlantis living somewhere in the remote Himalayas.[14]

These hidden masters the Thule Society — like so many other fraternities that claimed such continuity with an ancient elite — identified with the "white Lodge" or "White Brotherhood,"[15] never bothering to consider the other assertion of esoteric tradition: that there was a black Lodge or "Brotherhood" or elite as well, and that they might be in continuity with something whose agendas and moral compass were quite different than what was assumed of the "White" lodges from which they claimed descent.

In any case, by asserting their claims to mastery over the Earth grid, the early twentieth century German occultists could draw on a wide tradition of English and German Earth grid research. Alfred Watkins had already published his now famous study of the grid system of England, *The Old Straight Track*, and the famous astronomer, Sir Norman Lockyear, had extended the idea to include astronomical alignments of many ancient sites, including Stonehenge and the Egyptian temples in his books *Stonehenge* and *The Dawn of Astronomy*.

Not to be outdone, the Germans Josef Heinsch and Wilhelm Teudt published similar works concerning the grid system in Central and Western Europe and the layout of churches and monasteries over older sacred pagan sites. Studying Stonehenge, Heinsch discovered other alignments overlooked by Lockyear, and extended his observations to include all of Central Europe and its ancient sites, i.e., Germany.[16]

In 1933, excavations at the Choir in Xanten Cathedral in the Rhineland revealed an ancient geometrical mosaic pavement, Heinsch was called in to examine it. In form, it was a square crisscrossed with lines and diagonals. Heinsch measured its angle of orientation and found it to be the same as that of the Avenue at

---

[14] Pennick, *Hitler's Secret Sciences,* p. 28.
[15] Ibid.
[16] Ibid., p. 47.

Stonehenge — a misummer sunrise alignment. Its form echoed the ancient cosmic diagrams of the Chinese, Mexican, and Norse cosmology. Testing the pattern on a map of the district, he noticed that the lines of this cosmographic mosaic correspondence with the placement of the churches in the district. From this startling discovery, Heinsch was able to detect a major north-south axis on the Lower Rhine just like those studied in England by Duke, Bennett and Lockyear. He now had the key to the sacred geography of Europe.[17]

This, of course, was tailor-made to fit the esoteric beliefs of the Thule Society and the Nazis, who had assumed power that same year.

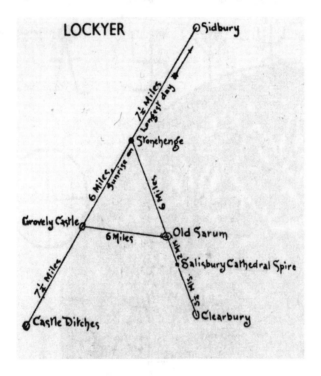

Sir Norman Lockyear's Simple Triangulation of Locations Around Stonehenge[18]

---

[17] Pennich, *Hitler's Secret Sciences*,, pp. 47-48.
[18] Ibid., photo insert.

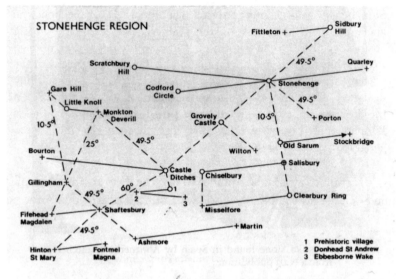

Heinsch's Survey of the Grid System Around Stonehenge[19]

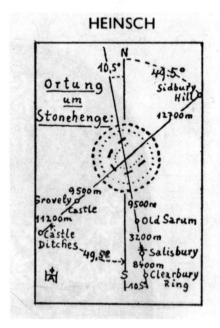

Heinsch's Grid Lines at Stonehenge[20]

---

[19] Pennick, *Hitler's Secret Sciences,* photo insert.

Heinsch's associate Gerlach[21] extended this system into a ley line system covering the whole of Central Europe, i.e., Germany and southern Scandinavia, based on the placement of churches in the area.

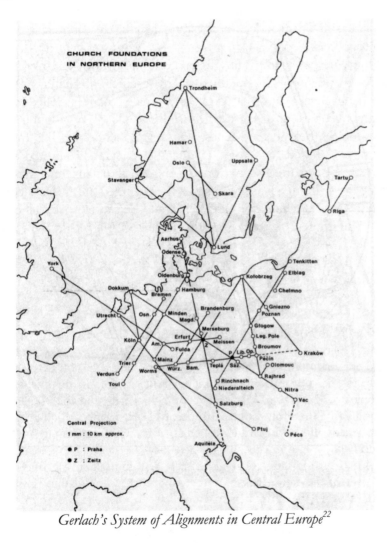

Gerlach's System of Alignments in Central Europe[22]

---

[20] Pennick, *Hitler's Secret Sciences*, photo insert.

[21] As far as I am able to determine as of this writing, there is no relationship to the Dr. Walther Gerlach who headed the Nazi Bell project.

[22] Pennick, *Hitler's Secret Sciences*, photo insert of the map by Michael Behrend, based on Gerlach's findings.

All of this work on the Earth grid by Heinsch, Teudt, and Gerlach, let it be noted, was being done in Germany in the period immediately prior to, and after, the Nazi assumption of power, which leads to the logical question: what exactly did the Nazis do with it?

With that question, the plot thickens considerably, though the clues are still enshrouded in mystery, leaving researchers to piece them together.

One clue lies in the outright esoteric nature of Nazi practice, a practice that can only be qualified as "geopolitical geomancy." As the Wehrmacht swept across Europe and smaller nations fell either to outright occupation, or were pressured into alliances with the Third Reich, the SS, behind the scenes, was quietly "collecting" all manner of things. Coupled with this activity, the Gestapo infiltrated secret fraternities, from the Freemasons to the Rosicrucians, and prepared lengthy dossiers on all of them, since they claimed "to possess certain universal secrets which Himmler felt could be put to better us by the SS."[23] The interest of these societies in Jewish Qabalistic esotericism was even held to be "a threat to state security" and "to Nazi magic itself."[24] This "magic" disclosed itself in two ways, the first being the collection of regalia:

> In order to consolidate his position as future Emperor of Europe, Hitler became an inveterate collector of regalia. At first, the regalia he presented himself were only replicas, but after the war began in earnest, he appropriated the authentic articles. In 1934, he obtained copies of the crown, orb, and sceptre that had been the imperial insignia of the Holy Roman Emperor Charlemagne. Although he had made this odd gesture on behalf of the German people — "I accept these into my keeping on behalf of the glorious Fatherland" — it is an indication that he actually saw himself in the role of Kaiser of the Third Reich. As the deposed Kaiser Wilhelm II was still alive at the time, it would not have been politic for him to proclaim himself Kaiser, but, had he won the war, it is likely that Kaiser Adolf I would have been crowned at the World's Fair and victory celebrations planned for Berlin in 1950.

---

[23] Pennick, *Hitler's Secret Sciences*, p. 138.
[24] Ibid.

As his conquests proceeded, Hitler continued to accumulate the trappings of sacral kingship. Six months after the *Anschluss* of Germany with Austria, Mayor Liebel of Nuremburg presented Hitler with more replica regalia, this time of a more overtly occult nature. When Hitler had re-entered his native land as its master in 1938, he had shown an inordinate interest in certain jewels among the Hapsburg regalia. These were the pieces made for the fifteenth century German King Frederick III. Frederick had been a lapidarian as well as an astrologer and alchemist, and, like Hitler, and many Kaisers before and since, had cherished notions of the conquest of other nations. Although Frederick III had failed in his dreams of megalomaniac grandeur, the gold settings of this collection of mystic gems were inscribed with the letters AEIOU. When Hitler was told that this cipher meant *Austria Est Imperare Orbi Universo* — it is for Austria to rule the whole world — he saw it as an omen for his dreams of the Greater Reich. So before the next Nuremberg Rally, the mayor presented Hitler with facsimile copies of these pieces.

When the war began, Hitler the occultist realized that he needed the real thing, so he personally took possession of all the regalia of the countries that the German Army overran. From Vienna they looted the coronation regalia of the Holy Roman Empire from the Imperial Treasure Room. This wealth included the jeweled crown of the Emperor Conrad, a magic shield, two swords and an orb. These was also the famed Spear of Destiny... Although the regalia had been kept in Vienna since 1804, the Nazis discovered a fifteenth century decreee by the Emperor Sigismund that they should be kept at Nuremberg... From Prague, the regalia of the ancient Bohemian kings disappeared into Germany, and from the bombed ruins of Warsaw Castle disappeared the Polish royal treasures.

In appropriating these regalia, Hitler continued the ancient magical tradition of conquerors taking away relics of national power as symbols of their victories, for possession of the emblems of rule is traditionally believed to ensure the continuance of that power. The Emperor Napoleon I took the emblems of sovereignty from his subject nations, and the practice was continued in the British Empire. The magical jewel of the Sikhs, the Koh-i-Noor diamond, whose name means *Mountain of Light* — was taken from India to grace the symbols of British monarchy.[25]

---

[25] Pennick, *Hitler's Secret Sciences*, pp. 139-140.

It is important to understand that this activity was not merely understood by Hitler as the mere exercise of the rightful possession of the victor over the treasures of the vanquished.

Something more was involved:

> The ancient tradition of the divinity of kings also applied to their regalia, which were not merely symbols *but actually instruments of a magical technology.* By appropriating the regalia of subject nations, he believed that the magical powers of rulership inherent in the symbols would be transferred to him.[26]

This belief in the divinity of Kings and the special powers inherent in their symbols of authority goes back, of course, to ancient Mesopotamia, and to The Cosmic War that was fought over the possession of the Tablets of Destinies.[27]

While this is not the place to review extensively the beliefs of the ancient Mesopotamian cultures, it is to be noted that two things about those beliefs would have immediately caught the Nazis' attention: (1) the belief that the ancient kings were chimerical human-divine offspring of a mingling with "the gods," a belief well in keeping with the Thule Society's belief that the Aryans originated from "Atlantis" and ultimately, off this planet entirely, and (2) the belief that the Tablets of Destinies and their magical powers showed all the signs of being a lost high *technology.*

All this breathtaking Nazi "regalia collecting" was accompanied by an even more sinister activity: actual geomancy. As we shall see in subsequent pages, the buildings and temples on sacred sites, sites whose locations were themselves determined by arcane methods,

> were specifically designed to channel and enhance those (Earth) energies to the exclusive use of the priesthood that owned then, for to possess these sites was to have control of the 'psychic body' of the whole country. In ancient times, the sacred layout of the country was held to be essential for the well-being of the fields, the

---

[26] Pennick, *Hitler's Secret Sciences*, p. 141.

[27] See my *The Cosmic War: Interplanetary Warfare, Modern Physics, and Ancient Texts* (Adventures Unlimited Press, 2007), pp. 139-274.

flocks, and mankind, so the government of a nation depended upon control over the country's geomancy.[28]

The origin of this Nazi interest in geopolitical geomancy was most likely Hitler's geopolitics guru, General Karl Haushofer, head of the *Institut für Geopolitik* at the University of Munich, and university mentor to Hitler's first deputy, Nazi Party *Reichsleiter* and occultist Rudolf Hess.

Hess, in command of the Nazi Party's own intelligence gathering organ, the People's Organization for Germans Living Abroad, or the so-called *Auslands* division, placed his mentor Haushofer at the head of this organization. In this twin role of the head of the premier geopolitical institution in the world as well as having access to the party's own considerable intelligence organization, Haushofer conceived of his grand geopolitical scheme. "His was the head which conceived of the plan by which Germany was to conquer the world."[29] A veteran of the Kaiser's General Staff, Haushofer was a military attaché to Germany's embassies in the Orient including a stint as the military attaché to the German Embassy in Tokyo. There, he learned Japanese and "became initiated into one of the most arcane Buddhist secret societies."[30]

But that was not all there was to the general. While in Japan he came to believe

> that the Germanic race had originated in Central Asia, and that, in order to preserve German superiority for ever, the Reich should expand to the east. This expansion should not only include Eastern Europe, argued Haushofer, but should encompass the Ukraine and Russia, Turkestan, Iran, Mount Pamir, the Gobi and Tibet.[31]

The reason for this modern-day expansion of the Teutonic Knights' *Drang nach Osten* was for more than just *Lebensraum*, an idea that also originated with Haushofer, but also because Tibet and Iran were also "places of great importance in sacred geography..."[32]

---

[28] Pennick, *Hitler's Secret Sciences*, p. 59.
[29] D. Sklar, *The Nazis and the Occult* (), p. 68.
[30] Pennick, op. cit., p. 29.
[31] Ibid., pp. 29-30.
[32] Ibid., p. 30.

This occult influence underpinned the massive research Haushofer's *Institut für Geopolitik* undertook.

> He had long believed that Germany would give birth to a leader who would rule the earth; and astrological predictions had convinced him that this leader would accomplish his mission in an alliance with Japan. He often had premonitions, upon which he acted. He convinced Hitler that the Institut(sic) must find out everything about its enemies: strengths, weaknesses, impending famine, religious sensibilities, the personalities and tastes of officials, the morals and corruptibility of even minor bureaucrats, the views of opinion makers. To collate, sift through, and interpret all this material on every country in the world, Haushofer enlisted a staff of more than a thousand students, historians, economists, statisticians, military strategists, psychologists, meteorologists, *physicists*, geographers, and other specialists, working in Germany and abroad.
>
> The researches apparently paid off. When, in 1938, the General Staff was worried that France would mobilize if Germany invaded Czechoslovakia, Haushofer assured them that it neither could nor would. He turned out to be right. He argued that Poland could be conquered in eighteen days. The military disagreed. They feared their armored trucks would bog down in the Polish mud. Haushofer said it was not likely to rain. It did not. The General Staff didn't believe Germany should invade Norway. Haushofer prophesied that it would be easy. The military wanted to invade France when war first started. Haushofer urged that they wait until German propaganda had made its full impact on the people. He also dictated when the campaigns in Africa and the Balkans would begin. It was his idea that the Nazis make temporary friends with Russia, despite widespread anxiety about collaborating with the Communists. He wooed Latin America for its usefulness against America.[33]

It is to be noted that among the types of experts that Haushofer gathered in his geopolitical institute were physicists, strongly suggesting that the Nazis knew there was something deeper to ancient geomancy than just peculiar alignments of structures on an astronomical grid. In short — and it is a crucial point to comprehend

---

[33] Sklar, *The Nazis and the Occult*, p. 69, emphasis added.

— Haushofer was attempting, and in a great measure succeeded, in bringing scientific rationalizations to ancient geomancy, transforming it into the modern "science" of geopolitics, a geopolitics that had something to do with physics. There are other clues suggesting this fact, and we shall return to them momentarily.

General Karl Haushofer, Mentor to Nazi Party Leader Rudolf Hess, and Geopolitical Guru of Adolf Hitler

The upshot of Haushofer's geopolitics, however, and of the Nazis' more generalized interest in all manner of claimed occult "powers," was that they were searching for modern scientific rationalizations of ancient legends and lore, and by finding such rationalizations, were attempting to restore lost technologies of power:

> ...Nazi occultists were deeply interested in all obscure manuscripts. They carefully investigated all the ancient archives they plundered in their rampage across Europe in a search for some further knowledge which could aid their creation of the 'New Order'.
> Amongst this welter of half-forgotten occult lore resurrected by the Nazis was the physical control of nations by means of the ancient science of geomancy which some call 'earth magic'. In ancient times, they found, a nation's most sacred place was also

invariably its seat of government. Possession of this sacred place, the psychic centre of the nation, meant dominion over it...

... (The) whole science of geomancy finally became an essential magical tool in the conquest of Europe.[34]

Thus, the "lines of force" which German grid researchers had uncovered in Central and Western Europe were understood by the Nazis as tools to be "used as lines of conquest."[35]

But why would Haushofer's geopolitical institute employ — amid its grab bag of meteorologists, geographers, psychologists, strategists and other specialists — *physicists?*

C. A Deeper Physics?
1. Ashlars and Engineering

The answer to that question brings us more directly into contact with the Earth grid, and the mysterious energies that may inadvertently have been tapped in the thermonuclear theurgy of those first h-bomb tests. In bringing down the thermonuclear fire of the gods-stars to the surface of the Earth, the scientists and engineers involved in designing and testing those devices were in fact engaged in a very ancient undertaking: alchemical architecture.

The conception of "alchemical architecture" — an architecture deliberately employing sacred geometries and numerology in an attempt to bring down to Earth the transforming powers of the heavens — is an old conception, and forms one of the pillars, pun intended, of Freemasonry. Those "transforming powers" however, are both of a purely *physical*, but also a purely *spiritual and social*, nature, and the two, as we shall see throughout this book, are closely

---

[34] Pennick, *Hitler's Secret Sciences,* p. 3. It should be noted that Haushofer and his son Albrecht were in constant touch, even after the war began, with upper echelons of the British elite, in hopes of ending the war with Britain. The general and his son grew increasingly disenchanted with Hitler, and his son was implicated in the July 20,. 1944 assassination and coup attempt against the dictator.

[35] Ibid., p. 78. One need only consider the Nazi invasion of the Low Countries and France in May of 1940. The German breakthrough at Sedan ran along a line from Sedan to the region around Reims, to Abbeville, and thence to the Channel Ports, Boulogne, the Pas de Calais, and, of course, Dunquerque.

connected in the ancient mind by what it considered to be the underlying physics of the medium.

One may understand the Masonic obsession with the *social* aspect of this alchemical architecture by a closer look at its conception of "ashlars." In my previous book *LBJ and the Conspiracy to Kill Kennedy* I noted both these aspects — the physics and social engineering aspects — of the symbolism of the Masonic ashlar, and it is worth citing those remarks at length here, for they are now germane to the wider context of the geomantic energies that such alchemical architectures seek to evoke in the Earth grid by the placement and design of certain types of temples and structures:

> According to Albert Pike, author of the Scottish Rite's "Bible" of Freemasonry, *Morals and Dogma,* an ashlar is a symbol of the whole philosophy of the Masonic Craft:
>
> > You will hear shortly of the *Rough* ASHLAR and the *Perfect* ASHLAR, as part of the jewels of the Lodge. The rough Ashlar is said to be "a stone, as taken from the quarry, in its rude and natural state." The perfect Ashlar is said to be "a stone made ready by the hands of the workmen, to be adjusted by the working-tools of the Fellow-Craft."... They are declared to allude to the self-improvement of the individual craftsman, — a continuation of the same superficial interpretation.
> >
> > The rough Ashlar is the PEOPLE, as a mass, rude and unorganized. The perfect Ashlar, or cubical stone, symbol of perfection, is the STATE, **the rulers deriving their powers from the consent of the governed**; the constitution and laws speaking the will of the people; the government harmonious, symmetrical, efficient, — its powers properly distributed and duly adjusted in equilibrium.[36]

It is to be noted that the context of this piece of Masonic ritual is understood to be a symbol of *people*, both in an unorganized condition — the "rough ashlar" — and in an organized, that is to say, a *socially engineered* condition — the "perfect ashlar." This will be an important interpretive context in a moment.

The second thing to be noted about the quotation is the double-edged sense in which many of its statements — particularly that about "the rulers deriving their powers from the consent of

---

[36] Albert Pike, *Morals and Dogma of the Ancient and Accepted Scottish Rite of Freemasonry* (Charleston, S.C.: 1871), p. 5, italicized and capitalized emphasis original, bold face emphasis added.

the governed" — can be interpreted. There is obviously the prosaic sense, namely, that Pike simply means to indicate the nature of the republican form of American government, and is mouthing pious patriotic platitudes. But there is the deeper sense explored in the previous chapter, that of the consent of the people to an obviously criminal act, and even more criminal "explanation" and cover-up, an act of consent which increases the powers of the occult rulers performing the ritual.

The deep connection between this "alchemical" social engineering and Masonic ritual is made clear by another reference to the "ashlar" occurring much later in Pike's tome in reference to citations from the ritual of initiating a Knight of the Sun, or Prince Adept, the twenty-eighth degree of the thirty-three degrees of Scottish Rite Freemasonry:

> A rough Ashlar is the shapeless stone which is to be prepared in order to commence the philosophical work; and to be developed, in order to change its form from triangular to cubic, after the separation from it of its Salt, Sulphur, and Merecury, **by the aid of the Square, Level, Plumb, and Balance,** and all the other Masonic implements *which we use symbolically.*
>
> Here we put them to philosophical use, to constitute a well-proportioned edifice, analogous to a candidate commencing his initiation into our Mysteries. **When we build we must observe all the rules and proportions: for otherwise the Spirit of Life cannot lodge therein. So you will build the great tower, in which is to burn the fire of the Sages, or, in other words, the fire of Heaven; as also the Sea of the Sages, in which the Sun and the Moon are to bathe.** That is the basin of Purification, in which will be the water of Celestial Grace, water that doth not soil the hands, but purifies all leprous bodies.[37]

This quotation requires careful attention and care in unpacking its carefully coded language.

The "philosophical work" referred to is precisely the alchemical operation of confecting the Philosophers' Stone, the transformation of matter, the bringing down of the *materia prima* into earthly form. But there is also an esoteric operation, that of the transmutation of base metals into gold, in this case, the base metal of unenlightened humanity into the pure gold of an illuminated

---

[37] Pike, *Morals and Dogma*, p. 787, italicized emphasis original, boldface emphasis added.

consciousness. The "philosophical work" is thus a code for these two types of operation.[38]

But our real interest in this passage lies in the bold face passages. Note the use of "Masonic implements," the square, level, plumb and balance. If one did not know that this was a nineteenth century Masonic text, one might conclude one was reading a bizarre description of the torsion physics experiments of Russian astrophysicist Nikolai Kozyrev. The passage hints, obliquely, that it is talking about an encoded physics, an encoded physics probably unknown even to a Masonic adept like Albert Pike.

This is darkly hinted at in the second paragraph. Masonry is an alchemical craft, for in the metaphor of constructing buildings according to the sacred geometry of Masonic "architecture" the real goal is to embody "the Spirit of Life" in those buildings. That one is dealing with a physics here is evidenced by the next part of the passage, referring to "the fire of the Sages" which is "the fire of heaven," the *energy of the sea of space-time itself*, the "zero point" energy of the vacuum.

That this is so is further reinforced by the use of a standard code often found in ancient texts for this physical medium of space-time, for in those texts deep space is referred to as "the abyss," the "primeval waters or primeval ocean," and this is what we see in this Masonic text where the sun and moon are said to "bathe" in this sea.

Finally, note the reference to building "the great tower." While this could be construed to mean the Masonic principle of embodying "rule and proportion" into physical buildings and thus embodying "the Spirit of Life," there is a deeper meaning. Recall that Hoffman stated one long term goal of such alchemical workings was to reinvoke the gods of old. The reference, in other words, is an ancient one, and at this level of meaning the "great tower" is the Tower of Babel itself, a tower which, according to the biblical story, would reach to heaven and allow men "to do whatever they imagined to do." I have argued elsewhere that the real purpose of this tower — and of all pyramidal structures in one

---

[38] For a further discussion of these two types of alchemy, see my *The Philosophers' Stone: Alchemy and the Secret Research for Exotic Matter* (Feral House, 2009), pp. 31-36.

form or another — was to access this energy of heaven, this energy of the vacuum, of space-time itself.[39]

On this reading of the passage, we are indeed dealing with a very ancient agenda, the agenda of turning the "rough ashlars" of stone into the "perfect ashlars" of structures able to summon the fire of heaven itself. We are dealing, in other words, with an encoded physics.[40]

Alchemical architecture, in other words, encompassed two aspects: the architecture or engineering of society, and the architecture or engineering of the physical medium itself, and notably, within Masonic tradition, these two were clearly seen as being connected.

2. Transmitters, Temples, Sacred Sites, and Nazis

Thus, with the SS's infiltration of fraternal societies, it should come as no surprise that there are some slight suggestions that the Nazis saw the connection between sacred sites and a potentially deeper physics, for Nazi German radio and radar stations were constructed on "ancient mark-points in the land's sacred geography."[41] Indeed, Nazi high-energy research seems to have been in part driven by physics considerations of various points on the Earth grid within the Third Reich:

> The place where the 'occult arts' and official science came closest together is in the real of earth-radio-magnetic-psychic energies. By the 1930s, luminaries like Nikola Tesla claimed that electronic research was close to perfecting the 'death ray'. German scientists saw this as the ultimate weapon which would guarantee world supremacy. Working with high-voltage X-rays the Nazi physicist Schieboldt attempted to develop a ray that wopuld destroy an aircraft in flight.[42] Code-named *Hdubrand, a similar device used intersecting beams of infrared energy to burn up enemy aeroplanes.* This line of study proved fruitless, but one of its spinoffs was the electron

---

[39] See my *The Cosmic War: Interplanetary Warfare, Modern Physics, and Ancient Texts* (Adventures Unlimited Press, pp. 204-212.

[40] Joseph P. Farrell, *LBJ and the Conspiracy to Kill Kennedy* (Adventures Unlimited Press, 2010), pp. 220-223.

[41] Pennick, *Hitler's Secret Scienes*, p. 171.

[42] See my *The Philosophers' Stone* (Feral House 2009), pp. .

microscope, now a fundamental research tool in both biology and materials science. Hitler had said "If we had more powerful microscopes, we would discover new worlds," and the electron microscope did just this. It has indeed been one of the few useful legacies of the Third Reich.[43]

In connexion with this high-energy research, various mysterious 'transmitters' were erected at several 'key points' in the Reich. In 1938, the Brocken, a celebrated peak in the Harz mountains, was the site of feverish construction work. Holy mountain of the goddess Freyja, the Brocken is best known for the curious optical phenomenon known as the 'Brocken spectre', which occurs when the shadow of a person on the summit is cast by the rays of the sun onto a cloud below. Under some conditions, this 'spectre' has a saintly halo around its head.

This 'transmitter' was a strange contraption, a tower surrounded by an array of posts with pear-shaped knobs on top. At the same time a similar system was erected on the peak of the Feldberg near Frankfurt. When it began operation, there were soon reports of strange phenomena in the vicinity of the Brocken tower. Cars travelling along the mountain roads would suddenly have engine failure. A Luftwaffe sentry would soon spot the stranded car, and tell the puzzled motorist that it was no use trying to get the car started at present. After a while, the sentry would tell the driver that the engine would work again now, and the car would then start up and drive away.

Years later, after the war, the 'car paralysis' phenomenon was reported time and again in association with UFO sightings. Whatever its function, this 'transmitter' was emanating a field of energy sufficient to short-circuit the electrical systems of nearby cars.[44]

An event during the war demonstrated that these transmitters were being used in some sort of weaponized capacity.

On January 24, 1945, two American P-38 twin-engine fighters were dispatched to investigate the reports of a Nazi "magnetic wave" weapon near Frankfurt. The P-38 of Lt. Hitt suddenly began to experience malfunctioning of all its electrical equipment as he drew

---

[43] For a picture of the German electron microscope, see my *Roswell and the Reich* (Adventures Unlimited Press, 2010), p. 486.
[44] Pennick, *Hitler's Secret Sciences*, pp. 168-169.

close to the transmitter installation near the Feldberg at Frankfurt, including his compass, which began to spin through 360 degrees, and his plane's two engines which began to sputter and run very rough. The other pilot, flying nearly a mile away from Lt. Hitt, experienced no such difficulties. Upon their return to base Lt. Hitt's difficulties generated an intelligence report entitled "Preliminary Report on Suspected Magnetic ray." A British engineer did calculations to determine how large such a facility had to be, and he concluded that it would have been a facility using such large ground-based coils as to render the idea impractical. The German transmitters, however, as we have seen, involved no such coils, but were, rather, a series of antennae laid out in circular fashion — almost mimicking the henge-like stone structures that dotted the European and British landscapes — with pear-shaped bulbs at their end. As I have observed elsewhere, "This implies that the German device operated on different principles than what the Allies expected, given that the description of these antennae (does) not resemble that of a huge set of coils."[45]

But if there were different principles involved, what were they?

One clue is perhaps afforded by the *postwar* conclusions of yet another German electrical engineer, Prof. Dr. Konstantin Meyl, who noticed not only that certain ancient Greek and Roman temples were built according to the principles of "sacred geometry," but also that they could, if viewed with the eye of an engineer, function as vast wave-guide cavities for simple radio telegraphy! Ancient temples, in other words, were deliberately constructed as simple radio transmitters![46]

The placement of such temples — and the Nazi transmitters — on world "grid" sites suggests that the Nazis did indeed discover or re-discover some aspects of long lost science. In this connection, it should also be noted that they showed immense interest in Nikola Tesla's schemes for the wireless broadcasting of electrical power.

---

[45] Joseph P. Farrell, *Secrets of the Unified Field: the Philadelphia Experiment, the Nazi Bell, and the Discarded Theory* (Adventures Unlimited Press, 2008), p. 242. For a fuller discussion of this incident, see pp. 240-242. Meyl's work does raise the speculative possibility that it might, somehow, be based on wartime Nazi research, though I have found no direct evidence to suggest such a connection.

[46] Joseph P. Farrell, *Babylon's Banksters: The Alchemy of Deep Physics, High Finance, and Ancient Religion* (Feral House, 2010), pp. 250-264.

While this is not the place to recount the nature of Tesla's wireless electrical power broadcasting technology in detail,[47] there are certain features that must be noted in terms of the Earth grid. Tesla's scheme was dependent upon making the *Earth itself* as the transmitting medium by establishing standing longitudinal electrical waves within it.

This requires some unpacking.

A longitudinal wave is *not* a typical sine or Hertzian wave, but rather, a *pressure* or pulse. We may understand the difference between the two types of waves by means of a simple analogy. If we imagine two people standing with a jump rope suspended loosely between them, and then one person jerking the rope up and down, that upward jerk will transmit a loose "S" shape down the rope to the other person. This would represent a standard Hertzian wave, the kind of electromagnetic energy that we are familiar with in light, radio signals, and so on. Notice, that *most* of the energy generated in creating the wave is lost in the creation of that initial jerking motion, and only a fraction of that energy is received by the person holding the rope at the other end, and it does so *some time later than the initial pulse.*

Now we replace the jump rope by placing a yardstick between the two people, and one of them repeatedly pushes or "pulses" his end of the yardstick. *Instantly*, that pulse transmits virtually *all* the energy of the pulse to the person at the other end of the yardstick. This is a longitudinal or pressure wave.

But what has this to do with the Earth grid, and with the Nazi transmitters? The answer is very simple. Recall that the British engineer consulted to run calculations on the amount of power that would be needed by the Frankfurt transmitter would have been enormous, and would have required enormous coils. This is our clue that he was thinking in terms of (1) only *one* transmitting antenna, and (2) of standard *Hertzian* or "jump rope" waves. Whereas, we have seen that the two Nazi transmitters at the Feldberg near Frankfurt and the Brocken were both composed of *several* antennae, and this is our clue that they were transmitters designed to send out not Hertzian "jump rope" waves, but longitudinal "yardstick" pulses. If

---

[47] For a fuller discussion of this technology, see my *Babylon's Banksters*, pp. 130-155.

we can imagine, for the moment, the Earth itself being a smooth pond, into which we toss a handful of pebbles, we will see immediately what is happening. As each pebble — representing one pulse from one antenna — hits the surface of the pond, it will send out a circular pressure wave which will overlap with all the other waves being created by all the other pebbles. *Where these waves overlap, we get nodal points, where the energy of all the waves meeting at that point is added together.*[48] Thus, one need not have a *single* installation with large coils, but in actual fact, the best system would be several smaller systems with several antennae each sending out overlapping pulses. It is thus possible that the Earth grid actually consists of nodal points created by such standing waves overlapping on the surface of the Earth, being guided by local landscape(which would function as wave guides).[49] It thus seems evident that the Nazis, working with some version of Tesla's wireless electrical broadcast technology, had discovered at least some aspects of the physics behind ancient geomancy and the world grid system.

D. A Review of the Building Case

So, at the end of these previous two chapters, what do we have?

Three salient facts emerge from the survey thus far, and they are each suffused with implications for Earth grid research:

1) The lithium-7 explanation for runaway yields on early hydrogen bomb tests is quite possibly a cover for a discovery of something else:
   a) In the case of the "Mike" test it fails utterly, since no lithium-7 was even involved, making its subsequent use as an explanation for the "Castle Bravo" test at best a partial explanation, and at worst, a lie; and
   b) In the latter case, the idea that the engineers and scientists did not know about the reaction until *after* the test occurred is also unlikely, since the "fraud" in Argentina,

---

[48] For a fuller discussion of this point, see my *SS Brotherhood of the Bell* (Adventures Unlimited Press, pp. 211-219.

[49] This is the basic idea behind Sesh Heri's book *The Handprint of Atlas* (Corvos Books, 2008).

Dr. Ronald Richter, clearly and unequivocally stated that he knew about it, and his Argentine interlocutor, Dr. José Balseiro, clearly did as well. The fact that a slightly asymmetrical conpression might have led to the rotation of the nuclear plasma, and thus to the induction of energy from unanticipated torsion effects into the reaction, squared fully with Richter's own explanations of his research, as well as with the research and statements of Dr. Kozyrev in the Soviet Union. In Kozyrev's case, the fact that his research disappeared into the deepest classification after a public denunciation in *Pravda* strongly suggests that Soviet thermonuclear engineers may have incorporated his insights into the design of the massive "Tsar Bomba" hydrogen bomb, tested with a yield of 57 megatons. By inducing torsion effects into the reaction, the placement of such devices, and the timing of a test vis-a-vis local celestial geometries, would effect the efficiency of such devices to greater or lesser degrees, determinable only by means of actual observation, and therefore, nuclear testing;[50]

2) These grid energies in turn were perhaps based upon interfering standing waves in the medium of the Earth itself, and possibly present at certain nodal points — places where such waves intersected — nodal points moreover located precisely at ancient sacred sites. In the case of the Nazis and their transmitters, it would seem to be indicated that they had at least understood that some aspects of ancient engineering were tapping into these energies, and they placed their transmitters accordingly, hoping to tap into it;

---

[50] The possibility must also be entertained that the Soviet MGB/KGB investigated Richter and his claims as well — in fact, it would have been highly unlikely for it *not* to do so, and this may also have been a factor in the subsequent "public denunciation" of Kozyrev and the secret classification of his research. This, tied with the fact that the Soviets certainly *knew* of the Nazi Bell device via SS General Jakob Sporrenberg's Polish War Crimes trial affidavit, makes it very likely that torsion research in that country was fueled in part by earlier Nazi wartime efforts, and the realization that those efforts were continued by the Nazis under the nominal aegis of Perón's Argentina in Richter's project.

3) It would not have been lost to the Nazi scientists, just as it was not lost to their English counterparts, that the early Grid research clearly and unequivocally demonstrated recurring astronomical alignments. But how such astronomical alignments figured into the actual physics and technologies remains to be seen, though again, a clue is afforded by the early H-bomb tests and the work of Drs. Richter and Kozyrev; and finally,

4) Especially in the case of German secret societies, one finds the notion of a hidden and esoteric continuity of institutions with ancient times and mystery schools, a belief that reinforced the idea that there was indeed a hidden wisdom and lost science to be recovered.

As we shall see, there was indeed a "quantum mechanical conundrum" to the Earth grid and ancient sites that, during the time of these early researchers, was not known nor anticipated. But first, an interlude...

3

ANGKOR WAT, ASTRONOMY, AND ARITHMETIC:

AN ENTRANCE INTO THE GRID AND ITS EXPLANATIONS

"Nobody sets out to build 50,000-plus pyramids and mounds around a planet just for the hell of it, or want of something to do. History teaches that these primitive people were hunter-gatherers who spent their waking hours running down their next meals. If that's true, then who built these monuments? These people didn't have the time. ...(These) things were not built at the whims of medicine men. There was enormous global planning behind it all."
Carl P. Munck[1]

C ataloguing all the *research* of various authors who have noticed the placement of ancient sites on a grid system spanning the globe would be a difficult, if not impossible task. Indeed, merely cataloguing all the *researchers* who have written on the subject would be nearly impossible, for virtually everyone in the field of "alternative research" has been compelled, by the nature of the field itself, to say something about it at one time or another. Well known and prominent names such as David Hatcher Childress, Graham Hancock, Alexander Thom, Sir Norman Lockyear and numerous others have commented or written whole books about the subject and in so doing have joined the ranks of grid researchers along with less well-known names. As we saw in previous chapters, those ranks were swelled even more by a panoply of Nazis, and a Soviet astrophysicist — Dr. Nikolai Kozyrev — whose work's implications touched directly on aspects of the phenomenon. Accordingly no attempt to do either will be made here.

But what, exactly, is the "Earth grid"?

We clearly need some sort of working definition, one capable of modification as our survey proceeds. Let us begin with a simple definition: *Ancient sites, temples, and structures are laid out upon a grid whose significance is determined by their placement at mathematically significant places*

---

[1] Carl P. Munck, *Whispers from Time: the Pyramid Bible* (Bellevue, WA: internet Marketing NW, 1999), p. 80.

upon the surface of the Earth, or in correspondence with celestial, astronomical alignments, or both, and often incorporate these and other mathematical analogues in the structures themselves.

A. Anomalies at the Temples of Angkor

We need only consider the famous site of Angkor Wat in Cambodia.

Angkor Wat in Cambodia

Well-known alternative researchers Graham Hancock and his wife Santha Faiia point out some very odd connections of Angor Wat to another well-known culture harboring many sites on the world grid, Egypt:

> The name 'Angkor', although supposedly a corruption of the Sanscrit word *nagara*, 'town', has a very precise meaning in the ancient Egyptian language — 'the god Horus lives'. Other

acceptable translations of 'Ankh-Hor' or 'Ankhor' are 'May Horus Live', 'Horus Lives' and 'Life to Horus'.[2]

Of course, such etymological coincidences are just that, coincidences. Or are they?

1. The Ancient Prime Meridian: Giza

Hancock and Faiia observe a very peculiar thing about the *placement* of the Angkor temples, a placement that ties them to Egypt in a very direct and unavoidable way, nor are they by any means alone in their observation, for it has been repeatedly observed by other grid researchers. It is apparent, they maintain, that when one studies the placement of various sites and monuments around the world — Angkor Wat, Teotihuacan, Tikal, Stonehenge, Avebury, and a host of others too lengthy to mention — that they are placed with Giza as the prime meridian, with that meridian in fact running through the apex of the Great Pyramid itself.[3] When this is done, Angkor Wat lies at almost exactly 72 degrees east longitude from Giza.[4]

That number, 72, requires some special commentary of its own. It is, of course, the exact measure of the spacing between points of a pentagon and pentagram if circumscribed by a circle. The years allotted to the various Hindu yugas — the four great world ages — are all divisible by 72:

1,728,000 years, the Satya yuga
1,296,000 years, the Treta yuga
  864,000 years, the Dvapara yuga
  432,000 years, the Kali yuga[5]

Dividing by 72 gives some very interesting results:

---

[2] Graham Hancock and Santha Faiia, *Heaven's Mirror: Quest for the Lost Civilization* (New York: Crown Publishers, Inc. 1998), p. 116.

[3] Ibid., p. 119.

[4] Ibid.

[5] See also my *The Cosmic War: Interplanetary Warfare, Modern Physics, and Ancient Texts*, p. 105f.

24,000
18,000
12,000
6,000

The yugas, in other words, are all harmonics, or multiples, of 72, in the orderly progression of 24, 18, 12, and 6. Interestingly enough, if one deals only with the coefficients of the Hindu yugas — the numbers themselves — by dropping three orders of magnitude, then one ends up with 1728, 1296, 864, and 432, all numbers which are encoded in the dimension of the temple at Angkor Wat![6] Nor are these the only things encoded there.

2. As Above, So Below: The Astronomical Correlation and the 10,500 BC
Mystery

In 1996, Hancock's and Faiia's research associate, John Grigsby, discovered that the layout of the temples of Angkor Wat corresponded with the northern constellation of Draco. Thus, there was another odd correlation to Egypt, for "just as the three Great Pyramids Giza in Egypt model the belt stars of the southern constellation of Orion, so too do the principal monuments of Angkor model the sinuous coils of the northern constellation of Draco."[7] By running astronomical programs, Hancock and Faiia determined that at sunrise of the spring equinox in 10,500 BC the constellation Draco was due north of the Angkor complex.[8] This corresponded exactly to the date of the three major Giza pyramids' alignment to the three stars of the belt of the constellation Orion: 10,500 BC.

However, there was a problem. If one accepted the conventional dating of the Giza compound to ca. 2500 BC,[9] how would one account for such a similar memorialization of a very ancient date —

---

[6] Hancock and Faiia, *Heaven's Mirror*, pp. 152-153.

[7] Ibid., p. 126.

[8] Ibid., p. 133, see also the discussion on pp. 131-132.

[9] As we shall see in a subsequent chapter, there are massive problems with this conventional date, and there is every reason to believe, based on geological evidence alone, that the Sphinx at least is several thousands of years older than this date, or, for that matter, dynastic Egypt.

10,500 BC, thousands of miles away, and nearly three millennia *later*, in Cambodia?

> Indisputable archaeological and inscription evidence proves that the temples of Angkor were built by named and known Khmer monarchs, almost all of whom reigned during the four centuries between AD 802 and AS 1200.[10]

Why were massive monuments being built in Cambodia to memorialize a date almost eleven millennia previous to the time of their construction? And why were such memorializations present in both Egypt and Cambodia?

The pattern of this Egypt-Cambodia link only deepened the closer Hancock and Faiia looked. For example:

1) Both in Cambodia and in Egypt, there was a tradition of an "architect of the gods" who was responsible for the building of such monuments and who taught architecture to men. In Egypt's case, this was Imhotep; in Cambodia's it was Visvakarma;

2) Both Egypt and Cambodia venerated the serpent as a sacred figure[11] (and, as we shall see, Meso-America as well!), and "in both cases it was the hooded cobra that was selected as the archetype, in both cases it could be depicted in art as a half-human, half-serpent figure."[12] Again, the same, as we shall discover, holds true for Meso-America as well;

3) Both in Egypt and in Cambodia this "serpent god" could also symbolize either the sky or the ground; and finally,

---

[10] Hancock and Faiia, *Heaven's Mirror*, p. 128.

[11] For a further discussion of the symbolism of the serpent in this connection, see my *The Cosmic War*, pp. 327-330; 347-348. The serpent, it should be noted, was often also a symbol of the planet Mars.

[12] Ibid., p. 174. The serpent thus becomes the natural symbol in Egypt of sacred Kingship, and the pharaoh's headdress is meant to reflect a hooded-cobra's hood in full extension. This too is paralleled by the Hindu *Nagas* or cobra-kings, supernatural beings counted as gods but who rule on earth. (q.v. Hancock and Faiia, pp. 134, 136.)

4) Both in Cambodia and in Egypt the serpent could symbolize immortality and the cycles of the universe;

5) Both in Cambodia and in Egypt, it was believed that when the king died, his soul would ascend to the heavens.[13]

All this raises the problem of explaining why such odd correspondences should be found in two such disparate cultures, and why that one date in particular — 10,500 BC — should be embodied in both:

> So the real questions at Angkor are not so much a matter of the absolute dates of the construction of the various temples, or even of the many substructures that are known to lie beneath them, but rather:
>
> 1. *Why* does the overall site-plan focus so insistently and specifically on the pattern of stars in the sky region surrounding the constellation of Draco as it looked at dawn on the spring equinox in 10,500 BC?
> 2. How can we explain the fact that this same precise date is signaled by the three great Pyramids and the Great Sphinx of Giza — monuments that are not thought to be linked in any way to the temples of Angkor?
> 3. Is it not amazing that all three groups of monuments use the same architectural technique to draw attention to that date, i.e. by modeling a prominent constellation that was present at one of the cardinal points of the sky on the spring equinox in 10,500 BC(Draco to the north, in the case of Angkor; Leo, to the east, in the case of the Great Sphinx; Orion to the south, in the case of the Pyramids)?
> 4. **Could there be some sort of hidden connection?**[14]

Hancock and Faiia have noticed the central mystery of the grid: why do so many disparate cultures appear to be building massive monuments, at different times and places, and yet, seem to be doing so as if following some sort of plan?

One answer immediately comes to mind: the grid-building activity was the program and product of a hidden elite:

---

[13] For these five points, see Hanock and Faiia, op. cit., p. 174.
[14] Ibid., p. 161, italicized emphasis in the original, boldface emphasis added.

Another explanation... (there) could be an undetected 'third party' influence, very discreet, very secretive and of very great antiquity. Such an influence — perhaps the long-lived and highly motivated society that referred to its initiates in ancient Egypt as the 'Followers of Horus' — does seem immensely improbable. Nevertheless, as Sherlock Holmes famously reminded Watson in *The Sign of Four*, 'when you have eliminated the impossible, whatever remains, however improbable, must be the truth.'[15]

Yet there is another clue as to the nature of this elite and its activities in a symbolism more universal than that of the "Followers of Horus."

3. Enter the Serpent

The symbol of the wise serpent in this case turns out to hold an answer — or at least, *part* of an answer — to the 10,500 BC mystery and to the possibility of a connection via a hidden elite.

Angkor Wat's western entrance is a place of shadows before dawn when the sun lies invisible in the east beneath the vast mass of the temple. Even in low light it is impossible to ignore the dominant presence of the Naga serpents which, with their stone bodies, and rearing, hooded heads, form sinuous balustrades lining the causeway. The same cobra motif in numerous different forms is frequently, almost incessantly, repeated — leading one authority to conclude that Angkor Wat 'was wholly dedicated to serpent worship. Every angle of every roof is adorned with a seven-headed serpent.'[16]

As we shall see elsewhere in this book, this is not the only time we will encounter a serpent motif in conjunction with the monuments of the world grid. We have already noted, however, the serpent motif is present in Egypt, in the hooded headdress of the pharaohs, representing the extended hood of a cobra. The pharaohs, in other

---

[15] Hancock and Faiia, *Heaven's Mirror*, p. 168.
[16] Ibid., citing Rooney, *Angkor*, p. 52.

words, were not only kings claiming descent from the gods, they were not only "Followers of Horus" but they were also in a certain sense "serpent-kings."

This chimerical human-serpent motif is found, curiously enough, in the Hindu conceptions underlying the symbolism of Angkor Wat, for these multi-headed serpents, the Nagas, represent a kind of trans-dimensional creature, "crossing the realms of sky and ground, time and space, this world and the next and although they intermingle — and sometimes intermarry — in the material realm of earth and men there is never any doubt that their true identity is as celestial and cosmic forces."[17] This Egyptian-Hindu link is further compounded beyond the point of coincidence when one examines closely the respective cosmologies of the two cultures.

Within Hinduism, Vishnu, the primordial "all-god" creates the universe through the sheer strength and force of his will. But this is accompanied by an explicit sexual metaphor, as Vishnu ejaculates into the primordial cosmic waters. This is paralleled in the Egyptian cosmology by Atum, who, coming forth from the primeval waters of the Nun, ejaculates into the cosmic waters.[18]

It is important to pause and consider the full implications of this cosmology and its explicit sexual metaphor. In both cases, the primordial condition, with the "Self-existent" Vishnu or Atum, is one where there is absolutely nothing else in existence. Thus, even the "primordial waters" are, to some extent, "part of" this self-existent "god" or "state" or "condition." The ejaculation of semen by this god into this ocean, from which He is not distinct, is, in effect, the injection of "seed" or *differentiating information* into himself.

The parallels do not end there however.

4. The Topological Metaphor

As we shall see subsequently, within the Egyptian cosmology, the self-differentiation of Atum gives rise to the first three *neters*, a "triad" or "primordial trinitarian differentiation." It is the same within the Hindu cosmogony, for in the *Padama Purana* we read:

---

[17] Hancock and Faiia, *Heaven's Mirror*, p. 137.
[18] Ibid.

In the beginning of creation the Great Vishnu, desirous of creating the whole world, became threefold: Creator, Preserver, Destroyer. In order to create this world, the Supreme Spirit produced from the right side of his body himself as Brahma then, in order to preserve the world, he produced from his left side Vishnu; and in order to destroy the world he produced from the middle of his body the eternal Shiva. Some worship Brahma, others Vishnu, others Shiva; but Vishnu, one yet threefold, creates, preserves, and destroys: therefore let the pious make no difference between the three.[19]

Note that neither in the Egyptian nor in the Hindu versions of this "primordial trinitarian homosexual ecstasy" are we dealing with any notion of a theological *revelation.*

We are dealing, rather, with the "topological metaphor" of the physical medium itself, as I noted in the appendix to chapter nine of *The Giza Death Star Destroyed,*[20] and again in *The Philosophers' Stone,*[21] and it is worth recalling what I stated there concerning the emergence of this "trinity" from the information-creating processes of the physical medium as viewed in yet *other* ancient traditions, in this case, the Neoplatonic and Hermetic.

In order to understand what the ancients meant by all the variegated religious and metaphysical imagery they employed to describe this topological metaphor — in order to *decode* it — let us perform a simple "thought experiment." Imagine an absolutely undifferentiated "something." The Neoplatonists referred to this "something" as "simplicity" (απλωτης). Note that, from the *physics* point of view *and from that of Hinduism itself,* we are dealing with a "nothing," since it has no differentiated or distinguishing features whatsoever.

Now imagine one "brackets" this nothing, separating off a "region" of nothing from the rest of the nothing(Vishnu's ejaculation

---

[19] W.J. Wilkins, *Hindu Mythology* (New Delhi: Heritage Publishers, 1991), p. 116, citing the *Padama Purana.*

[20] Joseph P. Farrell, *The Giza Death Star Destroyed* (Kempton, Illinois: Adventures Unlimited Press, 2005), pp. 222-245.

[21] Joseph P. Farrell, *The Philosophers' Stone: Alchemy and the Secret Research for Exotic Matter* (Feral House, 2009), pp. 43-48.

metaphor). At the instant one does so, one ends up with *three* things, each a kind of "differentiated nothing." One ends with:

1) the "bracketed" region of nothing;
2) the *rest* of the nothing; and,
3) the "surface" that the two regions share.

Note something else. From a purely physics point of view, this occurs without *time*, since time is measured only by the relative positions of differentiated things with respect to each other. The "regions of nothing" and their common surface are, so to speak, still eternal, and yet, at the same instant, a kind of "time" has emerged simultaneously with the operation of differentiating itself.

In short, from a non-quantifiable "nothing," information begins to emerge with the process of "bracketing" or "differentiating" itself, including the concept of *number*. On the ancient view, then, numbers do not exist in the abstract. They are, rather, functions of a topological metaphor of the physical medium.[22]

Now let us go further into this topological metaphor by notating our three differentiated nothings mathematically. There is a perfect symbol to represent this "nothing", the empty hyper-set, whose symbol is $\emptyset$, and which contains no "things" or "members." Now let our original "nothing" be symbolized by $\emptyset_E$. A surface of something is represented by the partial derivative symbol ∂, for after all, a "surface" of something, even a nothing, is a "partial derivative" of it. So, we would represent our three resulting entities as follows:

1) the "bracketed" region of nothing, or $\emptyset_{A-E}$;
2) the *rest* of the nothing, or $\emptyset_{E-A}$; and,
3) the "surface" that the two regions share, or $\partial\emptyset_{A-E|E-A}$.

---

[22] The similarity of this concept to Schwaller De Lubicz's understanding of numbers in ancient Egypt as *functions of geometry* is readily apparent. Schwaller, a mathematician, knew that he could have expressed this conception more deeply, in the form of numbers not as functions of geometry, but of an even higher-order, as functions of the topology of the physical medium itself. It is my opinion that he did not do so, not because he was unaware of it, but rather, because he was trying to popularize and render Egyptian cosmological thought understandable to lay audiences.

Note now that the three "nothings" are still nothing, but now they have acquired information, distinguishing each nothing in a *formally explicit* manner from each other nothing. Note something else: *the relationship between them all is analogical in nature, since each bears the signature of having derived from the original undifferentiated nothing; each retains, in other words, in its formal description, the presence of ∅.* And this will be true *no matter how many times one continues to "bracket" or "differentiate" it.* On this ancient cosmological view, in other words, everything is related to everything else by dint of its derivation via innumerable steps of "differentiation" from that original nothing. It is this fact which forms the basis within ancient civilizations for the practice of sympathetic magic, for given the analogical nature of the physical medium implied by these ancient cosmologies, in purely physics terms, everything is a coupled harmonic oscillator of everything else.[23] Finally, observe how this formal explicitness dovetails quite nicely with the Hindu conception that the created world is, in fact, illusion, a "nothing," but a differentiated nothing.

Now let us take the next step in the decoding of this topological metaphor in ancient texts and cosmologies. It is understood within the kind of mathematical metaphor that we are exploring here, that *functions* can be members of the empty hyper-set without destroying its "emptiness," for the simple reason that *functions* are not "things" or objects, but pure processes. Thus far, we have dealt with regions, and surfaces, now we add *functions.*

Here is what I wrote in *The Giza Death Star Destroyed* about the three entities when examined from the standpoint of a passage of the *Hermetica:*

The passage is the *Libellus II:1-6b,* a short dialogue between Hermes and his discipline Asclepius:

---

[23] Of course, everything is not necessary an *efficient* oscillator of any other given thing, but that is a more complex aspect of the ancient cosmologies and their topological metaphor than can be explored in this chapter. That is the purpose of the rest of this book.

"Of what magnitude must be that space in which the Kosmos is moved? And of what nature? Must not that Space be far greater, that it may be able to contain the continuous motion of the Kosmos, and that the thing moved may not be cramped for want of room, and cease to move? — *Ascl.* Great indeed must be that Space, Trismegistus. — *Herm.* And of what nature must it be Aslcepius? Must it not be of opposite nature to Kosmos? And of opposite nature to the body is the incorporeal.... Space is an object of thought, but not in the same sense that God is, for God is an object of thought primarily to Himself, but Space is an object of thought to us, not to itself."[24]

This passage thus evidences the type of "ternary" thinking already encountered in Plotinus, but here much more explicitly so, as it is a kind metaphysical and dialectical version of topological triangulation employed by Bounias and Krasnoholovets in their version in their model. However, there is a notable distinction between Plotinus' ternary structure and that of the *Hermetica*: whereas in Plotinus' the three principle objects in view are the One, the Intellect, and the World Soul, here the principal objects in view are the triad of Theos, Topos, and Kosmos (Θεος, Τοπος, Κοσμος), or God, Space, and Kosmos, respectively.

These three — God, Space, and Kosmos — are in turn distinguished by a dialectic of opposition based on three elemental functions, each of which in turn implies its own functional opposite:

$$f_1: \text{self-knowledge} \Leftrightarrow \text{-}f_1: \text{ignorance}$$
$$f_2: \text{rest (στασις)} \Leftrightarrow \text{-}f_2: \text{motion (κινησις)}$$
$$f_3: \text{incorporeality} \Leftrightarrow \text{-}f_3: \text{corporeality.}$$

So in Hermes' version of the metaphor, the following "triangulation" occurs, with the terms "God, Space, Kosmos" becoming the names for each vertex or region:

---

[24] *Libellus: 1-6b, Hermetica*, trans. Walter Scott, Vol. 1, pp. 135, 137.

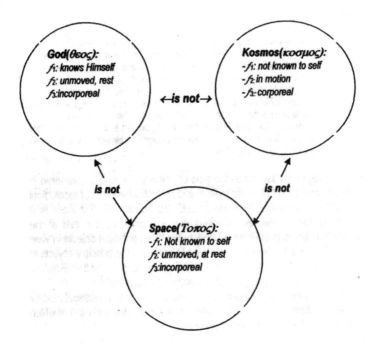

This diagram is significant for a variety of reasons. For one thing, theologically informed readers will find it paralleled in the so-called Carolingian "Trinitarian shield," a pictogram used to describe the doctrine of the Trinity as it emerged in the Neoplatonically-influenced Augustinian Christianity of the mediaeval Latin Church. Again, it must be recalled in this context that the Greek Fathers objected to this formulation of the doctrine in the strongest possible terms, and viewed this dialectical structure as not so much metaphysical, as "sensory," i.e., as more applicable to physical mechanics than to dogmatic theology.

More importantly in this context, however, the diagram illustrates how each vertex — God, Space, Kosmos — may be described as *a set of functions or their opposites:*

God $(\theta\varepsilon o\varsigma)$ $\{f_1, f_2, f_3\}$	Kosmos $(K o \sigma \mu o \varsigma)$ $\{-f_1, -f_2, -f_3\}$	Space $(T o \pi o \varsigma)$ $\{-f_1, f_2, f_3\}$
f_1: knowledge f_2: unmoved f_3: incorporeal	$-f_1$: ignorance $-f_2$: in motion $-f_3$: corporeal	$-f_1$: ignorance f_2: unmoved f_3: incorporeal

Hermes' version of the metaphor thus lends itself quite neatly to an analysis in terms of Hegelian dialectic, with Space itself forming the synthesis between God, the thesis, and Kosmos, the antithesis, described in terms of the functions f_1, f_2, f_3 or their opposites.

To see how, let us extend the formalism by *dispensing with* Hermes' metaphysical description of the *functions f_1, f_2, f_3* and take the terms God, Kosmos, and Space as the sigils of distinct or discrete topological regions in the neighborhood of each vertex in the diagram on the previous page, and model them as empty hyper-sets. Since it is possible for combinatorial functions to be members of empty sets, then letting $\varnothing_G, \varnothing_K, \varnothing_S$ stand for God, Kosmos, and Space respectively, one may quickly see the lattice work that results from entirely different sets of functional signatures, exactly as was the case in Plotinus, but via a very different route:

$$\varnothing_G = \{f_1, f_2, f_3\}$$
$$\varnothing_K = \{-f_1, -f_2, -f_3\}$$
$$\varnothing_S = \{-f_1, f_2, f_3\}.[25]$$

Note that space in Hermes' version of the metaphor, since it comprises functional elements derived from the other two regions — "God" and "Kosmos" — could be conceived as the common "surface" between the two. Thus, once again, we have our familiar three entities:

1) the "bracketed" region of nothing, or $\varnothing_{A-E}$, Hermes' "Kosmos";
2) the *rest* of the nothing, or $\varnothing_{E-A}$, Hermes' "God"; and,
3) the "surface" that the two regions share, or $\partial\varnothing_{A-E|E-A}$, Hermes' "Space"

---

[25] Joseph P. Farrell, *The Giza Death Star Destroyed*, pp. 239-241, see also my *The Philosophers' Stone*, pp. 44-47.

With this in mind, let us now look once again at the passage concerning Vishnu and the Hindu version of this primordial triad, from the *Padama Purana,* half a world and millennia removed from the *Hermetica* and related texts of Egyptian provenance:

> In the beginning of creation the Great Vishnu, desirous of creating the whole world, became threefold: Creator, Preserver, Destroyer. In order to create this world, the Supreme Spirit produced from the right side of his body himself as Brahmal then, in order to preserve the world, he produced from his left side Vishnu; and in order to destroy the world he produced from the middle of his body the eternal Shiva. Some worship Brahma, others Vishnu, others Shiva; but Vishnu, one yet threefold, creates, preserves, and destroys: therefore let the pious make no difference between the three.[26]

Once again, note that the three resulting entities, after Vishnu "differentiates himself," are described in *functional terms.* So we may substitute the names Vishnu, Brahma, and Shiva for Hermes' God, Kosmos, and Space. And again, one of these, Brahma the "preserver", appears to be a functional "set" of "nothing" that is a common surface of the other two, Vishnu the creator and Shiva the destroyer:

Androgynous Shiva

---

[26] W.J. Wilkins, *Hindu Mythology* (New Delhi: Heritage Publishers, 1991), p. 116, citing the *Padama Purana.*

Hermes: God ($\theta \epsilon o \varsigma$) $\{f_1, f_2, f_3\}$	*Hermes:* Kosmos($\mathbf{Ko\sigma\mu o\varsigma}$) $\{-f_1, -f_2, -f_3\}$	*Hermes:* Space ($To\pi o\varsigma$) $\{-f_1, f_2, f_3\}$
Padama Purana: Vishnu, the creator $\{f_4\}$	*Padama Purana:* Shiva, the destroyer $\{-f_4\}$	*Padama Purana:* Brahma, the "preserver" $\{\sqrt{-f_4}\}$
Hermes: f_1: knowledge f_2: unmoved f_3: incorporeal	*Hermes* $-f_1$: ignorance $-f_2$: in motion $-f_3$: corporeal	*Hermes* $-f_1$: ignorance f_2: unmoved f_3: incorporeal
Padama Purana: f_4: creation	*Padama Purana:* $-f_4$: destruction	*Padama Purana:* $\sqrt{-f_4}$: preservation

Note in the case of the *Padama Purana* that the functional set identified with each region or "manifestation of Vishnu" is described by a function(creation), its inverse(destruction), or the inverse of the other two(preservation). And again, we have the same three entities:

1) the "bracketed" region of Nothing, or $\varnothing_{A\text{-}E}$, Hermes' "Kosmos", and the *Padama Purana's* Shiva;
2) the *rest* of the Nothing, or $\varnothing_{E\text{-}A}$, Hermes' "God" and the *Padama Purana's* Vishnu; and,
3) the "surface" Nothing that the two regions share, or $\partial\varnothing_{A\text{-}E|E\text{-}A}$, Hermes' "Space" and the *Padama Purana's* Brahma.

The implications of this sort of analysis are profound and far-reaching, for they suggest that behind certain types of metaphysical texts, particularly those suggesting triadic structures, there is a much deeper topological metaphor that such texts are designed to encode and transmit. It suggests that all such texts are capable of a deep topological analysis, and that they have nothing, really, to do with metaphysics in the conventional philosophical or theological senses at all. They also suggest, as more and more differentiations are added to this process that account for the rise of physical creation, that there is a *physics* reason for the phenomenon of the world grid. They suggest that, as the physical medium is the information-creating and transmuting Philosophers' Stone itself, that the purpose of the world grid and its constructions is one of an "alchemical architecture," of the monumental manipulation and engineering of the medium itself, for after all, on the ancient view, once again, everything derives from that nothing and is a multi-differentiated nothing, directly tied in with everything else.

In these metaphysical and religious texts, in other words, we are looking at a profound topological and physics metaphor. We are looking at declined legacies of a very ancient, and very sophisticated, science.

5. Cosmology and History: A Hidden Elite, and a Hidden Physics?

With the "topological metaphor" in hand, let us return to Angkor Wat, and look more closely at other aspects of the Hindu cosmology memorialized in the grand and intricate stone edifice. One of the many stone reliefs at Angkor Wat portrays a Hindu cosmological conception called "the Churning of the Milky Ocean" by the five-headed Naga serpent, Vasuki.[27] On one of the panels depicting Vasuki, his long body is coiled around a mountain, Mount Mandera. Mount Mandera is, in turn, one of the four mountains butressing Mount Meru in Hindu cosmology.[28] These mountains are, like the "primordial mound" of Egypt's "Zep Tepi" or "first time," the primordial mountains of Hindu cosmology.

Vishnu himself is above this mountain, clutching Vasuki's body with two of his four hands "and seeming to control or direct its movement."[29] Vasuki is gripped on one side of his long body by an *asura* or a "high-ranking demon,"[30] and on the other by three gods

---

[27] Hancock and Faiia, *Heaven's Mirror*, p. 141.
[28] Ibid.
[29] Ibid., pp. 141-142.
[30] Ibid., p. 141.

and 85 *devas* "of lesser stature."[31] Between them, Vishnu is suspended, gripping Vasuki in the center of his body coiled around Mount Mandera, as if superintending this cosmic tug-of-war, as Mount Mandera "is being rotated, first one way then the other, by the opposing forces of the *devas* and *asuras*."[32]

As this back-and-forth churning and counter-rotation continues, eventually there arises a foaming mass, a "Sea of Milk" or "the Milky Ocean", from which the Moon and other celestial bodies appear, followed by the goddess Lakshmi, Vishnu's wife.[33] Mount Meru and its four buttressing mountains, including Mount Mandera, are the mountains at "the center of the world"[34] and thus, from their "churning," give rise to the physical world *from the action of rotation, from a vortex.*

This is a profound metaphor, and again, a distinctively *physics*-related metaphor, for what is being suggested is that one of the key methods by which things arise from that primordial nothing, and the means by which they are distinguished, is by complex systems of rotation and counter-rotation. Even "the Milky Sea" has a profound physics analogue in the "sea of quantum flux" or "vacuum energy," the sea of the void of space-time, which in quantum theory is literally teaming with vast energy potential, and which, in some versions of the theory, is *accessed by the rise of rotating systems.* In some versions of the theory, particles themselves are but systems of rotations with this otherwise inchoate sea of energy, and anyone familiar with the vast quantum mechanical particle zoo will know at once that particle families are distinguished by, among other things, their spin or rotation.

Once again, behind the seemingly irrational religious and mythological imagery lurks a profound metaphor of very contemporary and sophisticated physics.

These observations are worth comparing with those of Hancock and Faiia, who, looking at the stone reliefs of the Churning of the Milky Ocean at Angkor Wat, see yet another physical process:

---

[31] Ibid., p. 142.
[32] Ibid.
[33] Ibid., p. 143.
[34] Ibid., p. 144.

There *is* a cosmological process that fits the bill: precession — the slow, cyclical wobble of the axis of the earth that inexorably changes the positions of all the stars in the sky and shifts the 'ruling' constellation that lies behind the sun at dawn on the spring equinox. It is this process, according to Giorgio de Santillana and Hertha von Dechend in their landmark study *Hamlet's Mill*, that is the subject of a whole family of myths coming down to us from remotest antiquity. The Churching of the Milky Ocean, they say, is one of these myths.

The great contribution to scholarship made by *Hamlet's Mill* is the evidence it presents — compelling and overwhelming — that, long *before* the supposed beginnings of civilized human history in Sumer, Egypt, China, India and the Americas, precession was understood and spoken of in a precise technical language by people who could only have been highly civilized. The prime image used by these as yet unidentified archaic astronomers 'transforms the luminous done of the celestial sphere into a vast and intricate piece of machinery. And like a millwheel, like a churn, like a whirlpool, like a quern, this machine turns and turns endlessly.'[35]

But given all we've seen thus far, the answer of de Santillana and von Dechend, and of Hancock and Faiia, is not deep or complete enough. What we've observed thus far is that these mythological cosmologies are metaphors operating on *three* distinctive levels:

1) at the deepest level, of a topological metaphor of the physical medium itself, and of its "analogical" information-creating properties;
2) at a less deep level, of a *physics* metaphor of the emergence of creation, of particles, from the vast ocean or sea of quantum flux, whose emergence is described in terms of *rotation*;
3) similarly, at a less deep level, of a *physics* metaphor of the *astronomical* machine of precession.

With this in hand, we may propose a corollary thesis regarding the alchemical architecture of the world grid: any theory of the world grid

---

[35] Hancock and Faiia, *Heaven's Mirror*, p. 144.

which takes into account only one of these aspects is an incomplete theory.

But there is one final aspect of the cosmology enshrined at Angkor War that must be examined, and it is the most controversial of them all.

6. The Machine-Like Medium and Immortality

Hancock and Faiia ask a significant question: why, at Giza, and Angkor Wat — and as we shall see, in other structures of the world grid — is there such a focus and fascination with the astronomical phenomenon of precession? Precession was both for the Egyptians and the builders of Angkor a virtual immortal, eternal celestial machine. Accordingly, both in the Hindi cosmologies depicted at Angkor Wat and in the religious cosmology of distant Egypt, precession was the means to "seize the sky" and its immortal processes. Understanding it, the initiate could gain immortality.[36] This machine-like character of the celestial medium was, in other words, conceived also as a gate to immortality. While this may seem to the modern reader to be the flights of purest mythological fantasy and imagination, the Hindu cosmology so beautifully depicted in the stone carvings of Angkor Wat also contains a key, for in the "churning of the Milky Sea" the nectar of immortality is created.[37] This, as we shall see in a subsequent chapter, is a profound clue to the deeper physics behind the world grid.

However, it is worth mentioning at this juncture that such a "deeper physics" is implied by the Hindu cosmology, for it views this world — the world of our three dimensions, our senses and perceptions — as

> *not* real at all but rather a sinister sort of virtual reality game in which we are all players, a complex and cunning illusion capable of confusing even the most thorough empirical tests — a mass hallucination capable of extraordinary depth and power designed to distract souls from the straight and narrow path of awakening which leads to immortal life.[38]

---

[36] Hancock and Faiia, *Heaven's Mirror*, pp. 144-145.
[37] Ibid., p. 145.
[38] Ibid., p. 157.

This is the view implied by the "topological metaphor" we examined earlier in connection with the *Hermetica,* and it has yet another incarnation in the world grid, for "with a synchronicity that seems strange to anyone who has studied the mysteries of Central America," the Hindus named this hallucination "Maya."[39] Indeed, as we shall eventually discover, the connections go much deeper than just a name.

B. *The Master Plan of a Hidden Elite*

In addition to a "deep physics" implied by all this, there is also a "deep history" laying underneath the ground of Angkor Wat, a deep history testifying to the antiquity not only of the cosmological views of the Vedas but of the placement of the site itself. Hancock and Faiia note that Hindu tradition ascribes great antiquity to the actual *contents* of the Vedas, which were initially passed down for thousands of years as an oral tradition by Brahman priests before their codification into the books we know today. Even here, this oral transmission is not understood by the Hindu tradition to be the *original* transmission, but a "repromulgation" after the previous age of calamity and catastrophe. This work of repromulgating an earlier tradition was the work of the seven Rishis, or seven sages, who survived the previous cataclysm and "whose desire it was 'at the beginning of the new age... to safeguard 'the knowledge inherited by them as a sacred trust from there forefathers in the preceeding (sic) age.'"[40] Viewed another way, what the Rishis represent is a *surviving elite from a catastrophe,* doing what all such elites do in such circumstances: trying to preserve the knowledge that made a previous high state of civilization possible, in order to attain a similar development in the future.

Not surprisingly then, "all the major temples of Angkor also show similar traces of having been built directly on top of earlier structures which may in turn have been built on the sites of earlier

---

[39] Hancock and Faiia, *Heaven's Mirror,* p. 157.

[40] Ibid., p. 159, citing Lockamanya Bal Ganghadar Tilak, *The Artic Home in the Vedas*(Poona, 1956), p. 420.

structures still,"[41] dating back to the period when the constellation Draco, itself representing the great cosmic serpent, rose over the spring equinox in 10,500 BC. Once again, we shall discover in later chapters that the same can be said of many other sites on the world grid: while the structures themselves may be comparatively new, they are often built according to a preconceived plan dating back to remotest antiquity.

This activity of a surviving elite is encoded within Hindu tradition in yet another intriguing way, for many of Vishnu's incarnations follow a *pralaya*, a cataclysm that, interestingly enough, is most often a world-destroying flood. Hindu codices state unreservedly that Vishnu's objective on each of these occasions was precisely to save some of the knowledge "accumulated by antediluvian civilizations" and to secure its transmission to future generations.[42] In other words, Vishnu's activities on such occasions represent the activity of a surviving elite, decorated and disguised in the pious language of religion and mythology.

At Angkor Wat — as at Stonehenge, Giza, Teotihuacan and so many other places on the world grid — we are confronted with vast structures, temples, pyramids, monuments, all seemingly laid out in correlation with some astronomical alignment, and all seemingly related to each other, as Angkor Wat's placement at a certain longitude east of the Giza Prime Meridian testifies. This, as Hancock and Faiia state, is clearly suggestive of the activity of hidden players, of a hidden elite or elites:

> ...(We) have had the eerie sense of stumbling across the fragments of a strange and shadowy archaic master game — a game on a planetary scale that ran for thousands of years and that appears to have been played out in four principal dimensions:
> *First Dimension:* 'Above' — stars in the sky;
> *Second Dimension:* 'Below' — monuments on the ground, scattered around the world like pieces of an immense jigsaw puzzle, linked to one another through occult astronomical clues;
> *Third Dimension:* 'Time' — measured by the slow cycle of precession, the principal means by which the astronomical

---

[41] Hancock and Faiia, *Heaven's Mirror*, p. 159.
[42] Ibid.,p. 155.

signposts pointing from one monument to the next were hidden to the uninitiated;

Fourth Dimension: 'Spirit' — the point of it all, the quest for immortality.

The game — if game it was — has the feel of a beautifully *self-referential* system, one with interlocking and mutually interconnected features that bear all the hallmarks of an intelligent and highly organized design.[43]

Reduced to its basic level, Hancock and Faiia are stating that the world grid embodies the following four principal features:

1) A *celestrial* or *astronomical* reference, "as above;"
2) an *earthly* reference in the vertical dimension — "so below" — in which those astronomical references are embodied in the layout and dimensions of structures, each of which *also* appears to be linked to other such structure on the "horizontal" dimension by their placement on the earth's surface;
3) a *temporal* reference embodying the slow cycle of precession;
4) a *spiritual* reference suggesting that all this has something to do with immortality.

As we shall see, the deeper into history and further back in time we go, the connections to physics get even broader and deeper, encompassing monuments memorializing not only the physics of the very large in astronomical alignments, but also memorializing the physics of the very small in precise structural analogues to aspects of *quantum mechanics.* Additionally, we shall also discover *arithmetic* and *hyper-dimensional* properties embodied in these structures — and their placement on the globe — that point to a purpose *beyond* mere *memorialization* of certain aspects of physics, but to a purpose that suggests they were designed to *manipulate and engineer* it. We will, in other words, add the following things to the previous list:

---

[43] Hancock and Faiia, *Heaven's Mirror*, p. 162.

5) A *reference* to the *physical medium itself*, embodied, as we have seen,

    a) in certain topological metaphors contained in ancient texts,

    b) but also embodied in certain dimensional analogues of the principles of quantum mechanics, embodied in some ancient structures;

6) A reference to certain *arithmetic principles* that we may best describe as "sacred science" or "sacred arithmetic" or "sacred geometry"; and finally,

7) Indicators that this vast network was not only designed as a memorialization, as a *message*, but also as a *machine*, to engineer a deep physics that all of the above suggests. In short, we are looking at indicators that all this vast architecture, spread across the globe, is an *alchemical* architecture, a vast construction designed to embody and manipulate the Philosophers' Stone, the transmutative physical medium itself.

In view of all of this, "coincidence" is not an explanation that can be rationally entertained.[44]

But what elite is involved in all this activity, according to Hancock and Faiia?

> But the dimension of time still veils much: 10,500 BC is the astronomical dating of the ground plan of the Pyramids and the Sphinx; 2500 BC is the astronomical dating of the alignments of the Great Pyramid's shafts (supported by undisputed archaeological evidence of intense activity at Giza around 2500 BC); 10,500 BC is the astronomical dating of the ground plan of the Naga temples of Angkor Wat, with undisputed archaeological evidence that the entire complex of monuments at Angkor were built over slightly more than four centuries between AD 802 and AD 1220.
>
> What powerful common source of high knowledge and what shared spiritual idea; descending through what underground stream, could have been sufficiently global in manifestation, sufficiently ancient, and sufficiently sustained, to have made such a

---

[44] Hancock and Faiia, *Heaven's Mirror*, p. 173: "In our view, however, the range and sheer extent of the similarities is such that 'coincidence' can no longer be regarded as a safe explanation."

deep impact on the culture of Egypt at around 2500 BC and *3500 years later*, on the culture of the Khmers in Cambodia between the ninth and the thirteenth centuries AD?[45]

Their answer is simple, and ingenious, and faithful to the textual and mythological traditions represented by the various sites in whose cultures they occur:

> What better candidates could there be for the masters if a game with immortality as its goal than the Followers of Horus, the Shemsu Hor, the wielders of magic, the counters of the stars — who are said in the ancient texts to have come to Egypt in the First Time?[46]

We shall have occasion to comment on the *Shemsu Hor* or Followers of Horus in a later chapter, but for now it should be noted that this "good" elite — whether one calls it the Followers of Horus or the "Brotherhood of the Seven Rishis" or the "Society of the Incarnations of Vishnu" — is only part of the story.

There is another elite or elites, a "bad" or "evil" elite, as we shall see, that, fully in possession of the same knowledge, had rather different purposes, agendas, and uses for the monuments of the world grid.

For now, we have noted the curious anomaly of larger-than-expected yields from early hydrogen bomb tests, the curious placement of Nazi headquarters on points on the world grid, the activity of apparent elites placing ancient structures in astronomical alignments and positioning them according to a prime meridian running through Giza. We have noted the presence in Hermetic and Hindu texts and cosmologies of a profound "topological metaphor" of the physical medium, the fabric of space-time. And finally, we have noted the persistency and continuity of those elites over vast millennia, as evidenced by their common activity enduring through those millennia and cultures.

---

[45] Hancock and Faiia, *Heaven's Mirror*, p. 163.
[46] Hancock and Faiia, *Heaven's Mirror,* pp. 162-163.

But what of the *other* components of the world grid: the arithmetical and geometric?

Those answers will be explored in the next chapter, in connection with the two "mathematical masters of the global matrix."

4

THE MATHEMATICAL MASTERS
OF THE MYSTERIES:
MUNCK AND MICHELL

*"These monuments, capacitors to the ley lines, are multi-purpose
and they function on many levels."*
Carl P. Munck[1]

*"How much more worthy of cultivation and study is this most venerable of human
cultural possessions than the pretentious, mock-scientific metre! And yet how perfectly
adapted is the metre, with its inherent banality and meaninglessness, to represent the
values of the modern processes for which it was designed!"*
John Michell[2]

I f astronomical alignments form one crucial component of the
world grid of the gods, then *positioning* and mathematics form the
other, and no two mathematical masters have delved more
thoroughly into this aspect of the mystery of the global grid than
have Carl Munck and John Michell, Munck by a thorough — indeed,
one might say overwhelming — study of almost all sites on the grid
and their unique placements and mathematical properties, and
Michell by a Schwaller De Lubicz-like lifetime of study of the larger
issues implied by sacred numbers and sacred geometry.

As was seen in the last chapter, however, there is evidence from
the cosmologies depicted at Angkor Wat and the texts of Hermetic
and Neoplatonic tradition, that we may be looking at a profound
topological metaphor of the physical medium itself. There are in
addition to these indicators, traditions long associated with such
"power places" on the world grid, particularly in Europe and Great
Britain.

Paul Devereux is an Englishman who, along with his "Dragon
Project," has been attempting to conduct scientific investigation into
such locations on the grid where local tradition and lore ascribes
paranormal occurrences to them, including attempts to investigate

---

[1] Carl P. Munck, *Whispers from Time: the Pyramid Bible,* Volume 2
(http://www.pyramidmatrix.com/carl_munck.htm, 1999), p. 24.
[2] John Michell, *The New View Over Atlantis* (Thames and Hudson, 2001), p. 135.

the infrasonic and infrared properties of such places, which oftentimes returned anomalously high, or alternatively, low amounts of such sounds and radiations.[3] It should also be noted that Devereux and his research team often found that their readings of infrasound or infrared energies often *varied with the phases of the Moon, that is, in response to the wider celestial geometries!* Shades of Kozyrev![4]

Additionally, Devereux and his teams also discovered "noteworthy anomalies relating to background radioactivity and natural magnetism at certain monuments."[5] But beyond these anomalous findings, there is the matter of tradition and rumors themselves:

> Throughout the twentieth century, popular rumour has maintained that ancient sacred sites harbour strange powers. This belief has its origins in anecdotal reports of unusual happenings at such places, and centuries of folklore ascribing supernatural properties to old standing stones and mysterious earthworks.[6]

In Devereux's opinion, the ultimate source of these traditions comes from the ancient belief that "the earth was alive, with subtle but powerful forces flowing through its body, the land," forces which concentrated themselves according to the "spirit of the place", the *genius loci.*[7]

Accordingly, Devereux, more than most researchers of the world grid phenomenon and its ancient places, assembled a vast catalogue of traditions about such places, "in the hope that actual recall of the megalithic technology may be partially contained within it, however fragmented and distorted."[8]

---

[3] Paul Devereux, *Places of Power: Measuring the Secret Energy of Ancient Sites* (London: Blandford, 1999), p. 4.

[4] Ibid., pp. 76-77, 81.

[5] Ibid.

[6] Ibid.

[7] Ibid., p. 11.

[8] Ibid., p. 24.

A. Devereux and The Traditions of Places of Power
1. Moving and Immoveable Stones

One of the most persistent of these traditions is that movement, or, conversely, immovability, is attributed to the stones of such monuments. Stones were said to move to nearby brooks or rivers to drink, or alternatively, rise up at certain times of the day — in some cases heralded by the chiming of a nearby clock — or certain times of the year.[9] Alternatively, other traditions hold that certain stones cannot be moved at all or, "if they are so displaced, will either return automatically or else cause such problems that the person involved will obliged to return the stone, and will find it supernaturally easy to do so."[10] One may, and should, of course, view such traditions with due skepticism for very obvious reasons.

But viewed a different way, these traditions are actually describing something having profoundly to do with *physics* and with the properties of mass and inertia. As will be seen shortly, Devereux is alive to the possibility that there may be a much deeper, and older tradition, of cosmology and physics at work in such legends. In short, one may be looking at a decayed and declined legacy in such traditions, one that at a much older time might have entailed explanations shorn of totemistic and shamanistic imagery.

2. Uncountable Stones and Stones of the Giants and Gods

Other local traditions — at least in Great Britain — hold that some of the stone henges and circles that dot its landscape are populated by stones that refuse all attempt to enumerate or count. Each time a person tries to count them, a different answer will obtain. Similarly, "Many megaliths or large natural boulders are said, in folklore, to have been placed in their positions by giants of old."[11] Stonehenge itself was once known as the Giants Dance,[12] and similarly, the stone circles of Sanguli in far-off Africa were said by local tribal traditions to be "built by ancient people who were eight

---

[9] Paul Devereux, *Places of Power*, p. 26.
[10] Ibid., pp. 26, 28.
[11] Ibid., 28.
[12] Ibid., p. 30.

metres tall."[13] Yet another famous megalithic site, Baalbek in Lebanon, whose thousand-ton-plus stone "trilithion," was according to tradition said to have been built by Cain and an ancient giant race.[14] While this association of megalithic sites with giants is not universal, it does have echoes, as we shall see, in places as diverse as Meso-America, South America, and Egypt, where similar giant stone constructions are attributed to the gods or to the giants, or associated with them in some other fashion.

3. Desecration, Inhabitation, and Treasure Traditions

In other traditions, disturbing stones — in effect, desecrating them — are associated with various curses for doing so, among which are that the desecrator "can expect to be subjected to severe weather conditions such as freak winds or fierce electrical storms."[15] In this case, notes Devereux, there are actually examples in the modern record of this actually happening:

> In 1849, for instance, when Dean Merewether of Hereford and his team were digging at Silbury Hill near Avebury in Wiltshire, a 'dramatic high Gothick thunderstorm' broke out, and men working deep within the great mound felt it shudder to its base. The Dean wryly observed that the significantly timed storm was 'much to the satisfaction... of the rustics.'[16]

Similarly, in 1940 a farmer approaching the so-called Hobgoblin Stone near Lampeter in Wales with the intention of breaking it up to make gateposts was subjected to a violent thunderstorm which pursued the poor man as he ran for his home.[17]

In addition to these "desecration traditions," there are also traditions that maintained treasure was often associated with the site,

---

[13] Devereux, *Places of Power*, p. 30.

[14] Michel M. Alouf, *History of Baalbek* (Escondido, California: Book Tree, 1999), p. 52.

[15] Devereux, op. cit., pp. 30-31 (quotation from p. 31).

[16] Ibid.

[17] Ibid.

in a manner recollecting assertions of vast buried treasures of wealth and knowledge in the secret and ancient sites of South America.[18]

4. Divination, Animation, Healing, and Numerical Traditions

In other traditions, megalithic sites, in addition to their astronomical orientations, were apparently used for actual divination.[19] Local customs practiced in conjunction with this oftentimes "involve the numbers three, seven or nine."[20] We have already seen how the number three emerges as a function of the topological metaphor in the previous chapter, and we have already encountered the seven sacred sages or *Rishis* of the Hindu cosmology. We shall encounter these numbers, and the number nine, again when we turn to Egypt in a subsequent chapter.

In addition to these peculiar traditions, especially those depicting *moving* stones, there are also other legends suggesting that these monuments are animated and connected with life in other fashions, including traditions ascribing healing, virility, and fertility to various stones in such monuments.[21]

5. Gateway Traditions

Finally, as Devereux notes in the case of the traditions of the American Pueblo Indians, there are legends connecting such sacred sites to the flow of energies between this plane of reality and "other concurrent realities,"[22] as a kind of gateway or door between worlds of one reality or another. Strangely enough, this is reflected further south in the legends of the Maya and Aztecs, and also in Mesopotamia, where the very name *Bab-El* or Babylon means literally, "door" or "gate of the gods."

---

[18] Paul Devereux, *Places of Power*, pp. 32-33.
[19] Ibid., p. 35.
[20] Ibid.
[21] Ibid., p. 39.
[22] Ibid., p. 13.

B. Devereux: The Cosmology and Physics Implications of the Traditions of Places of Power

1. "Strange Radiation" Traditions

All of this potently suggests that we might be looking at not just a hodge-podge of entirely unrelated legends and lore about such places, but rather, at dim memories of their possible purpose and function, a purpose that was, moreover, attributable to some kind of *function* for such monuments beyond enshrining certain measures and astronomical alignments. They are strongly suggestive of an underlying *technological* purpose and meaning; they suggest we are looking at cogs in a vast machine.

This is made more evident, at least for Devereux, when one turns to consider one of the more widespread traditions associated with such sites, that of "strange radiations."

From the pyramids to Giza to those of Mexico, and from the henges and earthworks of Britain to those of North America and continental Europe, there are abundant traditions that associate the presence of strange lights or glowing aura around such monuments.[23] No one, for example, who has studied the lore associated with Giza in Egypt, or Teotihuacan in Mexico, can help but encounter such stories, for they are numerous and plentiful. In one sense, this is entirely to be expected in the case of the massive stone pyramids of Meso-America and Egypt, for the piezoelectric properties of quartz under stress are phenomena that are regularly scientifically studied. Quartz crystals, when shattered or subjected to stress, give off minute bursts of electricity, which show up as sparks of light. And the massive structure of the Great Pyramid, composed of enormous amounts of limestone and granite — both types of rock embedding tiny quartz crystals — is certainly in one sense a gigantic piezoelectric capacitor.[24]

So in one sense, such stories are to be expected, for the phenomenon is now well-known to science. Yet, this does not exhaust the anomalous nature of what sometimes is encountered at such sites. For example, Devereux uncovered evidence that Native

---

[23] Devereux, *Places of Power*, p. 4.
[24] For Devereux's discussion of these phenomena, see pp. 44, 59.

American Indians were familiar with concentrations of natural radioactivity and even marked such sites with distinctive petroglyphs:

> American researcher, Marsha Adams, has uncovered indications that a recurring symbol found in prehistoric Native America rock art in Arizona and Nevada may indicate locations of strong natural radioactivity. Adams has measured five sites where the rock art symbol in question appears. Increased amounts of radiation were found at four sites, while there were extremely strong radiation levels at one. Maximum radiation readings were found close to the symbol of interest. In at least one case, Adams had to undergo decontamination procedures when she returned home after fieldwork at the rock at sites.[25]

Of course, such abnormal and anomalous radiation readings could be rationally explained by the presence of high amounts of pitchblende or other radioactive minerals in the area. But no *conventional* model would explain how the Native American Indian populations knew about them, other than, perhaps, feeling a slight heat from the rocks.

2. Shamanism, Radiation, and Grid Sites

This leads Devereux into a very interesting line of speculation, a line of speculation mingling various versions of shamanistic tradition and lore with modern science. He begins by noting that in places of abnormally high background concentrations of radiation, concentrations often associated with such ancient grid sites, many people experience some form of "heightened awareness" or "increased consciousness."[26] This, he hypothesized, is due to some sort of unknown or little understood relationship between radiation and consciousness, a relationship he calls "radiation-psi."

This is not as wild as it at first might seem, for the Canadian neurologist Michael Persinger published a paper in the June 1995 professional journal *Perceptual and Motor Skills* entitled "On the Possibility of Accessing Every Human Brain by Electromagnetic Induction of Fundamental Algorithms." Additionally, there is a solid argument to be made that at least some temples of the much later

[25] Paul Devereux, *Places of Power*, pp. 4-5.
[26] Ibid., pp. 5, 199-202.

classical period relied explicitly on the knowledge of radio-engineering principles, in part for long-distance communications purposes, and in part for the possible manipulation of emotional and mental states.[27] In Persinger's case, the induction of visions and memories is produced by a special helmet which beams powerfully concentrated magnetic fields into a person's brain.

For Devereux, the implications of so many people having such experiences at so many ancient sites are clear, for they imply that *physical* energy effects "were deliberately and opportunistically employed at ritual sites," making them "simply one part of an ancient technology of consciousness manipulation that included initiatory ordeals, ritual activity, dancing, drumming, sensory deprivation, the use of drugs — and even the nature of (the) sites themselves."[28]

3. Devereux and the Possibilities of a Deeper Physics

For Devereux, all of this is a manifestation of the continuance within various local lore and tradition in Great Britain of the ancient Druidic philosophy of the *prime matter*, the physical medium itself.[29] The Druids, it seems, laid out all their sacred sites along straight lines, much as did Chinese practitioners of the geomantic art of *Feng Shui*.[30] Like Hancock and Faiia, whom we encountered in the previous chapter, Devereux began to understand that he was looking at more than just a philosophy confined to megalithic sites in northwestern Europe and Great Britain:

> At these monuments we are in the presence of *technology*, the impressive remains left by a group of races who were the founders of what has become today's 'Western culture', which has put its stamp, indeed has stamped, over most of the world.[31]

---

[27] See my *Babylon's Banksters* (Feral House, 2010), pp. 251-264, and *Genes, Giants, Monsters, and Men* (Feral House, 2011), chapter 3, "The Technologies of Special Revelation."

[28] Paul Devereux, *Places of Power*, p. 8.

[29] Ibid., p. 24.

[30] Ibid., p. 16.

[31] Ibid., p. 23.

For Devereux, this technology was designed to manipulate some "life force," the power of the physical medium itself: "It could be accumulated and controlled to some extent, and esoteric technologies were developed to this end."[32]

In short, we are looking at an *alchemical* technology, an alchemical *architecture* whose very blueprint is the entire grid itself.

But to understand just how intricate and carefully planned that grid was, and how that planning is further evidence of *a coordinated effort* on the part of a group or groups possessing the knowledge and techniques to do so, we must, inevitably, do a little mathematics, for it is in the numbers and measure of the placement of these sites, as well as the numbers inherent in the structures placed upon them, that we begin — at first dimly, then with growing light and illumination — to perceive just how deep the physics embodied in them might actually be, and how high a civilization actually left them.

C. Munck and the Grid

Grid researcher Carl P. Munck has been investigating the intricacies of the world grid with a mathematical precision that is unparalleled both in its breadth and in its depth, leaving almost no relationship unfathomed between virtually each place on that Grid and every other place on it. Indeed, Munck himself would object that his approach is not so much mathematical as it is arithmetical.[33] For Munck, who calls himself an "archaeocryptographer," numbers are indeed the code that links and decodes each component structure on the global matrix, not only in terms of its own unique position and purpose, but also in terms of decoding its relationship to the other localities on the grid. In this approach to the primacy of numbers as the key to the Grid system, Munck is not alone, as we shall see, but he is certainly alone in the degree to which he has carried out detailed calculations.

While more will be said in a moment about the details of Munck's method in decoding this complex numerical relationship embedded in the Grid, one component of it has already been mentioned in the

---

[32] Paul Devereux, *Places of Power*, p. 19, q.v. also p., 20.

[33] Carl P. Munck, *Whispers From Time: the Pyramid Bible,* Volume 1 (The Pyramid Matrix Bookstore, 1997), p. 18.

p̲.̲.̲ ̲ ̲us chapter in our examination of Hancock's and Faiia's study of Angkor Wait, and it must again be highlighted here: for Munck, as for other Grid researchers, *the Grid only makes arithmetical or numerical sense if one first uses Giza, or rather, the apex of the Great Pyramid itself, as the prime meridian of the ancient world,*[34] *and secondly, only makes arithmetical and numerical sense if one uses — astonishingly — the British imperial system of measures and not the metric one.*

When this is done, an astonishing set of precisely placed relationships between various sites on the world Grid emerges, between such seemingly culturally unrelated sites as:

1) The largest North American Indian mound at Grave Creek, Moundsville, West Virginia, and Sillbury Hill in England;[35]
2) Chichen Itza in southern Mexico and Giza;[36]
3) Teotihuacan, outside of Mexico City, and Giza;[37]
4) The Florida circles and the Avebury circle in England;[38]
5) Uxmal and Tikal in Meso-America, and Giza;[39]
6) The Nazca lines in Peru, and everything else, for according to Munck, this very old and strange monument — only visible from the air! — is a kind of Rosetta Stone to the global Grid system;[40]
7) Tikal in Central America, and everything else, for according to Munck, this site, like the Nazca Lines in Peru, is a kind of "directory" to the world Grid;[41]

---

[34] Munck, *Whispers from Time: The Pyramid Bible*, Volume 1, p. 15.
[35] Ibid., pp. 79-81.
[36] Ibid., p. 108.
[37] Ibid., p. 42.
[38] Munck, *Aquarius 10: The Metrology Origin*, p. 31.
[39] Ibid., pp. 9, 15, 20.
[40] Munck, *Whispers from Time: The Pyramid Bible*, Volume 1, p. 111.
[41] Munck, *Aquarius 19: Waldseemüller's Globe — 1507* (The Pyramid Matrix Bookstore, 2004), p. 25. Munck also notes numerical relationships between Stonehenge and the measures of Sumeria, and between numbers embedded at Stonehenge and the Mayan pyramids of Tikal. (Q.v. *Aquarius 10: Metrology Origin*, pp. 4-5).

And on and on we could go, almost endlessly uncovering new relationships, so long as the apex of Giza's Great Pyramid is used as the prime meridian. And to this we may add, as we saw in the last chapter,

8) Angkor Wat, and Giza.

At most of these sites, one encounters one of two types of construction: either a pyramid (or an earthen mound), or a stone or earthen circle.

When one estimates the total number of such structures throughout the world one obtains a rather astonishing figure: "85 in Egypt so far, more in the Sudan, over 100 in China, hundreds in Mexico, several dozen in Gautemala, several (unexplored) in Ecuador, estimates for 400 in Peru (all destroyed), the Akapana in Bolivia and reports of a super pyramid in Tibet."[42] To that, we may now add yet another, recently-discovered pyramid in Bosnia, unknown at the time Munck wrote his book.[43] When one adds to this number all the various mounds of effigies or totems of various animals and the various stone henges and earth circles, one is looking at literally tens of thousands of monuments, all precisely placed on a huge global matrix.[44] The purpose of all this placement according to Munck was, in part, precisely to *mark* significant locations on the matrix, but the reasons for doing so "are only partially clear at this time."[45]

There are, however, clues, and Munck, like Devereux, is not oblivious to the fact that something deeper is going on besides merely marking various locations on an abstract grid system. For Munck, the question is not *who, when, and how* these monuments were built, but "*why* they were built as they were, and *where* they are."[46] Citing the famous case of the submerged pyramid in Rock Lake, Wisconsin, Munck notes that this site — like some of the megalithic sites in Great Britain investigated by Devereux — is the home to

---

[42] Munck, *Whispers from Time: The Pyramid Bible*, Volume 1, p. 27.
[43] It should be noted that some still dispute the validity of this finding.
[44] Munck, op. cit., p. 28.
[45] Ibid., p. 27.
[46] Ibid., p. 7.

consistent reports of unusual phenomena. For example, local residents report seeing huge rocks *floating on the surface* of the lake, or outboard motors on boats that will not work at certain times, or how divers attempting to approach and film the submerged pyramid with their underwater cameras suddenly find they have malfunctioned. Munck even notes that some divers report a strange sense of dread as they prepared to dive to photograph the pyramid.[47] For Munck, the clue to the resolution of this riddle may lie in the fact that another submerged structure in the lake, a triangle-shaped stone called the "Delta," encodes the number 5.337 in its placement on the Grid, a number close to the frequency of 5.34 MHz, which is a frequency in turn that its known to be able to alter the emotional state of an individual.[48] In short, Munck, like Devereux, hints that at least part of the purpose in the placement of such structures might be *the alchemical transformation of consciousness.*

This possible hidden microwave engineering in such structures also becomes, for Munck, a physics rationalization behind the Tower of Babel story. Assuming the story to be true, Munck reasons that perhaps the builders simply built a structure that, when it reached certain dimensions, acted like a gigantic microwave collector and reflector, literally transforming the brainwave activity of the builders and as a result, confusing the tongues![49]

While the microwave explanation is a speculative possibility, as we shall see in subsequent pages, the precision engineering of so many of these structures suggests strongly that the designers of them, if not the builders, were at least aware of the power of such structures to manipulate energetic radiations, making such an "accidental" explanation of the "Tower of Babel Moment" unlikely, and the biblical version of some sort of intervention from political motivations much more probable.[50]

In addition to all this, Munck, like Hancock and Faiia at Angkor Wat, concludes that at least one of the major sites on the world Grid,

---

[47] Munck, *Whispers from Time: The Pyramid Bible*, Volume 1, p. 73.
[48] Ibid.
[49] Ibid.
[50] For my own approach to the "Tower of Babel Moment" see my *The Cosmic War* (Adventures Unlimited Press, 2007), pp. 210-212.

Teotihuacan in Mexico, shows all the signs of several epochs of construction.[51] This, suggests Munck, argues for a much earlier dating of the site than conventional archaeology would allow, placing the beginning epoch of construction to around 8000 BC, the same era as some alternative dating for Stonehenge.[52] While this is not yet the place to evaluate the specific arguments for such an early dating of Teotihuacan, it is worth noting that such a date and extended period of construction implies the presence of some group, an elite, with specialized knowledge and a long term agenda, an agenda considered to be so important that construction could not be abandoned over the long years of its undertaking.

1. Munck's Methodology

With all this in mind, a closer look at Munck's methodology is in order, for many aspects of it will form crucial components of our own examination of certain sites and structures in the remaining parts and chapters of this book. While Munck's voluminous work does examine the earthen mounds and earthen and stone circles of other megalithic sites, our focus is on his methodology in examination of pyramidal sites.

The first of these methods is to "reverse-engineer" each pyramidal structure as it "came off the drawing boards of remote antiquity."[53] But in Munck's hands this implies two very specific, and crucial observations:

1) True pyramids are five-faced objects, one side forming the base and the other four faces forming the sides of the structure. Thus, the only *true* pyramids in the world are the smooth-faced earthen pyramids in China, and the smooth-faced stone pyramids of Egypt.[54] All other pyramids are "corruptions" of this basic form through the additions of staircases, terraces, ornamentation, rectangular "temples" on

---

[51] Munck, *The Master Code Book* (The Pyramid Matrix Bookstore, 2004), p. 20.
[52] Munck, *Whispers from Time: The Pyramid Bible,* Volume 1, p. 25.
[53] Ibid., p. 17.
[54] Ibid.

their apexes or elsewhere on the structure, and by offsetting terraces on some structures;[55]

2) *Thus, when "reverse-engineering" a pyramid, it is important to count all the corners and faces, even on "corrupted structures."* When this is done, a certain series of numbers will *inevitably* emerge from any *smooth-sided* pyramid as a universal geometric law:

> 1 — An apex at the top.
> 3 — Each side of a true pyramid is actually a triangle with 3 sides or 3 corners.
> 4 –Ground corners, or number of sides...
> 5 — Total of 4 ground corners and the apex.
> 8 — All ground corners and all sides.
> 9 — Above 8 features plus the apex.[56]

Before commenting on the implications of this sequence of numbers, it is important to point out in the clearest possible terms the enormous implications of Munck's method, *for as we shall see in the final chapter, this method of counting corners and faces is a clue to a profound and deep hyper-dimensional physics and the formal mathematical and geometrical techniques employed to describe it.*

If the last comment seems odd or even far-fetched, look closely again at the *first two* numbers embodied in a smooth-sided pyramid: one, and three, the very numbers we saw emerge in the previous chapter *in the topological metaphor contained in the Hindu cosmology and in Hermetic texts, the very first two numbers that emerge as functions of the differentiated physical medium contained in the metaphor.* As we shall see in our subsequent examination of the cosmology of Egypt, the other numbers of a pyramid enumerated above by Munck, also emerge in that exact sequence within Egyptian cosmology! Egypt's preoccupation with smooth-sided pyramids would appear, then, to be anything but an accident, as it would also

---

[55] Munck, *Whispers from Time: The Pyramid Bible*, Volume 1, p. 17. Munck notes that the famous Pyramid of the Sun at Teotihuacan in Mexico has offset faces. Q.v. pp. 45-46.

[56] Ibid.

appear to have little to do with entombing dead pharaohs. It has everything to do with their view of physics and the physics of the information-creating, transumtative, alchemical physical medium itself. As we shall also discover in our examination of the Mesopotamian component of this mystery, it also has everything to do with *music, with sound.*

3) The next crucial component in Munck's methodology is his classification scheme of ancient monuments. We have seen one component of this scheme already, in the distinction between

a) Smooth-faced, or proper and true pyramids; and,

b) "corrupted" pyramids, to which alterations in the forms of terraces and so on (*and thereby the addition of more corners and faces to count*), have been added.

Within each of these two classes, four further classifications are to be distinguished: (1) structures embodying the geometric constant of π, (2) structures that "decode themselves" in only one aspect of their location, i.e., either by longitude or by latitude, (3) structures that "decode themselves" with respect both to latitude and longitude, and finally (4) structures that are not self-decoding in any respect of latitude or longitude, but that are decodable only by reading the presence of other significant numerical relationships present in the structure.[57] One thus has *eight* classes into which a pyramid on the Grid can fall:

a) Smooth-faced, or proper and true pyramids;

    (1) structures embodying the geometric constant of π;

    2) structures that "decode themselves" in only one aspect of their location, i.e., either by longitude or by latitude;

    (3) structures that "decode themselves" with respect both to latitude and longitude; and finally,

---

[57] Munck, *Whispers from Time: The Pyramid Bible*, Volume 1, p. 27.

(4) structures that are not self-decoding in any respect of latitude or longitude, but that are decodable only by reading the presence of other significant numerical relationships present in the structure.

b) "corrupted" pyramids, to which alterations in the forms of terraces and so on (*and thereby the addition of more corners and faces to count*), have been added:

(1) structures embodying the geometric constant of π;

2) structures that "decode themselves" in only one aspect of their location, i.e., either by longitude or by latitude;

(3) structures that "decode themselves" with respect both to latitude and longitude; and finally,

(4) structures that are not self-decoding in any respect of latitude or longitude, but that are decodable only by reading the presence of other significant numerical relationships present in the structure;

4) The final component in Munck's methodology is that it is necessary to "de-toxify" measurements of such structures from the metric system and to convert all measures into the British imperial system in order for the ancient numerical code present in and between structures on the Grid to emerge.[58]

While this point may seem at first glance to be purely arbitrary, it is in fact based on the careful and close study of ancient monuments themselves, and as I pointed out in my previous book *Genes, Giants, Monsters, and Men*, there is considerable evidence that there is nothing really "British" about the imperial system of measures, and that the system comes down from high antiquity.[59]

Within this constriction, there are a number of crucial techniques that Munck uses to derive the significant numbers, among them, the amount of cubic degrees in a sphere,

---

[58] Munck, *Whispers from Time: The Pyramid Bible*, Volume 1, p. 123.
[59] Joseph P. Farrell, *Genes, Giants, Monsters, and Men* (Feral House, 2011), chapter 2.

squaring or cubing, or finding the square or cubic roots, of numbers, the tangents of numbers, and so on.

A final component of this attention to specific numbers is the reliance upon gematria, the ancient technique of assigning specific numerical values to letters in an alphabet. In this respect, Munck points out that the gematrian numbers are all multiples of 36, a significant number in the Sumerian sexagesimal system. These "Sumerian" numbers — all multiples of 36, are found in almost all structure of the Grid, from Ohio's Sep Mound, Mississippi's Emerald Mound, the "Great Triangle" at Nazca in Peru, the Great Pyramid, Bent Pyramid, and Red Pyramid in Egypt, and even in the D&M Pyramid in the Cydonia region of Mars![60]

While we will deal more in detail with some of these structures in subsequent chapters, for our purposes here it is important to note what this vast list implies, for once again, one is in the presence of a *global* phenomenon, implying a group with global extent and a common mathematical and metrological heritage to conduct such a vast scale of constructions.

It also implies something else, something usually missed by Grid researchers, and that is, the technique of gematria and the numbers "sacred" to it, is something applied to *texts* as well as evidently to *monuments*. It thus strongly suggests that one may not separate textual or mythological traditions from the monuments themselves. This will become a crucially important point when we examine the Mayan and Aztec traditions of the monuments they found in their midst , and made use of.

3. Munck's Conclusions: The Work of an Elite

The conclusions that Munck draws from this precise and exacting methodology as he applied it to his years of research of the Grid clearly point to the existence of at least one elite, extensive across not only the space of the globe but also through untold millennia of time, for if sites of incomparable antiquity such as Stonehenge, and

---

[60] Munck, *Whispers from Time: the Pyramid Bible*, Volume 2, p. 322.

structures of purported later construction such as the El-Kola pyramid in Egypt or the pyramids of Mexico all are found to be speaking the same numerical and arithmetical language, then at least the *plan* of the world Grid is of great antiquity.[61]

There is, as Munck avers, also evidence of a suggestive sort that the Indian mounds of North America as well as the more massive Egyptian pyramids reach back into remote antiquity, for the Native Americans would have had to build such structures "at the steady rate of over 25 per year — everywhere."[62] Nonetheless, as Munck also points out, tribal traditions do not record any *construction* of these sites in many cases; they are already present when the Indians arrived. Thus, many of the mounds and similar structures, contrary to traditional archaeology, were there many years before the tribes arrived. Similarly, in Egypt, notwithstanding the great antiquity of writing in that country, *nowhere* is the construction of its grandest structure, the Great Pyramid, ever mentioned.[63]

For Munck, all this vast methodology, combined with the sheer *scale* not only of the individual constructions, and also with the sheer scale of its global sweep, testifies to an extraordinary fact:

> Nobody sets out to build 50,000-plus pyramids and mounds around a planet just for the hell of it, or want of something to do. History teaches that these primitive people were hunter-gatherers who spent their waking hours running down their next meals. If that's true, then who built these monuments? These people didn't have the time.... these things were not built at the whims of medicine men. There was enormous global planning behind it all.

In this assessment, the other great mathematical master of the earth matrix, concurs...

---

[61] Munck, *Whispers from Time: the Pyramid Bible,* Volume 1, p. 26.
[62] Ibid., p. 28.
[63] Ibid. Munck actually makes this claim for *all* of Egypt's pyramids.

D. *John Michell, "Sacred Geometry," "Sacred Science", The Grid, and the Ancient Elite*

While Carl Munck may have run into gematria after years of research on the global Grid, British researcher John Michell (1933-2009) did just the opposite, having spent many years plumbing the numerical and gematrian depths of ancient and sacred texts, only to find the same thing encoded in the monuments of the world Grid. As for many other researchers, for Michell the most prominent feature of the Grid system is its universal extent across the globe.[64] Of unquestioned antiquity,[65] there are, Michell maintains, perhaps even references to the system in the Old Testament.[66]

For Michell, the overriding perspective with which to view the earth Grid system is as a system of geomancy, that is, as "a science of landscape design based on the idea of a living earth."[67] Curiously, general widespread European awareness of this system only began in the nineteenth century, and due to a very curious circumstance:

A hundred years ago the practice of Chinese geomancy first became generally known in the West through the complaints of European business men, who found inexplicable resistance to their rational plans for exploiting the country. Continually they were informed that their railways and factories could not take certain routes or occupy certain positions. The reasons given were impossible to understand, for they had no relevance, economic, social or political, to the problem of laying out an industrial network. The Europeans were told that a certain range of hills was a terrestrial dragon and that no cutting could be made through its tail. Tunnels through dragon hills were forbidden, and a proposed railway to run straight across low, flat country was rejected on the grounds that the line would spoil the view from the hills. All this was laid down by practitioners of the science of *feng-shui*, 'wind and

---

[64] John Michell, *The New View Over Atlantis* (London & New York: Thames and Hudson, 1995), p. 8.

[65] Ibid., p. 25.

[66] Ibid., pp. 27-28. Michell cites the ley line research of O.G.S. Crawford, who in turn references Jeremiah 6:16, 31:2; 18:15; and Isaiah 58:14 and 2:2 as being possible indicators of the knowledge of the Grid system among biblical writers.

[67] Ibid., p. 7.

water', obscurely explained as 'that which can not be seen and can not be grasped'.[68]

It was during this same time period — the nineteenth century — that research into the grid system, or "ley lines," first began in earnest in England and continental Europe, as we have seen, an interest that in turn was based on earlier probes, among them those of Dr. William Stukeley, an eighteenth century Freemason, who modeled his investigations after the seventeenth century work of John Aubrey.[69] Nor was Aubrey alone, for as early as 1580, Elizabeth I's court "magician," the "Aleister Crowley" of Elizabethan England, Dr. John Dee, noticed that the earthworks around the famous Glastonbury abbey constituted a kind of "earthen Zodiac," thus becoming the first in modern times to notice the astronomical alignments and significance of ancient sites.[70]

Dr. Stukeley, however, was one of the first to observe the recurring presence in these ancient sites of certain numbers also found as universal constants in geometry and music, which in turn formed a crucial component of the hermetic tradition of illumination in Freemasonry, a tradition we shall examine in much more detail in the section on Mesopotamia.[71] In this, he anticipated the later research of Munck and Michell themselves.

But Stukeley and his forebear Dr. John Dee were not the first to notice the system *either*. The Spanish conquerors of Peru noticed the same "straight line" system in the far-flung Inca Empire, this time as a network of roads reserved for the Inca Emperor and his messengers:

> Fantastic efforts had been made to ensure that they ran dead straight. Stone causeways were laid across marshes, steps were cut over mountains, tunnels were bored through cliffs and amazing woven bridges spanned chasms. Obstacles were never bypassed, but a way was built through or over them. In a very short time

---

[68] Michell, *The New View Over Atlantis*, p. 59.
[69] Ibid., pp. 13-14.
[70] Ibid., pp. 21-22.
[71] Ibid., p. 16.

these roads conveyed the Spanish missionary and military power through every centre in the country.[72]

Nor were the Spanish even the earliest to notice the system, for according to Michell, the Romans ran into the same system of "straight line roads" as their empire expanded into Gaul and Britain, over the ancient system of ley lines in those countries, and soon paved these roads for Roman armies and commerce: "Unaware of any source of power except through trade and conquest, the Romans may have thought that in laying their roads along the lines of their predecessors they were reestablishing a lost political empire."[73] Here I must, however, dissent from Michell, for there is abundant evidence that the Romans — or at least *someone* in the Roman republic — was well aware of the significance of ancient sites and how to build temples that essentially functioned as simple radio transmitters.[74]

Adding all of the research together — that of Stukeley, Dee, Sir Normal Lockyear, Heinsch and the German researchers, Michell reached an astonishing conclusion concerning the British part of the Grid, and it is worth citing it here, for the same, as we have seen and shall see again, is true of Angkor Wat and virtually every *other* place on the system: "The whole landscape of Britain has been laid out to a celestial pattern. Every hill has is astrological meaning, every district its centre of symmetry from which its hidden nature can be divined."[75] This crucial point of "finding the center of a region" of land will be seen in a moment.

For now, however, there is another curious circumstance of the British component of the system observed by Michell, and that is the recurring presence of none other than the Egyptian god of wisdom, Thoth, and Baal, the ancient sun god, memorialized in place names along this ancient grid. Thoth was known as Theutates[76] by the Druids, and Baal is found in Ball Hill, and there is even a Baalbeg — shades of Baalbek! — as the name of a deserted Scottish village

---

[72] Michell, *The New View Over Atlantis*, p. 42.

[73] Ibid.

[74] Joseph P Farrell, *Babylon's Banksters*, pp. 251-264.

[75] Michell, op. cit., p. 47.

[76] The name "Thoth" would have been pronounced "Teh-HOO-Teh" or something similar in ancient Egyptian, hence the Druidic derivation is not as remote as it might first seem.

above Loch Ness. And hundreds of Toot or Tot hills can be found dotting the British landscape, testifying to Thoth.[77]

1. Finding the Center of the Land

Delving deeper into this mystery, Michell learned one important principle was, as previously mentioned, to "find the center of the region." The reasons for this, however, were more than geomantic, for the social order itself depended, in a certain sense, upon it. Here, as elsewhere, the alchemical principle of "as above so below" was operative, so that "social order is designed to reflect the order of the universe"[78] In short, there is for Michell a *social engineering* component to the Grid system.

For Michell this social engineering component is further manifest in the ancient conception of kingship being "lowered from heaven," a divine prerogative, as in the ancient Sumerian and Egyptian civilizations. But for Michell, this divine component is much more than just a claim of the ancient kings being chimerical offspring of the "gods" and of man, but is rather *a reflection of the celestial machine itself*:

> At the locus of divine law, the cosmic pole is the most powerful symbol of authority and is regarded as the only legitimate source of human laws. Its many images include the scepter, the measuring rod, the king post, and the central pillar. Kings and chiefs are installed upon the local world-center rock, which empowers their rule, and when the rightful lawgiver pronounces from it, his words have the same unchallengeable force as if the rock itself had spoken.[79]

Thus, it became a consuming compulsion for ancient societies and kingdoms to determine the center of their nation, the first component of this exercise being to find or determine the main north-south axis of a given region or country. It was a symbol, an

---

[77] Michell, *The New View Over Atlantis*, pp. 51-52.
[78] Michell, *The Sacred Center: the Ancient Art of Locating Sanctuaries*, p. 2.
[79] Ibid., p. 7.

image, of the universal axis of the world.[80] It was this principle of geomantic power as the basis of political power that lay behind the selection of Hitler's East Prussia headquarters, outlined in chapter two. The next step was to determine the "regional equator," the main east-west axis.

The principle is not entirely unknown to modern cartography, for "there are specialists known as centographers, whose business it is to locate centers."[81] In the United States, these specialists used what can only be called a "'center of gravity' approach. They pasted a map of America on a board, cut out the relevant area, and found its point of balance on a vertical pivot."[82] When this was done, the center of the lower forty-eight states was found to be near Lebanon, Kansas.[83] When Alaska and Hawaii were later added to the union, the same method located the new center eleven miles west of Castle Rock in Butte county, South Dakota, a short way north of the small town of Spearfish in the northern Black Hills.[84]

While such an approach may on the surface sound a trifle silly, it does suggest that the center of gravity approach to a given surface and site location might be hinting at a deeper physics to such locations, a physics having to do with gravity and the very nature of space-time itself, a view also reinforced by the astronomical alignments of many of these sites.

When this approach of finding the major north-south and east-west axes over the most land is taken with respect to the entire world, however, an interesting thing results, as the nineteenth century Scottish Astronomer Royal, Piazzi Smyth observed. Here, a map says it all:

---

[80] Michaell, *The Sacred Center*, p. 12.
[81] Ibid., p. 25.
[82] Ibid., pp. 25-26.
[83] Ibid., p. 26.
[84] Ibid.

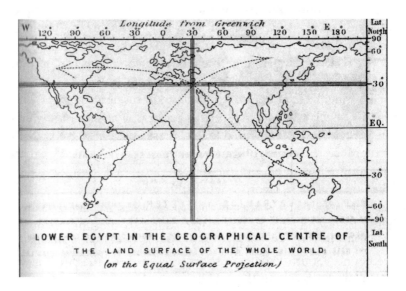

Piazzi Smyth's Map of the Center of the Surface of the World[85]

Giza, and more specifically, the Great Pyramid, are positioned as close to the north-south and east-west axes passing over the most land mass on the surface of the Earth, and additionally, over the northwest-southeast and southwest-northeast axes as well.[86] It was hardly accidental then that Giza's Great Pyramid was set as a marker for the prime meridian. The question is, was it something more than that, and if so, then what about the structures on the rest of the Grid, and particularly, the pyramidal ones?

[85] Piazzi Smyth, *The Great Pyramid: Its Secrets and Mysteries Revealed* (New York: Bell Publishing Company, 1978), Diagram insert beginning after p. 226.

[86] Michell, *The Sacred Center*, pp. 27-29 notes the placement of Akhenaten's "new center" near modern Tel al Amarna, and produces a map noting its close proximity to the Giza meridian, though he does not mention Piazzi Smyth's observation. Michell does refer to this map in *The New View Over Atlantis*, p. 140.

2. The Ancient Catastrophe, the Very High Civilization, and the Post-Catastrophe Elite

Part of the mystery of the Grid for Michell, as for Hancock, Faiia, Munck and other researchers, is its apparent antiquity. Particularly in northern Europe where such sites are evidently contemporaneous with, or even predate ancient Egypt, this phenomenon for Michell, as for the others, is "the relic of an ancient scientific enterprise, conducted over many centuries and presumably directed by a central college of astronomer-priests whose authority was everywhere accepted."[87] And this poses tremendous problems for the "*ex oriente lux*" standard model of cultural diffusion, in other words, the whole idea that

> cultural, scientific and technological innovations were made in the early civilizations of the ancient east, and reached Europe only in a dilute and etiolated form through a slow and gradual process of diffusion. In terms of this model, therefore, it is almost inconceivable that mere barbarians on the remote north-western fringes of the continent should display a knowledge of mathematics and its applications hardly inferior, if at all, to that of Egypt at about the same date, or that of Mesopotamia considerably later.[88]

The sheer antiquity and scale of the undertaking led Michell to suppose that the Grid was the undertaking of some survivors of a very high civilization lost in the mists of High Antiquity through some catastrophe.[89]

3. Michell on the Purpose of the Grid System

But what was the purpose of all this activity? Michell's answers to this question go far beyond the usual "archeo-astronomical" or "archaeo-astrological" measuring markers, and even far beyond the idea of geodetic markers. For him, there is a much deeper *functional*

---

[87] Michell, *Secrets of the Stones: New Revelations of Astro-archaeology and the Mystical Sciences of Antiquity* (Rochester, Vermont: Inner Traditions International, 1989), pp. 84-85.

[88] Ibid., p. 87.

[89] Ibid., see also *The New View Over Atlantis*, p. 36.

significance to the global grid, a functional purpose perhaps revealed in the fact that, after whatever catastrophe as had overwhelmed the civilization that constructed it, the Grid system appeared to have built to channel whatever energies it represented "to their own magical purposes."[90] Reviewing the work of the early twentieth century German Grid researcher Heinsch, Michell notes that Heinsch's conclusions were rather breathtaking, for "the laying out of a network of astronomical and geometrical lines across the face of the earth implies a technology which would hardly have been developed to no practical purpose."[91]

a. Alchemy

But if there *were* energies to be channeled, and if the grid *does* represent a technology of some sort with "a practical purpose", then what were those energies, and what was the technology designed to do with them? What was its "practical purpose"? The global extent of the Grid itself poses enormous implications for these questions:

Only within recent years, since the development of universal communications allowed us to compare the antiquities of our own countries with those of others, have we been able to see the extent of the vast ruin within which we live. If we ignore all alterations to the landscape arising within the last three thousand years and consider the world as it must have looked in prehistoric times, the pattern that emerges is one so incompatible with our idea of civilization that it is easy entirely to miss its significance. *For what we find is this.*

A great scientific instrument lies sprawled over the entire surface of the globe. At some period, thousands of years ago, almost every corner of the world was visited by people with a particular task to accomplish. With the help of some remarkable power, by which they could cut and raise enormous blocks of stone, these men created vast astronomical instruments, circles of erect pillars, pyramids, underground tunnels, cyclopean stone platforms, all linked together by a network of tracks and alignments, whose

---

[90] Michell, *The New View Over Atlantis*, p. 36.
[91] Ibid., p. 33.

114

course from horizon to horizon was marked by stones, mounds and earthworks.[92]

Note the hidden implication of Michell's remarks, for if the global Grid was truly only perceived as a *global* network with the rise of modern transportation and communications in the nineteenth and twentieth centuries, that implies that the elite or elites that constructed the Grid had at least a similar global awareness. Such an awareness would, of course, be natural if that elite or elites were survivors of a prior Very High Civilization.

But notice the real import of Michell's remarks: modern man is living not only in the midst of a vast ruin of planetary extent, he was also living inside a vast ruined *machine* of planetary extent, a machine to manipulate "something." What that "something" may be was suggested by the research of William Stukeley once again, who discovered "recurrent forms — the serpent and the winged circle — which he identified as the symboils of the former patriarchal religion, on which Christianity itself was constructed."[93] We have already encountered a similar "primordial patriarchal" image in the Hindu cosmology examined in the previous chapter in relationship to Angkor Wat, but here it is crucial to note that this winged serpent symbol is also common to Egypt, and as we shall see, to Meso-America as well. The image of "the serpent passing through the circle" is the alchemical symbol of fusion par excellence, and Stukeley observed this symbol at Avebury in England before the image was erased by encroaching civilization.[94]

As we saw in the previous chapter, this "serpent cosmology" contained a profound clue to Hindu cosmology, which in turn led to a profound and deep "topological metaphor" present in ancient texts, a metaphor of a primordial trinity arising from the transmutative and information-creating nature of the physical medium itself, as the ancients viewed it. It was this characteristic that made the medium the Philosophers' Stone as such, and thus, Michell is quick to perceive the deeply alchemical nature of the ruined architecture of the global grid, for the "prehistoric alchemists were dealing with the

---

[92] Michell, *The New View Over Atlantis*, p. 83, emphasis added.
[93] Ibid., pp. 14-15.
[94] Ibid., p. 15.

earth itself, which they regarded as the retort for the alchemical fusion between the 'sulfur' of solar or cosmic energies and the 'mercury' of the earth spirit."[95]

This point cannot be pondered too long, for if the "topological metaphor" of ancient cosmologies and texts has any grain of truth in it, then this means that something *more* is involved in this prehistoric "alchemy" than mere pseudo-science; one is looking not only at a ruined machine, but perhaps at a ruined machine of much more sophistication than popular imagination, whether ancient or modern, would admit.

b. Bloody Sacrifice

Leaving no aspect of this alchemical mystery of the Grid unturned, Michell also notes something else, something sinister connected to some sites on the matrix:

> The appearance of an organized spiritual technology, controlled by the priests, was attended in every country by a massive increase in human sacrifice. The Aztec massacres are notorious; the Druids in Ireland are said to have decimated the population. The innumerable sacrificial stones, carved with basins and channels for the flow of blood, and the traditional violent and bloody associations of so many ancient sites confirms what is recorded of the slaughter carried out by priests in the interests of necromancy.
>
> The practice of human sacrifice *flourished in the ruins of the universal civilization.* The secrets of spiritual invocation, once common property, had become exclusive to those appointed by the community to procure the seasonal renewal of fertility and interpret the will of god through the heavenly portents. The priests, thus established in a position of power, began, as do the members of all professions similarly placed, to extend their influence and activities and to make demands on the population for sacrificial offering.[96]

---

[95] Michell, *The New View Over Atlantis*, p. 8.
[96] Ibid., p. 95, emphasis added.

Not all sites on the Grid, however, were places where human sacrifice was practiced. This emerges in specific cultures — most famously in Meso-America with the Aztecs, as Michell mentions — and for specific reasons as will be seen in a subsequent chapter. For the moment it is important to note that those reasons may have something to do with the alchemical nature of the Grid itself, and what human sacrifice may have been designed, or at least, *perceived by some,* to do. The clue is provided by Michell's insight that the purpose of such a practice was *magical* and *necromantic,* that is, it was designed to manipulate, or intensify, whatever forces the Grid itself tapped into.

c. Number, Measurement, and Time: The Grimoire of the Cosmos

Michell, like Munck, sees the key to the Grid system to lie not only in its astronomical alignments, but also in the numbers incorporated into each site's location, and in the dimensions of the structures built on them. And like Munck and many other Grid researchers, he jettisons the metric system as being of any utility whatsoever for understanding these structures:

> Modern students of ancient metrology, or units of measure, have been hampered by their use of the irrelevant metric system in their researches. The French metre is a modern contrivance of the late eighteenth century, based on an inaccurately measured quarter of the earth's circumference through the poles, of which the metre was made a ten-millionth part. This new-fangled unit bears no relation to any ancient unit, and by using it for antiquarian research modern scholars have concealed from themselves the key to the elucidation of ancient metrology. The key is in number. All the ancient units relate to each other, and to the dimensions of the earth, by the same code of number as is found in every other ancient form of art and science.[97]

Note carefully what is being implied here: the ancient units of measure are derived from the earth, these in turn give rise to certain recurrent numbers, present in the dimensions of the Grid structures only if one used some form of ancient measure. And more

---

[97] Michell, *The New View Over Atlantis,* pp. 125-126.

these same numbers are "found in every other ancient
and science," namely in the numbers hidden by gematria
in texts.

Succinctly stated, Michell is saying that *texts are architecture, and
architecture is text,* and that when certain numbers are found, the
purpose of both is alchemical in that the ultimate purpose is the
manipulation of the physical medium — the Philosophers' Stone —
itself.[98]

A review — necessarily short — of Michell's research on number
and measure will show why this is so. One of the first points to be
observed is that the English imperial, Roman, and Greek units of the
measurement of length are all related to each other in the ratio of
24:25. Thus,

1) 24 English miles of 5280 feet equal 25 Greek miles of 5068.8
   feet; and in turn,
2) 24 Greek miles of 5068.8 feet equal 25 Roman miles of
   4866.048 feet.[99]

If one divides the Greek and Roman miles by 5000, one obtains the
measures of the Greek and Roman foot, and 6000 Greek feet and
6250 Roman feet in turn comprise "one minute of a degree of
latitude."[100] When the meridian circumference of the Earth —
24,883.2 miles — is measured by the Roman and Greek units, some
very interesting numbers begin to occur, for that measure converts
to:

> 135,000,000 Roman feet of .09732096 ft.
> 90,000,000 Roman cubits of 1.4598144 ft.
> 216,000 Roman furlongs of 608.256 ft.
> 27,000 Roman miles of 4866.048 ft.
> 129,600,000 Greek feet of 1.10376 ft.
> 84,400,000 Greek cubits of 1.152064 ft.
> 207,360 Greek furlnogs of 633.6 ft.

---

[98] We shall see in a later chapter Michell's profound gematrian analysis of one
famous text and the Great Pyramid.

[99] Michell, *The New View Over Atlantis*, p. 126.

[100] Ibid., pp. 126-127.

25, 920 Greek miles of 5068.8 ft.[101]

But that is not all; Michell observes that, "All these multiples are canonical numbers, representing powers and multiples of the number twelve."[102] Or put differently, all are multiples of the number *six* and *sixty*, the basis of the ancient Sumerian sexagesimal system of measures and numbers. Note also that the last number — 25,920 — is close to the amount of time for the precession of the equinoxes of the Earth to complete one revolution.

These numbers, essentially all multiples of six, composed a numerical canon that "was once possessed by civilizations world-wide"[103] as a kind of universal numerical "grimoire." For example, one such number, 5040, is divisible not only by six, but by all *other* numbers up to ten, and is moreover a peculiar number in another way, for $1 \times 2 \times 3 \times 4 \times 5 \times 6 \times 7 = 5040 = 7 \times 8 \times 9 \times 10$.[104] That bit of arithmetical magic would not be so extraordinary in and of itself, except for the fact that its harmonic, 50.4 feet, is the mean diameter of the lintel ring at Stonehenge, which incorporates many more such numbers into the dimensions of the structure.[105]

While it is tempting to get lost in these numerical excursions, the important point to bear in mind is that since most structures on the world Grid embody many of these numbers in their dimensions in a kind of "architectural gematria," the implication is rather obvious, namely, that "the ancient philosophers were concerned above all to seek out the patterns in number which correspond to those in nature, and to set them up as models in the conduct of human affairs."[106] However, since these numbers were viewed as cosmological processes, components of the great machine of the heavens, there was another purpose for embodying them in structures:

In the design of temples, to give human satisfaction was only one part of the architect's purpose. The chief object for which a temple was built *was to attract the gods or forces in nature to which it was dedicated.*

---

[101] Michell, *The New View Over Atlantis*, p. 127.
[102] Ibid.
[103] Ibid., p. 122.
[104] Ibid., p. 123.
[105] Ibid.
[106] Ibid., p. 121.

This was done by the use of the principle of sympathetic resonance or 'like attracts like'. Each temple was so framed as to include symbolic reference to the appropriate deity. It was oriented according to the season and the heavenly body corresponding to that deity, whose characteristic numbers were also expressed in the dimensions of the building. Certain patterns of number, each with corresponding musical and geometric types, represented certain aspects of universal energy.[107]

It is important once again to pause and reflect on what Michell is really implying here, given its context in the wider alchemical context of "as above, so below," *for this means that such architecture was a direct attempt — if one may be permitted to employ the modern physics term for "sympathetic resonance" and "sympathetic magic" — to construct coupled harmonic oscillators capable of manipulating the physical medium itself.*

We have come a long and winding trail from the first tests of hydrogen bombs with their anomalously high yields, through the glimmers of a political geomancy practiced by Nazis and other researchers into the Grid system, through a profoundly sophisticated "topological metaphor" of the primordial "masculine-adrogyous trinity" at Angkor Wat and various ancient texts, and finally to the beginning glimpses of an alchemical architecture on a truly global scale, an architecture encompassing numbers recurrent across the globe, an architecture that summons the image of modern man living inside a vast ruined machine of great antiquity. We have seen, too, the first stirrings of something dark and sinister in the form of bloody sacrifice hanging over some of this project. This program was so large, and so old, that one cannot help but entertain that this whole process was the product of some elite coordinating the project.

In the remaining chapters of this book, we will explore those cultures that said the most about numbers and music, that are so self-evidently identified with pyramids and antiquity, and that are even identified with human sacrifice. In short, we will focus our attention on the ancient sites of Central and South America, on Mesopotamia, and of course, on the center of it all, Egypt, to see if we can peel back the layers of this machine, and to see if, lurking underneath, there

---

[107] Michell, *The New View Over Atlantis*, p, 124,emphasis added.

may be the suggestions of a profoundly sophisticated, and all but lost, physics and technology of the manipulation of the medium and of consciousness.

Before we do so, however, a more detailed review of what we have encountered in previous chapters is in order.

The Mathematical Masters of the Mysteries

5

A CATALOGUE OF CLUES:
CONCLUSIONS TO PART ONE

"The intensity of energy varies with the seasons and times of day, with sunrise and sunset. It may, like the geomancers' ch'i, be influenced by other heavenly bodies."
John Michell[1]

Our overview and introduction of the earth Grid is now complete, and it now affords us a very high vantage point with which to view the problems and inquiries that will form the detailed examination of the remainder of this book, so it is best to highlight the components of this mystery, of this vast ruined machine of alchemical architecture, to bring them into stark relief and to reinforce them as the themes that now draw our attention. The clues that we have encountered are vast and different, and seemingly unrelated, but as we shall now see in this review, there is a common conception underlying them all.

1) *Anomalous Yields from Early Hydrogen Bomb Tests* revealed that the supposedly unaccounted-for fusion reactions of lithium-7 were the publicly-stated reasons for the enormous yield of the Castle Bravo test, which far exceeded the predicted yield. However, two facts revealed that this public explanation was probably a cover-up for something else:
   a) the first hydrogen bomb test, "Mike", was not fueled by any lithium component at all, thus rendering the lithium-7 explanation of its anomalous yield inapplicable in this case; and,
   b) the lithium-7 reaction *was* known prior to the Castle Bravo test, both by the Argentine physicist José Balseiro, and to the Nazi physicist, Dr. Ronald Richter, who was relying upon that very lithium-7 reaction in his so-called fusion experiments in Argentina.
   c) Further examination of Dr. Richter's project and his own statements made later in personal interviews to the U.S.

---

[1] John Michell, *Secrets of the Stones*, p. 117.

Air Force revealed that he believed that *rotating plasmas* functioned as transducers — as "gates" — of the zero point energy, or of the energy of the fabric of space-time itself. Reduced to its simplest form, this means that any rotating mass of a non-linear medium can act as a transducer of the energy present in the local geometric configuration of space-time, which, by the nature of the case, is ever-changing;

d) Thus it was speculated that any slight deviation from perfect symmetrical compression of an atomic core could conceivably introduce a minute rotation or torque into the plasma of a nuclear explosion, thus making it function as a gate or transducer, for a brief moment of time, of the local geometry of space-time, which is, of course, variable over time and dependent on the relative positions of celestial bodies;

e) This view was corroborated by the existence of the work of Dr. Nikolai Kozyrev in the Soviet Union, who noticed similar effects in the sun itself — a large rotating ball of plasma — and posited that these were due to the functions of time itself playing into the thermonuclear reactions of the sun;

f) Thus, the celestial machine with its component bodies functions in itself as a kind of a grid system, which is mirrored on the Earth by the placement of structures deliberately aligned with celestial markers. It is thus possible that thermonuclear testing, to some degree not fully understood, taps into the actual earth Grid system, as it in turn taps into the celestial one.[2]

2) *Similar Observations of Variable Readings at Grid Sites Depending upon Time* were made by Grid researcher Paul Devereux and his Dragon project, which recorded similar variances in

---

[2] It is important to understand what is being said here. The lithium-7 explanation for the anomalous yields of the Castle Bravo test *do* make sense, but possibly do not account for *all* the anomalous yield. The mere fact that the reaction was known *prior to* the test makes it unlikely that such an obvious component of fusion reactions was overlooked by American nuclear engineers. The exchange between Drs. Balseiro and Richter in Argentina, in other words, cast an aura of suspicion over the official Castle Bravo explanation.

infrared and infrasonic readings at various megalithic sites, depending upon the time of day (sunrise, sunset, etc) and in some cases the phases of the moon, thus suggesting that the site in question somehow was tapping into the energies of the geometries of local space-time;

3) *The Giza Prime Meridian, Metrology, and Number* occurred in connection with *the Ruins of a Global Machine of Alchemical Architecture*, these numbers and measures reflecting a positioning of sites with respect to an ancient prime meridian running through Giza, and more specifically, through what would be the apex of the Great Pyramid. With respect to the ancient systems of measure, it was seen that most Grid researchers are aware of the importance, and ancientness, of the British imperial system as well as of other ancient systems of measure for obtaining the numerical values connecting grid sites. It was also seen that the Greek, Roman, and British imperial measures were related to each other in the precise mathematical ratio of 24:25, yielding numerical coefficients of geodetic measurements that were based on a Sumerian sexagesimal system. Many of these numbers in turn are *gematrian* numbers which can be substituted for letters in ancient texts. This suggested that one was looking at a combined system of *texts and monuments* that both made use of the same systems of "sacred numbers."

4) *The Grid and the Social Engineering of Power and Consciousness* was also implied, not only directly by Michell with frequent allusions to the need to "find the center" of a region, but also in the regalia of royalty that suggested the "cosmic axis", such as the scepter. For Michell, the Grid was intended in some sense as a manipulation of consciousness, as the social engineering of society done in deliberate reflection of the celestial machine that the Grid was designed to emulate.

5) *Bloody, and Human, Sacrifices* were also associated with *some* aspects and sites on the world Grid — one need only think of the blood and gore of the Meso-American sites — but not with *all* of them. As noted, Michell suspected that this was due to the concept that somehow such sacrifices were able to intensify the magical manipulation of whatever forces the

ancients thought to be involved at the site. It was thus implied that the technology of such sites itself, which we have argued was for the ultimate purpose of the manipulation of the physical medium itself, may also have been involved in the manipulation of consciousness, and sacrifice was somehow a means to this end, though in ways we have yet to examine.

6) *Medium Manipulation, Consciousness Manipulation, the Topological Metaphor, and the Implications:* We saw also that contained within certain ancient cosmologies and texts was a "topological metaphor" that led to a primary initial "differentiation" creating a primordial "masculine-adrogynous" trinitarian or triadic structure — as in the metaphor of Vishnu's tripartite manifestation — of two differentiated regions in the physical medium, plus their common shared surface. This led to the view that the physical medium, in the ancient view, was a transmutative medium that created information, information that was *analogical* in its structure due to the fact that all differentiations derived from their common substrate. This "analogical structure" and metaphor suggests that on the ancient view there was a common understanding both of the physical medium and of consciousness, and a deep physics underlying the two.

In the coming chapters, we will attempt to unfold this deep relationship and its relationship to the Grid system and some of its monuments, with a view to further understanding of their, and its, possible designed purpose and function. In the course of this examination, we will have occasion to briefly suggest the possible reasons for human sacrifices, originating in a perverted understanding of the physical medium and its relationship to consciousness.

PART TWO:
THE MESO-AMERICAN AND SOUTH AMERICAN "PYRAMID PEOPLES"

"Again there comes a humiliation, destruction, and demolition. The minikins, woodcarvings were killed when the Heart of Sky devised a flood for them. A great flood was made; it came down on the heads of the manikins, woodcarvings."
The Popol Vuh,
Trans. Dennis Tedlock, p. 71.

"Then they tell how Quetzlcoatl departed. It was when he refused to obey the sorcerers about making the human payment, about sacrificing humans. Then the sorcerers deliberated among themselves, they whose names were Tezcatlipoca, Ihuimetcatl, and Toltecatl. They said, 'He must leave his city. We shall live there.'"
The Life of Topiltzin Quetzlcoatl: A.D. 817-95, p. 31,
History and Mythology of the Aztecs: the Codex Chimalpopoca,
Trans. John Bierhorst

6

PARADOXES AT PUMA PUNKHU:
THE ANTIQUITY OF MAN IN SOUTH AMERICA, AND ANCIENT MACHINING

"Tiahuanaco is a perfect illustration of a certain 'challenge' to all *the theories, namely that it experienced a period of uncanny technological progress, followed by an equally unexplainable period of deterioration."*
Igor Witkowski[1]

South America is famous for its huge cyclopean walls of massive stones, cut at impossible angles and all fitted together so precisely, and without mortar, that one cannot slide a penknife blade between them; it is famous for ancient ruins, thousands of years old, buried beneath deep jungle in the heart of its murky interior, for strange sites of great antiquity depicting figures on the ground only visible and discernible from the air, and for a megalithic site high in the lofty reaches of the Andes mountains, a site that evidences such paradoxes that any way one slices them, one is in the presence of a great historical and technological mystery, one with crucial bearing on any study of the world Grid.

That site is Tiahuanaco, and its sister site a few miles away, Puma Punkhu, both near the shores of Lake Titicaca in Bolivia.

But before looking closer at Tiahuanaco and Puma Punkhu, an overview of the general context — itself bizarre enough — is needed, in order to see just how strange Tiahuanaco really is in the midst of so much other strangeness.

In Peru, for example, it is well known that there are walls of stone, with two distinctive features or periods of construction in evidence. The first, and oldest of these, features large stones with irregular cuts, so precisely joined together, without mortar, that knife blades cannot be inserted into the cracks. The most famous of these is a twelve-sided stone with such irregular cuts as to defy the imagination, yet, it is fitted perfectly to all the surrounding stones.

---

[1] Igor Witkowski, *Axis of the World: The Search for the Oldest American Culture* (Kempton, Illinois: Adventures Unlimited Press, 2008), p. 203.

The Twelve-Sided Stone in an Ancient Wall near Cuzco.[2]

Note that all of the stones seen in the above picture are joined together without mortar, and the twelve-sided stone implies a measure of technological sophistication to even cut and fit the stone so precisely with the surrounding blocks. Oftentimes these cyclopean structures are topped with a later layer of construction made according to a more traditional "rectangular brick and mortar" approach typical of Incan construction.

But why would an earlier culture construct walls in such a complex way? One answer, given by engineers, is that in earthquake-prone Peru, the cavitation of an earthquake would certainly shake the walls, but, given the irregularity of many of the stone blocks in these walls, the stones would simply fall more or less back into their original position and the wall would remain intact. The later layers of Incan construction, built according to more conventional models, do not fare so well.

---

[2] The wall is located at Sacsayhuaan, near Cuzco. See David Hatcher Childress, *Technology of the Gods: The Incredible Sciences of the Ancients* (Adventures Unlimited Press, 2000), p. 70

Similar construction principles are found elsewhere in the world, as, for example, in the Gate of the *Nekromonteion* near the ancient city of Ephyra.

The Gate of the Nekromonteion in Greece

Again, the stones are irregularly cut and joined so precisely, that the structure, like the walls in Peru, has survived for centuries in spite of the many earthquakes in the region.

A. The Riddle of Sacsayhuaman
1. Indicators of Advanced Machining Technology

A closer look at the walls near Cuzco — at a place called Sacsayhuaman — are in order to see precisely how intricate this method of construction could be. Indeed, so intricate is it that the sixteenth century Spanish chronicler, Garcilaso de la Vega, described his own shock at discovering the wall, and his deeper shock over its implications:

Its proportions are inconceivable when one has not actually seen it; and when one has looked at it closely and examined it attentively, they appear to be so extraordinary that *it seems as though some magic had presided over its construction... It is made of such (enormous) stones, and in*

131

such great number, that one wonders simultaneously how the Indians were able to quarry them, how they transported them, and how they hewed them and set them on top of one another... They are so well fitted together that you could not slip the point of a knife between two of them. If we think, too, that this incredible work was accomplished without the help of a single machine... how may we explain the fact that these Peruvian Indians were able to split, carve, lift, carry, hoist and lower such enormous blocks of stone, which are more like pieces of a mountain than building stones? Is it too much to say that it represents an even greater enigma than the seven wonders of the world?[3]

A glance at a picture will demonstrate the enormity of the mystery, one that has not cleared up in the centuries between de la Vega's observations and the present.

The Irregular Cut Stones of the Wall of Sacsayhuaman

It is intriguing to note that the notion of machining these massive and irregularly cut stones did not originate in late nineteenth or twentieth century "pseudo-archaeology," the favorite term of the

---

[3] Garcilasco de la Vega, *The Royal Commentaries of the Incas*, 233-235, cited in Hancock and Faiia, *Heaven's Mirror*, p. 285, emphasis added.

academically-blinded, for de la Vega's observations were made in the sixteenth century, and even *then*, the implications were obvious and apparent. Indeed, one scientist calculated the weight of one of the enormous stone blocks in the wall and concluded it weighed approximately 355 tons, one of the heaviest such cut stones in the world,[4] and exceeded in weight only by some of the truly gigantic stones of Baalbek in Lebanon.

Conventional archaeological theory here as elsewhere seems unable, or afraid, to confront the obvious, and attributes these huge constructions to the Incas, who, it maintains, used a "trial and error" approach in cutting and then fitting these stones together so snugly. But having stated this nonsensical position, conventional archaeological theory admits that the Incas, for some inexplicable reason — just as the Egyptians — left no *records* nor even maintained any *traditions* about the construction of these huge walls![5] As Hancock and Faiia point out, the *only* record of the Incas even attempting to move such a huge stone, recorded once again in de la Vega's *Royal Commentaries of the Incas*, "suggests that they had no experience of the techniques involved — since the attempt ended in disaster."[6]

And there is one final, highly significant, fact to be noted about Sacsayhuaman, and that is, that the Inca name means, quite literally, "Satisfied Falcon." This, notes Hancock and Faiia, connects the site to the unlikely place of Egypt in a more direct way, since the name "Falcon" is a name of Horus, and suggests the secret "mystery school" or elite of Egypt, the *Shemsu-Hor*, the Followers of Horus.[7]

---

[4] Hancock and Faiia, *Heaven's Mirror*, p. 286.

[5] Ibid., p. 287.

[6] Ibid.

[7] Ibid., p. 285. As I point out in my book *The Cosmic War* (Adventures Unlimited Press, 2007), pp. 285, 293, the name Falcon is also attributable to another Egyptian god, the Sun-God Ra, and has distinctive connections to the planet Mars.

2. The Incas, the Grid, and Human Sacrifice

The scholar William Sullivan noted that, just as in the Old World, the ancient sites of the New World were used to convey complex astronomical information, in a "language of sacred revelation grounded in empirical observation,"[8] but like the Aztecs, the Incas, according to Sullivan, took the symbolism of the heavenly machine, and the individual person's ascent to it after death, literally, and thus were led "into the dark hell of black magic and human sacrifice."[9] In the Incas' case, these sacrifices were always offered along the system of their straight roads, roads that were laid out in the customary design of making structures on Earth correspond to celestial constellations,[10] the magical power thus conjured being concentrated at the place of sacrifice and "transmitted" throughout the empire by means of those roads and "ley lines."

The contrast is acute and compelling, and again, raises the central mystery:

> In Mexico and the Andes astronomically aligned, pyramidal monuments were used as part of the apparatus of sacrifice. In Egypt and Angkor astronomically aligned pyramidal monuments were used as part of a gnostic quest for immortality.[11]

In other words, from one and the same mythological cosmology, two entirely *different* practices subsequently emerged. This is a crucial point, and we shall have occasion to return to it in a later chapter, but for the present moment, it is important to understand the significance of this point, for *if* the ancient cosmology examined in conjunction with Angkor Wat and some ancient texts (examined in chapter three) conceals a sophisticated topological metaphor of the physical medium, whose principal property is the creation of information via an "analogical process," then the implication is that,

---

[8] William Sullivan, *Secret of the Incas*, pp. 247-248, cited in Hancock and Faiia, *Heaven's Mirror*, p. 294.

[9] Hancock and Faiira, *Heaven's Mirror*, p. 294.

[10] Ibid.

[11] Ibid., p. 295.

in the ancient view, there is a direct relationship between consciousness and that physical medium. It is this direct relationship that leads to the subsequent divergence of the religious practices — one contemplative, the other very murderous and brutal — in connection with it.

3. The "Aerial" Mysteries: The Transition to the Heart of the South American Riddle

There are other mysteries, equally imponderable, to be found in Peru.

The famous Nazca Lines in Peru, for example, are only visible from the air:

Part of the Nazca Lines in Peru. Note the Straightness of the Lines

135

This has led some in the "ancient astronauts" school to propose that the lines were direction markers in some ancient "spaceport." But then, how does one explain these parts of the Nazca Lines, also only visible from the air?

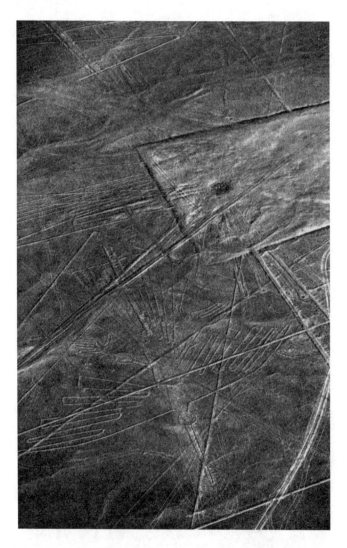

Nazca Lines in Peru with the Famous "Hummingbird" Glyph

More recent investigations have shown many of these glyphs, the "Spider"(not shown) and the "Hummingbird" to be configured, once again, to certain astronomical alignments.

Turning south from Peru towards Bolivia, the area surrounding Tiahuanaco is even stranger, for there the system of straight "ley lines" is even more in evidence from an aerial view of the Aymara Indian country surrounding Lake Titicaca, the site of Tiahuanaco.

Straight Ley Line System in Aymara Indian Country in Bolivia, Near Lake Titicaca.

And this brings us to the strangest ancient site in South America, and perhaps even the strangest of all sites on the world Grid, Lake Titicaca, and the curious ruins of Tiahuanaco and Puma Punkhu.

B. *Tiahuanaco and the Puma Punkhu Paradox: Ancient Machining*

No one visiting Tiahuanaco and Puma Punkhu can come away with anything less than awe and puzzlement, for there, amid the ruins of what was clearly an ancient city, high in the thin air of the lake, are the great stone remains of a civilization that clearly possessed an advanced technology able to machine the intricately cut stones. As we shall see, the presence of such clear evidence for a sophisticated stone-working technology raises in a clear fashion the possibility that one is looking at the debris of a very ancient civilization, remains that have led many to question the whole standard history and model of how mankind came to the South and North American continents.

Just a glance at some of these will demonstrate this point better than any words could possibly do.

Intricate Stone Cutting at Tiahuanaco[12]

---

[12] Igor Witkowski, *Axis of the World: The Search for the Oldest American Civilization* (Adventures Unlimited Press, 2008), p. 227.

More than any other of the huge stones at Tiahuanaco, the so-called "H Blocks" — huge stones intricately cut — testify to the existence of some sort of technology, to the existence of some sort of advanced ancient *machining* technology:

Trapezoidal Cuts in an "H-Block" at Tiahuanaco[13]

---

[13] Igor Witkowski, *Axis of the World: The Search for the Oldest American Civilization*, p. 226.

And not far away, at Puma Punkhu, are the famous "H-Blocks" themselves:

"H-Block" at Puma Punkhu[14]

[14] Witkowski, *Axis of the World*, p. 222.

Twin "H-Blocks" at Puma Punku[15]

When engineers carefully examined these huge, finely-cut blocks, they discovered something else: the cuts were so placed on each block that the bocks were meant to be joined together, as if they were three-dimensional pieces of an intricate jigsaw puzzle.

---

[15] Witkowski, *Axis of the World*, p. 224.

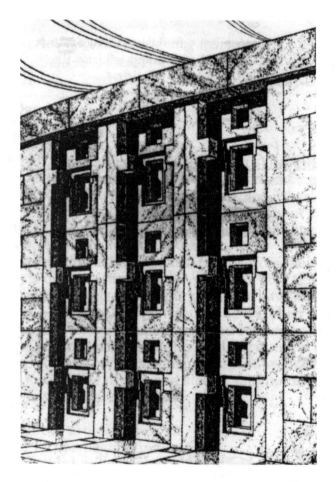

Artist's Rendition of the Joining of the H-Blocks[16]

The mystery only deepens, the closer one looks, and one researcher who *did* take a closer look was my friend and colleague in alternative research, Igor Witkowski.

Best known for his truly magisterial research in the field of Nazi technology, *The Truth About the Wunderwaffe*,[17] Witkowski turned his

---

[16] David Hatcher Childress, *Technology of the Gods: The Incredible Sciences of the Ancients*, p. 71.

[17] Igor Witkowski, *The Truth About the Wunderwaffe,* Trans. from the Polish by Bruce Wenham (European History Press, 2003). ISBN 838825916-4.

investigative talents to the question of human origins in the Americas in a fascinating study, *Axis of the World: The Search for the Oldest American Civilization,* a work we shall follow closely in this chapter, for Witkowski's conclusions are nothing less than stunning, and his book also makes available for the first time in the English language some of the investigations into these mysteries undertaken in Eastern Europe.

1. The Heart of All South American Mysteries

Witkowski justifiably calls Tiahuanaco and Puma Punkhu "the heart of all the South American and Transpacific mysteries."[18] We shall see presently why he says that it is at the heart of the "Transpacific" mysteries. As has already been seen with the pictures of the elaborate stone-work of Tiahuanaco and Puma Punkhu, however, the site "is a perfect illustration of a certain 'challenge' to *all* the theories, namely that it experienced a period of uncanny technological progress, followed by an equally unexplainable period of deterioration,"[19] for "the precision of stonecutting visible here and the level of its complexity are *evident* remains of some technological civilization's activity."[20]

This problem is compounded by Tiahuanaco's and Puma Punkhu's location at Lake Titicaca in Bolivia, at an altitude of nearly 10,000 feet above sea level, an altitude of such thin air that only the nearby Aymara Indians are accustomed to breathing and working in it; for Europeans such as Witkowski, the effort often produces nosebleeds, exhaustian, and pre-heart attack symptoms.[21] How could such a technologically sophisticated civilization emerge or settle in such an extreme place?

The problem is further compounded by the fact that the gigantic machined stones of Puma Punkhu are scattered chaotically over the

---

[18] Igor Witkowski, *Axis of the World: The Search for the Oldest American Civilization* (Adventures Unlimited Press, 2008), p. 197.

[19] Ibid., p. 203.

[20] Ibid., p. 212.

[21] Ibid., p. 213.

site, as if smashed by some heavy hand of destruction.[22] To Wiktkowski, when one considered all the various sites evident in South America and the varying degrees of technological sophistication they exhibited, it was evident that the most recent Inca period was the least sophisticated. The further back one went, the more the evidence suggested that the technology itself was far superior in remotest times, than more recent ones. This suggested something of great significance for the *chronological* development of the South American civilizations to Witkowski, when one compared the great technological sophistication of Puma Punkhu, to the less sophisticated level of technology evidenced by nearby Tiahuanaco:

> Looking at the site we have the overwhelming impression that we deal here with a *backward development* from an advanced, sophisticated technology in the remote past, through a moderately developed technology in nearer history, up to its almost complete atrophy presently.
>
> When taking into account modern construction achievements, we face the truth that *many of the construction methods that were applied in Puma Punkhu have absolutely no equivalent anywhere else in the world and would even be hard to reproduce in our time.*[23]

In other words, we have the following broad outlines of a tripartite structure of chronological and technological development:

1) *The most sophisticated* technological evidence, stretching back to "High Antiquity";
2) *A less sophisticated* layer of technological development, stretching back to "antiquity"; and,
3) *The least sophisticated* layer of technological development, comprising the known civilization of South America, the Incas.

This broad, tripartite chronological pattern is quite the crucial point, for we shall be returning to it later in this chapter in connection with

---

[22] Witkowski, *Axis of the World*, p. 213.
[23] Ibid., p. 214, emphasis in the original.

the actual *dating* of Tiahuanaco, but also in subsequent chapters when we consider the dating of places such as Teotihuacan in Mexico, and most importantly, Giza in Egypt.[24]

Witkowski outlines the complexity of attempting to machine the H Blocks and other stones found at Puma Punkhu, and just how precise the machined tolerances of these blocks really is:

A serial stonecutting of the blocks (of very hard andesite) was applied, characterized by a precision hardly achievable today! I cannot imagine a contemporary designer who would propose to build some large object of megalithic blocks having such complex shapes, reproduced with a precision of the order of one tenth of a millimeter (which is roughly the thickness of this sheet of paper), while the convex edges, formed by merging surfaces made with such a precision were to correspond with analogous concave two- or three-dimensional edges of other blocks. Such a designer would have to be crazy! But such precision can be found at Puma Punkhu!

The cutting machines currently in use (millers, for example) with rotating tools do not enable us to make such sharp concave edges, and in particular such sharp three dimensional concave corners merging three perpendicular surfaces — not to mention the serial production of them! Such a technology simply does not exist. You can make a precise surface and polish it, or connect two such surfaces with a convex or concave edge, but it would be quite a challenge to connect *three* such surfaces and create a 90° concave corner, still keeping the 0.1mm precision tolerance in the very corner![25]

But such precise tolerances are not the *only* technological problem posed by Puma Punkhu.

The *other* problem posed by the H Blocks is that they have "almost 80 surfaces each!" Witkowski quips — not inaccurately — "I suspect that a contemporary engineer could not even imagine

---

[24] I have already commented briefly on this tripartite pattern in connections with the observations of Alan Alford at Giza. Q.v. *The Giza Death Star* (Adventures Unlimited Press, 2003), pp. 24-38.

[25] Witkowski, *Axis of the World*, p. 214.

designing them without a computer."[26] For Witkowski, the mere presence of such technological sophistication, in addition to a globally aligned system of sites, constitutes "a very serious challenge" to conventional academic views of the evolution of human civilization. Indeed, the contemporary historical, archaeological, and anthropological sciences seem utterly unwilling even to consider the facts.[27]

And let us note one final thing by way of a question: why would one need such an almost *optical* precision in the H Blocks? Such precision by the nature of the case implies that it served some *functional purpose*, as in a machine.

2. The Traditions Concerning Tiahuanaco

However, in order to fully appreciate the deep significance and implications of Puma Punkhu, we must now turn our attentions to the second site at Lake Titicaca, and to the second, later and intermediate layer of technological evidence and chronological progression: Tiahuanaco. Here, interestingly enough, we discover many of the traditions that we found associated with megalithic sites elsewhere in the world.

The first of these is evident by the ancient name for Tiahuanaco: Taypicala. Not surprisingly, this means "the Stone at the Centre,"[28] giving yet another instance of the ancient "geomantic" practice of finding the center of a region. Indeed, the Inca tradition itself recognized that the ancient name of Tiahuanaco meant the Stone at the Center of the world.[29]

Even more interesting is the fact that when the first Spanish explorers arrived in the region and asked the local Aymara Indians if the structures at Tiahuanaco and Puma Punkhu had been built by the Incas, they were greeted with laughter. The Aymara explained that their ancestral tradition stated that the structures were built "long before the Inca reign" and that they had literally been built very

---

[26] Witkowski, *Axis of the World*, p. 215.
[27] Ibid.
[28] Hancock and Faiia, *Heaven's Mirror*, p. 270.
[29] Ibid., p. 274.

146

suddenly, in the span of one night![30] More interesting still, the site was also said to have been built by the first creations of the sun-god, Viracocha, who created a race of giants, who were later overthrown by a worldwide deluge when they had displeased him.[31] This is, of course, not the first time we have encountered such traditions concerning these cyclopean megalithic structures, for we have already encountered similar traditions already with respect to Stonehenge in England, Baalbek in Lebanon, and even stone circles in Africa.

The sun-god Viracocha requires a closer look, for once again, as in the case of Vishnu, the symbolism surrounding this god is multi-layered, and indicative of a possible deeper physics, though it should be made clear that, just as Vishnu, Viracocha is also manifested and precisely described in the Andean traditions as a bearded, blue-eyed white man of large stature, and the giver of civilization to the Incas, just as we shall discover Quetzcoatl to be when we turn northward to Mexico.[32]

As the sun-god, however, Viracocha like Atum in Egypt and Vishnu in India and Indochina, was the great self-generative power in, and of, the cosmos.[33] He is carved above the well-known "Gate of the Sun" at Tiahuanaco:

Viracocha's Image on the Gate of the Sun at Tiahuanaco

---

[30] Hancock and Faiia, *Heaven's Mirror*, p. 272.

[31] Ibid., p. 276.

[32] Ibid., p. 275.

[33] Ibid.

3. The Image of Vicacocha: A Schematic of a Technology?

There is something peculiar about this image, and it has haunted me ever since I first became aware of it many years ago. In *The Giza Death Star*, I observed the resemblance of this highly-stylized image to the schematic of a three-stage fission-fusion-fission hydrogen bomb.[34] Let us recall the schematic of such a bomb from chapter one, and compare it to the image:

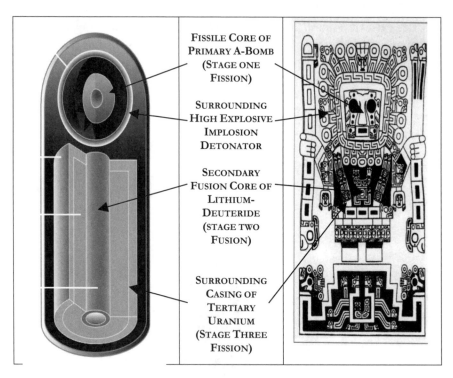

FISSILE CORE OF PRIMARY A-BOMB (STAGE ONE FISSION)

SURROUNDING HIGH EXPLOSIVE IMPLOSION DETONATOR

SECONDARY FUSION CORE OF LITHIUM-DEUTERIDE (STAGE TWO FUSION)

SURROUNDING CASING OF TERTIARY URANIUM (STAGE THREE FISSION)

Comparison of Three Stage Hydrogen Bomb Schematic with Viracocha

Of course, such comparisons are suggestive, if not fanciful, but they do give one pause especially considering that Viracocha was a *sun-*

---

[34] Joseph P. Farrell, *The Giza Death Star*, (Adventures Unlimited Press, 2001), pp. 25-26.

god. Even more suggestive is what happens when one rotates the Viracocha image 180 degrees on its vertical axis:

Viracocha Image Rotated 180° on its Vertical Axis

Upside-down, one cannot avoid the vague impression of the outlines of a bomb.

While such comparisons may be fanciful, there is a further tradition surrounding Viracocha that suggests that the comparison to modern technologies might not, indeed, be so questionable, and that is that Viracocha ushers in five new epochs, each one being heralded by a "new sun", each epoch being called a *pachacuti*. This word signifies a literal "'overturning of the world' (according to Sir Clements Markham's translation), and an *'overturning of space-time'* according to William Sullivan."[35] In other words, if one accepts the hypothesis that the anomalous yields of early h-bomb tests were in part the result of gating of energies from the variable conditions of the geometry of local celestial space-time, the peculiar resemblance of

---

[35] Hancock and Faiia, *Heaven's Mirror*, p, 275, emphasis added, citing Sir Clements Markham, *The Incas of Peru*, p. 43, and William Sullivan, *The Secret of the Incas*, p. 29.

the Viracocha image at the Sun Gate at Tiahuanaco to such devices, and the traditions of such over-turnings of space-time in the epochs or world ages that Viracocha destroys and then re-creates (one recalls Vishnu's similar role), then the comparison may not be all that fanciful.

4. Traditions Connected Half a World Away

There is one final tradition concerning Viracocha that is also worth mentioning, for it illustrates yet another very bizarre and unusual connection with traditions half a world away in Mesopotamia, for there are traditions which hail the engineering accomplishments of Viracocha *and* his companions, who are called, suggestively, "messengers," and *"the shining ones."*[36] If this sounds vaguely familiar, it should, this precise term, "the shining ones," was also used in some ancient Mesopotamian texts to describe the Annunaki, the Watchers, the race of "gods" that came to earth and, in some readings of the stories, helped to engineer the human race itself. They were thus designated because of the luminous character of their faces.[37]

As if this was not enough, there is another strange connection between the traditions of the Incas in the New World, and those of the Old World, for the Incas believed that the soul ascending to heaven after death was accompanied by black dogs, and in Egypt, the soul's ascension was accompanied by Anubis and Upuaut, symbolized by black dogs.[38]

5. The Difficulty of Dating Tiahuanaco

Conventional and standard archaeological dating of Tiahuanaco is unusually divided over the date of the site, assigning a *terminus ante quem* to the second millennium BC, and a *terminus post quem* to as late

---

[36] Hancock and Faiia, *Heaven's Mirror*, p. 288, emphasis added.

[37] See my *Genes, Giants, Monsters, and Men* (Feral House, 2011), chapter 3, section D, and D1. (Exact page references cannot be given as this book is being written prior to the release of *Genes, Giants, Monsters, and Men*.)

[38] Hancock and Faiia, op. cit., p. 282.

as the ninth century AD.[39] All standard archaeological models of Tiahuanaco are, however, agreed that the site has nothing to do with the Incas.[40] Even on the early dating of Tiahuanaco by conventional archaeology, this would make the site older than the Mayan ruins of Meso-America, and far older than the Inca empire.[41]

But these *termini ante et post quem* have always been challenged, even as early as the nineteenth century, by amateur archaeologists who have pointed out a number of problems even for the earliest dating. The French archaeologist Le Plongeon, for example, uncovered a layer of seashells after making some superficial excavations at the site, suggesting that it was once a seaport. He concluded from this that the site may have been antediluvian, a suggestion, notes Witkowski, that "turned out to be surprisingly long-lived."[42] This finding was echoed in the early twentieth century by the German-American Arthur Poznansky, who wrestled with the riddle of Tiahuanaco for almost thirty years.[43] Poznansky's reasons for this conclusion derived from his mapping of the site's barely-visible remaining canals, leading him to conclude the city had once been surrounded by the lake, and the shoreline higher.[44]

However, this method of dating by the level of the shoreline soon compounded the difficulty, and the mystery, of the entire Tiahuanaco-Puma Punkhu complex. When one examines the entire vicinity of the sites, there are clear indications that "the end of the 'Golden Era' must have had a rather sudden character," for scattered about it, "there were numerous large stone blocks just abandoned in various phases of cutting."[45] This was not the only indicator of sudden destruction, nor was it the only *problem*.

> The old shoreline was also clearly visible, as if the change came almost overnight. It was plotted on a map and with this came the first surprise. It turned out that the old shoreline was significantly

---

[39] Hancock and Faiia, *Heaven's Mirror*, p. 270.

[40] Ibid.

[41] Witkowski, *Axis of the World*, p. 204f.

[42] Ibid., p. 204.

[43] Ibid.

[44] Ibid., p. 205.

[45] Ibid., p. 206.

inclined to the present level... in the scale of the entire lake the difference amounts to around 1000 feet... It appeared, moreover, that the old coastline doesn't form a closed loop, but is open on the south; it simply ends, some distance from the ruins. It other words, had the lake's surface been that much higher, its waters would have spilled over the southern part of the altiplano, towards Lake Poopo; there was no natural barrier. But there must have been something! The only reasonable explanation in this situation was that there must have been a glacier, which could stop the waters. No one knew how long ago such conditions existed, but it was a kind of confirmation that the ruins were indeed quite old.[46]

The circumstantial evidence for a glaciers was not the only thing pointed to Tiahuanaco's "extreme antiquity," for also found on the Gate of the Sun — the Gate with the image of Viracocha discussed above — are the representations of elephant heads. And yet another relief at Tiahuanaco shows "quite clear bas-reliefs of *mastodons.*"[47] The youngest known fossils of mastodons in South America are some 10,400 years old.[48]

To make the dating of the site even more difficult, radiocarbon dating places the site to about 1500BC![49]

So on the one hand, the geological and indirect evidence points to a site of great antiquity, to the period of the end of the last Ice Age and to a period when the last mastodons were known in the region, that is, to a period of ca. 10,500 BC (there's that date again!), while the radiocarbon dating points to something much more recent, and hence, becomes the *terminus ante quem* for conventional archaeology. Before considering an extremely speculative resolution of this difficulty, however, it is worth looking at more recent moves within *conventional* archaeology to redate the site to a far earlier period than 1500 BC.

This shift began in ca. 1996-1997 when Dr. Oswaldo Rivera, the Director of Bolivia's National Institute of Archaeology, and "one of

---

[46] Witkowski, *Axis of the World*, p. 206.
[47] Ibid., p. 207.
[48] Ibid.
[49] Ibid., p. 198.

the world's leading experts on Tiahuanaco,"[50] made an announcement confirming his belief that the site was some 12,000 years old.[51]

Moreover, this new dating was based on an examination of *existing* structures at the site. But Rivero went on to explain that there was in all likelihood *another* Tiahuanaco buried beneath the present ruins.[52]

The implications of all this were and are enormous, for this means that if Tiahuanaco is some 12,000 years old, then Puma Punkhu is even older than that!

6. Back to the Technology of Puma Punkhu

So we return to Puma Punkhu, to observe even more mystifying evidence of advanced technological machining, bearing in mind we are now looking at a technology in use *before* Tiahuanaco.

> Examination of the blocks reveals also the use of one more unconventional technology. In some places one can observe groups (usually rows) of very precisely made holes. The precision is so great that it *rules out* manual processing. First and foremost, they generally have exactly the same diameter, the sides are very smooth (if the holes are not damaged, of course) and precisely parallel. The deviations in this respect — i.e., differences of the diameter between the top and the bottom of the hole — are on the order of 0.1 mm. This corresponds with drilling by a machine fixed on some mount, for it could not be done by holding the tool in one's hands, especially working a very hard stone.[53]

The evidence of such technology is, indeed, overwhelming, but Witkowski is acutely aware that there is a type of "scholarship" that balks at concluding the obvious, and that proposes ludicrous

---

[50] Hancock and Faiia, *Heaven's Mirror*, p. 305.

[51] Ibid., p. 306. Hancock and Faiia note that Poznanski had determined a date of 17,000 years ago.

[52] Ibid., pp. 307-308.

[53] Witkowski, *Axis of the World*, p. 216.

alternative theories. Witkowski's proposed method of persuading them of the error of their thinking is somewhat novel:

> From skeptical scientists, the "debunkers," we often hear that all the wonders of prehistoric construction were accomplished only (by) very simple stone or copper hand tools, accessible to primitive peoples. I would propose to chain such a scholar to a comparatively hard and large stone block, along with such primitive tools, until he turned it into a block such as one just described.[54]

Worse yet, Witkowski made a series of very exact measurements of the dimensions incorporated into the various surfaces of the H Blocks, and discovered, to his astonishment, that many of them incorporated a significant number: 3.1418, differing only from the ideal of π by .0002![55]

As if that were not enough, other recurring measures resulted in values that were exactly one fourth of the Sumerian unit of measure, the "ell".[56]

There is a final thing testifying to the high technology surrounding Puma Punkhu, and this time it comes from Andean tradition itself, and in it, we see the glimmer, perhaps, of a solution to the radiocarbon dating which was at such odds with the geological and indirect evidence for its antiquity. According to those legends, Puma Punkhu, with its large precisely-cut multi-faced stone blocks — some of which were simply abandoned in the middle of machining, as if some sudden catastrophe had overtaken the site — was "destroyed by Viracocha with 'deadly rays' before the deluge."[57]

In other words, its destruction was *deliberate and accomplished by means of a technology, and with an apparent suddenness.* One is, perhaps, looking at the South American version of some primordial "Tower of Babel Moment," when whatever was being constructed there was perceived as a threat to someone else, who intervened, and ended the project.

---

[54] Witkowski, *Axis of the World*, p. 217
[55] Ibid, pp. 218-219.
[56] Ibid., p. 221.
[57] Ibid., p. 217.

Moreover, the *type* of technology is even suggested by those legends; it was a technology involving electromagnetic *radiation.* Exposure to concentrated radiation would, indeed, massively distort radiocarbon dating efforts, making old things *appear far younger* than they actually were.

Maybe the comparison of the image of Viracocha on the Sun Gate at Tiahuanaco with a modern three-stage hydrogen bomb is not so fanciful after all.

C. The Axis of the World Across the Pacific
1. The Mystery of Easter Island

For the careful reader familiar with standard explanations of how mankind came to the Americas — the celebrated "land bridge" across the Bering Strait from Siberia to Alaska — the paradox of Puma Punkhu raises significant difficulties. Those difficulties are massively compounded when one considers the context of Tiahuanaco and Puma Punkhu within the context of the Grid system that stretches from South America, across the Pacific — in nearly a straight line as we shall see, or what Witkowski calls "the Axis of the World" — to the Indian subcontinent.

We have seen how local traditions concerning Puma Punkhu and Tiahuanaco conjoin two things: (1) a sudden and deliberate destruction by the means of an implied technology and an implied act of war, and (2) a subsequent catastrophe in the form of a flood.

One finds these two traditions coupled, once again, in the very unlikely place of Easter Island. There, the flood story is cast in the wider context of a lost land that sank under the sea, never to be seen again:

> The young man Tea Waka said:
> — In the old times our land was large, very large.
> Kuukuu asked him a question:
> — Why it turned small then?
> Tea Waka replied:
> — *Uwoke has lowered his stick on it.* He has lowered his stick on the Ohiro town. Big waves raised and the land became small. It has

been named Te-Pito-o-te-Henua. *Uwoke's stick was broken on the Puku-Puhipuhi mountain.*

Tea Waka and Kuukuu talked about the Ko-te-Tomonga-o-Tea-Waka village (the place where Tea Waka has reached the shore). Then the Hotu Matua king came ashore and settled on the island. Kuukuu said to him:

— Once this land was greater.

The friend Tea Waka said:

— The land sunk.

Then Tea Waka added:

— This town is now called Ko-te-Tomonga-o- Tea-Waka.

Hotu Matua Asked:

— Why the land sunk?

— *Uwoke did this, he has pushed the land* — replied Tea Waka. The land was named Te-Pito-o-te-Henua. *When Uwoke's stick was long, the land has collapsed into the abyss.* Puku-Puhipuhi — that's how the place where Uwoke's stick was broken is now called.

— The Hotu Matua king said to Tea Waka:

— My friend, it was not Uwoke's stick. *It was the thunder of the Make Make god.*[58]

While at first glance this Easter Island Flood legend might seem rather simplistic, a closer examination reveals some interesting details that parallel the Andean legends of Viracocha, the Flood, and the destruction of Puma Punkhu and Tiahuanaco:

1) The flood is brought about by the deliberate action of a god or gods, in this case, Uwoke, and Make Make;
2) Both gods use some sort of technology to do so, Uwoke a "stick," and Make Make uses "thunder;" and finally,
3) Note the association of Uwoke's *stick* with a *mountain,* an unusual association, for effectively this means we have the association of a *god* with a *weapon* with a *mountain.* This is a formula that has been seen before, for it is a formula seen in the ancient epics of Mesopotamia describing an ancient

---

[58] Witkowski, *Axis of the World*, pp. 19-20, citing A. Kondratov, *Tajemnice trzech iceanow (Mysteries of Three Oceans)* (Warsaw, 1980), emphasis added by me.

"cosmic war of the gods," where the same association of mountains with gods with *pyramids* occurs.[59] To put it succinctly, one is in the presence, once again, of more or less the same association and constellation of relationships in Easter Island, and far-off Mesopotamia. And that means that the loss of land spoken of in the Easter Island version of the legend somehow fits into the wider context of a global deluge and a war of the gods.

The end result of this technological intervention was the loss of a "large" land. One cannot help but think how closely this legend resembles Plato's allegory of Atlantis, where, following a devastating war, the fabled continent is overcome by disasters, and sinks into the ocean.

That such a legend would arise on such an isolated and small island with almost no resources, such as Easter Island, and that it would so closely parallel — even in its "formula" of associating gods with weapons with mountains — Mesopotamian myths and the Platonic allegory, highlights the problem, for the chances of these specific details arising by mere coincidence is almost nil. The problem is further compounded by the fact that Easter Island actually developed a rather sophisticated form of writing, well in advance of anything exhibited or developed in North America, which, if the standard theory of a "land bridge" by which the native populations of the Americas came to the continents, spreading from north to south, is true, meant that the northern tribes had far longer a time to develop sophisticated writing. Yet they did not do so, but the Easter Islanders did![60]

It is in fact this script that demonstrates that the original settlement of Easter Island was anything but an isolated affair, or that it was disconnected from civilization elsewhere. The connections to "civilization elsewhere" in Easter Island's case are, however, quite problematical, for the script connects it to one side of the Pacific, but the construction in evidence on it connects it to the other.

---

[59] See the discussion in my book *The Cosmic War*, pp. 74-75, 83, 239.
[60] Witkowski, *Axis of the World*, p. 14.

This may most easily be illustrated, again, by pictures of the type of "jigsaw" construction methods that we have already encountered in Peru:

Stone Wall at Easter Island[61]

Irregular Stone Cuts at Easter Island[62]

---

[62] Witkowski, *Axis of the World*, p. 32.

Witkowski points out that there are four distinctive features of the constructions of these walls on Easter Island that tie them directly to the walls of Sacsayhuaman, Tiahuanaco, and even the high Andean "Incan" fortress of Machu Picchu:

1. The stone blocks are very closely matched to each other, despite rounded, complex shapes;
2. They are polygonal;
3. Their external surfaces are convex; and,
4. The entire wall is inclined toward the center of the construction.[63]

All this evidences at least *some* sort of contact between these far-flung locales in historical times.[64]

Before looking at the script that ties Easter Island to the other side of the Pacific, it is worth mentioning that in 1956 the famous explorer and archaeo-navigator Thor Heyerdahl discovered a statue on Easter Island wholly unlike its more famous moai "Face" statues, in that this one was a bearded man closely resembling in style similar statues found at Mohenjo Daro in India. Two similar specimens were discovered in Bolivia near Tiahuanaco. This is the first beginning of some "cracks" in the "land bridge" theory that the Native American populations migrated across the Bering Strait thousands of years ago, for what these connections suggest is rather a migration across the South Pacific.[65]

The most telling evidence for such a connection, however, is the aforementioned script of Easter Island, the Rongo Rongo writing.

Rongo Rongo Script of Easter Island[66]

---

[63] Witkowski, *Axis of the World*, p. 26.
[64] Ibid.
[65] Ibid., p. 27.
[66] Witkowski, *Axis of the World*, p. 37.

Witkowski notes that his fellow countryman, the linguist Professor Benon Z. Szalek of the University of Szczecin, made a detailed study and comparison of the Rongo Rongo script with the writing of the Indus Valley civilization in India, the civilization centered around the mysterious ruins of Mohenjo Daro:

Comparison of Rongo Rongo Script to that of the Indus Valley[67]

---

[67] David Hatcher Childress, *Lost Cities of Lemuria and the Pacific* (Adventures Unlimited Press, 1988), p. 302. It is worth noting that the Rongo Rongo script, like that of Mohenjo Daro and ancient Sumer, was a syllabic writing. See Witkowski, *Axis of the World*, p. 53.

Compounding the difficulty that this astonishing resemblance represents is the fact that the Indus Valley-Mohenjo Daro civilization disappeared ca. 1000-1200 years BC according to conventional archaeology.

> It means that at the moment when Easter Island was inhabited, Mohenjo Daro's unique system of writing, its religion, etc.... lived only in human memory. It (had) been gone for over two millennia (at least according to officially accepted theories)! It was simply one of the three oldest civilizations on our planet, along with the Sumerians and the empire of the Pharaohs. Could Easter Island's culture reach that deep into the prehistory of mankind? Incidentally, these circumstances make the Rongo Rongo script the oldest system of writing in use in historical times, for no less than four thousand years.... In the case of this chain of traces, the truth seems so obscure, and so strange at the same time, that one has to ask himself a question: what really happened there, in the Pacific and Indian Ocean, all those thousands of years ago?[68]

As we shall see in a moment, that question becomes even more peculiar when one examines the ruins of Mohenjo Daro themselves, for they afford yet another connection with distant Tiahuanaco and Viracocha, and a very bizarre one at that.

Contributing to this mystery is the fact that Easter Island's own indigenous peoples are of apparent Polynesian descent, but their local legends tell of an earlier race of a "long eared" people with "taller skulls, brighter skin, and of course a very different cultural heritage. They spoke a non-Polynesian language and according to the known tradition, it was they and only they, who knew the secret of writing."[69] These "long-ears" were, according to local tradition, white skinned and red haired![70] This tradition was confirmed by the first permanent European settler on the island, the French priest Eugene Eyraud, who began a campaign of burning the wooden tablets containing the Rongo Rongo script. Eyraud observed that the local natives were not able to read the writing, confirming the idea that the

---

[68] Witkowski, *Axis of the World*, p. 28.
[69] Ibid.
[70] Ibid., p. 20.

"long-ears" kept the secret of reading the writing to themselves.[71] According to the islanders' traditions, "the first king, Hotu Matua, brought with him 67 most precious tablets from their land of origin in the west."[72]

This tradition is very suggestive, for it indicates not only that the Easter Islanders maintained that they came to the Island "from the West," i.e., across the Pacific, but that part of the purpose may have been to bring priceless records of some sort to the island, and perhaps from thence, elsewhere. In any case, this tradition is also suggestive of another possible connection to the West, and to the celebrated Sumerian "Tablets of Destinies," the terrible objects of power with which and over which the "gods" fought a tremendous war, upon the conclusion of which, some were destroyed and others were taken "elsewhere."[73]

If bringing some priceless records *was* the purpose of the migration to Easter Island, then there is a sort of logic to it, if the purpose was to prevent such records from falling into the wrong hands by hiding them in a remote place, for one cannot get much more remote than Easter Island.

That there *was* some sort of hidden purpose behind the migration to this remote and desolate place is evident from the fact that the semi-triangular island itself covers only about 45 square miles, and from the fact that its hard igneous rock contains little soil suitable for agriculture. Yet, the island contains several distinctive and famous statues of heads — the famous Maoi — weighing as little as 10 or as much as 200 tons,[74] all of which are facing the center of the island in order, according to local legend, to protect the island from sinking into the sea as had happened a previous time in the population's legends.[75] All this, of course, has prompted the question of how such

---

[71] Witkowski, *Axis of the World*, p. 30.

[72] Ibid.

[73] Joseph P Farrell, *The Cosmic War*, pp. 139-233. In my book *Genes, Giants, Monsters and Men*, in chapter 6, I indicate another *possible* connection of the Tablets of Destinies with an Eastern culture, that of China, and its system of divination, the *I Ching.*

[74] Witkowski, op. cit., p. 16.

[75] Ibid., p. 21.

a small population in such an isolated place could have quarried and then transported such enormous and finely-carved statues.

Maoi Heads on Easter Island

Maoi Heads on Easter Island

Local legend and tradition does not help much in answering this question, for on Easter Island, just as at various ancient sites on the Grid in Great Britain, the tradition states that the stones moved themselves!

There is, however, a clue as to the means of this movement in local tradition, but that clue opens up yet another mysterious connection between Easter Island and, of all places, Egypt:

> ...(According) to the legend the stony giants moved "on their own," to designated places thanks to the magical power called "mana." regardless of whether it's true or not, it is, however, nonetheless a fact that the same type of description of motive power emerges in the "second best" place of archaeological mystery in the Pacific, namely Nan Madol — some 10,000 km away to the west (around 6200 miles)...
>
> However this is by no means the end of the puzzling parallels. The mana power was symbolized by a sign that perhaps was supposed to concentrate is, and which was carved out on the backs of some statues. Strangely enough, it bears a striking similarity to

the Egyptian magic "ankh" cross, which was supposed to perform the same function.[76]

Nor is the presence of the strange "ankh-like" symbol the only connection to the distant cultures of the Middle East.

The idea of "bird-men" figured prominently into the cultus of Easter Island and its traditions.[77] This chimerical concept even appears as a heiroglyph in the Rongo Rongo script itself.[78] This bird-man symbol was perhaps the hieroglyph for the islanders' chief god, Make Make, who lived in the sky and who had such a command over the mysterious "mana" force that he was isolated, because his power over the mana was dangerous.[79] Make Make's dangerous control or use of the mana force was manifest in lightning, "exactly the same motif associated with the main Andean god, Viracocha,"[80] and, for that matter, the similar association of the principle god of Greece — Zeus — with thunderbolts, and the Mesopotamian gods Ninurta and Nergal with the same thing.[81]

Moreover, there are other strange connections of the "bird-men" gods to the Middle East. One need only think of the depiction of the Egyptian god of science and wisdom, Thoth:

---

[76] Witkowski, *Axis of the World*, p. 22.
[77] Ibid.
[78] Ibid., p. 23.
[79] Ibid.
[80] Ibid., p. 24.
[81] Q.v. my *The Cosmic War*, pp. 56-58.

Similar chimerical bird-man depictions are also found in Mesopotamia:

Mesopotamian Bird-Man

It would thus appear then that in addition to a world-wide *grid* phenomenon that we are also confronted with the global extent of more or less the same religious and mythological images accompanying it.

2. The Mystery of Mohenjo Daro

Nowhere is this better in evidence than in the suggestive ruins of Mohenjo Daro in India. We have already encountered the local legends of Viracocha suddenly destroying the civilization of Tiahuanaco by "deadly rays," with "lightning." Make Make, Easter Island's chief "sky god" similarly wields lightning, and its Rongo Rongo script connects it directly to the Indus Valley Civilization.

The ruins of Mohenjo Daro are gruesome testimony that such a deliberate act of mass destruction by some sort of technologically advanced means may have actually once happened, for at Mohenjo Daro one finds a city and citadel designed with modern plumbing, sewers, and an intricacy of planning and sophistication that boggle the imagination, as a glance at its street plan will demonstrate:

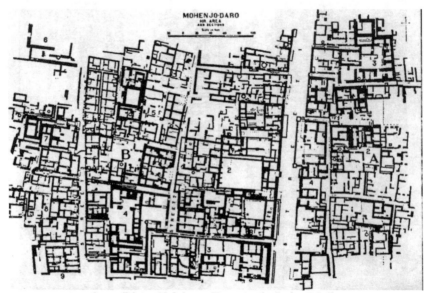

Street Plan of Mohenjo Daro in the Indus Valley

The Ruins of the Central Citadel of Mohenjo Daro

However, the most peculiar thing about the ruins of the city is the fact that, lying strewn about its molten, vitrified ruins are several human skeletons laying in the streets, some even holding hands, as if caught in some sudden catastrophe while going about their daily business:

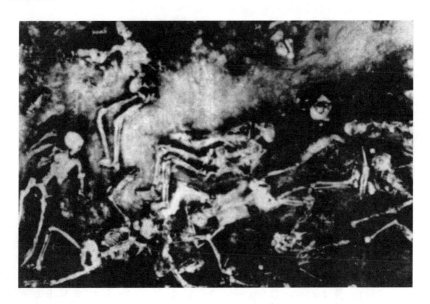

The Skeletons of Mohenjo Daro

Archaeologists investigating the area discovered a layer of radioactive ash near the region in Rajastan, India, covering an area of three square miles. So high were the levels of radiation that the Indian government cordoned the region off.[82] Digging further they discovered evidence of an atomic blast that occurred between 8,000 and 12,000 years ago.[83] One of the skeletons of Mohenjo Daro was discovered to have a level of radioactivity some "50 times greater than it should have been due to natural radiation."[84]

Vicacocha's "deadly rays," indeed!

Surveying this gruesome scene, one is reminded of the chilling words in the Indian epics, the *Mahabharata* and *Ramayana*, depicting an ancient "war of the gods":

> Gurkha, flying in a swift and powerful vimana,
> Hurled a single projectile,
> *Charged with all the power of the universe,*
> An incandescent column of smoke and flame,
> As bright as ten thousand suns,
> Rose with all its splendour.

> It was an unknown weapon,
> An iron thunderbolt,
> A gigantic messenger of death,
> Which reduced to ashes
> The entire race of the Vrishnis and the Andhakas.

> The corpses were so burned
> As to be unrecognizable.
> Hair and nails fell out;
> Pottery broke without apparent cause,

---

[82] Philip Coppens, "Ancient Atomic Wars: Best Evidence?" www.bibliotecapleyades.net/ancientatomicwar/esp_ancient_atomic_07.htm, p. 2.

[83] Ibid.

[84] Ibid., p. 3. See also Witkowski, *Axis of the World*, p. 47. The skeletons in general had levels of radioactivity commensurate with those at Hiromshima and Nagasaki. See my *Giza Death Star* (Adventures Unlimited Press, 2001), p. 97, n. 114.

And the birds turned white...[85]

(It was a weapon) so powerful
That it could destroy the earth in an instant —
A great soaring sound in smoke and flames —
And on it sits death...[86]

Dense arrows of flame,
Like a great shower,
Issued forth upon creation,
Encompassing the enemy....
A thick gloom swiftly settled upon the Pandava hosts.
All the points of the compass were lost in darkness.
Fierce winds began to blow.
Clouds roared upward
Showering dust and gravel
...
The earth shook,
Scorched by the terrible violent heat of this weapon.
...
From all points of the compass
The arrows of flame rained continuously and fiercely.[87]

In my book *The Giza Death Star* I noted that these texts "are more than suggestive of the effects and results of the use of nuclear weapons," including the loss of hair and teeth[88] and the reduction of glass and pottery to a fragile brittleness due to exposure to high neutron and gamma radiation.

But I also suggested that a closer examination of certain details of these texts hinted at some *other* kind of weapon, one that could indeed "hurl lightning" in a concentrated bolt of plasma, rather like squeezing the blast effects of a hydrogen bomb through a pipe, the "most significant" of those "suggestive phrases" being those which

---

[85] David Hatcher Childress, *Vimana Aircraft of Ancient India and Atlantis*, (Adventures UNlimtied Press, 1999), pp. 61-62, citing the *Mahabharata,* emphasis added.

[86] Ibid, p. 62, citing the *Ramayana,* emphasis added.

[87] Ibid. citing the *Mahabharata,* emphasis added.

[88] Jospeh P. Farrell, *The Giza Death Star,* p. 96.

clearly stated that one was dealing "not with many nuclear bombs," but with *"one single weapon."*[89] Additionally, other phrases suggested something *other* than nuclear or thermonuclear weapons:

1) "all the power of the universe" suggested a weapon somehow reliant upon the energy of space-time itself;
2) "the earth shook" suggests — if one take the phrase in the sense that "earth" means the entire planet, and not simply "land" — suggests that the entire planet's energy was utilized or affected;
3) "arrows of flame" that radiate "from all points of the compass" suggest, again, a radiant energy converging on a target by means of electromagnetic interferometry.[90]

I concluded that the Hindu epics, in addition to plausible descriptions of nuclear weaponry in the conventional sense, were also describing a weapon based upon the ability to manipulate the physical medium itself.[91]

We now have an odd constellation of facts indicating a relationship between whatever high civilization was behind the ruins of Puma Punkhu, Easter Island, and the Indus valley, among which are mythological parallels between Viracocha and the gods of the rest of the world, the similarity of construction methods between Easter Island and Tiahuanaci and Puma Punkhu on the one hand, and the Rongo Rongo script connecting it to the Indus Valley on the other.

To this high strangeness we may now add yet a further piece of evidence that suggests a common civilization of in high antiquity, dispersed, for whatever reason, across the globe, and that is liguistics. Witkowski points out that his countryman, Professor Benon Szalek, made a comparison of the common word roots of Basque, Hungarian, and...Japanese! From this he concluded that "these peoples must have been subjected to the influence of some single state organism — or that they were once part of it."[92] Or perhaps we

---

[89] Farrell, *The Giza Death Star*, p. 96.
[90] Ibid.
[91] Ibid., pp. 96-97.
[92] Witkowski, p. 45.

are in the presence of the influence of a hidden elite or elites with a common cultural origin?

Howsoever one answers that question, Prof. Szalek's linguistic investigations revealed something else, namely, that whatever connections as once existed between these groups was broken ca. 7000 BC.[93] In other words, if there was to be any "Tower of Babel Moment" in human history, it most likely occurred *prior to* 7000 BC.

By now one will have noticed a peculiar thing: all the dates with which we have been concerned point to something *pre-existing* the ancient high civilizations of Sumer, Egypt, and the Indus Valley, and over and over again there is the fixation upon the date of 10,500 BC, *within which* the atomic layer of ash in India fits. Even the linguistic evidence suggests that "something catastrophic" happened to put an end to whatever civilization as may have existed in this time frame. But there can be no doubt that *something* existed, and that it was something of great technological sophistication, for the ruins of Puma Punkhu clearly suggest it.

3. The Mysterious Connections Deepen: Nan Madol, Mohenjo Daro, and Easter Island

Nan Madol, which might justifiably be called the ancient Venice of the Pacific, and whose name means "in the middle of the way" in the ancient Dravidic tongue,[94] lies just slightly off-center of that "axis of the world" stretching from Mohenjo Daro to Easter Island. A veritable pile of ancient stone ruins and canals spread across islands in the southeastern Pacific, Nan Madol is another one of those places where the closer one looks, the more the mysteries multiply.

Dotted with stepped pyramids about 30 feet high and various stone platforms, one of the most curious features of Nan Madol is that basalt roads emanate from many of these pyramids and lead "straight into the ocean!" As if that were not enough, one of these roads emerges from its submerged journey one thousand miles away

---

[93] Witkowski, *Axis of the World*, pp. 45-47.
[94] Ibid., p. 51.

at the island of Rarotonga,[95] a fact that strongly indicates that the area was once above water.

Like other spots on the Grid, Nan Madol and the wider Polynesian culture also has its traditions associated with certain sites, and in this case, two traditions interest us. Like Easter Island, where the giant Maoi head statues were said to have moved by themselves by some mysterious force called "mana," the stone blocks of the pyramids at Nan Madol, weighting several tons, were said to have been "moved and raised by magic."[96]

The second tradition, however, brings into stark relief yet another mystery associated with the Grid. Viracocha, the "sun-god" whom we previously encountered, was also the great "civilizer" god of the Incas, and was said to be white-skinned, bearded, and blue-eyed. As we shall discover in the next two chapters, the same claim is made for the civilizing god of the Mayans and Aztecs, Kukulcan and Quetzlcoatl.

The Polynesians, as many other Asian peoples, have similar traditions. After the first European missionaries arrived in the islands, they discovered that the Polynesians referred to themselves as "aomata," a term that simply meant "humans." But the Europeans were called "te-i-matang," which meant "men from the land of the gods."[97] Other Polynesians referred to the white missionaries as "'gold-haired children of Tangaroa,' the god who according to their traditions came millennia before as a teacher and civilizer."[98] The idea is repeated in the Japanese legend of the ancient *Yamato*,[99] the white people who supposedly came to Japan, teaching civilization, in the legends of the Hopi tribe in North America, and even in the Hindu epic, the *Ramayana.*

But if this tradition is "so strong and important, and so common, then we cannot assume that it wasn't somehow anchored in reality."[100] However, if it is anchored in some "reality" lost in the

---

[95] Witkowski, *Axis of the World*, p. 150.

[96] Ibid., p. 158.

[97] Ibid., p. 148.

[98] Ibid.

[99] Ibid., p. 75

[100] Ibid., p. 149.

mists of pre-history, what sort of reality is it? Are we dealing with a vast dispersion, or the activity of an elite? Or both? The problem is compounded by recent genetic studies, which place the origins of mankind in Africa, and from the black races some 150,000 to 200,000 years ago. While this is not the place to explore possible resolutions of this dilemma, it is worth suggesting that perhaps the dispersion of this white group of peoples was done with a purpose, one suggested by the traditions themselves, for in each case they say that there was a purpose involved, an *agenda*, namely, to bring "civilization" to the rest of humanity. We might be looking at the purposeful dispersion of an elite, not a migration. In either case, given the extent of the traditions of such contacts across the globe, and the equally suggestive linguistic evidence mentioned earlier, we are looking at a global activity and dispersion of this group of people.[101]

In the middle of this historical conundrum sits Nan Madol, an ancient city covering an area of almost eleven square miles, the center of which is a complex of artificially made islands occupying about one square mile. These islands are connected by tunnels.[102] The site has also almost defied all attempts at a systematic exploration. The first explorer to do so — Kubary in the nineteenth century — committed suicide after a ship bearing artifacts recovered by him at Nan Madol sank on the way to Europe, and all his records and notes perished in a house fire. To this could be added dozens more who, visiting the site, perished, or were simply never seen again.[103]

Kubary was succeeded by the German Paul Hambruch in the early twentieth century, whose extensive survey of the site was popularized by Herbert Rittlinger in a book published in Germany in 1939.[104] Rittlinger also mentioned a story that platinum metal tablets, covered with an unknown form of writing, were recovered there. If this story is true, then it might be yet another possible connection to

---

[101] Witkowski, *Axis of the World,* p. 62. Witkowski also notes the discovery of white-skinned red-haired mummies in China, of all places, in connection with this idea. See pp. 63-64, 66.

[102] Ibid., p. 152.

[103] Ibid., p. 153.

[104] Ibid.

those lost Sumerian "Tablets of Destiny," and yet another possible connection to the activity of someone trying to preserve knowledge.

4. The Lost Civilization and the Flood: Polynesia, Egypt, and the Hopi

As has been noted, one of the curious features of Nan Madol is the many roads that emanate from its pyramids, and then disappear into the ocean, and we have already noted the Easter Island tradition of the Flood, the disappearance of a land to the west, and its faint suggestion that this was linked, somehow, to a deliberate action. Interestingly enough, Polynesian legends confirm this view, and even Egypt has a legend of "a great land in the east, among the waters of 'Uaj-ur' (as they named the eastern seas) that has been claimed by the sea."[105] Most interesting of these "lost land" legends, however, are those of the Hopi in North America, who maintain that they were evacuated to *South* America, whence they made their way to *North* America.[106]

5. The Land Bridge Collapses

The Hopi legends raise a number of questions about the standard "land bridge" model of Amerindian migrations to the Americas, across a land bridge on the Bering Straits between Siberia and Alaska, and thence gradually expanding southward from North America to South America. This theory was first formulated in 1938 by Dr. Alexd Hrdlicka of the Museum of Natural History in New York.[107]

But almost as soon as it was formulated the theory began to show cracks. The first and most obvious was apparent even when Hrdlicka formulated the theory, for the anthropological diversity among Amerindians was far greater than his theory would allow.[108] The most serious problem imposed by the theory, however, is that it carried with it the implicit assumption that the most advanced cultural traces

---

[105] Witkowski, *Axis of the World*, p. 77.
[106] Ibid., pp. 80-81.
[107] Ibid., p. 99.
[108] Ibid., p. 100.

should be found in North America, and as the migration spread further south, less developed cultures should have emerged. But as we have seen, the most advanced culture in evidence — that at Puma Punkhu and Tiahuanaco — are far in advance of anything further north.[109] The chronological progression of the facts is not that implied by the theory.

The discovery of human remains in 1963 in South America dating to 50,000 years ago, *along with tools*, was such an obvious contradiction to the theory that it is all but ignored by anthropology in North America.[110] Worse yet, remains of black, white, and mixed human skulls in Meso- and North America have added an element of racial diversity on the American continents that the standard land bridge theory is unable to sustain.[111] Even worse still, excavations in southern Chile of a human settlement — the oldest on *either* of the American continents — was found to be approximately 33,000 years old.[112] In other words, it was *South* America, and not *North* America, that "became the scene of the most interesting, even breathtaking achievements — the continent that supposedly was peopled at the very last."[113]

Worse yet, at Tafi del Valle, northwest of Buenos Aires in Argentina, there is a little-known megalithic site, that deserves attention. "the Argentine site wouldn't be anything unusual either, if not for the fact that it looked as if all the characteristic elements from Neolithic Europe were transferred there, as if by some magic force."[114] These included trilithions, aligned to the cardinal compass points, stone circles, and phalluses.

But the most fatal blow to the land bridge theory comes from mitochondrial DNA, the DNA that all humans inherit from their mother. When this DNA is sampled, the oldest human remains in the Americas shows that they belong to a distinctively *Pacific* group called haplogroup B, common to the Pacific and southern North America,

---

[109] Witkowski, *Axis of the World*, p. 101.
[110] Ibid., p. 104.
[111] Ibid., pp. 105, 106-107.
[112] Ibid., p. 108.
[113] Ibid., p. 113.
[114] Ibid., p. 146.

but *not* to Siberia or Alaska.[115] Worse still, blood-typing of South American mummies revealed a preponderance of Blood type A Rh negative, a feature common to Europeans predominantly.

6. Summary

We have journeyed far from the Paradoxes of Puma Punkhu, but the paradoxes there of advanced machining, and the genetic and cultural diversity of Amerindian peoples point to a very different picture than that of the standard land bridge theory. The almost unanimous traditions from Polynesia to the legends of the "white-skinned," bearded civilizing gods Virachoca and — as we shall see in the next two chapters — Kukalcan and Quetzlcoatl, point to a population that is very diverse, and to the possible activity of a group of people traveling throughout the globe with an *agenda*, for over and over those traditions insist that these people came to teach "civilization," to aid in its preservation and rebuilding after a great catastrophe.

That catastrophe was evident in that the traditions of a Flood abound in almost all these cultures, a tradition that in some cases implies that the catastrophe was in part brought about by the use of technology in conflicts. In some cases, the giant stone remains — as at Puma Punkhu — were clearly the products of an advanced machining technology well in excess of anything possessed even today. In other cases, legends and traditions ascribed a mysterious "force" to the placement of such gigantic stones, the force of "mana" on Easter Island.

Can any of these layers be peeled back still farther, to make some sense of the history of mankind, and why such monumental structures were undertaken at so many places? The answer is, yes, but in order to understand that answer, we must now journey northward, to Meso-America, and scrutinize the legends and structures of the Mayans and Aztecs.

---

[115] Witkowski, *Axis of the World*, p. 126.

7
MAYANS, MYTHS, AND MOUNDS:
THE MANIPULATION OF MATTER, MIND, AND MAN

"Their ancient day was not a great one,
these ancient people only wanted conflict,
their ancient names are not really divine,
but fearful is the ancient evil of their faces."
The Popol Vuh[1]

Having gone in the previous chapter from a survey of technological anomalies to a survey of the mythological and cultural contexts surrounding them, we now reverse the process, and go from the mythological context to the technological, to see if perhaps we can begin to peel back the layers of both to an understanding of the mysterious forces that people were trying to manipulate with them. Accordingly, we shall focus here upon three sites — Tikal, Chichen Itza, and Teotihuacan — and one mythology, the Mayan *Popol Vuh*.

The beginning of the Spanish conquest of Mexico and Meso-America in the sixteenth century saw the burning of many priceless records and books of the indigenous cultures, the records of the *Popol Vuh*, or *The Dawn of Life and the Glories of Gods and Kings*, among them.

Backed by means of persuasion that included gunpowder, instruments of torture, and the threat of eternal damnation, the invaders established a monopoly on virtually all forms of visible public expression, whether in drama, architecture, sculpture, painting or writing. In the highlands, when they realized that textile designs carried complex messages, they even attempted to ban the wearing of Mayan styles of clothing. Hundreds of hieroglyphic books were burned by missionaries, but they were still in use as late as the end of the seventeenth century in Yucatán and the beginning of the eighteenth in highland Guatemala.[2]

---

[1] Dennis Tedlock, trans. *The Popol Vuh: The Mayan Book of the Dawn of Life* (Simon and Schuster, 1996), p. 139.
[2] Ibid., pp. 23, 25.

In the midst of this destruction, the Mayans acted to preserve their culture by adopting a rather clever strategy, using Christian saints to disguise references to the ancient gods and using Roman alphabetic characters "as a mask for ancient texts."[3]

Humanity would know little, if anything, about the Mayan creation myths and legends were it not for these efforts, for the *Popol Vuh* as we have it now was the effort to preserve in alphabetic writing those myths, an effort undertaken by the three noble houses of the Mayans: "the Cauecs, the Greathouses, and the Lord Quichés."[4] The book itself, as extant today, is as much a mystery as its authors, and it is best to cite its English translator, Dennis Tedlock, at length here:

> At the beginning of their book, the authors delicately describe the difficult circumstances under which they work. When they tell us that they are writing "amid the preaching of God, in Christendom now," we can catch a plaintive tone only by noticing that they make this statement immediately after asserting that their own gods "accounted for everything — and did it, too — as enlightened beings, in enlightened words." What the authors propose to write down is what Quichés call the *Ojer Tzij*, the "Ancient Word" or "Prior Word," which has precedence over "the preaching of God." They have chosen to do so because "there is no longer" a Popol Vuh, which makes it sound as though they intend to re-create the original book solely on the basis of their memory of what they have seen in its pages or heard in the long performance. But when we remember their complaint about being "in Christendom," there remains the possibility that they still have the original book but are protecting it from possible destruction by missionaries. Indeed, their next words make us wonder whether the book might still exist, but they no sooner raise our hopes on this front than they remove the book's reader from our grasp: "There is the original book and ancient writing, but the one who reads and assesses it has a hidden identity." ...If they are protecting anyone with their enigmatic statements about an inaccessible book or an anonymous reader, it could well be themselves.[5]

---

[3] Tedlock, *Popol Vuh*, p. 25.

[4] Ibid.

[5] Ibid., p. 30. See also the discussion of the possible identity of one of its authors, Christóbal Velasco, on pp. 56-57.

Fascinating as the history of the *Popol Vuh* and Mayan culture are, however, our attention must remain fixed upon its contents and its implications for our study of the Grid. But before we examine its contents, one last point must be mentioned, for one of the things that clearly emerges from Mayan culture is that its frequent references to a place called "Tulan" or "Tula" mean precisely the ancient ruins of Teotihuacan, outside of Mexico City.[6] We shall have much to say about this site later in this chapter.

A. The Popol Vuh
1. The Primordial Triad and Differentiation: The Topological Metaphor, Mayan Style

Like the Hindu cosmology laid out in stone reliefs at Angkor Wat, The *Popol Vuh* begins in an abyss of mystery, an abyss laid out in eloquent and elegantly simple words and imagery whose power is made even more manifest by their poetic simplicity:

This is the account, here it is:
Now it still ripples, now it still murmurs, ripples, it still sighs, still hums, *and it is empty under the sky.*
Here follow the first words, the first eloquence.
There is not yet one person, one animal, bird, fish, crab, tree, rock, hollow, canyon, meadow, forest. Only the sky alone is there; the face of the earth is not clear. *Only the sea along is pooled under all the sky; there is nothing whatever gathered together. It is at rest;* not a single thing stirs. It is held back, kept at rest under the sky.
Whatever there is that might be is simply not there: only murmurs, ripples, in the dark, in the night. Only the Maker, Modeler alone, Sovereign Plumed Serpent, the Bearers, Begetters are in the water, a glittering light. They are there, they are enclosed in quetzal feathers, in blue-green.
Thus the name, "Plumed Serpent." They are great knowers, great thinkers in their very being.
And of course there is the sky, and there is also the Heart of Sky. This is the name of the god, as it is spoken.
And then came his word, he came here to the Sovereign Plumed Serpent, here in the blackness, in the early dawn.... Thunderbolt

---

[6] Tedlock, *Popol Vuh*, p. 45.

Hurricane comes first, the second is Newborn Thunderbolt, and the third is Sudden Thunderbolt.

So there were three of them...[7]

By now, this powerful, evocative imagery should recall the image of Vishnu at Angkor Wat, superintending the cosmic tug-of-war of the great *naga* serpent in the Milky Ocean.

Yet, this appears half a world away, in an entirely different culture!

Note too, that the *topological metaphor* of a primordial trinity is preserved. Everything begins as an emptiness "under the sky" and there is not yet any differentiation within it: "there is not yet one person, one animal" and so on. There is only an empty sky, and pooled water at rest beneath it. The only thing existing is Sovereign Plumed Serpent and a mysterious reference to "Bearers" and "Begetters in the water" who are described as "great knowers, great thinkers in their very being," who are later found, just like Vishnu, to be manifestations of Sovereign Plumed Serpent.

The *Popol Vuh* is telling us, in other words, the same thing we saw at Angkor Wat: there is a primordial "nothing", Sovereign Plumed Serpent, and then there is a primordial "trinity," of endless indistinct "sky" and below it a "sea", *and the implied common surface between the two*. Nothing else whatsoever, at this juncture, exists, except a faint "murmuring" and "rippling" in the night, implying somehow that *sound, frequency, vibration* give rise to all the fecund distinctions and variety to follow.

Indeed, at the very beginning, the *Popol Vuh* informs us that "This is the beginning of the Ancient Word, here in this place called Quiché. Here we shall inscribe, we shall *implant* the Ancient Word, *the potential and source for everything done*...in the nation of the Quiché people."[8] Note that the Ancient Word is something to be *implanted*, again recalling the imagery of Vishnu ejaculating into the primordial sea, which was but himself under another manifestation. Note too the very suggestive notion that this Word, this sound or vibration as it were, is "the potential and source for everything done," that is, that all the diversity that arises, arises from this pure and infinite potential.

---

[7] *Popol Vuh*, trans. Dennis Tedlock, pp. 64-65, emphasis added.

[8] Ibid., p. 63, emphasis added.

Consequently, it would appear that the *Popol Vuh*, in its very opening pages, is suggesting the very *same* topological metaphor of the physical medium that we encountered in chapter three, in connection with Vishnu's "trifurcation" and differentiation of himself as a primordial Nothing, and that we also discovered operative in some passages in the *Hermetica*, which were of *Egyptian* provenance, only here the metaphor of that "differentiated Nothing" is even more clearly suggested by the notion of an endless sky and endless sea, in neither of which nothing else exists; there is only the sky, the sea, and the surface touching, differentiating, or bracketing, both; again we have three entities of yet another primordial triad.

Thus, our chart from chapter three now looks like this:

Hermes: God *(θεος)*	*Hermes:* Kosmos*(Κοσμος)*	*Hermes:* Space *(Τοπος)*
Padama *Purana:* *Vishnu,* *the creator* *Popol Vuh* *Sky*	*Padama Purana:* *Shiva, the* *destroyer* *Popol Vuh* *Sea*	*Padama* *Purana:* *Brahma, the* *"preserver"* *Popol Vuh* *The Implied* *Shared* *Surface* *between Sky* *and Sea*

So now, we may add to what we stated about this topological metaphor of the medium in chapter three, for now we encounter yet more imagery — sky, sea, and the implied surface between the two — all saying the same thing: that we are dealing with a differentiated Nothing, whose first differentiation must always be triadic or trinitarian in nature:

1) the "bracketed" region of Nothing, or $\varnothing_{A\text{-}E}$, Hermes' "Kosmos", the *Padama Purana's* Shiva, and now, the *Popol Vuh's* "sky";
2) the *rest* of the Nothing, or $\varnothing_{E\text{-}A}$, Hermes' "God," the *Padama Purana's* Vishnu, and now, the *Popol Vuh's* "sea"; and,
3) the "surface" Nothing that the two regions share, or $\partial\varnothing_{A\text{-}E|E\text{-}A}$, Hermes' "Space," the *Padama Purana's* Brahma, and now, the *Popol Vuh's* implied common surface between "sea" and "sky".

However, the *Popol Vuh* goes on to make an even more interesting and suggestive set of statements that would seem to associate the creation of mankind itself with this process of emerging differentiation from some sort of *materia prima* or "primordial nothing."

2. The Engineering of Man

Very quickly after this account of the initial "trifurcation" of creation, the *Popol Vuh* moves to the creation of mankind himself, after the creation of land and animals,[9] and it does so once again, in equally evocative, elegant, and powerful poetic imagery:

Again there comes an experiment with the human work, the human design, by the Maker, Modeler, Bearer, Begetter:

"It must simply be tried again. The time for the planting and dawning is nearing. For this we must made a provider and nurturer. How else can we be invoked and remembered on the face of the earth? We have already made our first try at our work and design, but it turned out that they didn't keep our days, nor did they glorify us.

"So now let's try to make a giver of praise, giver of respect, provider, nurturer," they said.

"So then comes the building and working with earth and mud. They made a body, but it didn't look good to them. It was just separating, just crumbling, just loosening, just softening, just disintegrating, and just dissolving. Its head wouldn't turn, either. Its face was just lopsided, its face was just twisted. It couldn't look

---

[9] *Popol Vuh*, trans. Dennis Tedlock, pp. 66-68.

around. It talked at first, but senselessly. It was quickly dissolving in the water.

"It won't last," the mason and sculptor said then. "It seems to be dwindling away, so let it just dwindle. It can't walk and it can't multiply, so let it be merely a thought," they said.

So then they dismantled, again they brought down their work and design.[10]

Note that the rough order of creation in the Mayan mythology is that of the biblical Genesis: land forms, then animals of various types, and then finally this first "protohuman."

But what is very *different* about the Mayan version is the clear indication that mankind is the result of an *experiment*, one that was for the express purpose of creating intelligent servants to "the gods." In other words, the Mayans are reproducing, centuries later, and half a world and an ocean away, and what was first suggested in the texts of Mesopotamia: mankind was an engineered creation, created for the express purpose of servitude to the gods. He was *property.*[11] Life, on this view, was less a *gift,* than a *debt* to be paid in endless service.

The *Popol Vuh* gives a further hint of this concept of mankind as an experiment, and with it, the Flood is introduced:

This was the peopling of the face of the earth:
They came into being, they multiplied, they had daughters, they had sons, these manikins, woodcarvings. But there was nothing in their hearts and nothing in their minds, no memory of their mason and builder. They just went and walked wherever they wanted. Now they did not remember the Heart of Sky.
And so they fell, just an experiment and just a cutout for humankind. They were talking at first but their faces were dry. They were not yet developed in the legs and arms. They had no blood, no lymph. Their complexions were dry, their faces were crusty. They flailed their legs and arms, their bodies were deformed.

---

[10] *Popol Vuh*, trans. Dennis Tedlock, pp. 68-69.

[11] See my *The Cosmic War*, pp. 139-150. I note in those pages the Seven Sages of Mesopotamian legend. Thus, one has yet *another* connection between Mesopotamia and India, where the seven *Rishis* fulfill the same function.

And so they accomplished nothing before the Maker, Modeler who gave them birth, gave them heart. They became the first numerous people here on the face of the earth.

Again there comes a humiliation, destruction, and demolition. The manikins, woodcarvings were killed when the Heart of Sky devised a flood for them. A great flood was made; it came down on the heads of the manikins, woodcarvings.[12]

A little further on, there is even more commentary:

Such was the scattering of the human work, the human design. The people were ground down, overthrown. The mouths and faces of all of them were destroyed and crushed. And it used to be said that the monkeys in the forests today are a sign of this. They were left as a sign because wood alone was used for their flesh by the builder and sculptor.

So this is why monkeys look like people: they are a sign of a previous human work, human design — mere manikins, mere woodcarvings.[13]

In other words, there is no notion or conception of anything resembling evolutionary theory; rather, monkeys are the signs of another failed attempt at "the human work and design."

3. The Primordial "Masculine Homosexual Androgyny" of Man and the Tower of Babel Moment

The strangest aspect of the Mayan account of the creation of mankind is its suggestion of a kind of "primordial masculine homosexual androgyny" for the creature, and its coupling of the subsequent division of the sexes with a loss of human knowledge and intellectual power in a kind of Tower of Babel moment.

This part of the *Popol Vuh* begins by noting that at the beginning of the "conception of humans" there was a search for "the ingredients of the human body" by the "Bearer, Begetter, the Makers,

---

[12] *Popol Vuh*, trans Dennis Tedlock, pp. 70-71.
[13] Ibid., p. 73.

Modelers named Sovereign Plumed Serpent."[14] It is interesting to note that one is dealing with Quetzlcoatl again, but note that this deity is spoken of both in singular and plural terms, rather like a "council of the gods." This fashioning of mankind is called the making or modeling "of our first mother-father,"[15] and with that, we have encountered our first Mayan androgynous image for God Himself.

The *Popul Vuh* goes on to explain this androgyny in explicitly masculine terms: "They were good people, handsome, with looks of the male kind."[16] Then follows one of the most bizarre passages in the entire book:

> And then *they saw everything under the sky perfectly*. After that, they thanked the Maker, Modeler:
> " Truly now,
> double thanks, triple thanks
> that we've been formed, we've been given
> our mouths, our faces,
> we speak, we listen,
> we wonder, we move,
> our knowledge is good, we've understood
> what is far and near,
> and we've seen what is great and small
> under the sky or on earth.
> Thanks to you we've been formed,
> we've come to be made and modeled,
> our grandmother, our grandfather."
> they said when they gave thanks for having been made and modeled. *They understood everything perfectly, they sighted the four sides, the four corners in the sky, on the earth, and this didn't sound good to the builder and sculptor:*
> "What our works and designs have said is no good:
> "'We have understood everything, great and small,' they say."
> And so the Bearer, Begetter took back their knowledge.
> "What should we do with them now? Their vision should at least reach nearby, they should at least see a small part of the face of the earth, but what they're saying isn't good. Aren't they merely

---

[14] Ibid., p. 145.

[15] *Popol Vuh*, trans. Dennis Tedlock, p. 146.

[16] Ibid., p. 147.

'works' and 'designs' in their very names? Yet *they'll become as great as gods, **unless** they procreate, proliferate at the sowing, the dawning, unless they increase."*

"Let it be this way: now we'll take them apart just a little, that's what we need. What we've found out isn't good. *Their deeds would become equal to ours, just because their knowledge reaches so far.* They see everything," so said
the Heart of Sky, Hurricane,
Newborn Thunderbolt, Sudden Thunderbolt,
Sovereign Plumed Serpent,
Bearer, Begetter,
Xiyacoc, Xmucane,
Maker, Modeler
as they are called. And when they changed the nature of their works, their designs, it was enough that the eyes be marred by the Heart of Sky....

And such was the loss of the means of understanding, along with the means of knowing everything, by the four humans. The root was implanted....

*And **then** their wives and women came into being.*[17]

This passage requires careful scrutiny and unpacking in order for the full weight of its implications to sink in.

1) Note first of all that, just as in the Biblical story of the Tower of Babel,[18] there is no notion of morality in play, for the activities of mankind are not perceived so much as *immoral* but rather as an *implicit threat* to the power of the gods "just because their knowledge reaches so far." One is reminded of the biblical reason given for the confounding of languages at the Tower of Babel, for if the Tower was completed, mankind would be able "to do whatever it imagined to do;"

2) This human knowledge, in so far as the *Popol Vuh* is concerned, relates somehow to mankind's cosmological knowledge, to his understanding of the *physics* of the cosmos and being able to sight "the four corners in the sky, on the earth." Given the topological metaphor we have examined

---

[17] *Popol Vuh*, trans. Dennis Tedlock, pp. 147-148, all emphases added.
[18] Genesis 11:1-9.

previously, the metaphor here seems to be suggesting that mankind's knowledge was of the very way the physical medium itself was constituted and of how it operated. This too is mirrored in the biblical Tower of Babel story, where the purpose of the Tower is to "reach unto heaven;"[19] again implying that somehow human knowledge was of a deep physics;

3) In the *Popol Vuh*, all this knowledge and deep insight is coupled somehow to what can only be described as mankind's primordial "masculine homosexual-androgyny," a fact that seems also to be reproduced in the way that this creature refers also to the Sovereign Plumed Serpent, or God, both as grandmother and grandfather, as an androgyny; God, in other words, is viewed in the same way and this, somehow, suggests that in mankind, in his primordial masculine homosexual-androgynous constitution, had knowledge of some characteristic of the physical medium that he would not otherwise have had; this leads to the next point:

4) The *Popol Vuh* makes it very clear that this primordial "masculine homosexual-androgyny" had to be divided "just a little" in order to eradicate the threat posed by the knowledge he possessed in that original state; the division of the sexes is accomplished, and at *this* point "their wives and women came into being," causing procreation and the corresponding loss of human knowledge. This seems to imply that in mankind's primordial state, immortality was the natural consequence, and therefore with it, a commensurately wide knowledge. It is worth noting that a vaguely similar idea is even suggested in the biblical account of the Tower of Babel moment, where it says "And the LORD said, Behold, *the people is one.*" Again, the solution is to divide humanity; in the biblical instance, it is division through multiplication of languages; in the Mayan instance, it is division by the division of the sexes;

5) And lest it be thought that this primordial view of mankind as a kind of "masculine homosexual-androgyny" is far removed from the world of the Old Testament half a world and

---

[19] Genesis 11: 4.

centuries away, a closer look at Gen 1:27 is in order. In the standard English translation the verse reads "So God created man in his own image, in the image of God created he him; make and female created he them." But in the Septuagint Greek of the verse, the word "them" is actually *"them,"* but with one difference, the word "them" here is also masculine in gender, but lacks a second repetition of the word "them" in the feminine gender. Thus, while the verse can certainly be interpreted in the traditional manner with the masculine "them" as a *pars pro toto* usage designating a male and female "them," it is also worth nothing that it is capable of bearing a Mayan-like interpretation as well, as indicating a kind of "primordial masculine homosexual-androgyny," with the subsequent division of the sexes in Genesis chapter two representing a kind of "second creation;" this little-known possibility would in fact lead to many interesting speculations in the early centuries of Christianity, but this is not the place to delve into them.[20]

As we turn from this suggestive passage and all the previous allusions to the topological metaphor in the *Popol Vuh* to a consideration of the actual structures of Meso-America themselves, bear in mind that deep knowledge and the implied deep physics, for now it begins to come home to roost; and with it, we also see the beginning glimmers of the reasons for the practice in these societies of human sacrifice.

B. The Structures
1. Tikal and Chichen Itza

We will begin this technical exposition at Tikal in Central America. The first thing to be noted about Tikal is that it lies exactly 120 degrees longitude *west* of Giza, in other words, exactly one third the distance around the world from Giza. Here there are five large Mayan pyramids, which are unusual in that they are all *taller* than they are *wide*. In this, the Mayan Pyramids — like their mythology —

---

[20] The final version of the Documentary Hypothesis has the second chapter of Genesis and its creation account being the oldest, but earlier versions of the theory had the first chapter being the oldest.

suggests connections to India, where similar temples are in evidence at Madurai:

The Madurai Temples in Southern India

There are five such elongated pyramids at Tikal, and like the temples of Maduari in India, they all have a temple-like structure at the top of the edifice:

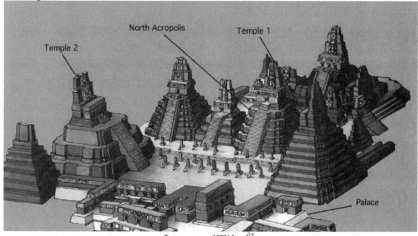

Layout of Tikal[21]

---

[21] http://www.authenticmaya.com/images/fig_21.jpg, from http://www.authenticmaya.com/tikal1.htm. This is an excellent website of information about the Mayans.

Munck gives the heights of these temples as follows:

1) Temple I: 154.8 feet;
2) Temple II: 142.7 feet;
3) Temple III: 177.8 feet;
4) Temple IV: 228.6 feet;
5) Temple V: 188 feet.[22]

Additionally, each of these Temples incorporates some harmonic of the number 656, usually at the level of the platform on which the temple atop the structure rests.[23]

Three of the temples — II, III, and IV — face east, temple V faces north, and temple I faces west, and again, the center of the compound is 120 degrees west of the Giza prime meridian. Moreover, each of these temples, with the exception of temple II, all have ten steps or terraces, with the temple atop the tenth. Temple II has three major terraces. But most importantly, all these temples are all, per Munck's classification, *corrupted* pyramids, that is, they are stepped pyramids with *corners and faces*, and all of them are *higher* than the width of their *base*. For the moment, we will forego the counting of corners and faces on these monuments to comment on the second fact concerning these pyramids: that they are taller than their base.

It is this fact that leads us into the deep physics that these structures were possibly designed to access, for all pyramids have one property in common: they all have some relationship of base-to-height proportional to π divided by two, that is, the basic formula of all pyramids is:

$$b/h \propto \pi/2, \text{ where h = height, b = base.}$$

This point recalls remarks concerning secret Soviet research into pyramids that I wrote years ago in *The Giza Death Star Deployed*, which are cited at length here in order to illuminate the relationship of the

---

[22] Carl P. Munck, *The Master Code Book*, p. 166.
[23] Ibid.

three basic types of pyramids and the deeper underlying physics possibilities that they embody:

> A much more substantial research into "pyramid power" was undertaken in the former Soviet Union where several large pyramids were built and their properties investigated at great expense. The research is being continued by Dr. Volodymyr Krasnoholovets of the Institute of Physics of the Ukrainian National Academy of Sciences in Kiev. Notably, Krasnoholovets has been led by his research to posit a "sub-quantum mechanics" with some peculiar properties that recall our own speculations about the tetrahedral properties of the medium
>
> Noting that the electromagnetic, the weak, and the strong forces of current quantum mechanics intersect at a scale of 10^{-28} cm, Krasnoholovets then takes this measure as the size of the building blocks of space itself. Space thus has a *cellular* structure... where particles appear as deformations of this structure.[24]

These elementary perturbations of space itself, these "fundamental particles", Krasnoholovets very suggestively calls "inertons." Without going into the complicated argument of his paper, it is worth noting that Krasnoholovets makes mention of the *"ex nihilo"* characteristics:

> "Of special is the approach proposed by Bounias (1990, 2000) and Bounias and Bonaly (1994, 1996, 1997). Basing on topology and set theory, they have demonstrated that the necessity of the existence of the empty set leads to topological spaces resulting in a "physical universe." Namely, they have investigated *the links between physical existence, observability, and information.* The introduction of the empty hyperset has allowed a preliminary construction of a formal structure that correlates with the degenerate cell of space supporting conditions for the existence of a universe. Besides, among other results we can point to their very promising hypothesis on a non-metric topologcial distance as the symmetric difference between sets: this could be a good alternative to the conventional metric distance which so far is still treated as the

---

[24] Joseph P Farrell, *The Giza Death Star Deployed*, pp. 267-268.

major characteristic in all concepts employed in gravitational physics, cosmology, and partly in quantum mechanics."[25]

I then observed the following:

> Behind the obtuse technical language lies a series of very unique insights:
>
> 1. The current mathematical "languages" used to describe the interactions of sub-atomic particles with space is inadequate;
> 2. It is inadequate *because* it is based on a form of mathematical language where *measurements of distance*, or more simply, *vectors* are the primary thing in view;
> 3. A more adequate way to account for the peculiarities of quantum and sub-quantum mechanics is via set theory, that is, a mathematical language that compares the properties of systems or sets wherein properties of distance and vectors are only sub-sets of a greater set of properties. Simply put, Krasnoholovets is saying that the fundamental language of physics must change from a *linear* mathematical language — points, lines, planes, vectors and so on — to a *non*-linear language inclusive of such things but not *limited* to them. Hence his emphasis on *information*. Sets of physical properties, on this view, are a much fuller description of the "information in the field."

Note now that Krasnoholovets is thinking in the same terms as our previously discussed topological metaphor, which also employed differentiations on the empty hyper-set — $\varnothing$ — to model the emergence of observable entities from a primordial Nothing.

> Thus...Krasnoholovets introduces the idea that the fundamental relationship between a particle and space itself is harmonic in nature, since a particle, by moving, exhibits inertia and sets up an oscillation in space itself. Or as he puts it, "It is the space substrate, which induces the harmonic potential responding to the disturbance of the space by the moving particle"[26] itself that is in primary view.

---

[25] Volodymyr Krasnoholovets, "Submicroscopic Deterministic Quantum Mechanic," p. 1, cited in *The Giza Death Star Deployed*, p. 268.

[26] Ibid., p. 13, cited in *The Giza Death Star Deployed*, p. 269.

Again, we must pause to note how well our topological metaphor corresponds to this idea of harmonic relationships between the various cells in space-time, for it will be recalled that by differentiating that primordial nothing — $\varnothing$ — we ended with two regions distinguished by a common surface: $\varnothing_{E-A}$, $\varnothing_{A-E}$, and $\partial\varnothing$. Note that each expression formally distinguishes $\varnothing$ but that *the signature of $\varnothing$* remains in each expression: each of the three entities is, in other words, analogically or harmonically related to the other two; each is an oscillator of the others.

But what has all this to do with pyramids? Krasnoholovets' answer is rather breathtaking:

"Let A be a point on the Earth's surface from which an inerton wave is radiated. If the inerton wave travels around the globe along the West-East line, its front will pass a distance $L_1 = 2\pi r_{earth}$ per circle. The second flow spread along the terrestrial diamater; such inerton waves radiated from A will come back passing distance $L_2 = 4\pi r_{earth}$. The ratio is:

$L_1/L_2 = \pi/2.$

If in point A we locate a material object with linear sizes (along the West-East line and perpendicular to the Earth's surface_ such that it satisfies (the above) relation, we will receive a resonator of the Earth's inerton waves.[27]

I then noted that the Great Pyramid, "because it is constructed in precisely such a fashion and geometric disposition with respect to the earth, is a coupled harmonic oscillator of the very inertial properties of the planetary space itself."[28]

But the same can now be said of *all* pyramidal structures, for *all* of them, without exception, bear some relationship to that fundamental ratio of $\pi/2$, according to that equation noted previously:

---

[27] Krasnoholovets, "Submicroscopic Deterministic Quantum Mechanic," p. 20, emphasis added, cited in *The Giza Death Star Deployed*, p. 269.
[28] Joseph P. Farrell, *The Giza Death Star Deployed*, pp. 269-270.

$/2$, where h = height, b = base.

As I observed in *The Giza Death Star Destroyed* every pyramid is in relationship to this ratio, and there are thus only three types of pyramids that can result, *depending* on their relationship to that ratio; I reproduced the following diagram:

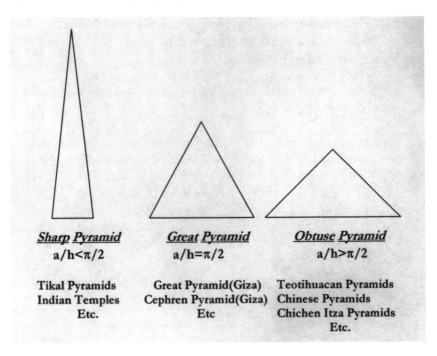

Sharp Pyramid	*Great Pyramid*	*Obtuse Pyramid*
a/h<π/2	a/h=π/2	a/h>π/2
Tikal Pyramids	Great Pyramid(Giza)	Teotihuacan Pyramids
Indian Temples	Cephren Pyramid(Giza)	Chinese Pyramids
Etc.	Etc	Chichen Itza Pyramids
		Etc.

Relationships of Pyramid Types to the Ratio π/2

Note that the temples of Tikal(as those at Madurai in India), are of the sharp pyramidal type, while all other pyramids — with the notable exception of the Great Pyramid and the Cephren Pyramid at Giza — are of the *obtuse* type.

But what would the functions of these different shapes be? Here is it best to cite what I wrote in *The Giza Death Star Deployed* once again:

> Krasnoholovets speculates that "the sharp pyramid plays the role of a radiator" and that it may also "function as an antenna

196

absorbing inerton radiation from outer space."[29] The obtuse pyramid "to the contrary... may rather function as a radiator that emits amplified interton waves into the Earth surface."[30] And thus, the most efficient shape to combine both functions would be in the dimensions of the Great Pyramid itself, "the happy medium."[31]

To put it succinctly, on this view of pyramids as resonators of the fabric of space-time, of the physical medium itself, then Tikal is an *antenna array.*

But it is that all-important method of Munck — the *counting of faces and corners* — that as we shall see in a later chapter, leads to the most astonishing confirmation of this view, and in a way that most Grid researchers never imagined. Before leaving Tikal, however, it is important to mention just a few of the significant numerical coding that Munck discovered there that confirm the view of Krasnoholovets that these structures are resonators of the Earth. In this case, the width of the "temple" atop the first pyramid at Tikal is 24.9015 feet, which is the equatorial circumference of the Earth in miles: 24,901.5 miles.[32] This, plus the fact that Tikal is exactly 120 degrees west of the Giza prime meridian — plus the counting of faces and corners that we shall examine later — tends to confirm the view of Michell that we are, indeed, living inside of, or in the midst of, a vast, ruined machine.

2. Chichen Itza and Human Sacrifice

We must now journey to Chichen Itza and Teotihuacan, to briefly view the massive pyramids of the other type: the obtuse pyramids of Meso-America. The most prominent feature of Chichen Itza is the massive pyramid of Kukulcan/Quetzlcoatl, an obtuse pyramid:

---

[29] Krasnoholovets, "On the Way to Disclosing the Mysterious Power of the Great Pyramid," p. 14, cited in *The Giza Death Star Deployed*, p. 271.

[30] Ibid.

[31] Krasnoholovets, "On the Way to Disclosing the Mysterious Power of the Great Pyramid," p. 14, cited in *The Giza Death Star Deployed*, p. 271.

[32] Munck, *Whispers From Time*, Volume I, p. 127.

Pyramid of Kukulkan, Photo Courtesy of Dr. Scott D. de Hart

The four staircases of this pyramid contain exactly 365 steps, the number of days in a year. But here, as at Tikal, the numbers conceal yet another connection to the Giza Prime Meridian.

Each of the four staircases up the pyramid are, of course, 90 degrees apart. If one divides 365 by 90, one obtains 4.055, and this is the "tangent of the surface distance of 7123.85 statute miles which separates the Kukulkan Pyramid from Giza's Great Pyramid."[33] Like Tikal, the numbers point to a consciously conceived and deliberately constructed system anchored upon Giza. Again, we are looking at a vast machine, and notably, the "sharp pyamids" of Tikal and the obtuse Kukulkan pyramid at Chichen Itza — and those of Teotihuacan as we shall see in a moment — are tied to the two grat Pyramids at Giza, which are in the "perfect" shape to be both antennae resonators and emitters.

There is, however, a darkness hovering over Chichen Itza, one we have mentioned before, and it is time to begin to address it more directly: human sacrifice. The *Popol Vuh* makes it clear that both males and females[34] were sacrificed within Mayan practice, and for

---

[33] Munck, *Whispers from Time*, Volume 1, p. 109.
[34] *Popol Vuh*, trans. Tedlock, p. 99.

the usual reasons, to guarantee fertility among the population, and so on.[35]

One passage of the *Popol Vuh* records the gods' twisted *delight* in the smell of the burnt offerings:

> "It has turned out well, your lordships, and this is her heart. It's in the bowl."
>
> "Very well. So I'll look," said One Death, and when he lifted it up with his fingers, its surface was soaked with gore, its surface glistened red with blood.
>
> "Good. Sir up the fire, put it over the fire,' said One Death.
>
> After that they dried it over the fire, and the Xibalbans savored the aroma. They all ended up standing here, they leaned over it intently. They found the smoke of the blood to be truly sweet![36]

A similar attitude to the aroma of sacrifice is recorded in the Book of Genesis:

> And Noah builded an altar unto the LORD; and took of every clean beast, and of every clean fowl, and offered burnt offerings on the altar. And the LORD smelled a sweet savor...[37]

But why, at least in Meso-America, would the practice of sacrifice even arise on its famous Grid sites?

There are only two clues. The first of these is that sacrifice is a kind of *payment* to the gods.[38] This follows from the idea of the creation account in the *Popol Vuh* itself: life was not a gift of the gods to man, but was merely a means to an end: mankind's perpetual service to the gods; mankind was a slave, property, a kind of collateral to perpetual debt, a concept with which we shall have much to say in the next chapter.

The second clue is provided by the quotation cited above, and by the following:

---

[35] *Popol Vuh*, trans. Tedlock, p. 97.
[36] Ibid., p. 101.
[37] Genesis 8:20-21a.
[38] *Popol Vuh*, trans. Tedlock, p., 134.

And this is the sacrifice of little Huanhpu by Xibalanque. One by one his legs, his arms were spread wide. His head came off, rolled far away outside. His heart, dug out, was smothered in a leaf, *and all the Xibalbans went crazy at the site.*[39]

Here the Xibalbans, the "gods," are "going crazy" at the site of the sacrifice, and this is consistent with the attitude cited earlier, that the aroma of the sacrifice was pleasing to them, an attitude we find echoed — over and over again in fact — in the Old Testament.

Viewed objectively, it would appear that bloody sacrifices are understood to induce some change in the state or attitude of *conciousness* in the "gods." This, plus the fact that at least in Meso-America's case these sacrifices are being performed at Grid sites, might be a profound clue as to why the practice arose in the first place.

To summarize: the practice of sacrifice appears to be tied to two distinct conceptions, as least, in so far as the *Popol Vuh* is concerned:

1) To the conception of humanity in perpetual slavery, servitude, and debt; and,
2) To the idea that bloody sacrifice somehow induces a change in the state or attitude of consciousness in the "gods."

When we add to this list the observations concerning the shapes of pyramids and their relationship to $\pi/2$, we have a very odd constellation of things indeed, for clearly the pyramidal shape, the numbers encoded in them, and the relationship of Tikal, Chichen Itza and virtually every other site on the Grid to Giza, means that we are living inside a ruined machine of planetary extent. We have furthermore seen that, insofar as the deepest physics is concerned, that machine was intended somehow to manipulate the physical medium itself.

So is there a relationship between that deep physics, consciousness, and sacrifice? And if so, what is it?

To answer that question, we need more data, and we will find it, further north, at Teotihuacan, and with the Aztecs.

---

[39] *Popol Vuh*, trans. Tedlock, p. 136, emphasis added.

8

HUMANITY IN PERPETUAL DEBT:
THE ANOMALY OF AZTECS AND ANSELM:
A SPECULATIVE THEOLOGY, ECONOMICS, AND PHYSICS
OF SACRIFICE

"...in fine, leaving Christ out of view (as if nothing had ever been known of him),
it proves, by absolute reasons, the impossibility that any man should be saved
without him."
Anselm, Archbishop of Canterbury (d. 1081)[1]

There is a dissonance — a discord, an unresolved suspension without a cadence, an unending stretto in a cacophonous fugue that reaches no conclusion - in this otherwise heavenly music of the spheres, and it is bloody sacrifice or, in the case of Meso-America and elsewhere, bloody *human* sacrifice. Why this practice should have arisen at some locations and within some cultures on the Grid remains a mystery, although, as we saw in the previous chapter, there are clues.

Perhaps no human culture has been so identified with the practice, however, than that of the Aztecs. It intrudes itself as a moral ugliness and incongruity into a society and culture in which — as with the Mayans — it seems out of place, an inexplicably bloody ugliness. Hancock and Faiia capture this terrible anomaly as best as anyone, in very evocative words:

> Travelers in Central America who have attempted to explore its monuments and its past have come away haunted by the intuition of a great and terrible mystery. A dark sorrow overhangs the whole land like a pall, and what is known of its history is filled with inexplicable contradictions.
>
> On the one hand there is tantalizing evidence of lofty spiritual ideas, of a deep philosophical tradition, and of astonishing artistic, scientific and cultural achievements. On the other hand we know that repulsive acts of psychopathic evil have become

---

[1] Anselm of Canterbury, *Cur Deus Homo* (*Why the God-man?*), Preface. http://www.ewtn.com/library/CHRIST/CURDEUS.HTM.

201

institutionalized in the Valley of Mexico by the beginning of the sixteenth century and that every year, amidst scenes of nightmarish cruelty, the Aztec empire offered up more than 100,000 people as human sacrifices. Two wrongs do not make a right, and the Spanish Conquistadores who arrived in February 1519 were pirates and cold-blooded killers. Nevertheless, their intervention, motivated exclusively by material greed, did have the happy side-effect of brining the demonic sacrificial rituals of the Aztecs to an end...

Their accounts reveal the dark side of a schizophrenic culture, addicted to murder, which also, with apparently quit staggering hypocrisy, claimed to venerate ancient teachings concerning the immortality of the human soul — teachings that urged initiates to seek wisdom and to be 'virtuous, humble, peace-loving... and compassionate' towards others.[2]

However, as we shall see, it was less the confrontation of one culture that *practiced* sacrifice with a culture that did *not*, but rather, the confrontation of two cultures, each with massive conceptual *parallels* where sacrifice was concerned, and in that confrontation, comes a further anomaly, for not only do both cultures conceive of sacrifice in almost exactly the same way, they even conceive of it to fulfill a similar purpose.

A. The Aztecs and Human Sacrifice:
1. The Original Teaching of Quetzlcoatl

The Aztec's principal god was the god Quetzlcoatl who, like the Mayan's Kukulcan, and the Incas' Viracocha, was a white-skinned, blue-eyed, bearded "civilizer god" who taught the Aztecs the basics of civilization. Like the Mayans' Sovereign Plumed Serpent, Quetzlcoatl was a feathered serpent. Ruling the Mexica in a past Golden Age when he taught the arts of civilization, he also stipulated, clearly and unequivocally, that living things were never to be harmed and, more importantly, that humans were never to be sacrificed. The only things to be sacrificed were various plants, fruits, and flowers of a particular season.[3] If one were to place this conception within the

---

[2] Hanock and Faiia, *Heaven's Mirror*, p. 3.
[3] Ibid.

cultural framework of the Old Testament, Quetzlcoatl would be the Old Testament's Cain — who offered God only sacrifices of plants — to its Abel, who offered the "more acceptable" sacrifices of animals.

We are looking, in other words, in all likelihood, at a common metaphor, a symbolic motif, that is not unique to one specific religion — in this case, that of the ancient Hebrews — but at a much more widespread idea, for in both cases, the earliest type of sacrifice is hardly bloody, but is later replaced by one which is. Indeed, as far as the Aztecs were concerned, their civilization — like the Egyptians' views of *their* civilization an ocean away — was a legacy received whole cloth from Quetzlcoatl.[4]

As if to reinforce this idea of common motifs spread over the planet and dispersed among distinct cultures, one can also observe a number of peculiar parallels between Quetzlcoatlt and, of all people, the Egyptian god Osiris. Like Osiris, Quetzlcoatl was buried in a sarcophagus, whence he was resurrected to ascend into heaven to become a star.[5]

But how, with such commonality, did the Aztecs derive the practice of human sacrifice? Laurette Sejourne, drawing on the vast legacy of Aztec culture left behind, concluded in 1956 that the whole apparatus and practice of human sacrifice was a badly understood metaphor, a metaphor of a ritual of initiation that had been taken literally by the Aztecs. Thus, for the "cutting out of the heart," a metaphor for the soul's "cutting out" from the body at death,, the "flailing of the heart" was a metaphor for spiritual detachment from the physical body and senses, and so on. All of these metaphors for spiritual processes were, argued Sejourne, massively misunderstood by the Aztecs, and became part of the ritual of sacrifice.

If this be the case, then it was a metaphor massively misunderstood by the Mayans and Incas as well. Moreover, Sejourne is not entirely correct, for the Aztec's own statements indicate that if there was misunderstanding involved, then it was not original to *them*, but rather, *a misunderstanding deliberately inculcated as an old order was overturned, and a new one ushered in to replace it.* Once again, the

---

[4] Hancock and Faiia, *Heaven's Mirror*, p. 13.
[5] Ibid., p. 20. In my *The Giza Death Star* I point out Hancock's observations of the parallels between Osiris and the Incan Viracocha, pp. 14-16.

chronological progression was from sacrifices of plants and flowers and grains, the original order of the civilizing god Quetzlcoatl, and a later order of bloody human sacrifices.

Curiously, their practice of sacrifice also has something to do with the Flood, for just as we saw in the previous chapter, Noah made bloody sacrifice after the Flood. The Flood, in Aztec cosmology, is in turn connected to their doctrine of the Five Suns, or if one prefer, the Five World Ages. Each of these ages is a "sun" and is ended by various catastrophes, and each requires the re-establishment of life and of humanity.[6]

The first sun ended with all life literally consuming itself. This was followed by the destruction of the sun itself.[7] The second sun age ended in a destruction by *wind*, when all life and even the sun itself was destroyed by a massive wind.[8] The third sun age was ended in a rain of fire.[9] The fourth sun age ended with the Flood,[10] ushering in this, the final and fifth sun age.

At this juncture, according to the Aztec creation and history, the *Codex Chimalpopoca*, the Sun refused to move for four days:

> Then the gods say, "Why doesn't he move?" Then they send the blade falcon, who goes and tells the sun that it has come to question him. It tells him, "The gods are saying, 'Ask him why he doesn't move.'"
>
> Then the sun said, "Why? Because I'm asking for their blood their color, their precious substance."
>
> ...
>
> Then all the gods get together: Titlacahuan, Nuitzilopochtli, and the women Xochiquetzal, Yapalliicue, Nochpalliicue. *And there in Teotihucan they all died a scarificial death.* So then the sun went into the sky.[11]

---

[6] *History and Mythology of the Aztecs: the Codex Chimalpopoca*, trans. from the Nahuatl by John Bierhorst (Tuscon: The University of Arizona Press, 1992), p. 25.

[7] Ibid., p. 142.

[8] Ibid.

[9] Ibid., p. 143.

[10] Ibid.

[11] Ibid., pp. 148-149, emphasis added.

In other words, the *celestial machinery was so broken it had stopped, and could only be restarted by the sacrifice of the gods themselves — notably at Teotihuacan.* In so far as the Aztec's cosmology was concerned, *sacrifice* was intimately connected to the *physics.* But again, why?

2. Curious Statements, The Human Payment, and Two Elites
a. Unusual Ritual Parallels

As one reads more deeply into the *Codex Chimalpopoca,* the mystery only deepens. For example, shortly before the account of the fall of Tollan, the Aztecs' version of Tula, Thule, or the land across the sea from whence they came, there is an account of the dedication of a temple of the King Ce Acatl in a ritual of blood sacrifice that, to some, will sound very familiar:

Now, Ce Acatl's uncles, who are of the four hundred Mixcoa, absolutely hated his father, and they killed him.

And when they had killed him, they went and put him in the sand.

Then the king vulture says to him, "They've killed your father. It's over yonder that he lies, that they've buried him."

So he went and dug him up and put him in his temple, Mixcoatepetl.

Now, his uncles, the ones who killed his father, are called Apanecatly, Zolton, and Cuilton, and they say, "How will he dedicate his temple? If there's only a rabbit, if there's only a snake, we would be angry. A jaguar, an eagle, a world would be good." And so they told him this.

Ce Acatl said — he told them — "Alright. It shall be."

Then he called the jaguar, the eagle, and the wolf. He said to them, "Come, uncles. They say I must use you to dedicate my temple. But you will not die. Rather you will eat the ones I use to dedicate my temple — they're those uncles of mine." And so it was without any real purpose that ropes were tied around their necks.

...

Then his uncles are furious, and off they go, Apanecatl in the lead, climbing quickly.

But Ca Acatly rose up and broke his head with a burnished pot, and he came tumbling down.

Then he seizes Zolton and Cuilton. Then the animals blow (on the fire). Then they sacrifice them.
... And after they've tortured them, they cut open their breasts.[12]

If one did not know better, one might think one was reading the rituals of the first three degrees of Freemasonry, for we find no less than these common elements between them:

1) a king, in the Masonic ritual, Hiram Abiff, king of Tyre, who is building the Temple, and in the Aztec version Ce Acatl;
2) his "three attendants," in the Masonic ritual, Jubelo, Jubela, and Jubelum, and in the Aztec version Apanecatl, Zolton, and Cuilton;
3) a temple, which in *both* cases, is "dedicated" by human sacrifice, in the Masonic ritual, by the murder of King Hiram by his three attendants, and in the Aztec case, just the reverse, by the king's murder of his three attendants; *and,*
4) torture, followed by the cutting open of the breast, which recalls the Masonic ritual once again, where the point of a compass is pressed to the left nipple of the candidate for initiation.

The ritual of the Blue Lodge of Masonry is of unquestioned antiquity, but what are its echoes doing here, in the Valley of Mexico, in the Aztec culture, and in connection with sacrifice? This, and the strange resemblance of Quetzlcoatl (and Kukulcan and Viracocha) to Osiris, removes such correspondences from the realm of coincidence and places them in to the category of evidence that we are looking at the remains of a common cultural inheritance, differently construed by the legacy cultures it left behind.

b. Giants and Cannibalism

Nor is this the only strange parallel between New World sacrifices and Old World legends. There is another strange connection, this time, in legends of cannibalistic giants:

---

[12] *History and Mythology of the Aztecs: the Codex Chimalpopoca,* trans. from the Nahuatl by John Bierhorst, p. 154.

Now, in Tollan the people were no more.

Huemac was ruler., The second was called Necuametl, the third was Tlaltecatzin, the fourth was called Huitzilpopoca. The four were lift behind by Topilzin when he went away. And the ruler of Nonoalco was called Huetzin...

Now then, an omen came to him; he saw an ash-bundle man, a giant. And it was the very one who was eating people.

Then the Toltecs say, "O Toltecs, who is it that's eating people?"

Then they snared it, they captured it. And what they captured was a beardless boy.

Then they kill it. And when they've killed it, they look inside it: it has no heart, no innards, no blood.

Then it stinks. And whoever smells it dies from it, as well as whoever does not smell it, who (simply) passes by. And so a great many people are dying.

Then they go to drag it away, but it cannot be moved. And when the rope breaks, those who fall down die on the spot. And when it moves, all those who come in contact with it die. It eats them all.[13]

This not only parallels accounts from the Old World identifying giants with the practice of cannibalism, but in the Aztec context, there is a subtle implication that the story has something to do with the practice of human sacrifice itself, with the literal consumption of the people being "cooked" as burnt sacrifices for the gods; the "giant," we are told, is opened up, and there is *no blood, no heart.* The giant, who consumes the lives of the people, is a heartless machine.[14]

c. Quetzlcoatl, Sacrifice, Payment, and "the Sorcerers"

We now come to confront the issue of human sacrifice in Aztec culture, as it is recounted in the *Codex Chimalpopoca*, directly. In one place, the account states that in the year 1487, or the year 8 Reed as

---

[13] *History and Mythology of the Aztecs: the Codex Chimalpopoca*, trans. from the Nahuatl by John Bierhorst, pp. 155-156.

[14] This Aztec giant resembles nothing so much as the descriptions of the so-called "grays" which according to some lack similar internal organs or blood in any conventional sense, leading some to posit that they are in fact genetically engineered bio-robots of some sort.

the Aztecs called it, some 80,400 prisoners were sacrificed on the top of the pyramid at Tenochtitlan, the Aztec capital.[15] Indeed, the numbers are so staggering that one begins to wonder if the whole vast program of Aztec conquest was really driven by a perceived "need" for a constant supply of sacrificial victims.

However, that same *Codex* makes it very clear that the god who was considered by the Aztecs themselves to have founded their civilization, Quetzlcoatl, forbade it. The following story of its origins is told, and with it, one has a further insight into the Aztec version of the Masonic ritual and dedication of the Temple:

> The Toltecs were engaged (in battle) at a place called Netlalpan. And when they had taken captives, human sacrifice also got started, as Toltecs sacrificed their prisoners. Among them and *in their midst the devil Yaotl followed along. Right on the spot he kept inciting them to make human sacrifices.*
>
> And then, too, he started and began the practice of flaying humans… Then he made one of the Toltecs named Ziuhcozcatl wear the skin, and he was the first to war a **totec** skin.
>
> Indeed, every kind of human sacrifice that there used to be got started then. For it is told and related that during his time and under his authority, the first Quetzlcoatl, whose name was Ce Acatl, absolutely refused to perform human sacrifice. It was precisely when Huemac was ruler that all those things that used to be done got started. It was the devils who started them. But this has been put on paper and written down elsewhere. And there it is to be heard.
>
> … Huemac sacrificed a human streamer, thus making payment.[16]

There are three things to notice here:

1) Sacrifice is considered a *payment*, i.e., something that is *owed*, and hence, the implied concept is that there is a *debt* to be paid, for whatever reason;

---

[15] *History and Mythology of the Aztecs: the Codex Chimalpopoca*, trans. from the Nahuatl by John Bierhorst, p. 118.

[16] Ibid., pp. 40-14, italicized emphasis added, boldface emphasis in the original.

2) Sacrifice was *not* the original order of society, but was instituted at some later period by *devils*; and,

3) it was instituted *by one devil in particular*, someone named Yaotl, whose name contains the root "Ya" and who both in name and in character sounds more than a little like the "Yahweh" of the Torah, the first five books of the Old Testament, who takes such delight in smelling the aroma of sacrificed animals.

One final thing should also be noted before we continue, and that is that the name "Quetzlcoatl" appears to be understood by the Aztecs to be a *titular* name, the name of an *office* as much as it is the name of a person, and office similar in nature to the Mayans' description, "Sovereign Plumed Serpent."

The idea of "devils" having been behind the institution of sacrifice is further elaborated:

> 7 Rabbit (1018). Here began the sacrifice of the human streamers. At that time, in the time of 7 Rabbit, a great famine occurred. What is said is that the Toltecs were seven-rabbited. It was a seven-year famine, a famine that caused much suffering and death.
> *It was then that the sorcerers requisitioned Huemac's own children* and went and left them in the waters of Xochiquetzal and on Huitzco and on Xicocotl, thus making payment with little children. This was the first time that the sacrifice of human streamers occurred.[17]

We have already encountered Huemac as one of the Aztec kings mentioned in the *Codex Chimalpopoca*, but now we learn of another presence behind the practice of human sacrifice: sorcerers, in addition to devils. In other words, the Aztec mythology is suggesting that we are looking at the activity of an initiated elite. And once again, sacrifice is referred to as a payment. It is thus difficult to avoid the conclusion that the "devils" were the ones demanding payment.

However, of all the suggestive passages in the *Codex* that refer to human sacrifice, one in particular stands out above all the rest for the breadth of its implications.

---

[17] *History and Mythology of the Aztecs: the Codex Chimalpopoca*, trans. from the Nahuatl by John Bierhorst, p. 39.

Well, it is told and related that many times during the life of
Quetzlcoatl, sorcerers tried to ridicule him into making the human
payment, into taking human lives. But he always refused. He did
not consent, because he greatly loved his subjects, who were
Toltecs. Snakes, birds, and butterflies that he killed were what his
sacrifices always were.

And it is told and related that with this he wore out the
sorcerers' patience. So it was then that they started to ridicule him
and make fun of him, the sorcerers saying they wanted to torment
Quetzlcoatl and make him run away.

And it became true. It happened.

...

Then they tell how Quetzlcoatl departed. It was when he
refused to obey the sorcerers about making the human payment,
about sarificing humans. Then the sorcerers deliberated among
themselves, they whose names were Texcatlipoca, Ihuimecatly, and
Toltecatly. They said, "He must leave his city. We shall live
there."[18]

This is a significant passage, for in it one finds the clear outlines of a
peculiar story emerging:

1) The "old order," represented by Quetzlcoatl, which refuses to
   institute human sacrifice;
2) The "new order" represented by three sorcerers, who
   eventually force Quetzlcoatl to abandon his city and take it
   over. These three sorcerers, along with King Quetzlcoatl,
   represent yet another variation, perhaps, of the Aztec version
   of the Hiram Abiff story, with the dedication of a temple by
   sacrifice;
3) Sacrifice is again referred to as a "payment," a debt, and
   Quetzlcoatl's refusal to institute the practice is, perhaps,
   suggestive of the fact that he did not accept the whole notion
   of payment and debt to begin with.

---

[18] *History and Mythology of the Aztecs: the Codex Chimalpopoca*, trans. from the
Nahuatl by John Bierhorst, p. 31.

To put it succinctly, it would appear that one is looking at two ideologies, two conceptions, of the place of mankind within the vast "cosmic machine," an older one, and a newer one, represented by Queztlcoatl and the sorcerers respectively. Those sorcerers were elsewhere called "devils," and one in particular, "Yaotl," was behind the practice.

All of this occurs in the post-Flood world of the Fifth Sun, so it is important to note one final thing. After the flood, the gods create "a new sun from the flames of the 'spirit oven' at Teotihuacan..."[19] The notion of sacrifice, in other words, was deeply tied to the most mysterious site on the world Grid in all of the Americas, as it was also tied to the notion of a recreation, a revitalization, of the sun and celestial machinery itself.

But before we look at the implications of these ideas at Teotihuacan, a closer look at the notion of sacrifice, payment, and debt in the culture that *confronted* the Aztecs is in order.

B. *Sacrificial Atonement in Latin Christianity:* *Anselm of Canterbury's* Cur Deus Homo

All across Western Europe, from whence the Conquistadores came, sacrifice was being offered in all the hamlet chapels, parish churches, deaneries, monasteries, and cathedrals of Europe: the sacrifice of the mass. Moreover, it would not take a great deal to show that many of these chapels, churches, and cathedrals were built over old pagan shrines or cult centers, occupying places on the world Grid. In brief, the sacrifice of the mass was understood to be a supremely alchemical act, the transubstantiation of earthly bread and wine into the heavenly body and blood of Christ, which had been sacrificed to God the Father at the Crucifixion. It was an act that made that sacrifice really present.

Two cultures, both of them practicing sacrifice of *some* sort, thus confronted each other, and though it could be said that the Spanish were hardly practicing actual human sacrifice, a closer look at the theological doctrine underlying Western Latin Christian belief will reveal that there was no great broad conceptual ocean dividing the

---

[19] *History and Mythology of the Aztecs: the Codex Chimalpopoca*, trans. from the Nahuatl by John Bierhorst, p. 9.

two cultures, but rather the reverse, that much of the language and conceptulization behind both cultures' practice and belief was the same.

For the western Latin Church, the constellation of ideas surrounding the sacrifice of Christ were most completely enunciated by the 11th century theologian, Anselm, Archbishop of Canterbury (1033-1109), in a work entitled *Cur Deus Homo*, or *Why the God-Man?* Here, the "logic" of sacrifice, debt, and payment is laid out clearly, and with a cold-bloodedness that lies just hidden beneath the surface language of piety.

The first indicator that even Christ Himself is viewed as but a cog in a vast sacrificial "machine" is found in the opening lines of the *Cur Deus Homo*, the very lines that formed the epigraph to this chapter: "...in fine, *leaving Christ out of view (as if nothing had ever been known of him), it proves, by absolute reasons*, the impossibility that any man should be saved without him."[20] In other words, once Christ is out of view, then it is the "absolute reasons" that form the basis of the machine of sacrifice into which Christ steps as "the essential cog."

A reading of a few select passages will make this clear.

1. Debt and Will

The *Cur Deus Homo* is laid out as a set of dialogues between Anselm and his pupil, Boso. We begin our examination of the logic of sacrifice in Anselm with this exchange between the archbishop and his student in chapter IX of the *Cur Deus:*

> **Boso:** ...How it was of his own accord that he died, and what this means: "he was made obedient even unto death; " and: "for which cause God hath highly exalted him;" and: "I came not to do my own will; " and: "he spared not his own Son;" and: "not as I will, but as thou wilt."
>
> **Anselm:** It seems to me that you do not rightly understand the difference between what he did at the demand of obedience, and what he suffered, not demanded by obedience, but inflicted on him, because he kept his obedience perfect.

---

[20] Anselm of Canterbury, *Cur Deus Homo* (*Why the God-man?*), Preface. http://www.ewtn.com/library/CHRIST/CURDEUS.HTM, emphasis added.

...

That man, therefore, *owed* this obedience to God the Father, *humanity* to Deity; and the Father *claimed* it from him.

Boso: ...For death was inflicted on him for his perseverance in obedience and he endured it; but I do not understand how it is that obedience did not demand this.

...

Anselm: ...It may, indeed be said, that the Father commanded him to die, when he enjoined that upon him on account of which he met death...And this, *since none other could accomplish it*, availed as much with the Son, who so earnestly desired the salvation of man, as if the Father had commanded him to die; and, therefore, "as the Father gave him commandment, so he did, and the cup which the Father gave to him he drank, being obedient even unto death."

Note the curious statement "since none other could accomplish it," a statement that many interpreters take as referring to the insufficiency and weakness of the human will and its inability not to sin. Christ, as a "perfect man" presumably does not suffer this weakness, and therefore, is able to offer a perfect obedience.

But this would be to reduce Anselm's argument, for this is not the only "absolute reason" that he has in mind.

2. Debt, Payment, and Satisfaction

That "absolute reason" is revealed by what Anselm has to say about the ideas of debt, payment, and satisfaction in chapter twelve of the *Cur Deus*:

Anselm: Let us return and consider whether it were proper for God to put away sins by compassion alone, *without any payment of the honor taken from him.*

...

But *if sin is neither paid for nor punished, it is subject to no law.*

Here the notion of payment and debt becomes more fully defined: it is a "payment for the honor taken" from God by man.

This is further elaborated in chapter nineteen:

Anselm: Therefore, *consider it settled that, without satisfaction, that is, without voluntary payment of the debt, God can neither pass by the sin*

213

unpunished, nor can the sinner attain that happiness, or happiness like that, which he had before he sinned; for man cannot in this way be restored, or become such as he was before he sinned.

Boso: ...For, if we pay our debt, why do we pray God to put it away? Is not God unjust to demand what has already been paid? But if we do not make payment, why do we supplicate in vain that he will do what he cannot do, because it is unbecoming?

Anselm: He who does not pay says in vain: "Pardon"; but he who pays makes supplication, because prayer is properly connected with the payment; for *God owes no man anything, but every creature owes God...*

Here the language of "debt" and "payment" has come fully out into the open, but note, that in the implicit logic of Anselm's argument, *both* God *and* man are caught as cogs in a machine of higher logic, that of an abstract justice demanding punishment and satisfaction for sin. Lest this point be missed, Anselm is really saying that there is *no intrinsic forgiveness whatsoever,* there is no fiat of forgiveness without the shedding of blood.

This gruesome logic is elaborated even further in chapters twenty through twenty-three:

> **Anselm:** Neither, I think, will you doubt this, that *satisfaction should be proportionate to guilt.*
>
> ...
>
> *When you render anything to God which you owe him, irrespective of your past sin, you should not reckon this as the debt which you owe for sin.* But you owe God every one of those things which you have mentioned....
>
> **Boso:** Truly I dare not say that in all these things I pay any portion of my debt to God.
>
> **Anselm:** How then do you pay God for your transgression?
>
> **Boso:** If in justice I owe God myself and all my powers, even when I do not sin, I have nothing left to render to him for my sin.
>
> **Anselm:** What will become of you then? How will you be saved?
>
> ...
>
> (We) set aside Christ and his religion as if they did not exist, when we proposed to inquire whether his coming were necessary to man's salvation.

(CHAPTER XXI)

...

Anselm: Therefore *you make no satisfaction unless you restore something greater than the amount of that obligation,* which should restrain you from committing the sin.

Here the implicit logic is finally revealed, for mankind owes a debt that he cannot repay, yet, since it is mankind that *owes* the debt, he *must* repay.

And this leads to the heart of the logic of Anselm's "machine of sacrifice."

3. Infinite Debt, Infinite Payment, and the Internal Logic of the Sacrifice of Christ According to Anselm

Mankind owes a debt that is, in effect, infinite, since his sin was — as was seen in the citations above — an affront to the honor of God, an honor one can only assume was infinite, like God Himself. Because of this, the infinite debt can only be "paid off" or "satisfied" by an infinite payment, yet, mankind had to pay it, since he himself owed it. And thus we come to the heart of the *Cur Deus Homo,* the *Why the God-Man,* for only God, by coming man, could both satisfy, and pay, the abstract infinite debt, as is enunciated in Book II, chapters six and seven of the *Cur Deus*:

> **Anselm:** But this cannot be effected, except the price paid to God for the sin of man be something greater than all the universe besides God.
> **Boso:** So it appears.
> **Anselm:** Moreover, it is necessary that he who can give God anything of his own which is more valuable than all things in the possession of God, must be greater than all else but God himself.
> **Boso:** I cannot deny it.
> **Anselm:** *Therefore none but God can make this satisfaction.*
> **Boso:** So it appears.
> **Anselm:** *But none but a man ought to do this, other wise man does not make the satisfaction.*
> **Boso:** Nothing seems more just.

(CHAPTER VII)

Anselm: ... *For God will not do it, because he has no debt to pay; and man will not do it, because he cannot. Therefore, in order that the God-man may perform this, it is necessary that the same being should be perfect God and perfect man, in order to make this atonement.*

And with those statements, Anselm has reduced God, man, and Christ as cogs in a kind of "accounting" adjustment as vast cogs in an impersonal machine of justice and sacrifice. Anselm "wins" the argument, and his disciple Boso summarizes this principle in chapter eighteen of Book Two:

Boso: ...And you, by numerous and positive reasons, have shown that the restoring of mankind ought not to take place, and could not, without man paid the debt which he owed God for his sin. And *this debt was so great that, while none but man must solve the debt, none but God was able to do it; so that he who does it must be both God and man.* And hence arises a necessity that God should take man into unity with his own person; so that he who in his own nature was bound to pay the debt, but could not, might be able to do it in the person of God.

Pause and consider quite carefully what this means. On Anselm's view, God is a banker, and Christ is less a person than an action of sacrifice balancing the books; all other aspects of the life and teaching of Christ are, really, merely superfluous to this overriding sacrificial necessity. On this view, even life itself is an indebtedness, and this reveals the flaw in Anselm's logic, for if life itself is an indebtedness, could mankind *ever* sufficiently "honor God" to pay back the debt of life?

There is, of course, a further flaw in Anselm, and it is a moral one, for it makes God the Father demand the death-by-torture of his own Son to satisfy an affront to His honor, an act that, even on human terms, seems neither just nor befitting a "God of Love," and an action few, if any, human fathers would ever demand.

We are dealing, in short, with a kind of closed "economico-theological" system, with God's honor as the interest, and mankind the principal and collateral on it.

With this view of mankind as a mechanism in a machine, let us now return to the Aztecs, to Teotihuacan, and look more closely at the possible physics connections.

C. Teotihuacan

Teotihuacan may rightly be said to be the Giza of the Americas. Its massive Pyramid of the Sun and Pyramid of the Moon dominate the Valley of Mexico, and their names themselves are both specifically mentioned in the local native lore, and were adopted by the Aztecs themselves when they moved into the Valley.[21] The name Teotihuacan itself means "city of the gods." Indeed, the emperor Montezuma himself thought that the Pyramid of the Sun was the "original primeval mound marking the spot where creation had been set in motion at the beginning of the present epoch of the earth."[22] In this, as we shall discover, the Aztecs echoed the Egyptians, who also regarded their great pyramids at Giza as representing the primeval mountains of creation.

In other words, the pyramids of Teotihuacan and in particular the Pyramid of the Sun were regarded as somehow fundamentally connected to the cosmological processes of creation itself. For the Aztecs, as for the Egytptians, they were, in some rudimentary sense, understood to be *machines* manipulating the physics of the cosmological process of creation and destruction itself at the highest, topological level.

However, for the Aztecs, unlike for the Egyptians, that manipulation was accomplished through the barbaric practice of human sacrifice, a practice overseen by priests who, according to Nahuatl tradition, directed sacrifices as part of the ritual of immortality and ascension connected with the pyramids.[23] Before

---

[21] Hancock and Faiia, *Heaven's Mirror*, p. 14.
[22] Ibid., p. 15.
[23] See the discussion on pp. 19-20.

proceeding to a more detailed examination, it is worth speculating on why sacrifice was thought, in some manner, to be connected with pyramids, immortality, and the manipulation of the medium.

We have already noted that pyramids were understood by the Meso-Americans, in some rudimentary form, as machines directly linked to the cosmological processes of creation, to a *physics*. As I have also noted in my book *The Cosmic War*, some of the ancient technologies seem to have been operable, or were *perceived* as being operable, only in close conjunction or actual physical contact with their possessors.[24] It is also known that the Aztecs in particular practiced human sacrifice with what may best be described as reckless abandon, as if, somehow, the sheer numbers and emotional trauma associated with them somehow enhanced the effect - whatever it was perceived to be - of the practice. Taking the Aztec and Mayan myths as our clue, we may conclude that at some point during the development of the Grid, that an elite arose - or perhaps simply asserted itself - that understood that there was a direct effect of consciousness upon the physical medium, and through the practice of massive human sacrifice, was attempting literally to "traumatize" or "shock" it.

Turning to Teotihuacan itself, it is to be noted that the site is very ancient, and bears the marks of several eras of construction.[25] The problem is, that no one *really* knows who built it, nor really, when it was built. Indeed, when the Conquistadors discovered the site,

> No one could tell them who had built the great ceremonial center, whence the builders had come, or whither they had gone. All they could learn was that two centuries earlier, when the Mexica had arrived in the valley, they had found the mysterious city already in an abandoned condition, *covered with earth and vegetation.*[26]

---

[24] Q.v. the discussion in *The Cosmic War: Interplanetary Warfare, Modern Physics, and Ancient Texts*, pp. 263-273. We have also noted that Montezuma viewed Teotihuacan's Pyramid of the Sun as being the primeval mound of creation, in yet another adaption of the "mountains ≈ pyramids" formula discussed at length in *The Cosmic War*.

[25] See for example, Munck, *The Master Code Book*, p. 20.

[26] Peter Tompkins, *Mysteries of the Mexican Pyramids* (New York: Harper and Row, Publishers, 1976), p. 11.

The presence not only of vegetation but of *earth* covering the monuments of Teotihuacan suggests that when the Aztecs came upon the site, it had been abandoned for some time.

There is loosely corroborating support for the antiquity of this site from Mayan texts, Aztec mythology and ritual practices. Peter Tompkins notes that the Aztecs and Mayans may have inherited the practice of human sacrifice from some contact with the Phoenicians, who were the ultimate practitioners of child sacrifice. Citing the work of archaeologist Hugh Fox, Tompkins notes that the practice of sacrifice in the Old World, emerged after the Flood in conjunction with an attempt to appease the gods and ward off another catastrophe, a conjunction of ideas also apparently at work in Mayan and Aztec thinking. [27] The Mayan Troano Codex spoke of a great catastrophe that had sunk an island in the Atlantic Ocean "extending eastward in a crescent as far as the Canary Islands" ca. 9937 BC. [28] The close proximity of this date to the 10,500 BC date mentioned elsewhere should be noted, for again it suggests that one is looking at a common cultural inheritance spanning the globe.

It is fairly certain that the Pyramid of the Sun at Teotihuacan was once dedicated to the Sovereign Plumed Serpent, Quetzcoatl, for the Mexican archaeologist Batras discovered many worked shells depicting snakes on and around the pyramid during his excavations of the site in the early twentieth century. [29]

However, there was a much deeper mystery concerning the Pyramid of the Sun, one suggesting that the structure was conceived for some machine-like function:

> An unpublished find on the fifth level has never been adequately explained. While the Sun Pyramid was first being probed by Batras in 1906, an archeologist working with him reported a thick sheet of mica covering the top of the fifth body. This material was apparently carried away during the course of the restoration.
>
> Coincidentally, a "Temple of Mica" was also found to the south of the Sun Pyramid about 350 meters down the Way of the Dead, where the local guard will still let one peek through a glass panel at

---

[27] Peter Tompkins, *Mysteries of the Mexican Pyramids* (New York: Harper and Row, Publishers, 1976), p. 353.

[28] Ibid., pp. 114-115.

[29] Ibid., p. 202.

the floor covered with mica slabs. Mica has two outstanding characteristics: high electrical resistance and opaqueness to fast neutrons. Hence it acts as an insulator or nuclear reaction moderator, which raises the question as to why two separate areas of Teotihuacan were covered with mica.[30]

In addition to these properties, mica may also be used in the manufacture of capacitors and as an insulator in high voltage machines.

While mica *was* used in ancient times for purposes other than these modern ones, its presence in the Pyramid of the Sun, plus the structure's possible antiquity, suggests that one may not too easily close the door on the possibility that its presence served some functional purpose. In this case, there are three possible properties:

1) as an electrical insulator;
2) as a dielectric in a capacitor; and
3) as a nuclear moderator.

Given these choices, one may speculate that perhaps the first two usages were intended by the structure's builders, but we will have to reserve any further commentary about this structure and its possible functional purpose for a possible future sequel on the Grid.

Munck notes that the Teotihuacan-Giza parallelism is quite acute, for the three main pyramids of Giza, Mycerinus, Cephren, and the Great Pyramid itself, are exact analogies to the Moon Pyramid, the Sun Pyramid, and the "Quetzlcoatl" complex at Teotihuacan.[31] And both these places with their three main structures are, as most know, laid out according to the patterns of the stars of the constellation Orion's "belt." For our purposes, however, we make an assumption, and note one thing. The assumption - which will be argued in chapter thirteen - is that we are looking an *machines* designed to engineer a hyper-dimensional physics. Once we have granted that assumption, then something immediately follows: Giza and Teotihuacan are designed according to the same basic plan, that is to say, they could be coupled oscillators to each other in some fashion.

---

[30] Ibid.
[31] Munck, *Whispers from Time*, Vol. 1, p. 42.

Munck makes some crucial observations regarding the most massive structure at Teotihuacan, the Pyramid of the Sun, and these play directly into our assumptions that we are looking at "hyper-dimensional engineering." A glance at this structure in side elevation, courtesy of the detailed line drawings of engineer Hugh Harleston, Jr., is in order.

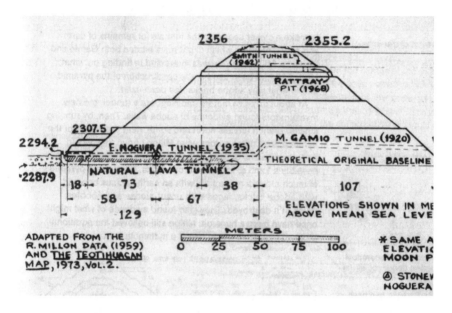

Hugh Harleston Jr's Side Elevation view of the Pyramid of the Sun. Note that all measures are given in meters.[32]

Note, says Munck, that the pyramid is *deliberately* offset, much like the "temples" of Tikal.[33] The offset, moreover, occurs on the level of the second terrace, and of all five terraces, only the lower two are centered. Following his method of counting faces and sides, this gives Munck the following interesting set of numbers:

1) Centered terraces:	2
2) Faces on one side elevation of the pyramid	6
3) Number of terraces	5

[32] Peter Tompkins, *Mysteries of the Mexican Pyramids*, p. 333.
[33] Munck, *Whispers from Time*, Vol. 1, p. 46.

4) Offset faces on one side elevation 4^{34}

Taking each of these numbers times π times each other, e.g., 2π x 4π x 5π x 6π yields 23,378,.18184, which translates to 19° 41' when converted to normal degrees measures.[35] This is, of course, our first clue that we are indeed dealing with a hyper-dimensional structure, for the first of the Platonic solids, a tetrahedron, is circumscribed in a sphere, with on vertex on the rotational axis, will have the other three vertices touching at 19 degrees 47 minutes north or south latitude, depending upon which rotational pole the fourth vertex is positioned. And was we shall see in chapter thirteen, this is a profound clue to hyper-dimensional geometries, to geometries done in more than three spatial dimensions.

Here we must begin, however, to take some issue with Munck, for from a strictly geometrical perspective, there is no difference between *terraces* and *faces;* for a geometer, they are both the same. Additionally, we would have to multiply his numbers by four, since there are four sides to the structure (remember, the terraces count as *one* face since they extend around the entire structure, so we do *not* multiply them by four).

We would get the following adjusted table of numbers:

1) Centered faces (i.e., faces and terraces)   10
2) Offset faces (i.e., faces and terraces)   19
3) total faces (i.e., all faces and terraces)   29

Note that we are counting only the faces of the basic structure, not the faces that would be added from the staircases and so on. Now there are two more numbers that should be added to this list: *corners* and *edges:*

4) Number of corners, or vertices   44
5) Number of edges   78

As we shall see in chapter thirteen, these sorts of numbers are strongly suggestive of strange sorts of hyper-dimensional objects

---

[34] Ibid., p. 45.
[35] Munck, *Whispers from Time*, Vol. 1, p. 45.

called compounds, though as we shall also see, there is a problem. But nonetheless, these sorts of numbers permit us to offer yet another speculation about what kind of machines they are: *by dint of the numbers of faces edges, and vertices embodied in their numbers, these objects appear to be constructed as three-dimensional analogues of higher-dimensional objects, as **resonators** of them.*

If this sounds like the flights of purest science fiction fantasy, it isn't, for the mathematician Hugh Harleston Jr, whose diagrams we have been utilizing, noticed the same thing about the musical and tetrahedral properties of Teotihuacan, and its relationship to the physics of the medium:

> The angles and perspectives in the Teotihuacan layout appear to Harleston to show the framework of an integrated earth and heaven - along with the megaspace of the heavens above - as being the work of a master mathematician. To Harleston the messages of Teotihuacan point to a new way of looking at time and space, and to some new source of energy from the cosmos, some new field fabric that our science has not yet isolated…
>
> Harleston says that once the student at Teotihuacan learned the important values of thirds, sevenths, and ninths, that squares and sqaure roots were basic mathematical tools, the next step was to understand the relationship of two simple geometric solids: the sphere and the tetrahedron.
>
> It was some time before Harleston found the clue to a tetrahedral geometry incorporated into the Teotihuacan complex, but he finally found it in the dimensions of the Pyramid of the Sun. Unlike the Pyramid of Cheops, which is a very exact scale model of the Northern Hemisphere (with the apex as the North Pole, the base as the equator, and its perimeter equal to one-half minute of arc), the Sun Pyramid does not fit such a system; it does, however, very accurately give the entire surface of the earth.[36]

Why is this so? because as we have already seen, the tetrahedral number of 19.5 is already approximated in the structure in terms of its number of faces and π. But there is also *another* way it is incorporated:

---

[36] Tompkins, *Mysteries of the Mexican Pyramids*, pp. 278-279.

Oddly, or coincidentally, the relation between a tetrahedron and a sphere constitutes the thrust of the work of Buckminster Fuller, who, in his book *Synergetics*, maintains that the tetrahedron gives the basic mathematical blueprint for the universe.

From what he calls his "isotropic vector matrix" Fuller obtains a constant of $\sqrt{9/8}$, which comes to `1.065066, so close to Harleston's 1.059 constant that it fits the Teotihuacan complex virtually as well.[37]

This tetrahedral redundancy that was built into Teotihuacan was not lost on Harleston:

> Pointing out that the carbon atom - which is the basic building block from which the material bodies of all living organisms are made - is a regular tetrahedron, and that the water molecule has characteristics that conform to the tetrahedral structure, Harleston concludes that the fundamental message conveyed by the Teotihuacanos is that the physical universe is tetrahedral from the microscopic level of the atom all the way up to the macroscopic level of the galaxies on a scale of vibrations *in which man stands about the center.* Man would thus have built into him, as suggested by Pythagoras and Plato, the tool for unlocking the geometry of the cosmos and recovering the knowledge of his role in the scheme.[38]

Those numbers, 9 and 8, and those mystics, Pythagoras and Plato, we shall encounter again in the next chapter, and man's unique position, as the microcosm and mediator in this cosmic, tetrahedral temple, we shall have much occasion to comment on in the fourth part of this book in connection with Egypt.

That positioning of man somewhere in the *middle* of all this physics, however, does suggest one final, significant clue as to why human sacrifice was practiced by *some* with a possible understanding of this physics, of the analogical nature of consciousness itself, and of the analogical view of the physical medium which the ancients held, for standing midway between the physics of the very small and the very large, man himself was the natural and most efficient *resonator* of all those things. For those intending to exercise power and influence

---

[37] Tompkins, *Mysteries of the Mexican Pyramids*, p. 280.
[38] Ibid., p. 281.

over the medium via its interface with consciousness, through the instrumentality of shock and emotional trauma induced within it by brutality and sacrifice, the selection of mankind is in some sense the manifestation of a twisted logic and a twisted music.[39]

But the original music, echoed from the Vedas down through Mesopotamia and Egypt, must now come into view, to see just how twisted that logic really was.

---

[39] We must also ask: Is there a connection to Kali, the destroyer who represents the final age, cycle for humanity? She comes consuming bodies, drinking blood, and particularly angry at the masculine force that has lost all sense of femininity? There is a final age, perhaps like the ages established with the suns (as mentioned in this chapter) and according to Hindu cycles, we are in the Kali age. It is an age of unsurpassed violence and masculine dominated force, detached from any feminine qualities.

Humanity in Perpetual Debt

PART THREE:
THE MESOPOTAMIAN "PYRAMID PEOPLES":
THE PYTHAGOREAN AND PLATONIC PRINCIPLES OF
SUMER, BABYLONIA, AND GREECE

"Creating the language of the philosophy of the future, Plato still spoke the ancient tongue, representing as it were, a living 'Rosetta stone.'...It comes from that 'Protopythagorean' mint somewhere in the Fertile Crescent that, once, coined the technical language and delivered it to the Pythagoreans (among many other customers, as goes without saying)."
Giorgio de Santillana and Hertha von Dechend,
Hamlet's Mill, p. 311.

"Ancient cosmology required just enough number theory and just enough musical theory to harmonize the heavens with the scale and the calendar."
Ernest G. McClain,
The Myth of Invariance: the Origin of the Gods, Mathematics and Music from the Rg Veda to Plato, p. 14.

9

PLATO, PYTHAGORAS, AND THE PHYSICS OF THE CAVE:

THE VEDAS, MESOPOTAMIA, AND THE MUSIC OF THE SPHERES

"Ancient cosmology required just enough number theory and just enough musical theory to harmonize the heavens with the scale and the calendar."
Ernest G. McClain[1]

No survey of the underlying physics of the world Grid system would be complete without a mention of Mesopotamia, for it is there, in the crossroads of the ancient Middle East, that the cultures of Egypt, Sumer, Babylon and India, met. Indeed, more than one author has commented on the peculiar links of Mesopotamian civilization to the ancient Vedic civilizations,[2] and it could be said with some justification that Mesopotamia owes its sophistication and cosmology to the legacy of the East. It is there that the planetary motions were fused with number theory and music to an extraordinary degree.

Plato himself, as we shall see, owed much of his numerical codes to the influence of Pythagoreanism, and that in turn owed much to Mesopotamian civilizations. A proper understanding of the Grid system and the cosmologies that underwrote it cannot therefore be had without a consideration of the massive influence that the civilizations "between the rivers" had on its development, and in particular, on the development of music. In this understanding, no work is more magisterial and important than that of Professor Ernest G. McClain.

---

[1] Ernest G. McClain, *The Myth of Invariance: The Origin of the Gods, Mathematics and Music from the Rg Veda to Plato* (York Beach, Maine: Nicholas Hays, Inc., 1984), p. 14.

[2] See for example David Frawley, *Gods, Sages and Kings: Vedic Secrets of Ancient Civilization* (Salt Lake City: Passage Press, 1991), and L. Austin Waddell, *Makers of Civilization in Race and History* (Kessinger Publishing. No date). Waddell is a good overview of the links between Sumer and the Vedic civilization but should be approached with some caution.

A. The Unified Intention of Symbol and Musical Codes

In my previous books I have spoken at length about a conception that I call "the unified intention of symbol," i.e., the idea that ancient myths were carefully composed, multi-leveled structures designed to encode a massive amount of technical information that could be decoded when science had advanced to a similar state of development as the society that originally created the myths.[3] It has been my assumption that this "mythological creation" was the *deliberate* act of a post-cosmic war elite or elites seeking a method to enshrine and transmit technical information in a form that would last over time. If studies such as De Santillana and Von Dechend's *Hamlet's Mill*, or Ernest G. McClain's *Pythagorean Plato* and *The Myth of Invariance* are any indicators, the program was wildly successful, for those myths, from Scandinavia to Polynesia, encode a wealth of astronomical, geometric, and musical data.

1. Music as the First Physical Unification and the Musical Meanings of Pantheons

I am not the only one, by any means, to have noticed this multi-leveled, almost paronomasial symbolism at work in ancient myths. Commenting on this phenomenon in the Vedic texts, McClain observes that there are at least four "languages" or modes of expression at work simultaneously:

1) the language of Non-Existence (*Asat*),
2) the language of Existence (*Sat*),
3) the language of Images and Sacrifice (*Yajna*), and
4) the language of Embodied (*Rta*) Vision (*Dhih*).
These four languages are the expressions of a sensorium which organizes itself primarily on a model of sound.[4]

---

[3] See my *The Giza Death Star Destroyed* (Adventures Unlimited Press, 2005), pp. 49-52; *The Cosmic War* (Adventures Unlimited Press, 2007), pp. 75-81.
[4] Ernest G. McClain, *The Myth of Invariance*, p. 2.

It is the recurrence of similar numbers, in a similar order, from the *Rig Vedas* of India, and on into Babylon, Egypt, and Greece that indicates an underlying, common spiritual and philosophical tradition. Indeed, for McClain, music was "the one force capable of projecting a philosophical synthesis" because music was the first physical unification.[5] This musical code manifests itself, within the Vedic tradition, as hymns and musical numerology that link Sun, Moon, the planets, to the Indian pantheon "in which sons create their own mothers and all are counted."[6]

In the effort to decode these musical-numeric codes, Plato is, for McClain, a kind of Rosetta Stone "to the more obscure science of earlier cultures."[7] Of all these cultures, the Vedic was by far the oldest, and its myths and hymns were, in fact, codes of a musical science:

> The numbers Rgvedic man cared about define alternate tunings for the musical scale. The hymns describe the numbers poetically, distinguish "sets" *by classes of gods and demons,* and portray tonal and arithmetical relations with graphic sexual and spatial metaphor. Vedic concerns were with those **invariances** which became the focus of attention in Greek tuning theory. Because the poets limited themselves to **integers**, or natural numbers, and consistently used the **smallest integers possible** in every tonal context, they made it possible for us to rediscover their constructions by the methods of Pythagorean mathematical harmonics.[8]

We may now add to the accumulated levels of meaning associated with the "unified intention of symbol" a new understanding of "gods:"

1) At the most prosaic level, the gods represent real "people" or beings who interact with humanity;

---

[5] Ernest G. McClain, *The Myth of Invariance*, p. xi
[6] Ibid., p. 1.
[7] Ibid., p. 3.
[8] Ibid., p. 4, boldface emphasis original, italicized emphasis added.

2) At a second, deeper level, the names of gods might be *titular*, as denoting a *planet* or its ruler, or ruling house;[9] and now we have, in addition to this,

3) At a third level, the names of classes of gods also represent sets of notes generated by certain mathematical relationships.

There is a clue here, for as was seen in my book *The Cosmic War*, there is yet another formula which emerges from Mesopotamian and Egyptian texts:

Mountains ≈ Planets ≈Gods ≈ Pyramids,[10] where the symbol ≈ means "is associated with."

We may now add a new component to this formula:

Mountains ≈ Planets ≈ Gods ≈ Pyramids ≈ Music.

But why associate music with mountains, pyramids and planets?

The answer to that question emerges from a careful consideration of McClain's decoding of the "musical paleophysics" of the myths of Pythagoreanism and Platonism. It is music that adds a hierarchy of order to the otherwise infinite and chaotic series of numbers:

> What we are investigating then, is actually a realm of number theory in which music sets the problems, since musical patterns elevate certain numbers to a prominence pure number theory would not accord them. Musical values introduce a hierarchy into the number field: as we shall show... *even* numbers which *define* the octave matrix are "female," *odd* numbers which *fill* the matrix with "tone-children" are "male," and the *smaller* numbers define intervals of *greater* importance.[11]

Or to put it into terms reminiscent of Rene Schwaller de Lubicz, music denotes the *functions* that numbers symbolize.

---

[9] Farrell, *The Giza Death Star Destroyed*, pp. 33-37.
[10] For a discussion of this formula, see my *The Cosmic War*, pp. 74-75, 83, 233
[11] McClain, *The Myth of Invariance*, p. 4, emphasis original.

What certain numerical relationships in ancient mythological texts are actually doing, in other words, are defining systems of *tuning* in the attempt to reduce the chaos of the harmonic series to an engineerable *order*. Why this is so requires a little explanation by way of a simple illustration.

Every musical tone has a natural harmonic series of overtones extending above and below it into infinity. The problem is, that each "overtone" or "harmonic" decreases in interval relationship to its fundamental the higher one goes. If one sits at an acoustic piano, presses the note "C" down silently, and then hits the note "C" an octave lower, one will hear this silently pressed "C" vibrating in sympathetic resonance with the struck note. Now, go up a *fifth* to the note "G", and repeat the experiment. Silently press down "G" while hitting the note "C". Again, one will hear the silently held note "G" vibrating sympathetically with the struck note "C". Again, go up a *fourth* — note that the interval is diminishing — to another note "C," press it silently, and hit the note "C" two octaves below it. Again, the silently held "C" will vibrate.

Repeating this process will inevitably lead to a note that does not exist on the piano keyboard, but that *does* exist in the natural harmonic series of "C", and that note lies in the crack between A and B^b. And as the intervals continue to diminish, more and more notes are added that do not exist on the keyboard. Our modern music, and particularly keyboard instruments, have been *tempered* or tuned to an artificially engineered overtone series that allows all twelve notes within an octave on the keyboard to function in any key of music, without having to stop to retune the whole instrument in order to do so.

Plato, in his *Republic*, encoded this "equal tempering" as a political philosophy: "The necessity of tempering the *pure* intervals, defined by the ratios of *integers*" that is to say, the harmonic series as it *naturally* occurs with its infinite overtones for each note, "is one of the great themes of Plato's *Republic*. In his allegorical form, 'citizens' modeled on the tones of the scale must not demand 'exactly what they are owed,' but must keep in mind 'what is best for the city.'"[12] That is to say, they must be willing to submit to a slight mathematical

---

[12] McClain, *The Myth of Invariance*, p. 11.

adjustment to allow them to function with each other in a harmonious fashion.

The number twelve here is a key, for it points directly to Mesopotamia and to its "sexagesimal" numerical system, a system that as we shall see was taylor-made to solve the tuning problem, and to a secret held by those cultures and passed down through the Pythagoreans. It points also to the twelve houses of the zodiac, and with that, the connection between music and astronomy comes a little closer into view.

B. Music, the Alchemical Medium, and Astronomy

The Vedic tradition is full of allusions to the "luminous nature of sound". Indeed, the word for light (*svar*) is similar to the word for sound (*svara*).[13] This, as I have observed elsewhere, is another clue that perhaps we are viewing a legacy of a lost sophistication in physics, for the idea of a "sound-light" can also be understood as "electro-acoustic," i.e., as longitudinal electrical waves in the medium, recalling the "Sound-Eye" spoken of in the Egyptian Edfu texts.[14]

The regularity of that physical medium was, for the ancient mind, expressed in the regularity of the cyclic nature of the heavens, and the precession of the equinoxes through a long cycle through the twelve houses of the Zodiac. Twelve, then, became the number of choice for expressing the musical harmony of the spheres. We may illustrate this by again sitting at an acoustic piano, and playing through the circle of perfect fourths and fifths:

Circle of Fourths (Asdending)
1) C
2) F
3) B^b
4) E^b
5) A^b
6) D^b
7) G^b/F$^\#$
8) B

---

[13] McClain, *The Myth of Invariance*, p. 7.
[14] Farrell, *The Cosmic War*, pp. 170-181.

9)E
10) A
11) D
12) G
13) (C)
Circle of Fifths, Descending (Reading the above chart bottom to top)

Again, the notes we play are not the result of the natural overtone series, but of a *tempering* or "tampering with" by means of a mathematical adjustment to harmonize with the celestial motions of precession through the twelve houses of the Zodiac. As McClain states it, "Ancient cosmology required just enough number theory and just enough musical theory to harmonize the heavens with the scale and the calendar."[15] The musical allegory is expressed in poetic terms in the *Rig Veda*

> Formed with twelve spokes, by length of
> time, unweakened, rolls round the
> heaven, this wheel of during order.

> Twelve are the fellies, and the wheel is single.[16]

This astronomical and calendrical correspondence is even evident if one plays the white keys of the C major scale: C, D, E, F, G, A, B, for these seven tones were understood to represent not only the seven day week, but, in Vedic tradition, the Seven Rishis or Seven Sages.[17]

The *Rig Veda* also knows and speaks of the primary "tripartation" that we discovered in connection with Angkor Wat and Vishnu's triadic self-manifestation:

> The Gods are later than this world's production,
> Who knows then whence it first came into being?[18]

That is to say, all the multiplicities of the god-notes follow upon that first tripartation.

---

[15] McClain, *The Myth of Invariance*, p. 14.
[16] *Rig Veda*, 1.164.11and 48, cited in McClain, op. cit., p. 9.
[17] McClain, op. cit, p. 15.
[18] *Rig Veda*, 10.129.6, cited in McClain, op. cit., p. 9.

But what happens, then, if we take thirds, or the powers of three, and follow those around "a circle of thirds"? The result is perplexing, for if we start again at C, and follow intervals of a major third, we get the following:

1) C
2) E
3) $G^{\#}/A^{b}$
4) C

We are far short of generating the twelve equidistant tones of the circles of fourths and fifths. In other words, the primary mathematical and musical problem faced by ancient civilizations, was how to reconcile the two "sets" of god-tones into a harmonious whole.

This leads us inevitably to a consideration of the "female" and "male" numbers of the ancient tuning systems.

C. The Male and Female Numbers and the Physical Medium

The image of the musical circle was one that haunted the Vedic literature.

> The chariot of the gods is actually a "wheel-less car... fashioned mentally" (10.135.3). The Celestial Race itself "was made by singers with their lips," and the same singers "with their mind formed horses harnessed by a word" to drive the chariot," a light car moving every way (1.20.1-3). Of the car itself, in what I assume to be an allusion to rotation and counter-rotation in the tone-circle, we hear that it "works on either side," the car-pole to which the horses are harnessed thus "turning every way" (10.102.1 and 10.135.3).[19]

In other words, the primary feature of the physical medium in view in the ancient cosmology was its *rotational frequency*, and the resulting "music" therefrom.

---

[19] McClain, *The Myth of Invariance*, pp. 10-11, references are to the *Rig Veda.*

Frequency is the key here, for it shows how and why the ancients approached the subject of tuning via whole number integers and ratios. Suppose you are sitting at the massive console of a pipe organ. Before you are five octaves on its various keyboards, beginning with the lowest note, "C" on your left. You pull an eight foot stop, say, the stop *Prinzipal*. On the stop knob there is a number 8 followed by a foot sign, thusly: 8'.[20] This means that the pipe, from the mouth to the tip, is exactly eight feet long, and will sound the note "C". Go up an octave, and the pipe will be exactly four feet long, and so on.

We thus have the ratio 8:4, which reduces to 2:1, which reduces even further, to 2. Two thus becomes the ancient number assigned to the octave of any note. It is a "female" number, and with this, occurs another problem:

> The number 2 is "female" in the sense that it creates the matrix, the octave, in which all other tones are born. By itself, however, it can only create "cycles of barrenness." In Socrates' metaphor, for multipication and division by 2 can never *introduce* new tones into our tone-mandala. In musical arithmetic, the powers of 2 $(2^{\pm n})$ generate cyclic identities; that is, they leave the musical relationship of the octave cycle invariant.[21]

Previously we saw how the primordial Nothing tripartitioned itself into Vishnu's primordial trinitarian manifestation.

McClain speaks of this same thing, and now we come to the musical application of our previous topological analysis. McClain obserfved that "the starting point of the *Rg Veda's* intentional life is the *Asat*, the non-existent, "the whole undifferentiated primordial chaos..."[22] Thus, the sexual metaphor also enters the picture:

> It is a theme of much ancient mythology that the Divine Unity is a hermaphrodite, producing a daughter, "2," by a process of division without benefit of of a mother. God is "1", but he cannot

---

[20] It should be noted that organ stops use the *imperial* and not the *metric* system of measurement!

[21] McClain, *The Myth of Invariance*, pp. 19-20.

[22] Ibid., p. 21.

preocreate except via his daughter, "2," the female principle and mother of all.[23]

But this, as we saw in our topological commentary on Angkor Wat, is not strictly true. It is not the number *two* which is first produced, but the number *three*, corresponding to the two regions of "differentiated Nothing" sharing a common surface. The common surface of the two regions becomes the topological symbol of the octave matrix, the regions defined by it.

To put it in terms of the numerical ratios that would have been used by the ancients, a primordial unity, once differentiated, gave rise to a primordial "triad," and two is the arithmetic mean between the two: $1+3=4/2=2$. In other words, our "ancient topological metaphor" is also a *musical* metaphor. The *odd* numbers are thus "male" numbers, including 1, 3, and especially 5, since these numbers, 3 and 5, generate the *differentiation* of tones within the octave "mother" or matrix.[24] In this, the "female principle was deified, but it was exclusively the male element on which the world developed and differentiated itself."[25] Thus, Plato could define a father as "'the model in whose likeness that which becomes is born.' The only fathers we need from here on are '3' and '5,' which appear to have meant in the *Rg Veda* exactly what they meant long afterward in the *Republic*."[26] The powers of three, and the multiples of three and five, define the eleven tones of our modern equally-tempered chromatic scale.[27]

But why would ancient cosmological-musical systems equate femininity with the octave, and masculinity with the differentiating process that gave rise to (tonal and topological) diversity? We are perhaps here in the presence of another clue to the degree of sophisticated scientific knowledge bequeathed as a legacy to these ancient civilizations, for as modern genetics now knows, females carry only the female sexual chromosome, but males carry *both* sexual chromosomes and are capable of biologically reproducing either a

---

[23] McClain, *The Myth of Invariance*, p. 21.

[24] Ibid., p. 24.

[25] Ibid., p. 25.

[26] Ibid.

[27] Ibid., pp. 25, 13.

male or female offspring. There is, as it were, a kind of inbuilt androgyny to the male that does not exist in the female. This might account for the assignation of "maleness" to those arithmetic ratios of odd numbers that produced *differentiation* in the generation of musical tones.

Why give such prominence to the "male" numbers? And what other numbers do they generate. Again, the answer is cosmological in nature:

> The male odd numbers take precedence over their female octave "doubles" not only because they lie closed to god = 1, but presumably because they permit the divine unity to be subdivided rigorously according to the principle of unity; if we limit generative ratios, as Greek musical theory did traditionally, to those between two consecutive intergers... then each odd number (oddness itself being due to an element of unity) functions as the arithmetic mean for an earlier superparticular ratio, and subdivides it according to the same principle. We can schematize this subdivision as follows:

1				2
2		3		4
4	5	6	7	8
8	9	10^{28}		

Note carefully the *implications* of this musical-topological metaphor, for clearly, it is not impaled on the horns of the either-or dialectic of having to choose between "pure monotheism" — a "feminine" principle in terms of the ancient worldview — nor a "pure polytheism", or "masculine" principle in terms of the ancient worldview. The metaphor is an acid drip on that conventional opposition, for what one is looking at is an "androgynous both-and," one encompassing both unity and diversity, and attempting to relate the two in a carefully conceived topological and musical metaphor.

The musical metaphor of the circles also lies behind the "churning of the Milky Sea", for the diversity of the universe, as we saw at Angkor Wat, arises from the tension created by Vishnu's original "tripartation" or differentiation. Rotation, understood in

---

[28] McClain, *The Myth of Invariance*, p. 24.

musical terms, in the terms of *frequencies*, is the key.[29] It goes without saying that *spin* and rotation moment are crucial concepts in distinguishing sub-atomic particles; thus as we shall see in chapter 13, there may be even deeper meanings to these ancient metaphors. There is even a dimension of Vedic teaching which relates all this cosmological topology and music to consciousness itself, for Soma, the magical food and drink of the gods that confers expanded consciousness, does so first of all by bringing insight into the musical experience as being comprised of the theory of numbers.[30]

From the musical point of view, however, the Vedic philosophy never completely reconciled the two cycles arising from unity, namely, the cycle of thirds, and the cycle of fifths. To put it differently, it never completely integrated the "female" octave with the "male" notes *within* that octave, and thus, any number of types of scales could be generated, all of which were, from the Vedic cosmological standpoint, equally valid.[31] The task of effecting that union and taking the first steps to our modern system of "equal tempering" or tuning was taken in Mesopotamia, and with its sexagesimal system of arithmetic.

D. *The Sexagesimal System, Music, and Cosmology*

It was in fact the famous Sumerologist Samuel Noah Kramer who located the fabled Sumerian "land of the gods," Dilmun, with the "Harappan culture of pre-Vedic India."[32] By the time of the high Mesopotamian cultures, however, Vedic mathematical prowess had grown to enormous sophistication.

> It is startling to learn...that the art of calculation in the third millenium (sic) Babylon — before the time of Abraham — was already comparable in many aspects with the mathematics "of the early Renaissance," thirty-odd centuries later. Computation was made easy by the possession of tables (of which we have many copies) of "reciprocals, multiplications, squares and square roots, cubes, and cube roots, the sums of squares and cubes...

[29] McClain, *The Myth of Invariance*, p. 22.
[30] Ibid., p. 49.
[31] Ibid., p. 53,
[32] Ibid., p. 129.

exponential functions, coefficients giving numbers for practical computation... and numerous metrological calculations giving areas of rectangles, circles," etc. The Pythagoran theorem was known in Babylon "more than a thousand years before Pythagoras." The foundations were laid for the discovery of the irrationality of √2 "exactly in the same arithmetical form in which it was obviously re-discovered so much later by the Greeks." Traditional stories of discoveries made by Thales or Pythagoras must be discarded as "totally unhistorical"; much of what we have thought was Pythagorean must now be credited to Babylon.[33]

The implications, for McClain, are enormous, for this means that

> The Hebrew Bible is thus the product of a Semitic culture which had mastered the fundamentals of music and mathematics a thousand years and more before its oldest pages were written. The stage was set for mathematical allegory on a grander scale than the relatively late Christian civilization has ever realized.[34]

Indeed, as will be seen, the Hebrew version of this mathematical and musical metaphor constitutes a step of trying to *edit and invert* the inherited Mesopotamian musical and mathematical metaphors of the "god of the mountain."

In this musical mathematical allegory, McClain notes that its sexagesimal system of whole number integers was "probably the most convenient language for acoustical arithmetic the world ever knew" until the rise of logarithmic computation introduced in the nineteenth century of our era.[35] Here we must also pause to note something that was observed in the previous book in this series, *Genes, Giants, Monsters, and Men,* namely, that the ancient systems of measures, and in particular, the Sumerian sexagesimal system, were also based *on astronomical and geodetic measures,*[36] in other words, one is not only looking at a musical system of numbering, but on a

---

[33] McClain, *The Myth of Invariance,* p. 130, citing Otto Neugebauer, *The Exact Sciences in Antiquity,* (New York: Dover Publications, Inc., 1969), p. 48, and Samuel Noah Kramer, *The Sumerians,* (Chicago: The University of Chicago Press, 1963), p. 291, and Neugebauer, op. cit., p. 36, respectively.

[34] Ibid., p. 130.

[35] Ibid., p. 131.

[36] Farrell, *Genes, Giants, Monsters, and Men* (Feral House, 2011), ch. 2, pp. 55-89.

cosmological and geodetic one. Quite literally, the three cannot be disentangled; one is literally looking at the music of the planets, the music of the medium itself. The musical advantage is that it allows one to retain the uses of the "female" even numbers generating the octave matrix and the male numbers, based on powers and multiples of 3 and 5, generating the rest of the twelve tones, as in the ratio 30:60, a ratio that is based on multiples of 2, 5 and 6. Note also that the ratio can be reduced to 3:6, which can be reduced to the female number of 2; and that 60:5 is, of course, 12, giving the 12 tones of the chromatic scale, and, for the Mesopotamians, the 12 houses of the Zodiac. Succinctly stated, it is in the sexagesimal system that cosmology, music, number theory, and physics all meet in a harmonious whole.[37]

But what of the "gods" themselves, and our formula "Mountains ≈ Planets ≈ Gods ≈ Pyramids ≈ Music?" Why did the gods become associated with mountains and music?

It so happens that within Mesopotamia numerological mythology, that the three principle gods, Ea-Enki, Enlil, and Anu, are all numerically, and therefore, musically related, Ea-Enki having the value of 40, Enlil the value of 50, and Anu the value of 60, which, in the sexagesimal system, is also representative of the primordial unity, or 1. In musical terms, if one assigns a fundamental tone — say in this case, the note D — to An, then Enlil represents a third up or down from that (f or b), and Ea-Enki a fourth down or up (A or G), and from Enki, then, the entire circle of fourths and therefore all twelve tones, would be generated.[38] Note that the ratio of these three gods is 40:50:60, or 4:5:6. From them, the whole modern twelve-note chromatic "tonal universe" is generated, as in our circle of fourths example above.[39]

---

[37] McClain, *The Myth of Invariance*, p. 131. It should be pointed out that we are, of course, massively compressing a great deal of numerical argumentation, and that, strictly speaking, the use of our modern chromatic scale is made for the ease of illustration, and that it is not, strictly speaking, an accurate representation of the subtlety of McClain's analysis of the ancient musical system, especially in the case of Mesopotamia. It nonetheless follows from McClain's argument that Mesopotamia was at least familiar *in theory* with our modern system of equal tempering of musical instruments.

[38] Ibid., p. 132.

[39] Ibid., p. 133.

If all this seems dense and obscure, it's about to become even more so, for in the ultimate example of the "unified intention of symbol," the numerical-musical allegory is reproduced in Berossus' version of the Kings' List of kings before the Flood:

King	Reign	Division by $60^2=3600$
Aloros	36,000	10
Alaparos	10,800	3
Amelon	46,800	13
Ammenon	43,200	12
Megalaros	64,800	18
Daonos	36,000	10
Euedoraches	64,800	18
Amempsinos	36,000	10
Opartes	28,800	8
Xisuthros	64,800	18
Total	432,000	120[40]

Note that the total, when divided by the quintessential Mesopotamian sexagesimal number of 3600, is 120, a harmonic of 12, our twelve chromatic tones once again.

In order to understand how all this relates to our musical tone circles, we have to look closer at Ea-Enki, whose numerological value is 40. To understand *how* this is so, it is important to remember that every whole number, when viewed *musically*, is viewed *in some ratio to the number sixty*, but the Mesopotamians do not actually *write* that second number. Thus, Enki's number, 40, is really the ratio 40:60, or 2:3, an essential musical relationship in generating the twelve tones, for as such, he is the "first born son" of Anu, that is, "the first odd, hence male integer."[41] As god of the "sweetwaters," Enki is also "the Sumerian counterpart to the Greek Poseidon" and thus intricately related to the myth of Atlantis.[42]

---

[40] McClain, *The Myth of Invariance*, p. 138.
[41] Ibid., p. 143.
[42] Ibid.

E. Music and Higher-Dimensional Geometries: The Musical Gods of the Musical Mountains

Enki, with 2:3 as his numbers, thus is a metaphor for the powers and multiples of 3 and 5, and here we come to the crux of the matter, for when these powers are graphed, a "numerical mountain" results, which we have followed by showing McClain's graph of the "irreducible" integers and the tonal "zigurrats," as McClain calls them, or mountains that result.

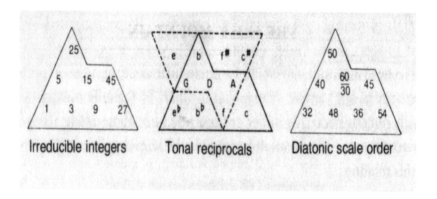

Irreducible integers   Tonal reciprocals   Diatonic scale order

McClain's "Tonal Zigurrats"[43]

---

[43] McClain, *The Myth of Invariance*, p. 51.

Similarly, Enlil, whose number is 50, that is to say, 50:60 in the Mesopotamian scheme of ratios, and Marduk, laying at 25, both generated their own numerical tonal mountains.

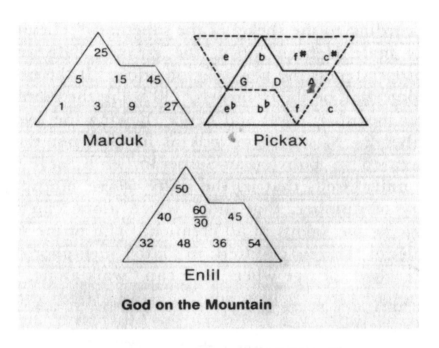

God on the Mountain

McClain's Babylonian Gods of the Mountain[44]

Note the "Pickax" form of tones and their reciprocals (represented by the dotted "upside down 'mountain'"), for if one does a rotation of that mountain on its side so that the numbers on Marduk's Mountain, which represent the tones generated in the pickax, can a common shared generating point in the number one, we get this:

---

[44] McClain, *The Myth of Invariance*, p. 141.

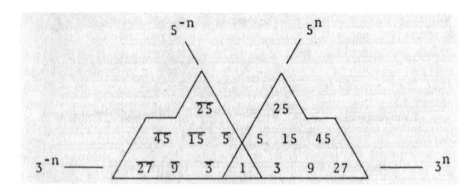

McClain's Diagram of Twin-Peaked Mt. Mashu[45]

Note that on the horizontal line extending in each direction we have the initial unity, its first "tripartation" represented by 3 and 5 on the horizontal and diagonal, and on the horizontal, powers of three extending into infinity, and on the diagonal, powers of 5 extending into infinity, and between them, multiples of 3 and 5.

If we overlay the extended version of these tonal mountains over each other, we obtain an analogue of a familiar, and very Babylonian, figure, the "Star of David:"

---

[45] McClain, *The Myth of Invariance*, p. 144.

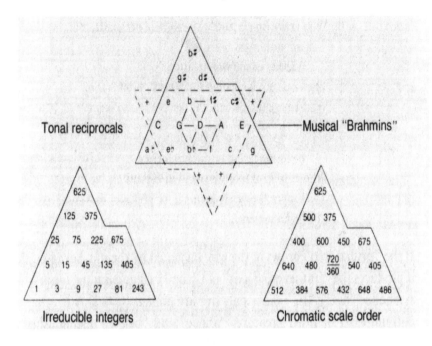

Musical Brahmins and Babylonian "Star of David"[46]

The significance of all this is that music and its mathematical codes, in McClain's view, played an inevitable role in the emergence of monotheism:

> Monotheism took as its God not the Great God 60(actually written in Babylonian-Sumerian as a large ONE), but the irreducible unity itself, that is, the unity whose multiplicity creates all the diversity of number, that unity which alone can subdivide prime numbers, the active agents of all creation.[47]

And of these, as we see from the previous page, the numbers 3 and 5 are the first two and most important prime numbers in the musical metaphor.

In other words, the ancient mathematicians performed what geometers would call a *rotation,* revealing a connection to another metaphorical mountain, the sacred tectratys of Pythagoreanism:

---

[46] McClain, *The Myth of Invariance*, p. 143.
[47] Ibid., p. 142.

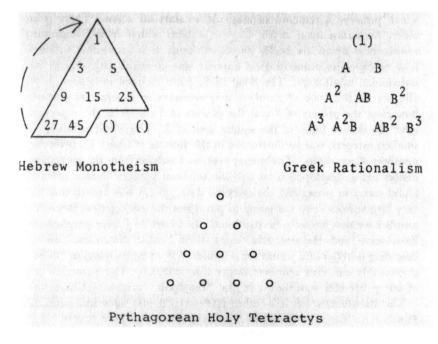

Hebrew Monotheism   Greek Rationalism

Pythagorean Holy Tetractys

McClain's Musical Evolution of Monotheism[48]

We will reserve comment on all the esoteric and physical principles embodied in the Pythagorean tectratys for chapter twelve. For now, it should be noted that, like the musical circle of tones itself, we have returned to that musical-topological metaphor that began the process we discovered at Angkor Wat, but now the metaphor has taken on an added richness, for specific numerical and musical functions have now been ascribed to the original primary "tripartition" or differentiation.

---

[48] McClain, *The Myth of Invariance*, p. 145.

248

The Grid of the Gods

1. Babylonian and Hebrew Flood Chronologies

There is another backdrop against which the ancient physics of the grid must be viewed, and that is the Platonic allegory of Atlantis and of the Flood itself, an account that McClain, with much humor and accuracy, says is a "kind of Pythagorean Grand Opera, complete with an all-star cast, a water show, dazzling scenery, and a tragic finale."[49] Yet, even here one finds that there are codes within the texts.

For example, there are hidden correspondences between the Hebrew and Babylonian chronologies of the Flood, correspondences that point to deeper numerical codes. McClain observes that the famous scholar of comparative mythologies, Joseph Campbell,

> ... discovered a correlation between the 432,000 years from the creation to the flood in Babylonian mythology and the 1,656 years from the creation of Adam to the flood in the Hebrew account. Campbell points out that these numbers have a common factor of 72, and that 1656/72 is 23. Now 23 Jewish years of 365 days plus five extra days for leap years equals 8,400 days or 1,200 seven-day weeks; multiplying by 72 to find the number of Jewish seven-day weeks in 1,656 (= 23 x 72) years yields 86,400 (1200 x 72). But the number 86,400 is 432,000/5, i.e., the number of Babylonian five-day weeks to the flood. Thus there is *no necessary contradiction* whatever in these different flood chronologies.[50]

To put it differently, it is possible that the standard views of conservative biblical scholars as to the relative recentness of the Deluge are thrown into a cocked hat, and that the actual meaning of the biblical numerical codes is that the Deluge occurred much farther back in time, in a context or chronological framework commensurate with its antiquity in Mesopotamian myths.

2. Babylonian Mathematics: Clues to a Higher-Dimensional Physics?

In this context, a closer look at the sexagesimal system of ancient Sumer and Babylon are in order, for as has been seen, various

---

[49] Ernest G. McClain, *The Myth of Invariance*, p. 163
[50] Ibid., p. 150, emphasis in the original.

numbers are ascribed to various gods in the pantheon. But there is another clue in Mesopotamian numbers, a clue that, oddly, resembles the modern numerical notations for higher-dimensional geometric objects: "In the sexagesimal system, 450,000 would be written as 2,5, meaning $2 \times 60^3 + (5 \times 60^2)$, perhaps a pun on Marduk $= 25$."[51] Note that in this system of notation, each number in {2,5} stands for that number in connection with some function that is a power of 60. One can, notes McClain, have a series of such numbers, such as {8,0,0} and so on.[52]

It is important to note what this notation means, for cubing and squaring a number — e.g. x^3 and x^2 — are, of course, *geometrical functions describing objects in two or three spatial dimensions*. Thus, the notation {2,5} mentioned above could be written this way more abstractly as {x, y}, and since the first number is multiplied by the cubic power of 60, and the second by the squared power of 60, the notation really would look like this:

$$\{(x \cdot 60^3) + (y \cdot 60^2)\} = n.$$

We can therefore imagine *extending* this notation to {x,y,z}, and extending the powers of 60 with which each number is multiplied, e.g. $\{(x \cdot 60^4) + (y \cdot 60^3) + (z \cdot 60^2)\}$; in other words, notations such as {8,0,0}, which are also within the realm of possibility in ancient Mesopotamian notation, conceivably may be understood as representing powers of 60 *greater* than the cubic, that is to say, as geometric and numerical representations of objects in *four* or more dimensions.

To state it as succinctly as possible, the very structure of ancient Mesopotamian numerical notation implies a basic familiarity with hyper-dimensional geometries and the basic mathematical techniques for describing objects in four or more spatial dimensions. Indeed, as we shall discover in chapter 13, *the exact same notation convention began to*

---

[51] McClain, *The Myth of Invariance*, p. 147.
[52] Ibid.

be used in nineteenth century geometrical techniques for describing objects in four or more dimensions.[53]

This contains a further, and very suggestive, implication, for it is to be noted that the Sumerian-Babylonian gods may be described by such notation. In other words, *the gods were being described peculiar union of physics and religion, as hyper-dimensional entities or objects.*[54] This new twist upon the "unified intention of symbol" we will encounter again in the next part of this book in conjunction with the Egyptian interpretation of this paleophysics of the physical medium, and its conjunction with religious cosmology. It is, however, a heritage that we have discovered is common to ancient Vedic India as well as Mesopotamia, and we have encountered suggestive parallels between Mesopotamian myths and those of Meso-America. It was, to paraphrase McClain, in India, Mesopotamia, Egypt and even Meso-America, that one is able "to watch the birth of the gods in the minds of musical poets and discover that continuity of tradition which maintains a perfect unity between music, mathematics, and metaphysics."[55] With Plato, the final step was taken, as the physics of the celestial harmonies and the gods was transformed into a technique of social engineering and political theory.[56] The ancient classical world had, in other words, moved quickly to outline all the implications of this musico-physical-metaphysical legacy that it had inherited, even though it may not have fully understood those implications, nor raised the technology to match in deed what its mythologies recorded.

3. Mesopotamian Music and the Fine Structure Constant

But does all this musical numerology actually contain any clue that the ancients were passing on a legacy that contained within it the seeds of a lost knowledge of a much deeper physics?

---

[53] The modern name for such notations is Schläfli numbers, and their appearance in notation is identical, with each number representing a particular type of geometric function. This will be explored further in chapter 13.

[54] McClain also observes that the Egyptian god of wisdom, Thoth, is also a sigil for various musical-numerical scales and harmonics; q.v. McClain, *The Myth of Invariance,* pp. 184-185.

[55] Ibid., p. 158.

[56] Ibid., p. 161.

There is indeed one such clue, and it's a whopper.

The Greeks, as noted above, inherited this musical-metaphysical legacy from Plato, who in turn gained it from the Pythagoreans and Mesopotamia. One may also point out that Plato was clear — in his "Atlantean dialogues," the *Timeus* and *Critias* — that there was also an Egyptian influence at work. All this was in turn encoded by Plato in many dialogues as a political theory, as a *means of social engineering.* Various "cities" are worked out — including Atlantis and Athens — along different numerical lines. In these attempts to divine the musical proportions of the "best" city, Plato proposes the city Callipolis, his

'absolutely best' city — his 'celestial city,' the *diatonic* scale sung by the Sirens in his planetary model — seven numbers required for the diatonic scale produce all eleven tones.

	384	432	486	512	576	648	729	768
rising	D	E	F#	G	A	B	C#	D
Falling	D	C	Bb	A	G	F	Eb	D[57]

McClain observes that within this octave-numerical scheme, that the largest "genetic element is 3^6, or 729.[58]

That number — 729 — may be one of the most significant in all of physics, for it is the decimal coefficient of the Fine Structure Constant, typically given a fractional value of 1/137 and usually denoted, coincidentally, and perhaps ironically enough, by the Greek letter alpha, α, for when one carries out the function of dividing 1 by 137, the result is .00729927007, an approximate harmonic of 729.[59]

Of course, the presence of only one occurrence of this coefficient does not mean that the Greeks — or for that matter those from whom they inherited their knowledge — were aware of this significance of this number. But as we shall discover in the next section on Egypt, there is strong and suggestive evidence that whatever Very High Civilization as preceded those cultures of the classic era(i.e., the Vedic, Mesopotamian, Egyptian and Greek

[57] McClain, *The Myth of Invariance*, p. 171.
[58] Ibid.
[59] For further speculations involving the fine structure constant, see *The Giza Death Star Deployed*, pp. 259-262.

civilizations), that civilization *did* know of the existence of these and other constants of modern physical mechanics, millennia before their (re-)discovery in our own era.

Why would the preservation of the numerical value of the fine structure constant, particularly in a musical-political context, be so significant? The answer lies in the deeply mysterious nature of the constant itself. First discovered in 1916 by physicist Arnold Sommerfeld, the constant is essentially a *dimensionless* constant — effectively, a scalar in mathematical terms, or a "pure magnitude" — possessing the same value in all systems or units of measure, and measuring the strength of electromagnetic coupling. But the problem is, while the constant "fits" the rest of physics like a glove, its own origins are so unique and inscrutable that it has puzzled physicists ever since. No less a physicist than Feynmann felt compelled to comment on its almost mystical nature and attraction for physicists ever since its first discovery:

> It has been a mystery since it was discovered more than fifty years ago, and all good theoretical physicists put this number[60] up on their wall and worry about it. Immediately you would like to know where this number for a coupling comes from; is it related to π or perhaps to the base of natural logarithms? Nobody knows. It's one of the greatest damn mysteries of physics: a magic number that comes to us with no understanding by man. You might say the "hand of God" wrote that number, and "we don't know how He pushed his pencil." We know what kind of a dance to do experimentally to measure this number very accurately, but we don't know what kind of dance to do with the computer to make this number come out, without putting it in secretly![61]

In other words, unlike most of the constants of physics, mathematics, and geometry, the Fine Structure Constant's relationship to geometrical functions was obscure. It explained a lot, but its own

---

[60] "This number," i.e., 137.

[61] Richard Feynmann, cited Peter Varlacki, Laszlo Nadai, Jozsef Bokor, "Number Archetypes and 'Background' Control Theory Concerning the Fine Structure Constant," *Acta Polytechnica Hungarica*, Vol. 5, No 2, 2008, 71-104, pp. 74-75.

basis remained obscure, unless one remembers the musical context in which it occurs in Plato.

The presence of this decimal basis of the coefficient of a constant of physics only discovered in the early twentieth century in writings that antedate it by over two thousand years suggests that its presence in those writings might be a legacy from High Antiquity, and a very sophisticated civilization.

One lone coefficient squatting otherwise anachronistically in an ancient text does not, however, constitute a case. If one were to encounter similar coefficients of quantum mechanics in decidedly ancient contexts, the case would become more solid, and the indicators that at least some of the structures of the world grid constituted parts or "gears" in a vast global hyper-dimensional machine, would become stronger.

Not surprisingly, one can find precisely such things at the center of the machine, at Giza, and in even older structures buried and only recently rediscovered in the deserts of Egypt.

PART FOUR:
THE PREMIER "PYRAMID PEOPLES," THE EGYPTIANS

"How does a complex civilization spring full-blown into being? Look at a 1905 automobile and compare it to a modern one. There is no mistaking the process of 'development'. But in Egypt there are no parallels. Everything is there right at the start. The answer to the mystery is of course obvious, but because it is repellent to the prevailing cast of modern thinking, it is seldom seriously considered. Egyptian civilization was not a 'development', it was a legacy."

"The implications of this alternative are obvious. If the coherent, complete and interrelated system of science, religion, art and philosophy of Egypt was not developed by the Egyptians but inherited (and perhaps reformulated and redesigned to suit their needs), that system came from a prior civilisation possessing a high order of knowledge. In other words, this alternative brings up the old question of 'Atlantis'."
John Anthony West,
The Serpent in the Sky, pp. 13, 197, emphasis added.

10

ALCHEMICAL COSMOLOGY AND QUANTUM MECHANICS IN STONE: THE MYSTERIOUS MEGALITH OF NABTA PLAYA

"...the history of science, like all other forms of history, is written by the winners. Thus, very few know that in the 17th century, an intellectual battle between supporters of the Hermetic Tradition and those of the school that would eventually produce our rationalistic, materialistic philosophy very nearly fell to the Hermeticists. Had they prevailed, we would most certainly still have an advanced science today, but it would look and 'feel' very different."

John Anthony West[1]

Approximately one hundred miles to the west of the great Nile River dam at Aswan, in the middle of nowhere in the Egyptian desert, one finds an "Egyptian Stonehenge" at a remote location called Nabta Playa. Discovered in 1973 by Fred Wendorf and his archaeological team, the site was soon excavated,[2] and with it, an almost inconceivable mystery was unearthed, for according to the astronomer Thomas G. Brophy, who undertook the most extensive examination of the structure's encoded physics, "a people living over seven thousand years ago may have possessed technical knowledge in astronomy and physics more advanced than our current understandings of the same subjects."[3]

As of this juncture, though it is difficult to say whether or not this site lies on a significant "grid" point, the site nonetheless commands our attention precisely because of the knowledge it demonstrates concerning advanced physics and astronomical knowledge it displays. There are, according to Brophy, at least three levels of sophistication involved in this ancient megalithic structure, the last two of which comprise the most serious difficulties for the standard academic models of history:

---

[1] John Anthony West, "Afterword," in Thomas G. Brophy, Ph.D., *The Origin Map: Discovery of a Prehistoric, Megalithic, Astrophysical Map and Sculpture of the Universe* (New York: Writers Club Press, 2002), p. 119.

[2] Thomas G. Brophy, Ph.D., *The Origin Map*, p. 1.

[3] Robert M. Schoch, Ph.D., "Foreword," Ibid., p. xiii.

1) Maps and markers denoting objects, alignments, and events that can be observed in the sky with the unaided (naked) eye.
2) Markers indicating celestial phenomena and events that cannot be observed (apparently) with the unaided eye.
3) Detailed astronomical and cosmological information, such as distances to stars, speeds at which stars are moving away from us, the structure of our galaxy (The Milky Way), and information on the origin of the universe, which we have either only just discovered in modern times, or possibly information (for example, concerning planetary systems around stars) that we do not even have available to us at the moment.[4]

Even worse for the standard academic models of history, all of this is positioned within a site whose astronomical alignments last occurred ca. 16,500 BC![5]

This is a significant point, for it corroborates ancient Egypt's own legends and historical records — Manetho among them — that its civilization is of much greater antiquity than standard academic historiography will allow, and it also corroborates the ancient Egyptians' view that theirs was a *legacy* civilization.

But this is not the only problem posed by the Nabta Playa megaliths, for they are intimately tied to that most famous site associated with Egypt: Giza, for *both* Nabta Playa, and Giza, have alignments pointing to the Galactic center, and in Giza's case, this alignment to the Galactic center occurred in 10,909 BC.[6] In Nabta Playa's case, argues Brophy, we are looking at a literal, and very sophisticated, "cosmology in stone."[7]

A. Celestial Alignments at Nabta Playa

One need only look at the celestial alignments Brophy detected at Nabta Playa to see how intricate and complex the megaliths there really are.

---

[4] Robert M. Schoch, Ph.D., "Foreword," Ibid., p. xiv.
[5] Ibid., p. xv.
[6] Ibid., p. xviii.
[7] Ibid., p. xxiii.

In its basic form, the Nabta Playa site is a circle of stone slabs — a "calendar" circle — similar to many other such sites in Europe and South America, and is of obvious antiquity. This "calendar circle"

> consists of an outer rim of sandstone slabs with four sets of larger gate stones that form two (lines) of sight "windows" in the calendar circle. Inside the circle are six larger stones. The largest of the slabs are almost three feet long, and the smallest are slight less than a foot. The circle is ten to eleven feet across.[8]

However, in addition to this, it was eventually discovered that the site possesses *two further subterranean* levels buried beneath the earth,[9] thus making the entire site a complex three-dimensional object that, as will be shown, exhibits an extraordinary degree of knowledge and deliberation in the way it was constructed.

1. The Celestial Alignments

The complex sophistication of the knowledge and deliberation that went into the construction of Nabta Playa is evident in the first level of the site, the surface "circle" itself, for there are a host of astronomical alignments and other celestial features encoded in the structure. The first, and most obvious, of these alignments also immediately confronts one with an anomaly:

> Three of those central six stones are a diagram of the constellation of Orion's Belt as it appeared on the meridian around summer solstice from 6,400 BC to 4,900 BC. The "meridian" is simply the line in the sky that passes north to south, and is thus the midway line or "meridian" across which stars pass in their nightly travels from rising in the east to setting in the west. Thus the inside of the calendar circle had a clear use as a star-viewing diagram.[10]

Therein lies the anomaly, and it is a somewhat anachronistic one, for as most people are aware, the Egyptian religion was fixated upon the constellation Orion and evolved a complex mythology of death and

---

[8] Thomas G. Brophy, Ph.D., p. 7.
[9] Ibid., p. 49.
[10] Ibid., p. 9.

resurrection fastened around the gods Osiris, Set, Isis, and Horus. The constellation became, for them, a veritable seal of the concept of Osiris' resurrection. The six megaliths in the center of the Nabta Playa circle were, when compared with reliable modern astronomical star charts, clearly meant to represent the six stars of Orion: Alnitak, Alnilam, Mintaka, Betelgeuse, Bellatrix, and Meissa.[11]

So what is a structure doing in the Egyptian desert that antedates the oldest Egyptian structures, and the Egyptian religion, itself? Or to put it differently: why the fixation on Orion?

To make the chronological anachronism and anomaly very much worse, Brophy soon discovered that there were *earlier* alignments encoded within the calendar circle. Three of the stones, as was noted, pointed to alignments ca. 4,900 to 6,400 BC. But there was a problem with the other three:

> The apparent significance of the other three central stones in the calendar circle is more difficult to reconcile with prevalent assumptions about prehistory. These other three stones are a diagram of the configuration of Orion's head and shoulders as they appeared on the meridian on summer solstice sunset in the centuries around 16,500 BC. That date is symmetrically opposite the 5,000 BC congruence of the Orion's Belt stars, in terms of the precession of the equinoxes, and both dates are at the extremes (maximum and minimum) of the tilt angle of the Orion constellation. *Thus the stone diagram illustrates the time, location, and tilting behavior of the constellation of Orion through the 25,900 year equinox precession cycle, and how to understand the pattern visually.*[12]

Lest one be tempted to use this earlier alignment as a means to date the structure, Nabta Playa has surprises in store, for it is a clear example of a *younger site clearly encoding alignments that antedate its construction by several thousands of years:*

> The case for the southern three stones in the diagram is also strong, but it is troubling to some investigators because there is no evidence yet of activity circa 16,000 BC at Nabta Playa, and the calendar circle couldn't be that old because it sets on younger

---

[11] Thomas G. Brophy, *The Origina Map*, p. 25.
[12] Ibid., p. 10, emphasis added.

sediments, and there is bias against the idea that ancient people could have known that the constellations change tilt long term due to the precession of the equinoxes.[13]

In other words, someone in pre-dynastic times in Egypt had accurate knowledge of the precession of the equinoxes and had encoded the entire cycle within the calendar circle.

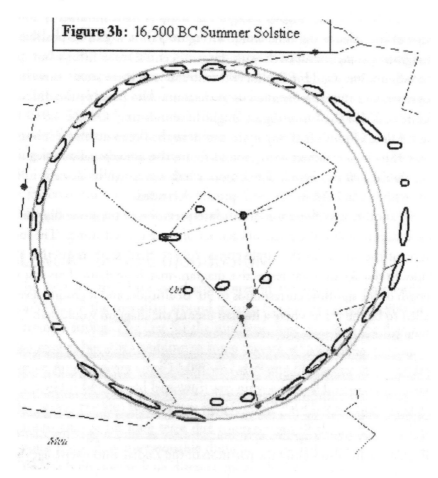

Figure 3b: 16,500 BC Summer Solstice

Brophy's Chart of the 16,500BC Summer Solsticial Alignment[14]

---

[13] Thomas G. Brophy, Ph.D., *The Origin Map*, p. 19.

[14] Ibid., p. 17. There is further discussion of the astronomical basis of these alignments on pp. 27, 29-35 in conjunction with declinations and ascensions.

None of this, however, was beyond the ability of primitive peoples either to observe or to enshrine in structures with their primitive technology:

> ...(It) should not be assumed that ancient sky watchers could not determine geometrical heliacal risings, even without the use of technology or mathematics, if they wanted to. An astute observer would simply watch the rising of the star for several days during the year while the star's rise was clearly visible. If the ancient sky watcher knew when vernal equinox was, he would simply extrapolate the star rise time of day to vernal equinox and determine if it would be a geometrical heliacal rising. That is a very achievable feat for an accomplished ancient megalithic astronomer even without technology or mathematics.
>
> Thus so far in this analysis of the Nabta megalithic astronomy these alignments could possibly have been designed by ancient peoples with the usually assumed low level of Stone Age technology. The designers displayed astonishing elegance and clarity, but plausibly they could have done it with primitive technology.[15]

But this easy explanation collapsed when Brophy then turned to deeper and closer analyses of the calendar circle.

One of the first clues that suggested to him that he was dealing with a structure requiring far more knowledge and sophistication than merely Stone Age technology was when he compared the analogues of *distances* between the stones in the circle that represented stars, and their modern astronomical measures, incorporating standard errors. The result? The measures of the Nabta Playa circle, when compared with modern astronomical measures, were astonishingly accurate.

> This is the first very important result of this analysis of the Nabta Playa megalith map. Star distances are difficult to measure. Modern science's best estimates of star distances, based on astrophysical

---

Brophy notes that the statistical probabilities for these alignments exceeds normal requirements for scientific hypothesis on p. 38.

[15] Thomas G. Brophy, Ph.D., *The Origin Map*, pp. 38-39. See also my *Genes, Giants, Mopnsters, and Men* (Feral House, 2011), pp. 55-89.

models of star evolution, were very erroneous until recently. Only with the launcing of the Hipparcos satellite observatory, above the atmosphere, have we been able to directly measure parallaxes (parallaxes are the different angles measured to a star as the Earth travels around the Sun) and achieve somewhat accurate star distances. If these star distances are the intended meaning of the Nabta Playa map, and are not coincidence, then much of what we think we know about prehistoric human civilizations must be revised. Further study of the Nabta Playa megalith map proves that this is in fact not coincidence.[16]

Behind Brophy's carefully chosen words is the extraordinary implication that such distances could *not* have been observed nor computed accurately by the naked eye or by means of Stone Age technology. By the nature of the case, they required *sophisticated technologies and mathematical techniques.*

Just how sophisticated was revealed to Brophy when, extending his analysis not only to star distance but to radial velocities, a new level of complexity was revealed (and remember, we are still only dealing with the surface structure; we have yet to encounter the truly astonishing things *buried* at Nabta Playa!). Observing that the placement of the megaliths in the northern half of the circle "indicate velocities" of stars receding from the Earth,[17] Brophy then makes a series of observations, each of which is massively disturbing to the conventional academic views of prehistory:

> In the Nabta megalith map so far, one megalith in each southern alignment represents the physical distance to that star, and one megalith in each corresponding northern alignment represents the radial velocity of that star. Also, each corresponding northern and southern pair of megalith alignments contain the same respective numbers of megaliths.
>
> ...
>
> If we continue to look at the site as an astrophysical map, and note that each alignment has one primary stone representing the primary star plus secondary stones, the obvious question to

---

[16] Thomas G. Brophy, Ph.D., pp. 42-43.
[17] Ibid., p. 45.

consider is whether the other megaliths in each line may represent *planets or secondary "companion" stars to the primary star.*

This hypothesis cannot yet be tested against observations because modern astronomers are not yet able to observe the planetary and companion systems of these stars. Extrasolar planet detection techniques are proceeding rapidly apace though and some day soon we may be able to observe these systems.[18]

However, we **can** test the physics of this hypothesis. If the hypothesis does apply to the stones, then the megaliths must be placed according to the astrophysical laws of planetary motion.[19]

In other words, Brophy proposed to "reverse engineer" the site according to the principles of standard celestial mechanics, in order "to test what astrophysical principles might have been used" to construct the site.[20]

When this was done, the physics of orbital dynamics were not only entirely consistent "with the dynamics or orbital motion," but the accuracy was better than many modern experiments. Brophy records his own astonishment at this result:

> Readers who have worked with actual scientific or engineering data will appreciate that I was nearly floored when I saw (the data) plot. Remember these megalith location markers are actual data from the site, constructed seven thousand years ago or longer, and they fit the physical theory better than many good modern experiments fit their theory the first time.[21]

In other words, one was not dealing merely with megalithic technology or techniques; whoever built the site was relying at some point and to some degree on a sophisticated knowledge of physics, knowledge that could only have predated the site's builders, and been handed down to them.

---

[18] In fact, since Brophy wrote those words, a number of planets orbiting distant stars have in fact been observed.

[19] Thomas G. Brophy, Ph.D., *The Origin Map*, pp. 45-46, italicized emphasis added, boldface emphasis in the original.

[20] Ibid., p. 46.

[21] IBid., p. 48.

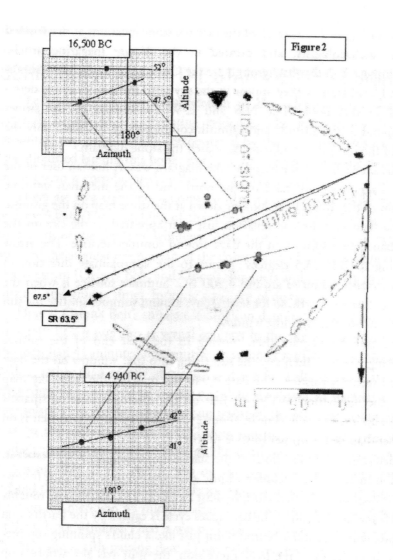

Brophy's Chart of the 16,500 BC and 4,940 BC Alignments[22]

---

[22] Thomas G. Brophy, Ph.D., *The Origin Map*, p. 11.

2. The Subterranean Structures and the Cosmological Meaning

We have already observed that the Nabta Playa site is a *three* dimensional structure, having subterranean layers or levels. These archaeology could not interpret along the lines of its usual, worn-out "tombs and religion" paradigm, and after digging around them hoping to find "bones and grave goods" but failing to do so, simply dubbed these subterranean megaliths as "complex structures."[23] These are more accurately "sculptures *carved onto the bedrock* 8 to 12 feet beneath the surface."[24]

One of these, dubbed by archaeologists Complex Structure A, contains a surface carving of an analogue of the entire Milky Way Galaxy.[25] That's not all:

> The Sagittarius Dwarf Galaxy, a recently discovered small satellite galaxy to our Milky Way may even be represented in the correct place on the sculpture as are the galactic spiral arms. In fact recent astrophysical analysis of the shape and location of the Sagittarius Dwarf Galaxy indicates that it more closely fits the Nabta sculpture representation than the Electronic Sky drawing... in *Monthly Notices of the Royal Astronomical Society.*[26]

Again, one must understand that this means no merely megalithic culture could have sculpted such a diagram without having access to refined and sophisticated scientific knowledge, knowledge that required for its very basis access to technologies commensurate with those possessed today.

Before proceeding further, a look at Brophy's sketches of Complex Structure A is in order.

---

[23] Thomas G. Brophy, Ph.D., *The Origin Map*, p. 49.
[24] Ibid., emphasis in the original.
[25] Ibid., pp. 50-51.
[26] Ibid., pp. 53-54.

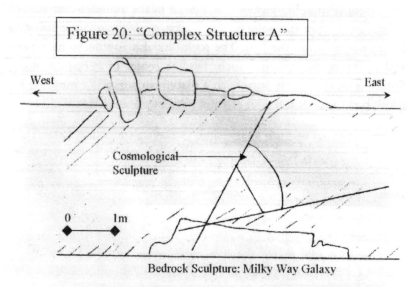

Brophy's Diagram of the Subterranean Complex Structure A, Looking West[27]

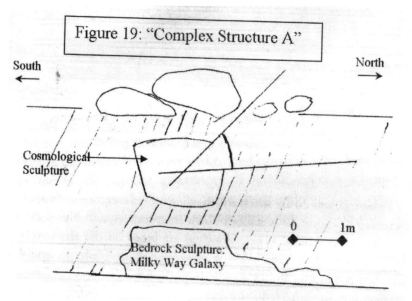

Brophy's Diagram of the Subterranean Complex Structure A, Looking North;
the "Cosmological Lens" is Clearly in Evidence[28]

[27] Thomas G. Brophy, Ph.D., *The Origin*, p. 57.

As is apparent from this diagram, with which we shall be concerned throughout the remainder of this chapter, Complex Structure A is, indeed, "complex," for it exists in three distinctive layers. When the bottom layer — the Milky Way sculpture itself — is considered, the result, again, is even more damaging to the idea that this site is the product of a primitive Megalithic culture:

> Astonishing as it may be, the bedrock sculpture underneath "Complex Structure A" at Nabta PLaya appears to be an accurate depiction of our Milky Way Galaxy, as it was oriented astronomically at a specific time: vernal equinox heliacal rising of the Galactic Center in 17,700 BC.[29]

Whoever built this structure, in other words, knew not only about the only recently discovered satellite dwarf galaxy to the Milky Way, but had accurate enough astronomical knowledge of the Milky Way's galactic center.

Brophy, however, was by no means finished with his list of amazing discoveries in the structure, and it is here that we start to approach the most paradoxical and anachronistic part of the Nabta Playa mystery. As he investigated the Complex Structures, Brophy discovered something else: that in addition to the *levels and layers* within the *physical* structures, there were also *more than one layer or level of scales employed* in the analogies between the structure and the celestial space it was encoding. There were, in fact, *three* scaling laws:

> 17.0 AU(astronomical units)/m (meter) for planets and companion stars; 0.799 LY (light years)/m for stars; and 17,600 LY/m for galaxies. The designers of the map needed to employ different scales to fit the different types of objects together on the map. Each type of object (planet, star, galaxy) is placed on the map according to the scale for that type. Different scales for different types of objects are called "scaling laws." Continuing with our astrophysical reverse engineering, to search for more information in the map at other scales, it is logical to look for a pattern in the scaling laws. If there is such a pattern, one might expect it to be a

---

[28] Thomas G. Brophy, Ph.D., *The Origin Map*, p. 58.
[29] Ibid., p. 54.

natural, nondimensional pattern. (Nondimensional meaning not depending on the use of an artificial measure like meters or feet.)

Nondimensionalizing the three scales (by expressing each in terms of meters on the ground to meters in the sky, thus eliminating the 'meters") and then taking the natural logarithm, yields a sequence of whole numbers: (29, 37, 47). These are prime numbers. And the numbers appear to fit a pattern given by selecting the next largest prime number in a log-linear sequence. In such a sequence, the next scale in the map is given by 59.

This next scaling law gives a new scale of one meter on the ground at Nabta equals 2.87 billion light-years in the sky.[30]

To put it differently, the complexity of the structures and the scaling laws involved mean, once again, that whoever constructed the site, they were doing so on the basis of knowledge and techniques handed down to them, for the ability to *observe* some of the objects depicted in the Nabta Playa map implied a technology sophisticated enough to do so.

We are looking, in other words, at a site constructed by the *legacy* of a Very High Civilization in High Antiquity, and therefore, once again, we are looking at a site whose very construction was probably done at the instigation of some surviving elite of that civilization.

This brings us to the megalith within the Complex Structure that can only be called "the cosmological sculpture" and the extraordinary astronomical and astrophysical information encoded within it, information that once again clearly points to a degree of physics sophistication commensurate with that of our own contemporary era.

Noting first that conventional archaeology persists in applying meaningless categories to the structure with little regard to its encoded mathematics, and speculating that it is "a ritual depiction of a cow,"[31] Brophy notes the odd mathematical correspondences, and it is worth citing them at length:

> The distance from the Sun to the outer spherical edge of the sculpture, according to the scaling law, is about 6 billion light-years. This is highly suggestive that the sculpted stone is a representation of the cosmological "Big Bang" of creation. Possibly it represents

---

[30] Thomas G. Brophy, Ph.D., *The Origin Map*, p. 56.
[31] Ibid., p. 59.

the age of the universe at the time of the origin of our solar system (which is roughly 5 billion years old). Or possibly the designers of the map meant for the diameter of curvature of the sculpture, rather than its radius of curvature, to represent the current age of the universe — 12 billion years. Or a third possibility is that it represents a current universe age of 6 billion years which would mean that our astrophysical models are in error by a factor of about 2.

...

More corroboration of the cosmological significance of this sculpture is found in its shape, size, and orientation. Except for the angular protrusion on one corner, the four curved, angled cornered sides of the stone may match a shape defined by two lines of declination on the sides, and on the top and bottom by two lines of right ascension. This is shown (on the diagrams on p. 267 of the current book) which is a drawing of such a declination window for the Galactic Center as viewed from Nabta Playa looking roughly east and up. Thus the shape of the sculpture, as it was placed facing outward from the sun location on the Milky Way Galaxy Sculpture, forms a "declination window" for the Galactic Center. The sculpture appears to have been carefully oriented such that this declination window subtends the full range of motion of the declinations of the Galactic Center.[32]

But the Nabta Playa "Complex Structures" held one final surprise, and it was the most breathtaking one of all.

B. The Biggest Problem for the Standard Model: The Analogues of the Constants of Quantum Mechanics at Nabta Playa

Dr. Brophy discovered, in addition to all the other encoded mathematics, codes that actually embodied within the Complex Structure the actual coefficients of the constants of quantum mechanics, *millennia* before their (re-) discovery in the early 20th century! It is best to allow Dr. Brophy to describe the process once again in his own words:

Finally, if we apply the scaling law sequence once more, the inverse natural log of the prime number 79 would give a scale that could

---

[32] THomas G. Brophy, Ph.D., *The Origin Map*, p. 58.

only represent objects much larger than the known universe. However, if we now reverse the scale from macro to microcosm, the scaling law sequence yields a scale that could represent extremely small things: 0.505 meters at Nabta equals one Plank Length.

The Planck Length is considered the fundamental length in physics. It is a fundamental constant of nature, and is the natural length that derives from three other fundamental constants of nature: Planck's constant, the Universal Gravitation constant, and the speed of light. At an almost unimaginably tiny 1.6×10^{-35} meters, the Planck Length is the size smaller than which all known physics breaks down. At this scale, the Cow Sculpture (Cosmological Sculpture) is close to one Planck Length thick. So the Cosmological Sculpture may double as a Planck Scale Sculpture.[33]

Note carefully what is actually being said here: the Cosmological Sculpture is a monument not only of the physics of the very large, but also of the physics of the very small, and this suggests that whoever constructed the site held or possessed the holy grail of modern physics, a physics that was *unified* and able to explain macro- and micro-physical mechanics all from the same set of conceptions and equations.

What is present at Nabta Playa, in other words, is strongly suggestive of an *engineered* physics construction suggesting an *engineered*, rather than a theoretical, physics unification, an idea I first broached in my *Giza Death Star.*[34] There I observed a similar phenomenon as Dr. Brophy: the Great Pyramid appeared to encode the numerical coefficients of various constants of quantum mechanics in dimensional measures *also* encoding large scale physics analogues.

All this led Dr. Brophy to the most sensational discovery of them all: the Complex Structure was, in fact, an analogue of a *hyper-dimensional physics:*

---

[33] Thomas G. Brophy, Ph.D.., *The Origin Map*, p. 61.

[34] See my *The Giza Death Star* (Adventures Unlimited Press, 2001), pp. i-ii, 218ff, 227.

... (The) angular protrusion on the Cosmological Sculpture is defined by two planes that are in a sense *orthogonal[35] to all of space-time*. In the galactic portion of the map, when an orthogonal plane was introduced it represented an entirely new coordinate system. Similarly the angular shape and/or size of the orthogonal plane protrusion on the Cosmological Sculpture may represent information *about physical dimensions orthogonal to space-time. Specifically it would be a natural way to represent aspects of multidimensional Planck scale physics such as how many physically meaningful hyperdimensions there are, eleven perhaps.[36]*

In other words, the engineers of Nabta Playa were constructing an *analogue* to hyper-dimensional objects and physics itself. Indeed, this is extraordinarily significant, for *any* attempt to unify the physics of the very large and the very small *has* to be hyper-dimensional in nature.

Again, the extraordinary nature of these discoveries cannot be overlooked and must be stated explicitly for their full significance to sink in: whoever built Nabta Playa in general and the Complex Structure A in particular, by definition, had to be in possession of physics and mathematical techniques *at least as sophisticated as those that began to emerge in our own times in the 19th and 20th centuries*. We are most definitely *not* looking at "ritual cows" and all the other nonsense that conventional archaeology claims for these structures. We are looking at a *legacy* structure of something that must of necessity be from High Antiquity and from an extraordinarily sophisticated scientific culture for Stone Age man most definitely did not possess knowledge of the constants of quantum mechanics.

---

[35] "orthogonal": i.e., perpendicular to. The technique Dr. Brophy is describing is that used in higher-dimensional geometries to describe objects that exist in more than three dimensions. It is easily imagined, for when one draws a straight line, one has one dimension. The second dimension emerges when one imagines a line, and thus a plane, existing perpendicular to that line. One thus, by creating an "orthogonal rotation" through 90 degrees, has created the second dimension. Repeating the process of creating a perpendicularity to *both* dimensions results in the *third* dimension. Creating a fourth spatial dimension thus requires perpendicularity, or an orthogonal rotation through 90 degrees to *each* of the three dimensions, and so on.

[36] Thomas G. Brophy, Ph.D., *The Origin Map*, p. 62, emphasis added.

C. Summary

What we are confronted with at Nabta Playa, when all is said and done, is an alchemical architecture in stone, an alchemical lithographical embodiment of sophisticated and only recently discovered constants — and therefore, *principles* — of quantum mechanics and astrophysical celestial mechanics. This suggests that whoever *built* this amazing structure so long ago did so not only from the basis of a survival of knowledge, a survival of knowledge that could only have been the provenance of an informed elite, but that this knowledge in turn viewed the physics of the very large and the very small as somehow deeply interconnected in a way that modern physics has yet to decipher. They might, indeed, have been in possession of the Holy Grail of physics: a unified theory that explained and unified all physical forces.

It is an alchemical structure, in short, because of the profound knowledge it embodies of the physical medium and all its manifestations from scales spanning the macrocosm to the microcosm.

To say that it is alchemical, however, is to suggest that the site had some *functional* purpose beyond merely memorializing certain mathematical constants and relationships. It is to say, rather, that it was designed somehow to *manipulate* the very medium it memorializes.

Could there have been such a functional purpose to the site? Brophy concludes that at the minimum the engineers of the Nabta Playa megaliths had the following three things:

1) "...Very advanced knowledge of astronomy, such that we are only able to achieve with modern high technology;"[37]
2) "...a basic understanding of physics, and knowledge of astronomy that rivaled or surpassed ours today;"[38] and,
3) "...knowledge of the astrophysical galaxy, and our situation in it, similar to our own such knowledge."[39]

---

[37] Thomas G. Brophy, Ph.D., *The Origin Map*, p. 102.
[38] Ibid.
[39] Ibid.

However, even Dr. Brophy sensed there was something more than merely memorialization at work in the functional purpose of the site:

...(Notwithstanding) the astrophysical and microphysical importance of the map, the most intriguing aspect of it may be that it appears to describe *some sort of function*. Such a function seems to involve certain alignments among the supermassive black hole at the Galactic Center, the Big Bang, the Sun (probably at vernal equinox sunrise), Earth's spin axis, and human beings. A unified understanding of this map, together with the alignments indicated in the Giza monuments, and probably with other megalithic structures yet to be deciphered, may pinpoint this function and indicate how to make use of it. This function may involve purely physical processes on one end of a spectrum, or involve human consciousness on the other end of the spectrum.

There are hints in some very ancient writings, such as the Sumerian, that might be interpreted as describing such a precise astrophysical-human interaction... (On) its 17,700 BC vernal equinox alignment date the Galactic Center rose very close with the Sun; thus both bodies entered the "declination window", defined by the Cosmological Sculpture, about 40 minutes after sunrise. Such "galaxy gates", if they really exist, must entail some mechanism of interaction between human consciousness and physical reality that is as yet unknown.[40]

But we have already seen what the clues are.

The Nabta Playa complex encodes a hyper-dimensional physics, one suggesting a unification of the physical mechanics of the very large with the very small. It thus encodes a physics of dynamic torsion, of rotating systems within cyclic systems within rotating systems. As most readers of my book *Babylon's Banksters* are also aware, this also encompasses cyclic systems in aggregate human behavior.

Could there, however, be a more direct link to consciousness, as Brophy suggests? And if so, how does hyper-dimensional geometry and physics fit into the picture?

...Brace yourself...

---

[40] Thomas G. Brophy, Ph.D., *The Origin Map*, p. 105, emphasis added.

11

THE *MA'ATERIA PRIMA*:
SCHWALLER DE LUBICZ AND THE EGYPTIAN VIEW OF THE PHYSICAL MEDIUM

"The Chinese sages said: One always equals three. The Egyptian sages placed the triad at the origin of each line, as they placed the triangle at the origin of geometric forms. Two irreducible magnitudes are necessary to determine a third. The sages have never taught otherwise."

"Do you care to translate this as Father, Spirit, and Son or Osiris, Isis, and Horus? Or Brahma, Siva, and Visnu?...You may, but if you are wise and wish not to be led astray, you will say: One, Two, which are Three. This has been represented *by initiates for those who need images, so that they may* rally around a tradition, *and be bound by what is called 'religion'."*
R.A. Schwaller de Lubicz[1]

In response to our epigraphs above, we are justified in asking, if the sages "have never taught otherwise" than to make reference to a primordial "trinity" of some sort, then *why* is that the case? Why do we find trinities not only in Christianity, but more anciently, in the Vedas? In China? In *Egypt?* And what has that to do with the world Grid and physics?

These questions may be answered by a consideration of the cosmology — the physics and mythological context — surrounding the Egyptian pyramids, and may be summed up in one word, *ma'at*, their word for the *materia prima* from which all else derives, and the sacred science they associated with it.

The question assumes importance for another reason, namely, that if one is to understand fully and completely the unique nature of the Egyptian contribution or component of the world Grid, then one must understand the cosmology that lay behind it. Once again, merely looking at numbers and engineering is not enough. One must look also at the texts and the cultural context.

---

[1] R.A. Schwaller de Lubicz, *Esotericism and Symbol* (Rochester, Vermont: Inner Traditions, 1985), p. 26, and R.A. Schwaller de Lubicz, *The Egyptian Miracle: An Introduction to the Wisdom of the Temple* (Rochester, Vermont: Inner Traditions, 1985), pp. 66-77, emphasis in the original.

A. The Physical Medium and the Nature of Hieroglyphic Symbols

No one performed the task of penetrating deeply into the meaning and spirit of Egyptian cosmology than the twentieth century's most accomplished esotericist-scholar, Rene Schwaller de Lubicz. Schwaller begins where most would not, namely, with the one most obvious fact about Egypt: hieroglyphs:

> Each hieroglyph can have an arrested, conventional meaning for common usage, but it includes (1) *all the ideas that can be connected to it*, and (2) the possibility of personal comprehension. This accounts for the cabalistic character of the hieroglyphs and requires the determinative in the writing.[2]

Just what Schwaller means by "all the ideas that can be connected" to a hieroglyph, he explains a little further on:

> Hieroglyphic writing has the advantage over the Hebrew of utilizing images that, without arbitrary deviations, *indicate the* qualities and *functions inherent in each sign.*
> Cabalistic writing maintains secrecy but offers a clue by accentuating the principal idea, inexpressible by fixed concepts. It always employs a form of transcription *with several possible meanings,* using an ordinary fact as a **hook** to catch the thought: a geographic site, for instance, a historical fact, a function, a gesture related to a profession, even a well-known theological form or myth.[3]

That is to say, each hieroglyph represents an "ideological" or "conceptual complex" whose principal feature is its *analogical, multi-leveled nature.*

1. Hieroglyphs and the Analogical Nature of the Physical Medium

It is crucially important to understand what this means, for in the Egyptian cosmology, a hieroglyph is much more than just a *symbol* of

---

[2] R.A. Schwaller de Lubicz, *The Egyptian Miracle: An Introduction to the Wisdom of the Temple* (Rochester, Vermont: Inner Traditions, 1985), p. 7, emphasis added.
[3] Ibid., p. 8, italicized emphasis added, boldface emphasis in the original.

the physical medium, it is an actual *operation and manifestation of it.* As will be seen a little later in this chapter, the Egyptians held to substantially the same view of the physical medium as did the ancient Vedic culture of India, and in fact, the Egyptians reproduce the topological metaphor describing that cosmology in almost exactly the same way, as an initial primordial triad that results from a "primary scission" or differentiation. Thus, everything that *is* a differentiable object is, on the Egyptian view, derived from the physical medium, and that includes, of course, hieroglyphs. But the hieroglyphs are also connected much more directly to the physical medium than just by being products of it, by dint of the fact that the medium, as we have noted in previous chapters, is analogical in nature, that is, that everything produced within it by a process of repeated differentiations still retains some signature of its original archetype, especially in terms of any overlapping *functions* shared between any of its products. In this sense, a heiroglyph, as Schwaller observed, is meant to be a collection of specific *functions;* they are designed as psychotronic objects — if we may use that term — as magical talismans or objects to manipulate not only the consciousness of their observer, but also of the physical medium itself. They are, as such, quintessentially magical and alchemical in their intention and design. There is nothing haphazard about them. The hieroglyphs are analogical in nature, because in the ancient view, in the topological metaphor, the medium itself is analogical in nature.

Schwaller thus views hieroglyphs as functions of the physical medium itself in their deepest analogical nature:

> In order to understand the meanings of a hieroglyph, *the qualities and functions of the represented object must be sought out;* if a sign is a composite, the living meaning of its parts must enter into the synthesis.
>
> This presumes an absolute exactitude in the figuration, and excludes any possibility of malformation or negligence. It should also be observed that symmetry is one of the modes of expression, but not to any aesthetic end.[4]

---

[4] Scwhaller de Lubicz, *The Egyptian Miracle,* p. 9, emphasis added.

Because of this close relationship between the hieroglyph and the actual medium itself, Schwaller points out that the difficulty for moderns in comprehending it arises from its deeply analogical nature; we fail to comprehend the nature of a hieroglyph because "out of laziness, or routine, we skirt this analogic thought process and designate the object by a word that expresses for us but a single congealed concept,"[5] rather than the deep and multi-layered complex phenomenon and manifestation of the medium that it is.

2. The Hieroglyph, the Unified Intention of Symbol, and the Hidden Elite

Egyptian hieroglyphs thus function as a prime example of the deliberate "unified intention of symbol," but in a much more deliberate way than they may at first seem to do, for given the analogical and multi-layered levels and associations of meaning in them, any given hieroglyph can, as Schwaller notes, "address itself simultaneously to all as well as to a chosen few;"[6] it is, in other words, the writing of an elite, of a group of initiates, who are by dint of that fact, privy to all the hieroglyph's encoded meanings. It is also the writing of an elite intending to manipulate or socially engineer the wider culture by means of the very system of writing it employs, through manipulations of the analogical thought process that each hieroglyph engenders.

B. The Physical Medium and the Role of Sympathetic Magic

As such, the hieroglyph not only links directly to the Egyptian view of the physical medium, but also to its practice of sympathetic magic, an alchemical process that would better be described as "analogical magic."[7] The hieroglyph is the "concretizing image" *of a specific subset of functions or ideas within that medium,* and hence, as Schwaller puts it once again, "All the qualities and *functions* it contains must therefore be sought out."[8] The reason for this view of hieroglyphical symbols as analogical symbols, as actual implements in

---

[5] Schwaller de Lubicz, *The Egyptian Miracle*, p. 9.
[6] Ibid., p. 34.
[7] Ibid., p. 10.
[8] Ibid., p. 40, emphasis added.

the practice of analogical magic, follows again from the Egyptians' nature of the physical medium itself, for indeed, it was itself a gigantic symbol, a "macro-analogy."[9]

Function or *action* is the key here, for the hieroglyph was not understood to be something static or frozen in time, but an actual activity. In one of his more abstruse passages, Schwaller has this to say about it:

> ...(The) analogy is not the symbol, it is the gesture that will be the symbol *evoking* the analogy; it summons it forth. This is the directive for the thousand forms of sympathetic sorcery about which much could be written, but it is also the key to sacred magic. The latter, however, demands more than a simple consideration of analogies.
>
> *In addition to knowledge of the analogues, sacred magic demands mastery of the proper gesture in the consonant ambiance and of the corresponding cosmic moment.*
>
> He labors in vain who does not take this into account.[10]

In decoding this crucial passage, it is important to remember that Schwaller was both a practicing esotericist, but also a *mathematician.* Thus, while most people would read this passage as referring to conventional occult magical practices, they ignore the mathematical clues that Schwaller plants in it: by stressing "gesture" and "function," in addition to a proper *timing* for the performance of "analogical magic," Schwaller is pointing, once again, to the "topological metaphor" contained within ancient cosmologies:

> To know how to make the proper gesture in the correct milieu at the right cosmic moment: this is sacred magic. The consequence of this gesture is then subordinated to neither time nor space: the effects it has caused will be manifested everywhere and in everything that is harmonically related to the cause.
>
> In this way, often unconsciously, we are magicians. Wisdom consists in knowing how to become consciously so.
>
> ...

[9] Schwaller de Lubicz, *The Egyptian Miracle*, p. 10.
[10] Ibid., p. 22, emphasis in the original.

279

For this the only guides are analogy and signature. This fact has led to the establishment of "analogical tables" such as the zodiac and planetary relationships with metals and, further, with the various parts of the human body and with plant and animal types. This is not a whimsical fantasy or even simply a conclusion based on coincidences observed over long periods of time: there does exist a science based on Numbers that reveals the reasons for these coincidences.[11]

Or to put Schwaller's words into slightly different diction, once again, there is a direct relationship between consciousness and the physical medium on the ancient view, and analogical magic was, as it were, a process designed to hone the consciousness to manipulate it more efficiently. The hieroglyph, that is to say, the symbol, the physical medium itself, and the performer of the magical act, exist in a complex system that is open-ended with respect to each of its three components.

De Lubicz's final comments about number should be noted carefully, for what he is actually implying is that, behind all the tables of analogical correspondences that one finds in ancient, mediaeval, and modern esoteric literature, there lies a *hidden grammar*, an actual analogical calculus that, once known, allows one to perceive the deep mathematical relationships of analogies clearly, and therefore also allows one to dispense with the tables of analogical correspondences themselves. The possession of such a grimoire or "grammar" would make analogical operations formally explicit, and, as Schwaller also implies, be deeply related to mathematics and to *numbers as functions of the emergent topology of the medium.*

This last statement requires further elaboration.

The physical medium as the Egyptians understood it was of primary importance to Schwaller, who summarized its philosophical presuppositions and implications in a manner that directly reveals the "topological metaphor" we have previously spoken of in context with the Vedic literature of India and the legends of Meso-America:

> 1. Faith in an origin that cannot be situated in time and space. This is reality absolute, not to be grasped by our intelligence. This

---

[11] Scwaller de Lubicz, *The Egyptian Miracle*, p. 21.

cannot be regarded as a mystery: it is the eternal Present Moment, indivisible Unity.

2. Through an internal act, the irrational source undergoes a polarization that manifests itself in spiritual substance. This substance appears as the energy of which the universe is constituted. Such is the *mystery* of the division into two, which, with the irrational origin, comprises the mystic ternary.

3. The phenomenon of universe in all its aspects is made up of this energy substance to the various degrees of its positive (north) polarity going toward its negative (south) polarity. This becoming is accomplished by alternation, a positive-negative and negative-positive oscillation. Hence the point of equilibrium must be the return to the nonpolarized source, the Present Moment, which cannot be situated.[12]

Schwaller is here speaking more as a mathematician than as a magician, for the image that he is invoking is that of the primordial "sameness," that primordial nothing-everything in which no distitions exist, and which therefore exists in a timeless and spaceless or "placeless place." By an internal function, that Nothing differentiates itself, and at once there arises what De Lubicz calls the "mystic ternary." Each broken off or "bracketed" region of an increasingly and repeatedly differentiated "Nothing" "comprise the phenomena composing our universe."[13] The implication of this analogical view of the medium is further revealed when one adds one more presupposition into the mix, namely, that the physical medium, in many ancient cosmologies, *was* consciousness. It is important that one understands the vast implications of this, for it means that consciousness is not an either-or affair, either one all-encompassing "I" or "Ego," nor a potentially infinite series of "I's" or "Egos," but a both-and: a consciousness able to endlessly differentiate himself into consciousnesses, each with their own unique "I" while remaining part of a greater "I".[14] To put it in terms of our topological

---

[12] Schwaller de Lubicz, *The Egyptian Miracle*, p. 11.

[13] Ibid., p. 14.

[14] Ibid., p. 18, Schwaller says that "The dialectics between Ego and Self is the enclosing wall that separates unitary paradise from the universe of creation," or in other words, the "either-or" way of construing the metaphor results in a separation of "Ego" and "Self," whereas the other method of construing the metaphor does not.

metaphor once again, the $\varnothing$ remains in each differentiation, *yet each differentiation of it possesses its own irreducibly unique signature.*

So how, in Schwaller's terms, would Number emerge as a function of this metaphor? We have already seen how with the "bracketing" or "regionalization" of the primordial "nothing," for the creation of a common surface $\partial\varnothing_{A,B}$ between $\varnothing_A$ and $\varnothing_B$ means that the common surface has the function of 2, a mean between 1, and 3, and so on. Number also emerges thus as a specific topological *function* in Schwaller's understanding of the Egyptian cosmology, for one designates the primordial nothing, or *first stage*, two designates the first differentiation of it, what Schwaller calls the "primary scission," and three the end result of the process which ends in three unique versions of the same nothing.

Egypt, in other words, was functioning with the exact same topological metaphor as was Vedic India, and Mayan and Aztec Meso-America.

A closer look at this "primordial" or "primary" mystic triad or ternary is in order.

C. The Primary Scission and the Primordial Triad
1. The Primordial Triad

The primordial differentiation, which Scwhaller calls the "primary scission," is evident in the Memphite myth, which we may understand as yet another "paleophysical metaphor," i.e., as a profoundly sophisticated physics metaphor disguised in religious terms. There, the primary scission is, as in the Vedic tradition, expressed in the generation of the gods from the primordial ocean, or Nun:

> The revelation of Heliopolis... is the mysterious divine action of the scission of Unity in Nun (the milieu likened to the primordial Ocean), which coagulates into the first earth, incarcerating the invisible fire of Tum.
> This is the heavenly fire fallen into earth, which in the mystery of Memphis takes the name Ptah. This metaphysical fire produces its effects in nature by materializing the principles enunciated at Heliopolis, but not as yet manifested.

The appearance of Tum implies the becoming of the three principles and the four essential qualities philosophically called the constituent elements of matter, but their "corporification" takes place only upon the appearance of the first Triad: Ptah, Sekhmet, and Nefertum.[15]

While the emergence of the number four may, at this juncture, seem ad hoc and completely arbitrary, we shall see in a little while that it contains yet another physics metaphor.

For the moment, however, our focus must remain on the emergence of the primordial triad of Ptah, Sekhmet, and Nefertum, for "Immanent in every being is a faculty of numbering that is an *a priori* knowledge of Number. The very fact of distinguishing between the I and the other is an enumeration."[16] In other words, for Schwaller, implicit in the primary scission is its relationship to consciousness and its Unity-in-Diversity. Schwaller explains the primary scission this way:

> Thus, at the origin of all creation, there is a Unity that, incomprehensibly, must include within it a chaos of all possibilities, and its first manifestation will be through division. At the origin of all concepts, there is One and Two, being Three principles where one explains the other, incomprehensible in itself.
>
> …
>
> Here is the divine Trinity that is infallibly found at the origin of all things, all arguments and reasoning; the Trinity that supports everything, the foundation on which the world is built, as everything stems from it.
>
> The original Unity contains all possibilities, of *being* and of *nonbeing*. Consequently, it is of androgynous nature.[17]

We have already made reference to this peculiar "primordial androgyny" — the subject of a whole other book — but again, what Schwaller is pointing out is that in the topological metaphor of the "differentiation of a primordial Nothing," the inevitability of a One-

---

[15] Schwaller de Lubicz, *The Egyptian Miracle*, p. 41.

[16] Ibid., p. 43.

[17] Ibid., p. 75, emphasis in the original.

Three always results: two regions of bracketed nothing sharing a common surface.

Thus we may add the names Ptah, Sekhmet, and Nefertum to our previous table, indicating a common conceptual inheritance lays behind Egypt and the Vedic culture:

1) Ptah = $\varnothing_A$;
2) Sekhmet = $\varnothing_B$;
3) Nefertum = $\partial\varnothing_{AB}$.

Our table now looks like this, revealing the commonality of the metaphor:

Hermes: God $(\theta\epsilon o\varsigma)$ $\{f_1, f_2, f_3\}$	*Hermes:* Kosmos($\mathbf{Ko\sigma\mu o\varsigma}$) $\{-f_1, -f_2, -f_3\}$	*Hermes:* Space $(To\pi o\varsigma)$ $\{-f_1, f_2, f_3\}$
Padama Purana: Vishnu, the creator $\{f_4\}$ *Memphite Myth:* Ptah	*Padama Purana:* Shiva, the destroyer $\{-f_4\}$ *Memphite Myth:* Sekhmet	*Padama Purana:* Brahma, the "preserver" $\{\sqrt{}-f_4\}$ *Memphite Myth:* Nefertum
Hermes: f_1: knowledge f_2: unmoved f_3: incorporeal *Padama Purana:* f_4: creation	*Hermes* $-f_1$: ignorance $-f_2$: in motion $-f_3$: corporeal *Padama Purana:* $-f_4$: destruction	*Hermes* $-f_1$: ignorance f_2: unmoved f_3: incorporeal *Padama Purana:* $\sqrt{}-f_4$: preservation

As already mentioned, why the ancients should so consistently view this primordial differentiation in androgynous terms is the subject of another book which we eventually hope to write, but for now it is worth noting in this regard something else that Schwaller points out:

> Do you care to translate this as Father, Spirit, and Son or Osiris, Isis, and Horus? or Brahma, Siva, and Visnu?
>
> You may, but if you are wise and wish not to be led astray, you will say, One, Two, which are Three. This has been *represented* by initiates for those who need images, so that they may *rally around a tradition*, and be bound by what is called "religion."[18]

In other words, once one comprehends the fact that the assignation of various gods' names to the topological metaphor is just that, an assignation, then one understands that any assertion of a primordial trinity is, in fact, not the consequence of religious revelation or metaphysics, but a scietifico-philosophical first principle needing no faith, but rather, a kind of belief in the character of the formally explicit metaphor, for that metaphor can be described in the highly abstract symbolisms of topology itself.

Which again raises an important question, one that Schwaller touches upon, and that we have already noted: why do the ancient cultures and civilizations insist on assigning predominantly *masculine* images to describe what is otherwise understood as an androgyny, including, as he avers, even the Christian doctrine of the Trinity? Again, any commentary on this aspect of the perplexing choice of images would require another entire book in order to reconstruct the process of reasoning that led to it, but it is important at this juncture to point out that Schwaller was indeed alive to the fact that this was both a *topological* and a *sexual* metaphor:

> Absolute Unity is the hidden God of the Jews, the unknown God who is incomprehensible; the Unutterable of the Egyptians. It is *sat*, the "Being" of the Brahmans...
>
> ...
>
> **A surface, the first incomprehensible form,** must have at least three sides. Three sounds form the perfect chord; male, female, and issue form the species; two elements and one mean

---

[18] Schwaller de Lubicz, *The Egyptian Miracle*, pp. 76-77, emphasis in the original.

term are the fundament of all reasoning, all aesthetics, all calculation, and so forth.

...

It is the God of Gods.[19] The world emanates from the God of Gods by the mere fact that "he contemplates his own face," which is the *splitting in two*, the scission, the first of all functions: *division*. This much holds for all living things...[20]

Note the close connection, once again, between the physical medium in this metaphor, and to consciousness itself in Schwaller's view. As soon as the first primordial differentiation occurs, there arises, in Schwaller's words, "generation, cause, and condition of becoming, and hence there is harmony," that is to say, analogy.[21] The medium in effect, in this process, creates information, and becomes par excellence the transmutative "Philosophers' Stone." It is because of this constant activity of differentiation, of the endless creation of more and more information, that one may speak of the primary scission or differentiation as being the ultimate metaphor of non-equilibrium, and of the fact that information, once created, is never lost. This is the basis for the ancients' belief that immortality was less a matter of faith, than of fact, or, as Schwaller put it, "it is impossible to kill a being *born within Nature*, be it mineral or man,"[22] for such creations emerge first as ever more refined differentiations of Nothing; they have specific information content.

Schwaller's emphasis on number as a *function of the topological metaphor* and of geometry is crucial. Number is a function because it emerges simultaneously with the first primordial trinity: "it has its *function* because it exists only as relationship."[23] It thus inhabits that Platonic world of the "eternal ideas," for number-as-topological function "shows us intelligibly that all proceeds from Unity and

---

[19] Schwaller notes that this "God of Gods" is, in Egypt, known as the Neter of Neters.(Q.v. p. 78)

[20] Schwaller de Lubicz, *The Egyptian Miracle*, p. 78, italicized emphasis original, boldface emphasis addded.

[21] Ibid., p. 113.

[22] R. A. Schwaller de Lubicz, *Esotericism and Symbol*, (Inner Traditions, 1985), p. 20.

[23] Schwaller de Lubicz, *The Egyptian Miracle*, p. 67.

returns to it through *diversity*. This diversity is precisely our world created in the image of the Eternal World's example."[24]

2. The Tectratys, and Pyramids as Analogical Machines

At this juncture, we must consider the origin of the number four, and what *its* function is within the esoteric Egyptian cosmology. No esoteric symbol more perfectly epitomizes the *functional* significance of this number than does the Sacred Tectratys of the Pythagoreans, which Schwaller discusses at length. The symbol is simplicity itself:

This symbol, as we shall see, contains within it yet more deeply encoded "paleophysics" and is yet another expression of the topological metaphor.

The first thing to observe is that the Tectratys is a two dimensional analogue of a Pyramid; it symbolizes, therefore, the primordial mound or Mount Meru of the Hindus, the primordial mound of the Egyptian *Zep Tepi* or "first time." As such, it is a symbol of the primary scission or differentiation and the process of creation as it emerges in the physical medium. "We can already understand," says Schwaller, "that the pyramid with square base best represents the square (base) of the four triangular Elements (its faces). Four times the triangle — this by necessity is the pyramid."[25]

Esoterically, then, the four layers of the Tectratys represents the emergence of the four elements — Fire, Air, Water, Earth — from which the ancients maintained the rest of the world, and all its

---

[24] Ibid., p. 69. For the implications of the Platonic turn (περιαγωγη) from the images of the physical world to the ideal world of "mathematicals" or, to put it in terms of the metaphor, to topology, see the table in my *The Giza Death Star Deployed*, p. 91.

[25] Schwaller de Lubicz, *The Egyptian Miracle*, p. 85.

differentiations, were created by various admixtures and combinations of those four elements:

Fire Air Water Earth	• • • • • • • • • •

Scwhaller De Lubicz's Table of Correspondences of the Four Elements with the Pythagorean Sacred Tectratys[26]

Schwaller comments on this as follows:

> Why are the four numbers of the decade called "Elements"?
> To answer, we must first of all set aside the arithmetic habit so as to see in each of these numbers, no longer the *addition* of units, but **a new entity altogether, a new unity.** There is the unity One, the unity Two, the unity Three, the unity Four. Each is a unity that in turn can give birth as a unity.
> ...
> ... the metaphysical Decade and formed matter begins only with the number four.[27]

Leaving aside once again the "androgynous metaphor" that a "unity" gives birth, what does Schwaller mean by each number being a new entity, a new unity unto itself? And why should the number four signify the beginning of the material creation for this esoteric symbol and doctrine?

Let us recall a remark that Schwaller made earlier, namely, that the elemental symbol for the primordial differentiation or "primary scission" was *fire*. In other words, Schwaller, the mathematician, is saying that the Sacred Tectratys is a symbol of the topological metaphor, *and its first three differentiations or derivatives.* The number defines the *derivative* of a specific set of information, what Schwaller calls an "entity" or "unity," in the continual process of ever more

---

[26] Schwaller de Lubicz, *The Egyptian Miracle,* p. 82.
[27] Ibid., p. 82, italicized emphasis in the original, boldface emphasis added.

differentiations. The number, in short, describes a node in the tree of topological descent of an entity from the medium.

But why does four symbolize, in this system, the emergence of the actual *material* creation? In my book *The Giza Death Star* I pointed out that the Sacred Tectratys also functioned not only as a symbol of the topological metaphor, but also of the emergence of *geometrical dimensions:*

Point	•
Line	• •
Plane	• • •
Three Dimensional Solid	• • • •

The Tectratys as a Metaphor of the Emergence of Geometrical and Physical Dimensionality[28]

Additionally, I also pointed out it can function as a metaphorical symbol of particle physics:

Physical Medium, or Aether	•
Sub-particles	• •
Particles	• • •
Atom	• • • •

The Tectratys as a Metaphor of Particle Physics[29]

These two charts exhibit the fact that the Sacred Tectratys functions *as* a symbol of "unified intention,"[30] that is, it is yet another legacy from a Very High Civilization with a sophisticated physics. With that in mind, let us look again at the assertion that the material creation emerges with the number four, and is connected to combinations of the four "primal elements," Fire, Air, Water, and

---

[28] Joseph P. Farrell, *The Giza Death Star* (Adventures Unlimited Press, 2001),p. 210.

[29] Ibid., p. 211.

[30] For my conception of the "unified intention of symbol," see my *The Giza Death Star Destroyed* (Adventures Unlimited Press, 2005), pp. 49-52, and my *The Cosmic War* (Adventures Unlimited Press, 2007), pp. 75-80.

Earth, for these things could *themselves* be understood as metaphors for the four basic forces of the standard model of quantum mechanics: the strong and weak nuclear forces, the force of electromagnetism, and the force of gravity:

Weak Nuclear Force Strong Nuclear Force Electromagnetism Gravity	⦁ ⦁ ⦁ ⦁ ⦁ ⦁ ⦁ ⦁ ⦁ ⦁

The question inevitably arises, why need one stop with a tectratys? Why not have a Pentactys?:[31]

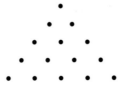

The answer, of course, is that there *is* no reason this cannot be done. It is, however, important to understand what *doing so* means: it means nothing less than that the Tectratys-Pentactys symbolism is a metaphor for the technique of *hyper-dimensional geometry*, as the extension of our previous table showing the geometrical-dimensional symbolism shows:

Point Line Plane Solid Hyper (four-)-dimensional Solid	⦁ ⦁ ⦁ ⦁ ⦁ ⦁ ⦁ ⦁ ⦁ ⦁ ⦁ ⦁ ⦁ ⦁ ⦁

As we shall see in chapter thirteen, there is actually a mathematical technique for describing objects — "solids" — in more than three spatial dimensions, and we shall discover profound clues

---

[31] Schwaller de Lubicz, *The Egyptian Miracle*, p. 93. Schwaller points out on this page that the Pentactys is the origin of the Pythagorean 3:4:5 triangle.

that some pyramidal structures are deliberately designed as *analogues* — there's that key word again! — of these things.

However, we can safely say at this stage that, from the *esoteric* viewpoint, pyramids *are* analogically-conceived hyper-dimensional machines, for as Schwaller has pointed out, they are three dimensional versions of the Sacred Tectratys, and all the multi-layered symbolism and *implied hyper-dimensionality* and subtle physics metaphorically embodied in that symbol. As it is a symbol of the primary scission, of the primordial differentiation within the physical medium, as a symbol of the topological metaphor itself, this means that by implication, they are analogically-conceived machines designed to manipulate the information-creating processes of the physical medium itself.

Are there other indicators that pyramids can function as such devices? A trip to Giza will provide an astonishing answer.

Rene Adolphe Schwaller de Lubicz

12
THE GEARS OF GIZA:
THE CENTER OF THE MACHINE

"There is no doubt that within the Pyramid's fabric are encoded many scientific laws and formulas, but the preservation of such knowledge can scarcely have been the only motive of its builders. Its numerical properties must surely have had some practical purpose in relation to the form of science which the Pyramid was designed to serve."
John Michell[1]

Giza lies at the center of the machine that was the world grid, for as we have observed, the ancient world prime meridian, and the placement of so many sites on the world Grid, are oriented with Giza being the prime meridian, and more specifically, with the prime meridian running through what would have been the apex of the Great Pyramid. Giza is, so to speak, the transmission gears at the center of the "machine" of the Grid, a great alchemical machine to manipulate the Grid itself.

But Giza and its pyramids are more than just gears in a machine; it is also an alchemical working of a very different sort, for they have exercised a transforming fixation on the human imagination itself.

As was seen in the previous chapter, the Sacred Tectratys of the Pythagoreans provided an entrance into a consideration of the profoundly analogical nature of ancient thinking, and suggested that the Pyramid builders — at least of Egypt and Mesopotamia — may have been conceiving of the structures as analogical machines to manipulate the physical medium itself. The Tectratys, we also observed, could also be understood as a symbol of the techniques of manipulating higher dimensional geometries, and thus, the symbol, as a two dimensional analogue of the Pyramid itself, implies that, from the esoteric perspective at least, the actual pyramids of that part of the world may have been intentionally conceived as hyper-dimensional "machines."

However, it may be objected that reading Pythagoreanism's most sacred symbol *back into* Egypt and its pyramids is a bit of an anachronism, and hence, begging the question. This problem

---

[1] John Michell, *The New View Over Atlantis*, p. 149.

deserves some attention, for it directly addresses the problem of the relationship of the post-Cosmic War elites, the monuments — or machines — they left behind, and the attempts of their successors in the mystery schools to interpret and understand them. Schwaller understood this process well, for he was not reading Pythagoreanism back into Egypt, but rather, arguing that their teachings were based both upon their long heritage and connection with a lost and vanished civilization, and upon *observation* of and reflection upon the man-made mountains of stone that surrounded them. The machines were the texts, and the Pythagoreans their interpreters.

A. The Pyramids as Texts:
Gematria and Esoteric Approaches to the Pyramids

But if this be the case, is there any further evidence that the Pyramids were the source for other types of esoteric speculation, and, if so, does that speculation disclose further clues corroborating the idea that they were conceived, esoterically at least, as analogical, alchemical, and hyper-dimensional machines?

These is indeed such evidence, and it comes from the ancient esoteric science of gematria.

Gematria is the practice of assigning numerical values to certain letters of an ancient alphabet. Anyone who has studied ancient Greek, or Hebrew, for example, knows that the letters of those alphabets were also assigned numerical values and, indeed, were *used* as numbers. This fact gave rise to a practice of looking for numerical codes embedded within ancient texts. Not surprisingly, there were numerous examples of the phenomenon.

We noted in the previous chapter that the pyramidal form was a three dimensional analogue to the primordial mound from which, in the ancient cosmologies, everything arose. It is thus also symbolic, as it were, of the primordial "phallus," symbolic of the

> instruments of the union between cosmic and terrestrial force by which the earth is made fertile. The same symbolism is apparent in the word πυραμις (pyramid), of which the number in gematria is

831, this number being also obtained by the addition of the values of the letters in the word φαλλος (phallus).[2]

The point, once again, is not the anachronistic reading of Greek gematria *into* the time of the Giza pyramids, but rather the fact that for esoteric tradition, there was evidence that they exercised a hold over the imagination, which sought to explain them in *functional* terms, as machines manipulating the cosmic forces of creation itself.[3]

Michell himself, whom we have cited above, also points out another esoteric significance, represented by the Great Pyramid and its nearly perfect construction:

> It has, however, often been observed that the Great Pyramid is not apparently of native Egyptian construction. Like the earliest and most perfect temples of Mexico, it related to world geography in a way which indicates that it belonged to some universal system in the forgotten past. Ever and again, studies of ancient civilizations trace them back from their declines to their high origins — beyond which the trail ends, with no trace of any previous period of cultural development. The great riddle in the quest for the origin of human culture is that civilizations appear suddenly, at their peak, as if ready-made.[4]

The Great Pyramid — and to a lesser extent as we shall see, the other large pyramid of Giza — thus symbolizes, in its perfection, the riddle of the rise of civilizations itself, for it one grants it an antiquity predating Egypt itself, then who built it, and why? That question, as we shall discover, is intimately related to the cosmological and quantum physics knowledge encoded at Nabta Playa.

However, given that the esoteric tradition was capable of viewing the pyramids of Giza in general and the Great Pyramid in particular in *functional* terms, as manipulators of the cosmic forces of creation,

---

[2] John Michell, *The New View Over Atlantis*, p. 160.

[3] Michell also notes that there is a tradition that the casing stones of the Great Pyramid were "said to have been engraved with letters and symbols expressing the entire knowledge of antiquity." Ibid., p. 137.

[4] Ibid., p. 162.

one is entitled to view them as alchemical works, on a planetary scale.[5]

It was, in fact, one of Napoleon's scientists and scholars, who accompanied the future French Emperor on his abortive expedition to Egypt, E.-F. Jomard, who first observed that the Great Pyramid's builders had to have had "an accurate knowledge of the earth and the solar system, and that its inner King's Chamber was air-conditioned by vents to hold an even temperature, thus making it an ideal repository for standards of weight and measure."[6] Indeed, as I observed in *The Giza Death Star*, the Great Pyramid functions as an analogue of nearly every known property of local physical and celestial mechanics, including, in my opinion, encoding various coefficients of the constants of quantum mechanics, just as Nabta Playa also encoded stunning astronomical and quantum mechanical data.[7]

A review of some of these analogues in the Great Pyramid is in order, for they point, at the minimum, to its heavily alchemical and functional purpose:

1) The structure appears, like so many other structures from ancient times, to embody systems of measure closely approximating the modern British imperial system of measurement, with the "pyramid inch" equal to about 1.0011 American, or 1.00108 British inches;[8]

2) The ratio of the apothem (the face slant to height) and the base of the Great Pyramid yields the value of the constant ϕ, which is 1.61818, the basis of the Fibonacci sequence (1,1,2,3,5,8,13..etc), a sequence not known until ca. 1200 A.D.;[9]

3) The approximate length of the base of the Pyramid, expressed in "pyramid cubits," is 365.24 cubits, an analogue of the

[5] Ibid., pp. 156-157.
[6] Michell, *The New View Over Atlantis*, p. 137.
[7] See my *The Giza Death Star* (Adventures Unlimited Press, 2001), pp. 161-179.
[8] Ibid., p. 174.
[9] Ibid., pp. 174-175.

number of days in a year, which requires knowledge of celestial mechanics;[10]

4) The approximate height of the Pyramid times 10^9 is close to the mean radius of the Earth's orbit around the sun;[11]

5) Doubling the perimeter of the bottom of the Coffer in the King's Chamber, and multiplying it by 10^8 yields the mean distance to the Moon;[12]

6) The scale of 1:43200 is embodied in the pyramid, which, if one takes an approximate measure of its height, multiplies it by 43,200, yields 3938.684 miles, the approximate polar radius of the Earth.[13]

To top all this off — and it is but a short review of a much longer list — as I also pointed out, there are analogues of the coefficients of the Plank Constant, the Planck Length, and the Planck mass present in the structure, constants that would not be (re-) discovered until the early twentieth century.[14]

The confluence of the fact that so many analogues of celestial mechanics and of quantum mechanics are built into both the Great Pyramid and Nabta Playa, plus the fact that the three large pyramids of Giza conform to the placement of the three stars in the belt of Orion, suggest that one and the same basis of knowledge, if not the same group, was involved in the construction of both places.

That raises the chronological problem posed by Giza.

B. The Dating and Design of Giza, and the Chronology Problem

The problem of the dating of the Giza compound is complex, and recently became much more so with the revelation by Dr. Robert Schoch that the water-erosion on the Sphinx meant that it was far older than dynastic Egypt, requiring a date of between 5000-7000

---

[10] Ibid., p. 176.

[11] Farrell, *The Giza Death Star*, p. 176.

[12] Ibid.

[13] Ibid.

[14] Ibid., pp. 207-209, 217-221, see also *The Giza Death Star Deployed*, ch. 9.

BC.[15] But this, according to alternative researcher Alan Alford, implied that the whole question of dating the Giza compound itself had to be re-thought, for the compound itself as a whole was laid out according to an intricate geometrical plan, a plan which included the Great Pyramid, and that

> encompassed the Sphinx, its temples, the causeway and Khafre's pyramid, for it would seem that the position of the two Sphinx temples was determined by two intersection lines drawn from both of the two giant pyramids. Indeed, when we add to these relationships the common use of megalithic-style masonry in the temples of both (sic) Sphinx and pyramids, it is easy to see why Egyptologists view all the structures of Giza as intimately linked, and thus roughly contemporary. The important implication of this is that one reliable dating has the potential to date all structures on the Giza plateau, hence the redating of the Sphinx is not an isolated issue, but has fundamental implications for our understanding of Egyptian history, and particularly the so-called 'Pyramid Age.'[16]

Close comparison of the construction quality evident in the structures at Giza revealed to Alford that there are at least three levels, or periods, involved, and it is worth citing what I remarked about Alford's conclusions in *The Giza Death Star Deployed:*

> The Sphinx, the temples, and the two giant pyramids at Giza were already present at the beginning of the Fourth Dynasty, and (the pharaohs) Khufu and Khafre simply adopted and refurbished them, accounting for the radiocarbon dating anomalies. The society that designed and built the structures disappeared long before the Egyptians occupied them, *with an intervening period where the site was maintained by a small and elite priesthood.* Thus, in Alford's scenario, there are three distinct levels of the cultural occupation of Giza:

---

[15] Farrell, *The Giza Death Star Deployed*, p. 26. For our purposes here, I will review the dating and arguments of Alan Alford presented in that book. For a fuller discussion of the chronological issues there presented, see pp. 25-38.

[16] Alan Alford, *The Phoenix Solution: Secrets of a Lost Civilization* (London, New English Library [Hodder and Stoughton], 1998), p. 6, cited in my *The Giza Death Star Deployed*, p. 27.

- The first level, responsible for the original construction of the major structures...
- The second level, a "remnant" or elite priesthood left behind at, or that came to occupy, the site...
- The third level, the Egyptian civilization itself.[17]

Thus, adopting Alford's conclusions and modifying them somewhat, I came to the conclusion that there were three levels, represented by three increasingly *declining* levels of construction perfection evident at Giza:

1) The oldest level, comprising the Great Pyramid itself, antedating ca. 10,000:
   a) since the re-dated Sphinx belongs to the *second* "less perfect" level of construction evident at Giza;
   b) since the Sphinx had been re-dated by Dr. Robert Schoch, based on its water erosion, to ca 5000-7000 BC; and,
   c) since there are ancient traditions that record the fact that when the Great Pyramid did have its casing stones on it, that a water mark was visible halfway up the structure, indicating that it antedated the agreed-upon date among alternative researchers for the flood, ca. 10,000 BC;
2) The second, younger, but still pre-Egyptian level, lying somewhere between 10,000 BC and the Fourth Dynasty millennia later, represented by the Second Pyramid, the Sphinx, the various Sphinx temples, and possibly the third large Pyramid, Menkaure; and,
3) The final, youngest, and purely Egyptian level, represented by the remainder of the structures at Giza, the causeways and the six smaller pyramids and also possibly by the third large Pyramid, Menkaure.[18]

But now the problem of dating grows more acute, for if one dates the first and second levels of Giza to antedate Egypt itself, the problem becomes one of *fixing Giza* within the wider context of the rest of the Grid, and especially in terms of the context and implied technologies

---

[17] Farrell, *The Giza Death Star Deployed*, pp. 29-30.
[18] Farrell, *The Giza Death Star Deployed*, pp. 31-32.

evident at such sites as Puma Punkhu, for one and the same technological skill is implied at both sites, and in both chronological levels of construction.

A closer look at Alford's logic is in order, for now it obtains truly global proportions. Let us recall his words, and then unpack the logic contained in them, to see how it applies to the question of the world Grid:

> Indeed, when we add to these relationships the common use of megalithic-style masonry in the temples of both (sic) Sphinx and pyramids, it is easy to see why Egyptologists view all the structures of Giza as intimately linked, and thus roughly contemporary. The important implication of this is that one reliable dating has the potential to date all structures on the Giza plateau, hence the redating of the Sphinx is not an isolated issue, but has fundamental implications for our understanding of Egyptian history, and particularly the so-called 'Pyramid Age.'[19]

Unpacking the logic reveals the implications:

1) Egyptology views the structures of Giza as being intimately related and "roughly contemporary," i.e., as stemming from Egyptian culture, *because of* the geometrical design of the site and "the common use of megalithic-style masonry" evident in the Sphinx, the Valley Temples, and the three large pyramids;
2) But redating the Sphinx threw all those structures back into a period *prior* to Egypt, and into what Alford calls a Pyramid Age.

In short, to say, as does Alford, that the Sphinx and Valley temples at Giza represent megalithic constructions is to raise the question of their relationship to other such structures around the world, *for those too are worked out according to a grand plan with respect to Giza itself; they were executed over a prolonged time, and they thus exhibit the same three declining levels of constructional expertise.* It is to highlight the even greater

[19] Alan Alford, *The Phoenix Solution: Secrets of a Lost Civilization* (London, New English Library [Hodder and Stoughton], 1998), p. 6, cited in my *The Giza Death Star Deployed*, p. 27.

antiquity of the Great Pyramid, upon whose apex the rest of the Grid was laid out, using it for a prime meridian!

We thus tentatively advance the following expansion of Alford's thesis, realizing the enormous difficulties that it represents. We do so, however, on the basis that the *levels of constructional expertise and precision* should be the primary determinants of assigning a site and its construction to one of the three periods or "levels":

1) The oldest level, comprising the structures *that reveal extreme precision of dressing and fitting stones, and a technology to do so, not obtainable today*, or *exhibiting precision alignments* not obtainable today. This level would thus include sites such as Titicaca and Pumu Punkhu in Bolivia, and the Great Pyramid, both antedating 10,000 BC, since:

   a) The re-dated Sphinx belongs to the *second* "less perfect" level of construction evident at Giza;

   b) since the Sphinx had been re-dated by Dr. Robert Schoch, based on its water erosion, to ca 5000-7000 BC;

   c) since there are ancient traditions that record the fact that when the Great Pyramid did have its casing stones on it, that a water mark was visible halfway up the structure, indicating that it antedated the agreed-upon date among alternative researchers for the flood, ca. 10,000 BC;

   d) Native traditions in South America place the dating of Pumu Punkhu to a period that also antedates the flood, as was seen in previous chapters;

   e) It should be noted also that one might be looking at yet a fourth level, represented by structures such as the great henges of Europe and Britain, and sites such as Nabta Playa. One is in the presence of a dilemma here, which we mention, but, at this juncture, do not speculate upon, namely, that of the relationship of these sites to those of the Great Pyramid and Puma Punkhu: which is older? the high-tech productions of Puma Punkhu and the Great Pyramid, or the megalithic constructions of Europe and Nabta Playa?[20]

---

[20] My own intuition, as of this writing, is to ascribe great antiquity to Puma Punkhu at least, and possibly to the Great Pyramid as well, and to view the

2) The second, younger, but still pre-Egyptian level, lying somewhere between 10,000 BC and the Fourth Dynasty millennia later. This level is represented by a *decline in the quality of construction, but still exhibiting great sophistication and precision*, and would represented by the Second Pyramid, the Sphinx, the various Sphinx temples, and possibly the third large Pyramid, Menkaure, in Giza, and possibly by Teotihuacan and similar sites elsewhere, since Native American Indian tradition ascribes that site to the construction of "the gods," and it exhibits correspondingly similar sophistication; and,

3) The final, youngest, level, represented by the remainder of the structures at Giza, the causeways and the six smaller pyramids and also possibly by the third large Pyramid, Menkaure, and also represented by constructions such as Tikal, Chichen Itza, Anghkor Wat, and the various temples in India.[21]

The positioning of all three levels with respect to a "Giza Prime Meridian" suggests that there was a continuity of ideology among those building the various structures around the world, and that suggests the presence and continuity of a hidden elite.

There is further testimony of the presence of an elite at Giza, an elite of great antiquity, and this comes, once again, from the astronomical work of Dr. Thomas G. Brophy.

Led by the data of Nabta Playa to consider a similar approach to Giza, Brophy minced no words as to the antiquity, if not of all the *structures* at Giza, then at least of the *design* by which they were laid out, which, like Nabta Playa, were aligned to the Galactic Center:

- The monuments function as ground and sky maps to signify the time and location in the sky of the culmination of the Galactic Center.

---

megaliths of Nabta Playa and Europe as the constructions of an elite undertaken in the aftermath of a catastrophe. There are, of course, problems occasioned by that view.

[21] Farrell, *The Giza Death Star Deployed*, pp. 31-32.

- The monuments function as a clock to mark the passage of the Zodiac Age of Leo, and to calibrate the start of the precession cycle to the culmination in the sky of the Galactic Center.[22]

These considerations led to the all-important question:

When were the monuments designed? The data evidences that the Giza plateau monuments *design plan was either created more than 12,900 years ago and developed over a several thousand year period;* or it was created by a people a people with astronomical calculation and conceptual design abilities rivaling our own, at some time before or contemporary with the large construction events at Giza around 2,400 BC.[23]

As is now evident, the perfection and technological skills in evidence at the plateau's first two levels of construction, the redating of the Sphinx, and the presence within the Great Pyramid itself of such overwhelming analogies to modern scientific knowledge point strongly to the first idea, that the site was designed and laid out in high antiquity, by a society or an elite whose scientific and technological knowledge rivaled our own.

C. Petrie and Clues to the Machine:
The Two Large Pyramids of Giza: Imperfections, or Torsion Analogues?
1. The Vedic Clue: Dynamic Torsion

Angkor Wat, as we saw, disclosed a profound clue into the ancient Vedic cosmology, a cosmology that we have also seen was closely mirrored by that of the ancient Mayans, as well as the Egyptians. But as was also observed, the Vedic cosmology was also worked out in close conjunction with the idea of counter-rotation, of *torsion.* There is a further confirmation of this view, again from the Vedic literature, as Brophy points out:

As one example, Vedic Scholar S. Yukteswar noted that the original Vedic description of the yuga ages gave the yuga durations in 2 sets of four periods with ratios 4:3:2:1 (4800:3600:2400:1200). adding

---

[22] Thomas G. Brophy, Ph.D., *The Origin Map*, p. 90.
[23] Thomas G. Brophy, Ph.D., *The Origin Map*, p. 90, emphasis added.

up to 24,000 years. Modern translations of the Vedas insert the word "divine" before "years" to create 360 times 24,000 (or 8,640,000) years as the full yuga epoch. The modern changing of "years" to "divine years" thus allows the denigration of the ancient Vedas to merely symbolic fantasy that can't have anything to do with actual human cultural history.

    ... According to Yukteswar, very ancient Vedic atsronomy conceived of planets revolving around the sun, and *"the sun also has another motion by which it revolves around a grand center called Vishnunabhi, which is the seat of the creative power, Brahma, the universal magnetism. Brahma regulates dharma, the mental virtue of the internal world...*[24]

The last highlighted portion exhibits the connection to physics in the proper sense, for the most stable means of creating physical systems from the primordial soup is via *rotation*, in this case, the idea of rotating systems within rotating systems is a concept known as dynamic torsion. Yet, the outline of the basic concept is present in the Vedic cosmology centuries if not millennia before, and it is from the rotation of the primordial nothing that everything arises.

2. The Twists in The Two Large Pyramids

With the concept of dynamic torsion, we begin to approach the end of our examination of the Grid, and of the functional nature of at least some of the structures — the pyramidal ones — upon it.

    In chapter one, the anomalous yields of early thermonuclear testing led us to speculate that these yields might have other explanations than the standard explanations being given at the time, namely, that those bombs were gating energy, for a brief moment, from higher dimensions. In that respect, the torsion research of Russian astrophysicist Nikolai Kozyrev was mentioned, and it is worth recounting what I wrote about him in *The Philosopher's Stone*, for the concept now enters the picture as a possible explanation of the functions of pyramids as alchemical machines to manipulate the physical medium itself:

Torsion may be defined as a spiraling motion within the fabric of space and time that folds and pleats the fabric by twisting it. The

---

[24] Thomas G. Brophy, Ph.D., *The Origin Map*, p. 91, emphasis Brophy's.

simple analogy of emptying a soda pop can, and then wringing it like a dishrag, illustrates what torsion does. The spirals in the can literally fold and pleat, and the can's length contracts. This, essentially, is what torsion does to space-time.[25]

In Korzyrev's thinking, however, torsion is not an abstract, static thing, but rather a constantly changing, dynamic thing,

> for if the basic idea of torsion is that it is related to a rotating system, then it will be apparent that the universe is composed of rotating systems within other rotating systems, producing a continuously changing system with a changing *flow* of time... time *itself* takes on dynamic properties.
>
> Such complex, interlocked systems of rotation may be thought of as "knots" of space-time that are so intensely concentrated that they form the objects observed in the physical universe. As such, *all systems are in fact "space-time machines," and since they "contain" space-time they are not ultimately "constrained" by it, but rather, interact constantly, and in some cases, instantaneously, with it.*[26]

The Vedic cosmology says essentially the same thing, and consequently, if one presses the speculation a great deal, one may say that it is saying that torsion forms the ultimate basis for the declined alchemical analogical magic so prevalent in the legacy civilizations.

With these thoughts in mind, we now take a closer look at the two large pyramids of Giza, for there we find the idea of torsion, of a *twist*, present in the structures themselves. It was the renowned Italian metrologist Stecchini who observed that the Great Pyramid's four sides were all of slightly different lengths and angles from each other, producing a slight twist to the northwest corner of the structure.[27] Many who have studied the Great Pyramid have commented on this feature, calling it a "slight imperfection" and other such phrases.

But is it?

---

[25] Joseph P. Farrell, *The Philosophers' Stone: Alchemy and the Secret Research for Exotic Matter* (Feral House, 2009), p. 156.

[26] Ibid., p. 158, emphasis added.

[27] Michell, *The New View Over Atlantis*, p. 147.

Given all the other extraordinary perfection in the structure, we must ask whether this is a likely explanation, or if this twist in the structure is there *intentionally?*

There are two things arguing for its intentionality. The first is, as we have seen, the deeply esoteric connection between Egyptian cosmology and the more ancient topological metaphor contained within it, a metaphor connecting it to other ancient cosmologies. Within that metaphor, as we saw, the pyramid itself is seen as an analogue to the whole cosmic process of differentiation. If, as we also suggested, the Great Pyramid could possibly stem from a time of construction somewhere in High Antiquity, such scientific concepts might have been very well-known and deliberately built-in to the structure.

But there is a much stronger argument that suggests this twist was fully intentional, and that is the fact that the *second* large pyramid of Giza *also* has such a twist. The great archaeologist and surveyor of Giza, Sir William Flinders Petrie, whose *The Pyramids and Temples of Gizeh* form the "bible" for any serious Giza research, detailed a number of curious features about the *Second* Pyramid. Observing that the top of the Second Pyramid still has some of its casing stones on it, and taking theodolite readings on the angles, Petrie stated that "From this it is seen that the builders skewed round the planes of the casing as they went upward; the twist being +1'40" on the mean of the sides; so that it is absolutely — 3'50" from true orientation at the upper part."[28] Additionally, unlike the Great Pyramid, whose alignment to the four cardinal compass points are almost perfect, the Second Pyramid is twisted even further off alignment to the true compass points; in short, the structure itself is twisted, and in addition, twisted off center relative to the compass points.[29]

The significance of the two large pyramids being twisted is not, in our opinion, accidental, for there is a *third* consideration that points, once again, very deliberately to the idea that the compound was designed as an analogue of torsion. In *The Giza Death Star Deployed* I pointed out that when one runs an axis of rotation through the apex

---

[28] W. M. Flinders Petrie, *The Pyramids and Temples of Gizeh* (Elibron Classics, 2007), p. 97.
[29] Ibid., p. 99.

of the Great Pyramid, and then rotates the compound through 120 and 240 degrees, two familiar forms result.

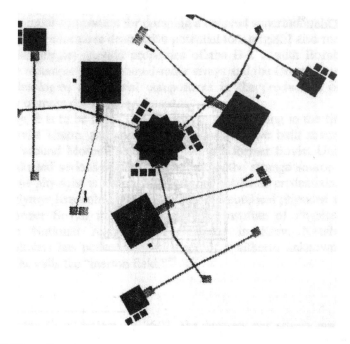

Middleton-Jones' and Wilkie's Overhead Rotation of Giza through 120 Degrees[30]

Note that the slight offset of the three large pyramids (remembering that the Great Pyramid is the center of rotation in the above diagram) yields a three-armed swastika, a common symbol of rotation in the Vedic tradition, and if the compound were rotated through 90 degree increments, the resemblance would be even more palpable.

Rotation through 120 and then 240 degrees yields an even more striking symbol, and clearly indicates that the Giza compound was deliberately designed to be *rotated*, if not in reality, then at least conceptually:

---

[30] Howard Middleton-Jones and James Michael Wilkie, *Giza-Genesis: the Best Kept Secrets* (Tempte, Arizona: Dandelion Books, 2001), p. 211.

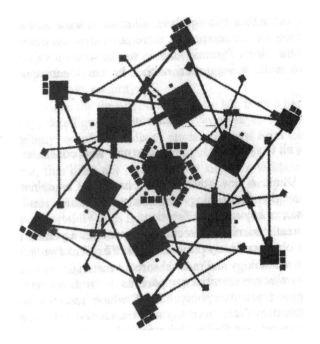

Middleton-Jones' and Wilkie's Rotation of Giza Through 240 Degrees[31]

So what do we have? We have at least *three* levels of rotation taking place at Giza:

1) Each of the two large pyramids is *twisted* from bottom to top, with the Great Pyramid being oriented slightly off center and toward the northwest corner;

2) In addition, both large pyramids deviate from true alignment to the four compass points, a divergence particularly true in the case of the Second Pyramid; that is, each is *twisted with respect to the Earth itself*;

3) Finally, the whole compound is also designed to rotate.

In other words, we have rotation within rotation within rotation, all on the surface of the Earth, which is rotating on its axis, revolving

---

[31] Middleton-Jones and Wilkie, *Giza-Genesis: The Best Kept Secrets*, p. 213. For further commentary on these two figures, see my *The Giza Death Star Deployed*, pp. 132-134, 244-250.

around the Sun, which is revolving around the Galactic center.[32] To put it succinctly, *the Giza Compound is an analogy of the concept of dynamic torsion.*

If, therefore, as engineer Christopher Dunn has argued so persuasively in *The Giza Powerplant,* that the Great Pyramid was a *machine* for the production of power, or as I have argued in the *Giza Death Star Trilogy* that it might actually have been designed or utilized as a weapon of some sort, then this fact, plus the *three chronological levels of construction* evident at Giza, and its overall design, indicate that the entire compound may have been designed as some sort of machine, perhaps even one that *modified* the original function of the Great Pyramid, the first structure present at the compound on Alford's alternative scheme of dating. And if the Grid is laid out with respect to Giza, then the *machine* of which Giza is the center, is truly massive.

The only questions that remain are, what was this vast machine designed to do, and how did it do it?

This is where the "answers" become highly speculative, and very technical...

---

[32] For the presence of these three levels of celestial rotation at Giza, see again Thomas G. Brophy, Ph.D., *The Origin Map,* p. 99.

PART FIVE:
THE PHYSICS OF THE "PYRAMID PEOPLES"

"From the relics of the Stone-Age science practised by the adepts of the ancient world it appears: first, that they recognized the existence of natural forces of whose potential we are now ignorant, and learnt to manipulate them; second, that they gained thereby certain insights into fundamental questions of philosophy, the nature of the universe and the relationship between life and death."
John Michell,
The New View Over Atlantis, p. 197.

13

SPECULATIONS:
THE PRINCIPLES OF ALCHEMICAL ARCHITECTURE AND ENGINEERING

"According to an adopted theory, every ponderable atom is differentiated from a tenuous fluid, filling all space merely by spinning motion, as a whirl of water in a calm lake. By being set in movement this fluid, the ether, becomes gross matter. Its movement arrested, the primary substance reverts to its normal state. It appears, then, possible for man through harnessed energy of the medium and suitable agencies for starting and stopping ether whirls to cause matter to form and disappear."
Nikola Tesla[1]

"In this system that I have invented it is necessary for the machine to get a grip of the earth, otherwise it cannot shake the earth. It has to have a grip on the earth so that the whole of this globe can quiver."
Nikola Tesla[2]

We have come a long way since the first chapter, and those early, anomalous yield returns of early hydrogen bomb testing, that suggested some aspect of the world Grid was in play. The journey has taken us from Angkor Wat and an interesting, if disconcerting, masculine-yet-androgynous imagery used to symbolize the physical medium, to Tiwanaku and Puma Punkhu in Bolivia and anachronistic displays of advanced technology, to Tikal, Chichen Itza, and Teotihuacan in Mexico, to even more disconcerting practices of human sacrifice connected to the structures, and to bizarre mythological correspondences between Mesopotamia and the Mayans regarding the engineering of mankind,

---

[1] Nikola Tesla, quoted in "Mr. Tesla's Invention: How the Electrician's Lamp of Aladdin May Construct New Worlds," *New York Times*, April 21, 1908, citing a letter of Tesla to the *New York Times* dated April 19, 1908.

[2] Nikola Tesla, Trial transcript, in answer to a question from the bench; New York State Supreme Court, Appellate Division, Second Department: Clover Boldt Miles and George C. Boldt, Jr.., as Executors of the Last Will and Testament of George C. Boldt, Deceased, Plaintiffs-Respondents, versus Nikola Tesla, Thomas G. Shearman, et al. as Defendents-Appellants, 521-537, at line 529, cited in David Hatcher Childress, ed., *The Fantastic inventions of Nikola Tesla* (Adventures Unlimited Press), p. 177.

to curious musical codes in Plato, Pythagoras, and the Vedas, to the sands of the Egyptian desert where a strange megalithic structure encodes quantum mechanical and astrophysical data, to the plateau of Giza, and to yet another example of a "topological metaphor" present in Egyptian cosmology. Along the way we've encountered Nazis building on the grid, Nazi and Soviet physicists implying "something was wrong" with standard models, and we've encountered a strange topological metaphor and mythological parallels concerning the creation, or better put, the engineering of mankind and "Tower of Babel" moments of history, from to Meso-America to Mesopotamia. We have implied along the way that at least *some* of these structures — the pyramidal ones — on the world Grid system were alchemical hyper-dimensional machines. Certainly in the case of Egypt the case can be made that, at least from the *esoteric* point of view, they can be, and possibly were, viewed as such.

But can a stronger case be made that this is the case from a mathematical and scientific standpoint? Can one argue that at least *some* of these structures were more deliberately and scientifically conceived as "hyper-dimensional" machines, and, if so, what was their purpose?

Indeed such a case can be advanced, and that is the task of this final, and most technical, chapter, but before that case can be fully appreciated and understood, a reprise of the arguments of the previous chapters is now, finally, in order.

A. Summary of the Arguments and Conclusions of the Previous Chapters
1. Historical Arguments and Mythological Parallels

Our historical arguments and mythological parallels can be summarized as follows:

1) There are three overall *levels of construction* evident throughout the world in conjunction with constructed structures on the world Grid, and paradoxically, the older the structures, the higher the technological skill and scientific knowledge encoded in them is. Yet, the placement of such sites as Tikal

and Teotihuacan on a Grid system that evidently placed the prime meridian through the Great Pyramid's apex indicates that some consistent body of knowledge survived into the later periods of construction, and that this knowledge may have been the proprietary intellectual culture of a hidden elite or elites constructing them.

2) The consistency of the building and placement of objects on the world Grid system, plus the consistency of the mythological *Leitmotifs* over time and area also suggests that a detailed plan was in place that arose from that common proprietary intellectual culture of that elite.

3) The high level of scientific knowledge represented by such sites as Giza or Nabta Playa, or for that matter, Teotihuacan, indicate a degree of scientific knowledge that could only have come down from High Antiquity from a civilization and scientific culture equally, if not more, sophisticated as our own. Additionally, some sites, such as Puma Punkhu, exhibit stone working technology equally as if not more sophisticated than our own, and thus a technological sophistication equal if not exceeding our own. It is thus reasonable to seek scientific rationalizations for the functions of these structures on the world Grid.

4) Curiously, as we also saw, the Mayan mythology parallels that of the Mesopotamian in its assertion that mankind was an engineered creature to function basically as the slave or servant of the gods. There is even present in the Mayan mythology a Tower of Babel moment in which mankind is embarked upon a project that somehow threatens the gods' power over it, and accordingly, a *political* decision is taken to end that project, whatever it was. It is my speculation that this project was intimately connected to the pyramid building and other constructions associated with the world Grid. The consistent esoteric association of pyramidal structures with "the gods" is an indicator that such structures were associated with the knowledge — that is to say, the *science and technology* — of "the gods", and this is particularly the case with the esoteric traditions surrounding the Giza complex, Teotihuacan, and the sites of Meo-America. Again, this

argues that scientific rationalizations for the functional purpose of such structures should at least be entertained.

5) In more modern times, the lithium-7 explanation for the anomalous yields of early hydrogen bomb testing was suggested to be a smokescreen and a deliberate lie on the part of the U.S. government, for the following reasons:

a) Lithium-7 fusion reactions were clearly known, and openly talked about, by Nazi-Argentine scientist Dr. Ronald Richter in connection with his "fusion" project for Argentine President Juan Perón. This project attracted world attention, and, as I demonstrate in my book *The Nazi International*, the considerable covert attention of American military and scientific authorities, such that his explanations of lithium-7 reactions were known *months before the USA claimed it had not considered its fusion reactions when it designed and tested the Castle Bravo device.* In the historical context proffered by Richter's project in Argentina, in other words, the post-Castle Bravo explanations seem ridiculous, for we are being asked to believe American scientists did not account in their design for a reaction that was well-known to other nuclear engineers, Nazis, Soviets, and Argentines among them!

b) Richter made it clear in his explanations both to Argentine and American authorities that he regarded a rotating and stressed plasma to be a key for tapping into the zero point energy itself, that is to say, he viewed fusion reactions within rotating and precessed plasmas as hyper-dimensional geometries gating energy into the fusion reaction itself. Similar suggestions were, as noted in chapter one, made by the Soviet astrophysicist Dr. Nikolai Kozyrev in connection to observations made about the sun itself. In short, it was suggested that the early h-bomb tests were returning anomalous yields because they tapped into geometries of the local physical medium itself, and since those geometries changed constantly, the yields of thermonuclear devices of the same design would also change slightly depending on the time and place of the test, i.e., depending upon the geometry of space time itself, and in conjunction with the energies of the earth Grid. It consequently became a highly and deeply classified secret of an "off-the-books" physics.

c) It was also shown that, apparently, the Nazis prior to and during World War Two had at least *some* knowledge, howsoever rudimentary it may have been, of this system, since they placed their transmitters and other installations are key points along that part of the Grid that fell under their control.

6) Finally, we also noted in the case of Meso-America and South America that at some *later* point the practice of human sacrifice arises in connection with certain sites on the Grid, as *one elite is replaced by another*, thus signaling the presence of *two* elites, with different understandings of how to manipulate the world Grid. How, then, does one rationalize this practice — if it can be rationalized at all — in connection with the speculative scientific rationalizations of the functional purpose of such structures and sites? To put it as bluntly as possible, why does sacrifice arise in conjunction with the pyramids of Mexico and Meso-America, and not in conjunction with those of Egypt?

a) While this is not the book to address either this bizarre and cruel fact, nor that of the disconcerting and curious imagery of "masculine-androgyny" associated with the topological metaphors in some cultures, its presence in one place and its absence in the other does tend to suggest that one elite prevailed in one place, and the other in the other place.

b) We also saw that the logic used to justify the practice of sacrifice was curiously similar in the case of the Aztecs, and the Christian archbishop Anselm, and that in each case, that logic relied upon the idea of a debt mankind owed to the gods, a "spiritual economics" that was impossible for mankind ever to repay, a step that

317

effectively made "the gods" or "God" nothing but banksters.

2. The Strange Topological Metaphor

We also encountered, in conjunction with the cultures — Vedic, Mayan, and Egyptian — that have built pyramidal structures and associated them with the gods, and with their activities and knowledge, a strange mythological and cosmological parallel that we have called simply "the topological metaphor":

7) In the Vedic, Mayan, Egyptian, and even Hermetic cosmology, all creation arises out of differentiations in a primordial "nothing" which is variously described as a primordial ocean or sea, an imagery consistently used in ancient literature to describe the fabric of space-time itself. While we saw evidence of that disconcerting "masculine-androgynous" imagery operative both in the Vedic and Mayan mythologies in conjunction with this topological metaphor, further explorations as to the reasons for its presence would require a book of its own to explore to the degree it requires. But for the present moment, viewing this primordial Nothing as undergoing a process of differentiation resulting in two regions with a common surface exhibited the rise of a "primordial triad," the regions and common surface themselves, with the names for each of these three entities varying according to the local mythology:
   a) For the Vedic, the names for these three entities within the topological metaphor were Vishnu, Brahma, and Shiva;[3]
   b) For the Hermetic, God, Space, and Kosmos;[4]
   c) For the Mayan, Sky, Sea, and the implied common surface between the two;[5] and,
   d) For the Egyptian, Ptah, Sekhmet, and Nefertum.[6]

---

[3] See pp. 71-79.
[4] See pp. 71-79.
[5] See pp. 181-184.

The presence and persistence of this metaphor throughout such disparate cultures — all of them engaged in pyramid building of one sort or another — argues strongly from the cultural context that they viewed these structures in the same way as Nikola Tesla — whose words were cited in the epigrams at the beginning of this chapter — viewed his own technological quest, as the means "to get a grip on the earth" and to cause the movements of the aether to stop and start, i.e., as the machines by which to manipulate the physical medium itself.

8) The strong association of the topological metaphor of the physical medium with consciousness itself also implies that, for these ancient cultures, the pyramidal structures esoterically associated with the physical medium were also viewed as *consciousness* manipulators, or, to put it slightly differently, that these were also alchemical machines for the transformation of consciousness and social engineering itself.[7]

3. The Types of Numerical Coding

9) In our survey in previous chapters of the pyramidal portions of the world Grid, we also encountered not only three levels of construction activity and corresponding scientific and technological sophistication, but also three distinct kinds of numerical coding involved:

a) The geographical coding, elaborated by Carl Munck, Graham Hancock, and other capable Grid researchers, that discloses that Giza and its Great Pyramid were used as a prime meridian.

    i) Additionally, as Thom, Munck, and others have also pointed out, use of English imperial measures also seems to have been at work in the measuring and

---

[6] See pp. 282-287.

[7] I have suggested such interfaces between consciousness and biology and these technologies in two previous books, *The Cosmic War*, pp. 243-271, and *Genes, Giants, Monsters, and Men* (Feral House, 2011), pp. 161-169.

positioning of some of these sites long before the system was actually "English;"[8]

b) The esoterical numerical coding, embodied in at least three distinct ways:

   i) The emergence of number itself as *functions* of the topological metaphor, as in the examination of the topological metaphor conducted by R.A. Schwaller de Lubicz in conjunction with the Egyptian version of the metaphor;

   ii) The use of numerical codes in the Platonic, Pythagorean, and Vedic tradition to denote not only certain gods in their respective pantheons, but also as *musical* codes to denote various schemes of tuning, and the use of these codes in turn to denote the astrological and astronomical data of the celestial "music of the spheres;" and,

   iii) The use of gematria, or numerical coding in texts.

From all these esoteric points of view, once again, the tradition tends to view pyramidal structures as the primordial mounds of "the first time" whence creation in all its diversity emerges. They are, so to speak, the metaphorical phallic symbols of that disconcerting image of androgyny one also so often encounters in the ancient cosmologies.

c) The strictly *scientific* numerical encoding, which occurred, as was seen, at two levels in the same structures:

   i) Codes referring to *macrocosmic* processes, or to the physics of large systems, that is to say, encoded astronomical data; and,

   ii) Codes referring to *microcosmic* processes, or to the physics of small systems, that is to say, encoded numerical data of *quantum mechanics* in the form of references to the coefficients of the constants of quantum mechanics, or, in the case of the Pythagorean tectratys, the four "elements" or forces

---

[8] See the discussion in *Genes, Giants, Monsters, and Men*, pp. 31-65.

320

of the standard model of physics, the electromagnetic, gravitational, and the strong and the weak nuclear forces. Such knowledge could only come down fdrom a civilization in High Antiquity with a similar or greater pitch of scientific development as our own. In this, we are indeed looking at the presence of alchemical machines in the proper sense, for if these ancient structures such as Nabta Playa can only reveal their secrets in accordance with a certain level of scientific sophistication, then indeed it becomes possible that other such codes await to be unlocked in these structures as our own scientific knowledge advances; it is thus possible that some of these sites on the world Grid will thus *provoke* a transformation and expansion of consciousness by actually yielding scientific information as yet unknown, if they can but be properly decoded. The association of these structures with consciousness manipulation should not seem so surprising by now, for as I noted in *Genes, Giants, Monsters and Men*, piezoelectric effects are used in modern mind manipulation technologies,[9] and some ancient temples from classical times also appear to have been deliberately engineered to be in resonance with certain frequencies of the human brain.[10]

It is, oddly enough, point 9)b)ii) above — the use of musical codes in the Platonic and Pythagorean traditions — rather than the quantum mechanical and astronomical encoding, that points directly to the next necessary stage in our speculative case that pyramidal structures are hyper-dimensional machines, designed to manipulate the medium itself, in all its effects, including consciousness.

In this respect, let us recall something stated in chapter nine:

It is important to note what this notation means, for cubing and squaring a number — e.g. x^3 and x^2 — are, of course, *geometrical*

---

[9] Farrell, *Genes, Giants, Monsters, and Men*, pp. 77-87.
[10] Ibid., pp. 87-90.

functions describing objects in two or three spatial dimensions. Thus, the notation {2,5} mentioned above could be written this way more abstractly as {x, y}, and since the first number is multiplied by the cubic power of 60, and the second by the squared power of 60, the notation really would look like this:

$$\{(x \cdot 60^3) + (y \cdot 60^2)\} = n.$$

We can therefore imagine *extending* this notation to {x,y,z}, and extending the powers of 60 with which each number is multiplied, e.g. $\{(x \cdot 60^4) + (y \cdot 60^3) + (z \cdot 60^2)\}$; in other words, notations such as {8,0,0}, which are also within the realm of possibility in ancient Mesopotamian notation, conceivably may be understood as representing powers of 60 *greater* than the cubic, that is to say, as geometric and numerical representations of objects in *four* or more dimensions.

To state it as succinctly as possible, the very structure of ancient Mesopotamian numerical notation implies a basic familiarity with hyper-dimensional geometries and the basic mathematical techniques for describing objects in four or more spatial dimensions. Indeed, as we shall discover in chapter 13, *the exact same notation convention began to be used in nineteenth century geometrical techniques for describing objects in four or more dimensions!*

This contains a further, and very suggestive, implication, for it is to be noted that the Sumerian-Babylonian gods may be described by such notation. In other words, *the gods were being described peculiar union of physics and religion, as hyper-dimensional entities or objects.*[11]

As I noted in that chapter in the footnote: "The modern name for such notations is Schläfli numbers, and their appearance in notation is identical, with each number representing a particular type of geometric function. This will be explored further in chapter 13."[12] This is now chapter thirteen, and a closer look at those mysterious Babylonian notations, so curiously identical to modern Schläfli

---

[11] McClain also observes that the Egyptian god of wisdom, Thoth, is also a sigil for various musical-numerical scales and harmonics; q.v. McClain, *The Myth of Invariance,* pp. 184-185.

[12] p. 251, n. 11.

notations, is in order, for in them is contained a profound clue to some of the ancient pyramids, *particularly* the ones in Mexico and Meso-America.

B. Hints of a Hyper-Dimensional Engineering:
A Cursory Excursion into Geometry in More than Three Dimensions

It has been suggested in some circles that some of the pyramids of the ancient world, in particular those of Meso-America and Egypt, represent structures designed to engineer the hyper-dimensional physics of the medium. Richard C. Hoagland, for example, performed simple experiments on television recently, using a Bullova watch, powered by a minute tuning-fork, to take measurements of changes in the tuning fork's frequency of vibration at various places near the pyramids of Tikal. When Mr. Hoagland moved away from the structures, the vibrations would return to normal, but near or on the structures, the vibrations varied greatly from their normal frequency, suggesting to him that that structures were manipulating local inertial effects. I myself have suggested that at least the Great Pyramid was a complex sort of phase conjugate howizter manipulating longitudinal waves in the physical medium itself.

But to argue that the pyramids of Mexico and Egypt *in general* are designed as hyper-dimensional machines — *analogues* of objects in higher-dimensional spaces — requires an additional type of analysis, and this can only be had by doing a bit of hyper-dimensional geometry. Unfortunately, presenting the mathematical techniques that geometers use to analyze such objects to a lay readership is no easy task, but inevitably, *some* degree of familiarity with these mathematical techniques is required, howsoever cursory.

Fortunately, we have already encountered, through the work of Carl Munck, *the* essential analytical conception used by geometers to describe hyper-dimensional objects, and that is *the simple technique of counting three things:*

*1) lines, or **edges**;*
2) points, or corners, or, as the geometers call them, vertices; and,
3) sides, or faces.

For our purposes, we shall attempt to summarize crucial conceptions in hyper-dimensional geometry using what may justifiably be described as the single best mathematical treatment of the subject: mathematician H.S.M. Coxeter's *Regular Polytopes.*

1. Geometry in More than Three Dimensions: H.S.M. *Coxeter's* Regular Polytopes
a. A Brief Biography

Harold Scott MacDonald Coxeter, 1907-2003

One of the twentieth century's greatest mathematicians, Harold Scott MacDonald Coexeter, is virtually unknown outside of mathematics, for the speciality that earned him his fame — hyper-dimensional geometry or geometry in more than three spatial dimensions — requires, needless to say, a powerful pictorial imagination and the ability to put that imagination into formally explicit and reproducible equations. Coexter had both, in abundance. Like so many who dwell on that fuzzy boundary between mathematics and the arts, Coxeter was a talented musician, being an accomplished pianist by the age of ten.[13]

Born in London in 1907, Coxeter attended the University of Cambridge, receiving his B.A. in the subject in 1928 and his P.D. in 1931. He spent a year at the Princeton University in 1932 as a Rockefeller Fellow, working with the famous mathematician and physicist Hermann Weyl. As the war clouds of World War Two were gathering, Coexter moved to the University of Toronto in 1936, eventually becoming a professor there in 1948. His hyper-dimensional geometry work inspired the famous Dutch artist Maurits Escher, whom Coxeter met.[14]

Coxeter published but few books and papers during his long and distinguished career, but that is hardly surprising, for anyone who has read any of his books or papers knows that each of them is a higher-dimensional tour-de-force, whose very equations and diagrams are themselves exercises in alchemical transformations and expansions of conciousness, working an almost magical effect on the mind. Of these few publications, *Regular Polytopes* is his distilled masterpiece, a model of mathematical rigor and yet, an essay of profound beauty. It is this book, and in particular its all-important opening pages, that we shall follow closely here, for they contain profound clues to unravel the mystery of the pyramids, *particularly those that depart from the smooth-faced Egyptian model.*

---

[13] "Harold Scott MacDonald Coxeter," *Wikipedia*, http://en.wikipedia.org/wiki/Harold_Scott_MacDonald_Coxeter, p. 1.
[14] Ibid.

b. The Essential Imaginative Technique

Coxeter's approach to higher dimensional geometry and its techniques was a profoundly intuitive and experiential one, notwithstanding the formal mathematics in which it is couched, relying upon the ability of the human imagination to grasp the basic conceptual principle on which the formal mathematical techniques were based. Typically, his intuitional experiential approach may be grasped in a series of short, pithy expressions that require deliberate thought to unpack. Indeed, Coxeter almost writes as an alchemical poet, crowding numerous layers of thought into extraordinarily short sentences.

The basic intuitive or experiential technique behind all the more formal principles and techniques of higher dimensional geometry may be glimpsed by the sentence that begins the seventh chapter of *Regular Polytopes*, "Ordinary Polytopes in Higher Space." One may, at this point, be asking, "What *is* a 'polytope' anyway?" Coxeter answers the question, and in doing so, reveals the intuitive or imaginative technique in play: "*POLYTOPE* is the general term of the sequence *point, segment, polygon, polyhedron...*"[15] Remember the "dimensional analysis" of the Pythagorean Tectratys of chapter 12? Coxeter is here saying the same thing: as one adds dimensions, one is able *to describe more and more things*, so that in zero dimensions, one can only describe a point, in one dimension, only a segment of a line, in two dimensions, polygons such as triangles, squares, octagons, and so on, and in three dimensions, polyhedra, such as tetrahedra, cubes, octrahedra, and so on. Coxeter puts this imaginative point more precisely as follows:

> In space of no dimensions the only figure is a point, Π_0. In space of one dimension we can have any number of point; two points bound a *line-segment*, Π_1, which is the one-dimensional analogue of the polygon Π_2 and polyhedron Π_3. By joining Π_0 to another point, we construct Π_1. By joining Π_1 to a third point (outside its line) we construct a *triangle*, the simplest kind of Π_2. By joining the triangle

---

[15] H.S.M. Coxeter, *Regular Polytopes*, p. 118, all emphases in the original.

to a fourth point (outside its plane) we construct a *tetrahedron*, the simplest Π_3. By joining the tetrahedron to a fifth point (outside its 3-space!) we contruct a *pentatope*, the simplest Π_4... The general case is now evident: any *n* +1 points which do not lie in an (n-1)-space are the vertices of an *n*-dimensional *simplex*...[16]

The term "polytopes" (Π) thus denotes *what happens to polyhedra when they are rotated into more than three dimensions.* Or to put it differently, the term "polytope" denotes the common mathematical elements of the same figure in various dimensions, such as the progression in the above quotation from Coxeter, of "triangle, teatrahedron, pentatope" and so on. Notice also, that in each of the two previous examples — polygons in two dimensions and polyhedra in three — that the shapes of the polyhedra result from performing what geometers call an "orthorotation," or a rotation from two dimensions into a third dimension that is perpendicular or at 90 degree angles from the other two. The same thing happens in the rotation from three to four, and from four to five dimensions: each dimensional orthorotation simply adds another spatial dimension to the previous ones, in a dimension at right angles to all the previous dimensions.

Obviously, this cannot exist in a three dimensional space any more than a three dimensional polyhedron can exist in a two dimensional space, but they can be *pictured* or represented in a two dimensional space, and more importantly, they can be exactly mathematically described by certain specific techniques that we will get to in a moment. To put Coexter's point about polytopes of certain types being analogues — there's that crucial word again! — somewhat differently, *all polytopes* of a specific type — say, triangles, tetrahedra, and pentatopes — share certain properties in common *regardless* of how many dimensions in which they occur; *they are, in "physics terms," all coupled harmonic oscillators to one another across dimensions, and the "coupling" occurs in the numbers themselves, numbers that in turn result from the regular geometry of their shape.* To boil it all down, all polytopes of a particular species have a "shape" in n-dimensions, and that shape is

---

[16] H.S.M. Coxeter, *Regular Polytopes*, p. 120, all emphasis in the original. The use of the capital pi, Π, simply means the "polytope" which the subscribted number after it means the number of dimensions in which it occurs.

projected into the dimensional space in which it exists — say, two, three, or four dimensions — by certain regular mathematical laws.

Now let us observe yet another implication of Coxeter's always deceptively simple remarks, namely, that *the simplest way to describe the orthorotation of **any** polytope or "shape" from one type of dimensional space to another is **tetrahedrally**.* Coxeter puts this point with his customarily deceptively simple statements: "Two-dimensional polytopes are merely polygons... Three-dimensional polytopes are polyhedra..."[17]

A "triangular" shape in two dimensions is a natural oscillator of the same shape in three, four, and more dimensions, and *this* is the real encoded secret in the Sacred Tectratys and Pentactys of the Pythagoreans, for the simple symbol is also a symbol of this mathematical technique, yet another legacy from High Antiquity, for it is essential to recall that the Pyragoreans regarded it as a key cosmological secret:

Tectratys		
O Dimensions	•	Point
1 Dimension	• •	Segment
2 Dimensions	• • •	Polygon
3 Dimensions	• • • •	Polyhedron
Pentactys		
4+ Dimensions	• • • • •	Polytope

The Pythagoreans, in other words, were preserving a secret of hyper-dimensional geometry, whether they knew it or not, and given all the indications that they knew the image concealed a great a various multi-leveled meaning, they may, indeed, have had an inkling of it.

c. The Essential Mathematical Techniques

With these things in mind, we are ready to address the next question: what are the *exact* mathematical techniques used to describe

---

[17] Coxeter, *Regular Polytopes*, p. 1.

polytopes in more than three, or >3, dimensions? Coxeter begins *Regular Polytopes* by describing one such technique in detail:

> To be precise, we define a *p*-gon as a circuit of *p* line-segments A_1A_2, A_2A_3,..., A_pA_1, joining consecutive pairs of *p* points A1, A2, ..., A_p. The segments and points are called *sides* and *vertices*. Until we come to Chapter VI we shall insist that the sides do not cross one another. If the vertices are all coplanar we speak of a *plane* polygon, otherwise a *skew* polygon.
>
> A plane polygon decomposes its plane into two regions...

(Remember our topological metaphor, and that initial differentiation of the dimensionless Nothing into two regions, joined upon a common surface? Coexter is now describing *the same process* in *two* dimensions, via a process of differentiation of a two dimensional Nothing, a "plane", by means of a regular polygon whose surface joins its finite interior with its infinite exterior! In other words, you have been doing higher-dimensional geometry all along, in the topological metaphor, the only difference between topology and geometry being, that topology is not dealing with geometrical objects, but the spaces themselves! To return to Coxeter):

> ...
>
> A plane polygon decomposes its plane into two regions, one of which, called the *interior*, is finite. We shall often find it convenient to regard the *p*-gon as consisting of its interior as well as its sides and vertices. We can then re-define it as a simply-connected region bounded by *p* distinct segments.[18]

Before we distill all this *lingua mathematica arcana*, there is one more statement, again from the beginning of the book, worth citing:

> *A polyhedron may be defined as a finite, connected set of plane polygons, such that every side of each polygon belongs also to just one other polygon,* with the proviso that the polygons surrounding each vertex form a single circuit(to exclude anomalies such as two pyramids with a common apex). The polygons are called *faces,* and their edges *sides.* Until Chapter VI we insist that the faces do not cross one another. Thus

---

[18] H.S.M. Coxeter, *Regular Polytopes*, p. 1.

the polyhedron forms a single closed surface, and *decomposes (three dimensional)*[19] *space into two regions, one of which, called the interior, is finite.*[20]

Again, Coxeter has described a process of three-dimensional differentiation of a three-dimensional space by means of a polyhedron.

So what is the first basic mathematical principle in evidence in the transition of any polytope from one system of dimensional spaces to another?

It's so simple that you, the reader, *know it already*, and have known it since elementary school: *one counts the*

1) points, or vertices of an object;
2) the edges, or *lines* of an object; and
3) the *faces* of an object.

Thus, a triangle has three vertices, three edges, and one "face"; a teatrahedron four vertices, six edges, and four faces, and so on. A square has four vertices, four edges, and one "face"; a cube has eight vertices, twelve edges, and six faces, and so on.

To this technique there is added yet another, and this one is a bit more complicated, but it is also the crucial technique. We begin, once again, with Coxeter's own summation of this technique:

> A regular polygon is easily seen to have a *centre*, from which all the vertices are at the same distance $_0R$, while all the sides are at the same distance $_1R$. This means that there are *two concentric circles, the circum-circle and in-circle*, which pass through the vertices and touch the sides, respectively.

And, notes Coxeter in the very next sentence, anticipating a physics application:

---

[19] I have added the parenthetical expression "three dimensional" for clarity.
[20] H.S.M. Coxeter, *Regular Polytopes*, p. 4, emphasis added.

It is sometimes helpful to think of the side of a *p*-gon as representing *p* vectors whose sum is zero.[21]

In other words, for any regular polygon, such as a square, it is possible to draw a circle whose center shares the center of the square, and whose circumference touches upon, or is tangent to, the four vertices of the square, which is the circumscribing circle, and it is also possible to draw a circle whose circumference touches upon, or is tangent to, the *edges* of the square, which is the circuminscribed circle.

But note that Coxeter is describing a process that, like the polygon itself, can be orthorotated into three or more dimensions, in which case, the circuminscribing and circumscribed circles, become cicuminscribing and circuminscribed *spheres,* and *hyper*-spheres. But the *numbers* will be preserved in all dimensional spaces.

Now we consider the next most difficult component of these circumscribing and circumscribed *n*-circles.[22] If we imagine a circle in two dimensions, and a square within it, obviously the square will touch on four points of a circumscribing circle. If we now instead circuminscribe an octagon, there will be eight points on touching on the circle. Dividing the octagon again will produce sixteen touching points, and with each such division, the regular polygon assumes a shape closer and closer to the circuminscribing circle. Similarly a process in three dimensions with regular polyhedra will more and more approximate the shape of the circuminscribing sphere. Notably, the circumference of the circle is, as everyone knows, C=2πr, where C is the circumference and r is the radius of any given circle. Thus, as the regular polygons circumscribed in a circle more closely approximate the circle itself, the closer they get to that crucial relationship of 2πr. In other words, the relationship of 2π and its multiples becomes a crucial component of rotations into more than three dimensions.[23]

---

[21] H.S.M. Coxeter, *Regular Polytopes*, p. 2.

[22] I am using the term *n*-circle simply to describe the circular shape in any number of dimensions.

[23] For the more mathematically inclined, the author is acutely aware of the garish nature of this summary, but begs their indulgence for a more general readership. Coexter's formulation of the relationship of exterior angles of a plane polygon and the complete turn is given on pp. 2-3 of *Regular Polytopes*. Coxeter notes that this method of increasing the number of edges circumscribed was the

This point about "squaring the circle" is also quite an important technique for this type of higher dimensional mathematical technique, for it allows geometers to determine the numerical relationships of objects in more than three dimensions to their circuminscribing and circuminscribed hyper-spheres. It is, along with the counting of vertices, edges, and faces (in order to determine what *type* of object one is dealing with), the essential technique.

It is this fact that, at least with respect to the Great Pyramid, also means that the structure was deliberately conceived as a higher-dimensional analogue, for as most investigators are aware, the Great Pyramid is built as an example of "squaring the circle" and "cubing the sphere,"[24] it is built, in other words, according to the very technique of higher-dimensional geometry.[25]

d. Tetrahedral and Octahedral Groups

We noted, previously, that there was a peculiar connection between Sumerian notation and the type of notation used by geometers in higher-dimensional mathematics. Before exploring that connection, it is worth mentioning that there is another deep connection between the Sumerian sexagesimal numerical system, based upon multiples of the number 6, and that of higher dimensional geometry. Coxeter notes that in the rotation groups of polyhedra, that there are three groups in particular:

---

means by which Archimedes estimated the value of π. Coxeter discusses the rotation groups for the Platonic solids on p. 33, and the three primitive transformations, translation, rotation, and reflection, on pp. 34-37.

[24] See, for example, Peter Tompkins, *Secrets of The Great Pyramid* (New York: Harper and Row, 1971), pp. 195-200.

[25] This fact also suggests something else about the world Grid itself, though it will require much more careful investigation on the part of researchers to determine if, in fact it is true. It is possible that various points of the Grid are laid out on *different coordinate systems that depict the surface points where regular polyhedra intersect with the idealized circumscribing surface of the Earth itself.* To my knowledge, no such investigation has been undertaken, though the work of some Russian investigators comes close to it.

...(we) have the *tetrahedral* group of order 12, the *octahedral* group of order 24 (which is also the rotation group of the cube) and the *icosahedral* group group of order 60 (which is also the rotation group of the dodecahedron).[26]

While consideration of rotation groups would far exceed the technical limitations of presenting higher-dimensional geometries to a general audience, it is worth noting that all these numbers are "Sumerian" in that they are all multiples of 6! And this brings us at last to the other peculiar Sumerian connection.

e. Schläfli Numbers, the Platonic Solids, and Their Extensions

Ludwig Schläfli (1814-1895) was the Swiss mathematician who first investigated regular polytopes in more than three dimensions, deriving a simple method of representing the counting of the numbers of vertices and faces.[27] Schläfli's notation convention, for regular polyhedra in three dimensions, is a symbol comprising two numbers, p and q, which looks like this:

$$\{p,q\},$$

where p is the number of sides of a face of a regular polygon and q is the number of faces around each vertex. A cube would thus look like this:

$$\{4,3\}$$

with the four denoting the equal sides of a square's face, with three such faces around each vertex.[28] The notation convention is strongly

---

[26] H.S.M. Coxeter, *Regular Polytopes*, p. 47.

[27] For a general discussion of Schläfli's importance and role in the elaboration of higher dimensional geometrical techniques, see Coxeter, op. cit., pp. 142-149, 152-153. For the mathematically-inclined, note particularly the recurrence of "sexagesimal" numbers — 120, 720, 1200, 600, on p. 153, which emerge in consideration of the regular polytope {3,3,5}.

[28] For Coxeter's discussion of the Schläfli numbers of each Platonic solid, see *Regular Polytopes*, p. 5.

reminiscent of Schwaller de Lubicz's understanding that numbers represent geometrical functions, and of the Sumerian notation convention where, similarly, the numbers denote functions of cubing or squaring, or of some other function of multiplication.[29] As more dimensions are added, the number expands: $\{p, q, r...\}$.

C. Counting Faces and Vertices In Mexico and Meso-America

We have already observed that the Great Pyramid in particular is an actual analogue of the technique of squaring the circle, a crucial step in the kind of analysis and technique geometers utilize to describe higher-dimensional objects. But expressed in terms of a Schläfli number, there is nothing so unique about them; they have five vertices, four triangular faces, and one square face. One would have to "adjust" the notation to reflect this fact, but it could be easily done.

It is when one turns to the pyramidal structures in Mexico and Meso-America that one is confronted with something *very* interesting, as the following charts and diagrams of the various pyramids of Teotihuacan and Tikal demonstrate.

---

[29] Again, for the mathematically-inclined, as Coxeter also notes, the Schläfli number can also denote a regular map, or, to put it differently, a regular polyhedron "is a special case of a regular map." For this discussion see pp. 8-11 of *Regular Polytopes*.

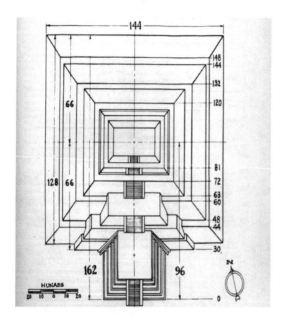

Harrelson's Overview of the Pyramid of the Sun at Teotihuacan[30]

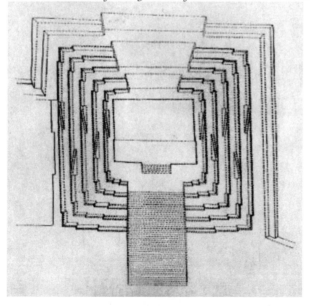

Overview of Small Pyramid At Tikal[31]

[30] Peter Tompkins, *Mysteries of the Mexican Pyramids*, p. 245.

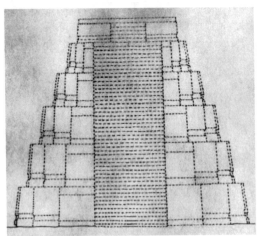

Small Pyramid At Tikal: Front View

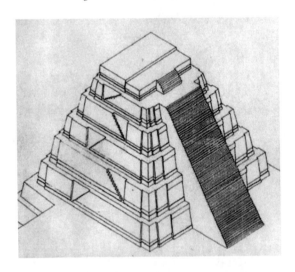

---

[31] Finding detailed sketches of the pyramids of Tikal was a difficult task, and I would like to thank Mr. James Kelly for procuring a copy of Ignacio Marquina's *Arquitectura Prehispanica.* 2nd Ed. Cordova, Mexico: Institiuto Nacional de Antropoligia e Historia Secretaria de Educacion Publica, 1964 [1950], from which these diagrams and sketches are taken, pp. 541-543.

Perspective View of Small Tikal Pyramid

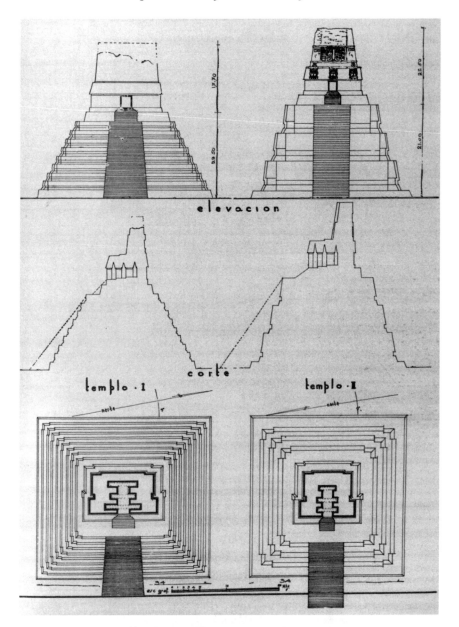

Tikal: Temples I & II: Front, Side, and Overhead Views

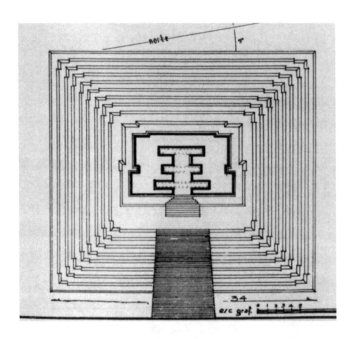

Tikal Temple I: Overhead

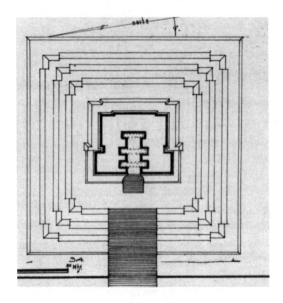

Tikal Temple II: Overhead

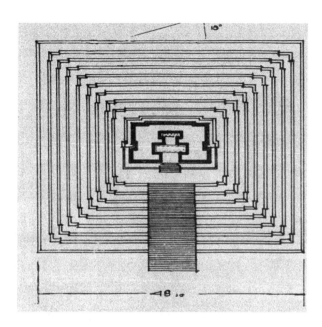

Tikal Temple III: Overhead

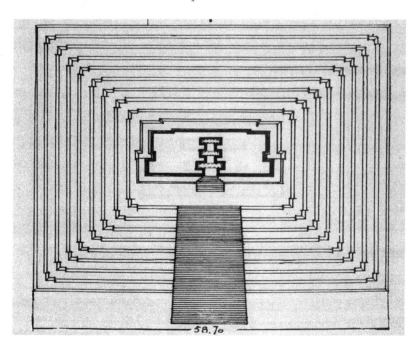

Tikal Temple IV Overhead

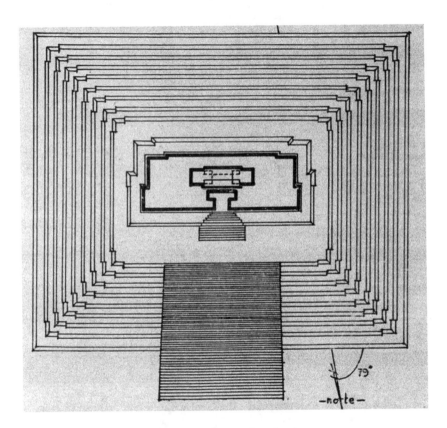

Tikal Temple V Overhead

What is immediately apparent in all these examples is that these are not true regular pyramids, they are elongated, in many cases their vertical orientation is not symmetrical, being skewed off center, and most importantly, as Carl Munck observed, they also have *numerous corners, edges, and faces.*

Why is this so important?

For one thing, just as the two large pyramids at Giza, the skewed off-center vertical alignment *suggests* once again that they were

340

deliberately conceived as structures with a *twist* or rotation, in short, as structures analogous to torsion.

And it is important for another reason, because, as Coxeter pointed out, higher dimensional polytopes — and we realize a pyramidal structure is already a departure from a regular polytope — have numerous vertices, faces, and edges.[32] And atop each of these structures is a "temple" that, if one looks at them closely, appear to be designed as some sort of resonant cavity.[33] What this strongly suggests or implies is that, just as a tetrahedron can be represented or "squished" into a two-dimensional representation or analogue, so too can higher-dimensional pyramidal objects or constructs be "squished" into a three-dimensional structure that is an analogue of them. This fact, coupled with Mr. Richard Hoagland's simple torsion experiments conducted at Tikal near these very pyramids, strongly suggests these structures were deliberately designed as hyper-dimensional analogical, alchemical structures designed to manipulate the physical medium, and to respond to it.

With this in mind, let us return to Sir William Flinders Petrie's observations concerning the *Second* Pyramid at Giza, remembering the context that the plan of the compound is *to rotate*, producing all those tetrahedral structures seen in the previous section of this book. Petrie notes that "The lower two courses of the casing" of the Second Pyramid "are of granite, very well preserved where it is not altogether removed."[34] In addition to this, "the builders made the face(of the granite casing stones)[35] drop down for some depth vertically from the edge of the slope, building the pavement against the vertical face."[36] Consider what this means.

---

[32] See again, H.S.M. Coxeter, *Regular Polytopes*, p. 153 ff.

[33] To make this qualitative speculation hard and fast, one would have to have accurate dimensional measures of these structures, and all my attempts to find such measures as this book was being researched turned up nothing. If such dimensional measures are available, then an analysis of possible frequency resonances with these cavities would have to be undertaken to make this speculation quantitative and conclusive.

[34] W.M. Flinders Petrie, *The Pyramids and Temples of Gizeh*, p. 96.

[35] I have added these words in parentheses to clarify that Petrie is still commenting about the lowest course of granite casing stones on the Second Pyramid.

[36] Petrie, op. cit., p. 96.

It is known that granite possesses very active piezoelectric properties, given all the small quartz crystals embedded in it. Thus, in a certain sense, one has the piezoelectric analogue of the primary to a Tesla magnifying impulse transmitter, for the enormous weight pressing down on these casing stones places them under constant stress. Furthermore, just as Tesla stated of his own technology in the trial transcript cited as an epigraph at the beginning of this chapter, it was necessary for his Wardenclyffe Tower to "grip the earth" in order to make it quiver. It is equally the case that it is necessary to grip it in order to *respond to* its natural vibrations.

So what do we have, when we combine all these observations about Giza, Mexico, and the wider cosmological myths we have examined in this book?

1) Present in the Mexican and Giza Pyramids are structural analogues of rotations and torsion;
2) The Mexican pyramids also appear, with their multi-cornered edges and faces, to be some sort of analogues of irregular higher-dimensional objects, contained within an overall normal pyramidal structure;
3) The Mexican Pyramids appear to have "temples" atop them that resemble — *qualitatively* — resonant cavities;
4) Their placement and position on the globe is oriented to Giza as a prime meridian, suggesting that any machine-like function they have is designed to work in conjunction with that site;
5) At Giza itself, the compound is designed to rotate, and each of the two larger pyramids there also is slightly twisted and skewed, thus producing an analogue of dynamic torsion, that is to say, of rotating systems within rotating systems;
6) The Second Pyramid of Giza appears to be a piezoelectric analogue of a Tesla magnifying impulse transmitter, a technology in turn based upon manipulating longitudinal electrical waves.[37]

---

[37] For this point, see my *Babylon's Banksters*, pp. 130-155.

The conclusion, though tentative, seems inescapable, for we are in the presence of a machine of planetary extent, designed, at the minimum, to manipulate planetary energies, if not more, to respond and manipulate the wider system of ever-changing torsion dynamics in the solar system, as would seem to be implied by all the careful astronomical alignments and data preserved in various sites, particularly at Teotihuacan and Giza. The end result of all of this symphonic coordination of all the moving parts of this massive globe-spanning construction in a vast counterpoint, was the transformation of the entire planet Earth itself into an alchemical laboratory, a temple of initiation, into the deep physics of the medium of the material creation and of consciousness itself.

For now, our examination is concluded: at least some of the structures of the Grid, if not the Grid itself, were conceived, designed, and executed over a prolonged period of time as genuinely alchemical objects and analogues of the transmutative information-creating physical medium itself, to manipulate it for whatever purpose, including the manipulation of consciousness, for they exercise their mysterious hold over the human imagination still. They thus embody an awesome, little understood, power, both for destruction, and very possibly, for protection.

As we sincerely hope has been shown throughout this book, any effort to understand the Grid and its function will now have to proceed much more cautiously than previous research has undertaken. Measurements of dimensions of structures with an engineer's eye to potential resonances will have to be undertaken; exacting study of the positioning of sites on the Grid will have to be made with a view to determine if these locations correspond to spherically circumscribed objects; their positioning in time, and within the overall scheme of the three chronological levels of construction will have to be fixed, and above all, due consideration of the mythological and cosmological context in which various cultures explained these structures by Grid researchers will have to be given, for as we have seen throughout this work, those "myths" contain a profoundly sophisticated higher-dimensional topological metaphor of the physical medium itself.

Conclusions: The Principles of Alchemical Architecture and Engineering

One thing, however, *has* clearly emerged: there is a definite correspondence between those cultures possessing some version of the topological metaphor in their cosmologies, and the activity of building pyramids or pyramidal structures, and it is this fact, above all, that suggests these structures' ultimate purpose and function was for the manipulation of the physical medium.[38]

Though we have encountered the disconcerting imagery of a "masculine androgyny" in many of those mythological cosmologies and the "topological metaphor" associated with the cultures surrounding these structures, though we have also encountered the strange idea of immortality also associated with them, and though we have also encountered, in Mexico, the inescapably immoral practice of human sacrifice associated with them, beyond this, for the present moment, we cannot go, as those subjects will require a book of their own to explore fully. But rest assured, those disconcerting images themselves contain profound clues not only into the mind of the ancients, but also into the physics and cultural consciousness that produced them; those images include profound clues into the nature of the topological metaphor itself, and into its ethical and even aesthetic ramifications.

But even though those are subjects for another book, there is one final, tantalizing bit of evidence concerning that disconcerting image of androgyny, and of sacrifice, to consider...

---

[38] This is true even of the two other pyramid-building cultures — Mesopotamia and China — though we have not examined them here, having already commented about them elsewhere.

14

A GOTHIC EPILOGUE:
ALCHEMY AND THE CATHEDRALS
(Joseph P Farrell and Scott D. de Hart)

"It is enough for us to know that the wonders of the Middle Ages hold the same positive truth, the same scientific bases as the pyramids of Egypt, the temples of Greece, the Roman catacombs and the Byzantine basilicas.... The hermeticists...will recognize here that it is from the confrontation of the Book and the Building that the Spirit is released and the Letter dies."
E. Canseliet[1]

I t was St. Anselm who first exposed the logic of the alchemy of perpetual debt when he raised the question, *cur deus homo* or "why the God-man?" Indeed, the medieval apologist answered his own question as to why God should leave a throne of universal authority and become the Lamb (of God) led to a slaughter. His answer: an infinite crime requires a corresponding judgment of infinite proportion; a punishment that would literally shake the foundations of the earth; an execution so horrific that the sun would take cover in the shadows of darkness. Humanity was on trial with an offended God and nothing less than a perfectly *innocent* victim of infinite worth being subjected to a false trial, bodily torture, and an agonizingly slow execution was deemed satisfactory to ameliorate the insult of disobedience and "zero balance the books."

We have raised in these pages more than a few counter arguments to the revered Saint Anselm; respectful but not as naïve as the defenseless Boso, for there are literally pyramidal mountains of evidence that are not so haphazardly scattered across the earth and over the span of centuries if not millennia. Boso, the curious and open minded disciple may have been finally silenced by the blood-curdling logic of Anselm of Canterbury, but how differently might he have countered his master if he were given a chance to survey the ancient monuments, open the sacred Mayan texts, and to make a

---

[1] E. Canseliet, "Preface to the First Edition," Fulcanelli, *Le Mystère des Cathédrales*, trans. Mary Sworder (Lsa Vegas, Nevada: Brotherhood of Life, 2007), pp. 6-7.

comparative study of human history with its echoed tales of innocent victims bleeding to appease an offended all powerful heavenly ruler? How differently might Boso have answered his master if he had been privileged to see into the future and gaze at the alchemical symbols that would adorn the great Gothic cathedrals raised only a few hundred years later?

The logical lid to Pandora's box has been swept off with hurricane winds of modern research. It is now impossible to reseal this once mysterious box with a simplistic theological "final word"; a word that was once sufficient to satisfy the medieval doubting Thomas' minds. The 21st century winds of time, historical inquiry, and archaeological evidence unquestionably raise a voice of doubt concerning the credibility of Anselm's apology. Perhaps even more disconcerting to modern unbelievers is the seemingly *im*moral appeal of the medieval apologist's insistence upon a once-for-all debt and payment theology which, as has now been shown, was hardly an isolated once-for-all incident. Careful research now reveals that the debt and payment ritual espoused by Anselm was little more than his own preferred bloody event among *many* innocent blood lettings to *this* or *that* god demanding endless sacrifices. The debt and payment ritual on the outskirts of a Jerusalem hillside in or about 33 C.E was gruesome and historically significant, but it was undoubtedly neither the first nor the last one made to an offended god demanding payment of a debt.

If Anselm's adversary in this dialogue were an atheist rather than his disciple it is certain that more poignant questions might have been asked, such as why would a *loving* god insist on the *un*loving ritual of draining the blood of victims for the appeasing of feelings that arose from an *insult*? What moral value is actually attached to the death of an innocent substitute victim? How is *insult* turned to satisfaction when the punishment seems to far outweigh the ostensible crime? Is it possible that the actual lust for recompense has less to do with insult and more to do with the payment over an assumed debt far more significant than the insult of disobedience?

Indeed, morality and innocence are hardly in play in this drama, other than in the tear filled eyes of the onlookers and next victims. This drama, for all practical concern, lacks any human morality; if any morality could be wrestled from this drama one might think they were watching an alternative version of Oscar Wilde's *Picture of Dorian Gray*; the chicanery of an angry god with blood dripping from his hands, scars and wrinkled brow, clinched fists, morphing into a loving and pure young man as all the sins of the world are infused into him rather than sins committed by him. Oddly enough, Victorian England condemned Wilde as propagating immorality in verse for a novel where the protagonist turns *from* his lust for blood and dies remorsefully, driving death's blade into the image of something evil. Aztecs and Anselm, conversely, wrote the climax to their drama with an innocent virgin dying to appease a blood thirsty god, and somehow this makes the world a better place. In the one case, it was a twisted "spiritual economics" that set the sacrificial drama into motion; in the other, a twisted physics, and both come together in some black alchemy designed to transform man's soul into the mindset of a perpetual slave.

"The world is a stage," stated Oscar Wilde, "but the play is badly cast." The stage for this tragedy is no quiet hillside nor a Victorian neo-gothic mansion with a magical portrait inside a nursery, but rather it is a far more sinister and unsuspecting place. This tragedy is one of debts, pure and simple. Gods with a thirst for more than moral uprightness; gods with an unquenchable need to eliminate competition; gods demanding nothing less than control over property and establishing ownership by threat and force. A quid pro quo played out from start to finish, a chilling tale of servitude and sacrifice for satisfying a debt, and manipulating the physical medium. This is the story of *The Grids of the Gods*, it is the story of human history and some of the monuments left behind on that grid as memorials!

The Grid did not die; the magical and alchemical music of the spheres, and the possible hyper-dimensional engineering with which it was engineered, did not die. It survived in the unlikely place of western Europe, in the breathtaking Gothic cathedrals, and the ambiguous, but clearly alchemical natures of the symbolism sculpted in them. No one better understood the ambivalent nature of these symbols than the enigmatic "Fulcanelli," a man as ambiguous, ambivalent, and alchemical as the symbols of the cathedrals whose esoteric and alchemical meanings he dared to expose. Lest we become lost in the mystery of the man,[2] however, we remain concentrated upon his work, or rather, upon just one of the many symbols he decodes.

We have seen that there was alchemy at work in this attempt to manipulate the physical medium through a "spiritual economics" of debt and sacrifice. But the practice of sacrifice, alchemy, and "spiritual debt" did not die with the Aztecs and Montezuma, for one need go no further as an epilogue to this survey of the Grid than these great Gothic cathedrals, where yet another ritual of sacrifice was played out amid the backdrop of a scarcely perceived alchemical symbolism. Those great, soaring, buttressed cathedrals are, as many know, purposefully laid out on points of the Gird; what many do not know, however, are the calculated depths of ambivalent alchemical symbolism that is employed within and through them.

We mention only one of the many bas reliefs of *Notre Dame de Paris*, pointed out by Fulcanelli in his monumental study. In many ways, it is the key to his work, as it is also the key to the alchemy of the cathedrals, and the deeper symbolisms that would eventually come bursting forth in European literature and art once the necessity for disguising them behind a veneer of Christianity was no longer necessary, and independent thought had begun to liberate itself to examine these symbols with more objectivity.

Fulcanelli was alchemy's answer to Anselm.

Or rather, he was the decoder of alchemy's symbolism which adorned the gothic cathedrals of France.

Consider the ambiguous nature of the following bas relief found in *Notre Dame de Paris*, the first such relief and symbolism Fulcanelli discussed in his book.

---

[2] That mystery has never been adequately solved. "Fulcanelli" appeared in 1920s France, and just as quickly, disappeared, after entrusting the manuscript for his now famous alchemical study of the gothic cathedrals to his disciple. There are those that believe that there is a strong case to be made that "Fulcanelli" was none other than the famous esotericist Rene Schwaller de Lubicz, and one of us, Joseph P. Farrell, inclines to this view.

The Ambiguous Bas Relief At Notre Dame de Paris: King of Heaven? or Androgynous Alchemy?[3]

The relief is found on the Great Porch of the famous Paris cathedral.

At first glance, the dictates of Christian piety will perhaps decode the relief in a predictable way: a figure is seated on a throne, holding a scepter in the left hand, and two books — one open, and the other closed — in the right, with the curious figure of a ladder between the knees. This, piety will suggest, is Christ, the King of Heaven, seated

---

[3] Fulcanelli, *Le Mystère des Cathédrales,* trans. from the French by Mary Sworder (Las Vegas: Brotherhood of Life, 2007), photo insert betwen pp. 70 and 71.

on the throne of Heaven, holding open the Book of the Gospels, perhaps, and the closed Book of Life, to be opened by Him at the apocalypse. The ladder is, perhaps, a symbolism of Jacob's ladder, by which heaven and earth were united, and thus a fitting symbol of Christ. It is a testimony to the skill of the symbolists that the figure can be interpreted in this fashion.

But to one schooled in esotericism, the symbol is capable of a very *different* interpretation. A closer glance at the figure reveals a carefully executed androgyny, neither fully masculine, nor fully feminine. Or rather, it is both fully masculine and feminine simultaneously. As such, it is equally an alchemical, as well as a Christian symbol, for it thus functions as a symbol of the physical medium itself, as alchemy understood it. Fulcanelli writes elsewhere "The spirit cannot but feel troubled in the presence of this even more paradoxical antithesis: the torch of alchemical thought illuminating the temple of Christian thought."[4]

From this vantage point, the rest of the relief decodes itself in very different terms. Fulcanelli notes that the famous cathedral, "like most French cathedrals, is dedicated to the Blessed Virgin Mary or the Virgin Mother."[5] However, there is an esoteric and alchemical significance even in this, and the bas relief on the Great Porch reveals it:

> In the place of honour, facing the parvis, alchemy is represented by a woman, with her head touching the clouds. Seated on a throne, she holds in her left hand a sceptre, the sign of royal power, while her right hand supports two books, one closed (esotericism) the other open (exotericism). Supported between her knees and leaning against her chest, is the ladder with nine rungs — *scala philosophorum* -hieroglyph of the patience which the faithful must possess in the course of the nine successive operations of the hermetic labour...[6]

Beyond the fact that Fulcanelli has glossed the androgynous nature of the relief, the symbol could be taken straight from Vishnu's first "tripartation," the primordial nothingness standing over against him

---

[4] Fulcanelli, *Le Mystère des Cathédrales*, p. 104.
[5] Ibid., p. 69.
[6] Ibid., p. 70.

after that initial "tripartation" in all its stark, undifferentiated femininity.

It is, Fulcanelli observes, "the seal of the secular Great Work" of alchemy "on the very face of the Christian Great Work."[7] This Virgin Mother depicted here is "stripped of her symbolical veil" and thus

> is none other than the personification of the primitive substance, used by the Principle, the creator of all that is, for the furtherance of his designs. This is the meaning (and, indeed, a very clear one) of this strange epithet, which we read in the Mass of the Immaculate Conception of the Virgin, of which the text reads:
> "The Lord possessed me at the beginning of his ways. I existed before he formed any creature. I existed from all eternity, before the earth was created. The abysses were not yet and already I was conceived...."[8]

For Fulcanelli, the bas relief was a therefore also a clue to the profoundly different alchemical and esoteric meaning of familiar passages of the Bible, meanings at variance with the popular meanings ascribed to them by piety.

The meaning was clear: the Virgin Mother was a symbol of that primordial *mater*, the primordial "mother" or matter, the physical medium from which, according to alchemy, all else derived. Small wonder, then, that alchemical symbolism should adorn the great cathedrals where, according to the dogmas of the mediaeval church, another transmutation called "transubstantiation" was performed in a ritual act understood by the Church to be sacrificial, for behind the exoteric dogma and ritual, a hidden esotericism was perhaps at work, biding its time behind Christian symbols, until it could once again re-emerge as itself, and freed from the necessity of having to disguise itself. The very fact that these symbols *are* alchemical, and boldly emblazoned on France's most famous Gothic cathedrals, is testament to something else, namely, that an alchemical, hermetic elite continued in Europe throughout the centuries, overseeing and guiding their construction.

---

[7] Fulcanelli, , *Le Mystère des Cathédrales*, p. 70.
[8] Ibid.

During his most recent research in Paris, as with his spine tingling pilgrimage to Chichen Itza, at least one thing was quite clearly revealed to Scott de Hart; both at Notre Dame as well as within the dark catacombs of the City of Lights, he was a witness to the ritual and alchemical march of humanity into the hidden chambers of the gods' playground. It is well to heed the warning for posted in the catacombs when taking this journey:*"Arrête! C'esticil'empire de la mort,"* Stop! This is the empire of death.

Finally, there is, as we also saw, a deeper reality to this ancient view of the physical medium, to the view that existed *before* it became twisted into rituals of spiritual debt and sacrifice, and that is the view that the medium was an overflowing fecundity, a primordial androgynous "Nothing" from which all else flowed. It was a primordial "divine simplicity," an empire of life, that created a very strange set of symbols, a set of symbols we have only briefly touched upon in these pages, and whose full range of expression and implications have yet to be plumbed.

But plumbing *those* depths is a task for another book. For now, this task, this survey, and the hints of its implications, is completed.

Joseph P. Farrell
Scott D. de Hart

The Main Arch of the Great Porch of Notre Dame de Paris

BIBLIOGRAPHY:
WORKS CITED OR CONSULTED

Alouf, Michel M. *History of Baalbek*. Escondido, California. The Book Tree. 1999. ISBN 1-58509-063-8.

Balseiro, Dr. José Antonio. "Report of Dr. José Antonio Balseiro Referring to the Inspection Carried out in Isla Huemul in September 1952," Buenos Aires: National Atomic Energy Commission, 1988, Nuclear Energy: History: Argentine: 621.039(091)(82), www.ib.edu.ar/informes-huemul/reports-huemul-principal.html.

Bierhorst, John, trans. *History and Mythology of the Aztecs: The Codex Chimalpopoca*. Tucson, Arizona: The University of Arizona Press. 1992. ISBN 978-0-8165-1886-9.

Brophy, Thomas G., Ph.D., with Schoch, Robert M., Ph.D., and West, John Anthony. *The Origin Map: Discovery of a Prehistoric, Megalithic, Astrophysical Map and Sculpture of the Universe*. New York: Writers Club Press. 2002. ISBN 0-595-24122-0.

Childress, David Hatcher. *Anti-Gravity and the World Grid*. Kempton, Illinois: Adventures Unlimited Press. 2001. ISBN 0-932813-03-8.

Childress, David Hatcher. *Lost Cities of Lemuria and the Pacific*. Kempton, Illinois: Adventures Unlimited Press. 1988. ISBN 0-923813-04-6.

Childress, David Hatcher. *The Technology of the Gods: the Incredible Sciences of the Ancients*. Kempton, Illinois: Adventures Unlimited Press. 2000. ISBN 0-932813-73-9.

Collin, Rodney. *The Theory of Celestial Influence*. Sunset Valley, Texas: Mercury Publications, Inc. 2006. ISBN 0-9754079-0-2.

Bibliography

Coppens, Philip. "Ancient Atomic Wars: Best Evidence?" www.bibliotecapleyades.net/ancientatomicwar/esp_ancient_ato mic_07.htm

Coxeter, H.S.M. *Regular Polytopes*. New York: Dover Publications, Inc. 1973. ISBN 0-486-61480-8.

Devereux, Paul. *Places of Power: Measuring the Energy of Ancient Sites*. London: Blandford. 1999. ISBN 0-7137-2765-9.

Dunn, Christopher. *Lost Technologies of Ancient Egypt: Advanced Engineering in the Temples of the Pharaohs*. Rochester, Vermont: Bear & Company. 2010. ISBN 978-159143102-2.

Hancock, Graham, and Faiia, Santha. *Hevean's Mirror: Quest for the Lost Civilization*. New York: Corwn Publishers, Inc. 1998. ISBN 0-517-70811-6.

Heath, Richard. *Matrix of Creation: Sacred Geometry in the Realm of the Planets*. Rochester, Vermont: Inner Traditions. 2004. ISBN 978-80892811946.

Honoré, Pierre. *In Search of Quetzalcoatl: The Mysterious Heritage of American Civilization*. Kempton, Illinois: Adventures Unlimited Press. 2007. ISBN 978-1-931882-57-6.

Hunter, Keith M. *The Lost Age of High Knowledge: Evidence of an Advanced Civilisation Prior to Recorded History*. 2009. ISBN 978-0-9564563-0-4.

Kreisberg, Glenn, ed. *Lost Knowledge of the Ancients: A Graham Hancock Reader*. Rochester, Vermont: Bear & Company. 2010. ISBN 978-159143117-6.

Malkowski, Edward F. *Ancient Egypt 39,000 BCE: The History, Technology and Philosophy of Civilization X*. Rochester, Vermont: Bead & Company. 2010. ISBN 978-159143109-1.

Malkowski, Edward F. *The Spiritual Technology of Ancient Egypt: Sacred Science and the Mystery of Consciousness.* Rochester, Vermont: Inner Traditions. 2007. ISBN 978-159477186-6.

Marquina, Ignacio. *Arquitectura Prehispanica.* 2nd Ed. Cordova, Mexico: Institiuto Nacional de Antropoligia e Historia Secretaria de Educacion Publica, 1964 [1950].

McClain, Ernest G. *The Myth of Invariance: the Origin of the Gods, Mathematics and Music from the Rg Veda to Plato.* York Beach, Maine: Nicolas-Hays, Inc. 1984. ISBN 0-89254-012-5.

McClain, Ernest G. *The Pythagorean Plato: Prelude to the Song Itself.* York Beach, Maine: nicolas-Hays, Inc. 1984. ISBN 0-89254-010-9.

Michell, John, with Brown, Allan. *How the World Is Made: The Story of Creation According to Sacred Geometry.* Rochester, Vermont: Inner Traditions. 978-159477324-2.

Michell, John. *City of Revelation.* New York: Ballantine Books. 1973. ISBN 345-23607-6-150.

Michell, John. *Secrets of the Stones: New Revelations of Astro-archaeology and The Mystical Sciences of Antiquity.* Rochester, Vermont: Inner Traditions. ISBN 978-089281337-7.

Michell, John. *The Dimensions of Paradise: Sacred Geometry, Ancient Science, and the Heavenly Order on Earth.* Rochester, Vermont: Inner Traditions. 2008. ISBN. 978-1-59477-198-9.

Michell, John. *The Dimensions of Paradise: The Proportions and Symbolic Numbers of Ancient Cosmology.* Kempton, Illinois: Adventures Unlimited Press. 2001. ISBN 0-932813-89-5.

Michell, John. *The New View Over Atlantis.* New York: Thames and Hudson. 2001. ISBN 0-500-27312-X.

Michell, John. *The Sacred Center: The Ancient Art of Locating Sanctuaries.* Rochester, Vermont: Inner Traditions. 2009. ISBN 978-159477284-9.

Middleton-Jones, Howard, and Wilkie, James Michael. *Giza Genesis: The Best Kept Secrets.*

Munck, Carl P. *Aquarius 10: Metrology Origin, the Square Root.* Pyramid Matrix Bookstore. 2003. No ISBN.

Munck, Carl P. *Aquarius 19: Waldseemüller's Globe — 1507.* Pyramid Matrix Bookstore. 2004. No ISBN.

Munck, Carl P. *The Code 1997.* Self-published manuscript. Carl P. Munck. Pyramid Matrix Bookstore. 1996. No ISBN.

Munck, Carl P. *The Master Code Book.* Pyramid Matrix Bookstore. 2004. No ISBN.

Munck, Carl P. *Whispers from Time: The Pyramid Bible, Volume 1.* Pyramid Matrix Bookstore. 1997. No ISBN.

Munck, Carl P. *Whispers from Time: The Pyramid Bible, Volume 2,* Pyramid Matrix Bookstore. 1999. No ISBN

Pennick, Nigel. *Hitler's Secret Sciences: His Quest for the Hidden Knowledge of the Ancients.* Suffolk: Neville Spearman. 1981. No ISBN.

Petrie, W. M. Flinders. *The Pyramids and Temples of Gizeh.* Elibron Classics. 2007. ISBN 1-4212-6403-X.

Schwaller de Lubicz, R.A. *The Egyptian Miracle: An Introduction to the Wisdom of the Temple.* Rochester, Vermont: Inner Traditions International. 1985. ISBN 978-089291008-6.

Schwaller de Lubicz, R.A. *Esotericism and Symbol.* Rochester, Vermont: Inner Traditions International. 1987. ISBN 978-089281014-7.

Schwaller de Lubicz, R.A. *A Study of Numbers: A Guide to the Constant Creation of the Universe.* Rochester, Vermont: Inner Traditions International. ISBN 978-0-89281-112-0.

Schwaller de Lubcz, R.A. *The Temple In Man: Sacred Architecture and the Perfect Man.* Rochester, Vermont: Inner Traditions International. 1977. ISBN 978-0-89281-021-5.

Tedlock, Dennis, trans. *Popul Vuh: The Definitive Edition of the Mayan Book of the Dawn of Life and the Glories of Gods and Kings.* New York: Simon and Schuster. ISBN 978-0-684-81845-0.

Tompkins, Peter. *Mysteries of the Mexican Pyramids.* New York: Harper and Row. 1976. ISBN 0-06-014324-X.

Vail, Gabrielle, and Aveni, Anthony, eds. *The Madrid Codex: New Approches to Understanding an Ancient Maya Manuscript.* Boulder, Colorado: The University Press of Colorado. 2009. ISBN 978-0-87081-939-1.

Witkowski, Igor. *The Axis of the World.* Kempton, Illinois: Adventures Unlimited Press. 2009. ISBN 978-1-931882-81-1.

About the Authors

Joseph P. Farrell is from South Dakota, receiving his B.A. in Biblical Studies and Philosophy in 1979, and his M.A. in Historical Theology in 1983. He went up to Pembroke College of the University of Oxford in 1984, and received his doctorate in Patristics in 1987. Scott D. de Hart received his M.A. in Historical Theology in 1993, and went up to the University of Oxford that same year, receiving his doctorate in Theology from Wycliffe Hall, the University of Oxford, in 1997. His dissertation *Anglo-Catholics, Authority, and Ritualism* was published as an ebook in 2010. Dr. de Hart has four sons, Wesley, Calvin, Alexander, and Bennett. Dr. Farrell and Dr. de Hart met in 1993, and from that time since have been friends and colleagues in research, lecturing, and writing, discussing many of the historical, scientific, and religious subjects represented in this book. *The Grid of the Gods* is their first official collaboration. They are planning a series of future collaborative books as sequels to stand in the arch of *Genes, Giants, Monsters and Men* (Feral House), and *The Grid of the Gods.*

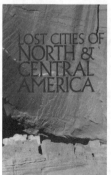

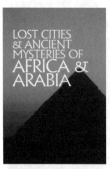

LOST CITIES & ANCIENT MYSTERIES OF AFRICA & ARABIA

by David Hatcher Childress

Childress continues his world-wide quest for lost cities and ancient mysteries. Join him as he discovers forbidden cities in the Empty Quarter of Arabia; "Atlantean" ruins in Egypt and the Kalahari desert; a mysterious, ancient empire in the Sahara; and more. This is the tale of an extraordinary life on the road: across war-torn countries, Childress searches for King Solomon's Mines, living dinosaurs, the Ark of the Covenant and the solutions to some of the fantastic mysteries of the past.

423 PAGES. 6x9 PAPERBACK. ILLUSTRATED. $14.95. CODE: AFA

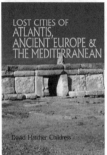

LOST CITIES OF ATLANTIS, ANCIENT EUROPE & THE MEDITERRANEAN

by David Hatcher Childress

Childress takes the reader in search of sunken cities in the Mediterranean; across the Atlas Mountains in search of Atlantean ruins; to remote islands in search of megalithic ruins; to meet living legends and secret societies. From Ireland to Turkey, Morocco to Eastern Europe, and around the remote islands of the Mediterranean and Atlantic, Childress takes the reader on an astonishing quest for mankind's past. Ancient technology, cataclysms, megalithic construction, lost civilizations and devastating wars of the past are all explored in this book.

524 PAGES. 6x9 PAPERBACK. ILLUSTRATED. $16.95. CODE: MED

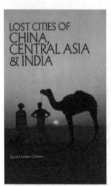

LOST CITIES OF CHINA, CENTRAL ASIA & INDIA

by David Hatcher Childress

Like a real life "Indiana Jones," maverick archaeologist David Childress takes the reader on an incredible adventure across some of the world's oldest and most remote countries in search of lost cities and ancient mysteries. Discover ancient cities in the Gobi Desert; hear fantastic tales of lost continents, vanished civilizations and secret societies bent on ruling the world; visit forgotten monasteries in forbidding snow-capped mountains with strange tunnels to mysterious subterranean cities! A unique combination of far-out exploration and practical travel advice, it will astound and delight the experienced traveler or the armchair voyager.

429 PAGES. 6x9 PAPERBACK. ILLUSTRATED. FOOTNOTES & BIBLIOGRAPHY. $14.95. CODE: CHI

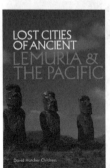

LOST CITIES OF ANCIENT LEMURIA & THE PACIFIC

by David Hatcher Childress

Was there once a continent in the Pacific? Called Lemuria or Pacifica by geologists, Mu or Pan by the mystics, there is now ample mythological, geological and archaeological evidence to "prove" that an advanced and ancient civilization once lived in the central Pacific. Maverick archaeologist and explorer David Hatcher Childress combs the Indian Ocean, Australia and the Pacific in search of the surprising truth about mankind's past. Contains photos of the underwater city on Pohnpei; explanations on how the statues were levitated around Easter Island in a clockwise vortex movement; tales of disappearing islands; Egyptians in Australia; and more.

379 PAGES. 6x9 PAPERBACK. ILLUSTRATED. FOOTNOTES & BIBLIOGRAPHY. $14.95. CODE: LEM

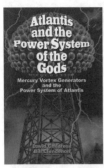

ATLANTIS & THE POWER SYSTEM OF THE GODS
by David Hatcher Childress and Bill Clendenon
Childress' fascinating analysis of Nikola Tesla's broadcast system in light of Edgar Cayce's "Terrible Crystal" and the obelisks of ancient Egypt and Ethiopia. Includes: Atlantis and its crystal power towers that broadcast energy; how these incredible power stations may still exist today; inventor Nikola Tesla's nearly identical system of power transmission; Mercury Proton Gyros and mercury vortex propulsion; more. Richly illustrated, and packed with evidence that Atlantis not only existed—it had a world-wide energy system more sophisticated than ours today.
246 PAGES. 6x9 PAPERBACK. ILLUSTRATED. $15.95. CODE: APSG

THE ANTI-GRAVITY HANDBOOK
edited by David Hatcher Childress

The new expanded compilation of material on Anti-Gravity, Free Energy, Flying Saucer Propulsion, UFOs, Suppressed Technology, NASA Cover-ups and more. Highly illustrated with patents, technical illustrations and photos. This revised and expanded edition has more material, including photos of Area 51, Nevada, the government's secret testing facility. This classic on weird science is back in a new format!
230 PAGES. 7x10 PAPERBACK. ILLUSTRATED. $16.95. CODE: AGH

ANTI–GRAVITY & THE WORLD GRID
Is the earth surrounded by an intricate electromagnetic grid network offering free energy? This compilation of material on ley lines and world power points contains chapters on the geography, mathematics, and light harmonics of the earth grid. Learn the purpose of ley lines and ancient megalithic structures located on the grid. Discover how the grid made the Philadelphia Experiment possible. Explore the Coral Castle and many other mysteries, including acoustic levitation, Tesla Shields and scalar wave weaponry. Browse through the section on anti-gravity patents, and research resources.
274 PAGES. 7x10 PAPERBACK. ILLUSTRATED. $14.95. CODE: AGW

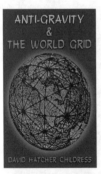

ANTI–GRAVITY & THE UNIFIED FIELD
edited by David Hatcher Childress
Is Einstein's Unified Field Theory the answer to all of our energy problems? Explored in this compilation of material is how gravity, electricity and magnetism manifest from a unified field around us. Why artificial gravity is possible; secrets of UFO propulsion; free energy; Nikola Tesla and anti-gravity airships of the 20s and 30s; flying saucers as superconducting whirls of plasma; anti-mass generators; vortex propulsion; suppressed technology; government cover-ups; gravitational pulse drive; spacecraft & more.
240 PAGES. 7x10 PAPERBACK. ILLUSTRATED. $14.95. CODE: AGU

THE TIME TRAVEL HANDBOOK
A Manual of Practical Teleportation & Time Travel
edited by David Hatcher Childress
The Time Travel Handbook takes the reader beyond the government experiments and deep into the uncharted territory of early time travellers such as Nikola Tesla and Guglielmo Marconi and their alleged time travel experiments, as well as the Wilson Brothers of EMI and their connection to the Philadelphia Experiment—the U.S. Navy's forays into invisibility, time travel, and teleportation. Childress looks into the claims of time travelling individuals, and investigates the unusual claim that the pyramids on Mars were built in the future and sent back in time. A highly visual, large format book, with patents, photos and schematics. Be the first on your block to build your own time travel device!
316 PAGES. 7x10 PAPERBACK. ILLUSTRATED. $16.95. CODE: TTH

THE SS BROTHERHOOD OF THE BELL
The Nazis' Incredible Secret Technology
by Joseph P. Farrell

In 1945, a mysterious Nazi secret weapons project code-named "The Bell" left its underground bunker in lower Silesia, along with all its project documentation, and a four-star SS general named Hans Kammler. Taken aboard a massive six engine Junkers 390 ultra-long range aircraft, "The Bell," Kammler, and all project records disappeared completely, along with the gigantic aircraft. It is thought to have flown to America or Argentina. What was "The Bell"? What new physics might the Nazis have discovered with it? How far did the Nazis go after the war to protect the advanced energy technology that it represented?

456 pages. 6x9 Paperback. Illustrated.References. $16.95.
Code: SSBB

SECRETS OF THE HOLY LANCE
The Spear of Destiny in History & Legend
by Jerry E. Smith

Secrets of the Holy Lance traces the Spear from its possession by Constantine, Rome's first Christian Caesar, to Charlemagne's claim that with it he ruled the Holy Roman Empire by Divine Right, and on through two thousand years of kings and emperors, until it came within Hitler's grasp—and beyond! Did it rest for a while in Antarctic ice? Is it now hidden in Europe, awaiting the next person to claim its awesome power? Neither debunking nor worshiping, *Secrets of the Holy Lance* seeks to pierce the veil of myth and mystery around the Spear. Mere belief that it was infused with magic by virtue of its shedding the Savior's blood has made men kings. But what if it's more? What are "the powers it serves"?

312 PAGES. 6x9 PAPERBACK. ILLUSTRATED. BIBLIOGRAPHY. $16.95.
CODE: SOHL

MAPS OF THE ANCIENT SEA KINGS
Evidence of Advanced Civilization in the Ice Age
by Charles H. Hapgood

Charles Hapgood has found the evidence in the Piri Reis Map that shows Antarctica, the Hadji Ahmed map, the Oronteus Finaeus and other amazing maps. Hapgood concluded that these maps were made from more ancient maps from the various ancient archives around the world, now lost. Not only were these unknown people more advanced in mapmaking than any people prior to the 18th century, it appears they mapped all the continents. The Americas were mapped thousands of years before Columbus. Antarctica was mapped when its coasts were free of ice!

316 PAGES. 7x10 PAPERBACK. ILLUSTRATED. BIBLIOGRAPHY & INDEX. $19.95. CODE: MASK

PATH OF THE POLE
Cataclysmic Pole Shift Geology
by Charles H. Hapgood

Maps of the Ancient Sea Kings author Hapgood's classic book *Path of the Pole* is back in print! Hapgood researched Antarctica, ancient maps and the geological record to conclude that the Earth's crust has slipped on the inner core many times in the past, changing the position of the pole. *Path of the Pole* discusses the various "pole shifts" in Earth's past, giving evidence for each one, and moves on to possible future pole shifts.

356 PAGES. 6x9 PAPERBACK. ILLUSTRATED. $16.95. CODE: POP

THE COSMIC WAR
Interplanetary Warfare, Modern Physics, and Ancient Texts
By Joseph P. Farrell

There is ample evidence across our solar system of catastrophic events. The asteroid belt may be the remains of an exploded planet! The known planets are scarred from incredible impacts, and teeter in their orbits due to causes heretofore inadequately explained. Included: The history of the Exploded Planet hypothesis, and what mechanism can actually explode a planet. The role of plasma cosmology, plasma physics and scalar physics. The ancient texts telling of such destructions: from Sumeria (Tiamat's destruction by Marduk), Egypt (Edfu and the Mars connections), Greece (Saturn's role in the War of the Titans) and the ancient Americas.
436 Pages. 6x9 Paperback. Illustrated. Bibliography. $18.95. Code: COSW

TECHNOLOGY OF THE GODS
The Incredible Sciences of the Ancients
by David Hatcher Childress

Childress looks at the technology that was allegedly used in Atlantis and the theory that the Great Pyramid of Egypt was originally a gigantic power station. He examines tales of ancient flight and the technology that it involved; how the ancients used electricity; megalithic building techniques; the use of crystal lenses and the fire from the gods; evidence of various high tech weapons in the past, including atomic weapons; ancient metallurgy and heavy machinery; the role of modern inventors such as Nikola Tesla in bringing ancient technology back into modern use; impossible artifacts; and more.
356 PAGES. 6x9 PAPERBACK. ILLUSTRATED. BIBLIOGRAPHY. $16.95. CODE: TGOD

VIMANA AIRCRAFT OF ANCIENT INDIA & ATLANTIS
by David Hatcher Childress, introduction by Ivan T. Sanderson

In this incredible volume on ancient India, authentic Indian texts such as the *Ramayana* and the *Mahabharata* are used to prove that ancient aircraft were in use more than four thousand years ago. Included in this book is the entire Fourth Century BC manuscript *Vimaanika Shastra* by the ancient author Maharishi Bharadwaaja. Also included are chapters on Atlantean technology, the incredible Rama Empire of India and the devastating wars that destroyed it.
334 PAGES. 6x9 PAPERBACK. ILLUSTRATED. $15.95. CODE: VAA

LOST CONTINENTS & THE HOLLOW EARTH
I Remember Lemuria and the Shaver Mystery
by David Hatcher Childress & Richard Shaver

Shaver's rare 1948 book *I Remember Lemuria* is reprinted in its entirety, and the book is packed with illustrations from Ray Palmer's *Amazing Stories* magazine of the 1940s. Palmer and Shaver told of tunnels running through the earth—tunnels inhabited by the Deros and Teros, humanoids from an ancient spacefaring race that had inhabited the earth, eventually going underground, hundreds of thousands of years ago. Childress discusses the famous hollow earth books and delves deep into whatever reality may be behind the stories of tunnels in the earth. Operation High Jump to Antarctica in 1947 and Admiral Byrd's bizarre statements, tunnel systems in South America and Tibet, the underground world of Agartha, the belief of UFOs coming from the South Pole, more.
344 PAGES. 6x9 PAPERBACK. ILLUSTRATED. $16.95. CODE: LCHE

THE TESLA PAPERS
Nikola Tesla on Free Energy & Wireless Transmission of Power
by Nikola Tesla, edited by David Hatcher Childress

David Hatcher Childress takes us into the incredible world of Nikola Tesla and his amazing inventions. Tesla's fantastic vision of the future, including wireless power, anti-gravity, free energy and highly advanced solar power. Also included are some of the papers, patents and material collected on Tesla at the Colorado Springs Tesla Symposiums, including papers on: •The Secret History of Wireless Transmission •Tesla and the Magnifying Transmitter •Design and Construction of a Half-Wave Tesla Coil •Electrostatics: A Key to Free Energy •Progress in Zero-Point Energy Research •Electromagnetic Energy from Antennas to Atoms •Tesla's Particle Beam Technology •Fundamental Excitatory Modes of the Earth-Ionosphere Cavity

325 PAGES. 8x10 PAPERBACK. ILLUSTRATED. $16.95. CODE: TTP

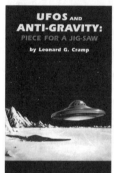

UFOS AND ANTI-GRAVITY
Piece For A Jig-Saw
by Leonard G. Cramp

Leonard G. Cramp's 1966 classic book on flying saucer propulsion and suppressed technology is a highly technical look at the UFO phenomena by a trained scientist. Cramp first introduces the idea of 'anti-gravity' and introduces us to the various theories of gravitation. He then examines the technology necessary to build a flying saucer and examines in great detail the technical aspects of such a craft. Cramp's book is a wealth of material and diagrams on flying saucers, anti-gravity, suppressed technology, G-fields and UFOs. Chapters include Crossroads of Aerodynamics, Aerodynamic Saucers, Limitations of Rocketry, Gravitation and the Ether, Gravitational Spaceships, G-Field Lift Effects, The Bi-Field Theory, VTOL and Hovercraft, Analysis of UFO photos, more.

388 PAGES. 6x9 PAPERBACK. ILLUSTRATED. $16.95. CODE: UAG

THE COSMIC MATRIX
Piece for a Jig-Saw, Part Two
by Leonard G. Cramp

Cramp examines anti-gravity effects and theorizes that this super-science used by the craft—described in detail in the book—can lift mankind into a new level of technology, transportation and understanding of the universe. The book takes a close look at gravity control, time travel, and the interlocking web of energy between all planets in our solar system with Leonard's unique technical diagrams. A fantastic voyage into the present and future!

364 PAGES. 6x9 PAPERBACK. ILLUSTRATED. BIBLIOGRAPHY. $16.00. CODE: CMX

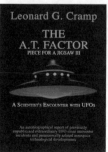

THE A.T. FACTOR
A Scientists Encounter with UFOs
by Leonard Cramp

British aerospace engineer Cramp began much of the scientific anti-gravity and UFO propulsion analysis back in 1955 with his landmark book *Space, Gravity & the Flying Saucer* (out-of-print and rare). In this final book, Cramp brings to a close his detailed and controversial study of UFOs and Anti-Gravity.

324 PAGES. 6x9 PAPERBACK. ILLUSTRATED. BIBLIOGRAPHY. INDEX. $16.95. CODE: ATF

THE FREE-ENERGY DEVICE HANDBOOK
A Compilation of Patents and Reports
by David Hatcher Childress

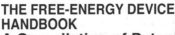

A large-format compilation of various patents, papers, descriptions and diagrams concerning free-energy devices and systems. *The Free-Energy Device Handbook* is a visual tool for experimenters and researchers into magnetic motors and other "over-unity" devices. With chapters on the Adams Motor, the Hans Coler Generator, cold fusion, superconductors, "N" machines, space-energy generators, Nikola Tesla, T. Townsend Brown, and the latest in free-energy devices. Packed with photos, technical diagrams, patents and fascinating information, this book belongs on every science shelf.

292 PAGES. 8x10 PAPERBACK. ILLUSTRATED. $16.95. CODE: FEH

LBJ AND THE CONSPIRACY TO KILL KENNEDY
By Joseph P. Farrell

Farrell says that a coalescence of interests in the military industrial complex, the CIA, and Lyndon Baines Johnson's powerful and corrupt political machine in Texas led to the events culminating in the assassination of JFK. Farrell analyzes the data as only he can, and comes to some astonishing conclusions. Chapters include: Oswald, the FBI, and the CIA: Hoover's Concern of a Second Oswald; Oswald and the Anti-Castro Cubans; The Mafia; Hoover, Johnson, and the Mob; The FBI, the Secret Service, Hoover, and Johnson; The CIA and "Murder Incorporated"; Ruby's Bizarre Behavior; The French Connection and Permindex; Big Oil; The Dead Witnesses: Jack Zangretti, Maurice Gatlin, Guy Bannister, Jr., Mary Pinchot Meyer, Rose Cheramie, Dorothy Killgallen, Congressman Hale Boggs; LBJ and the Planning of the Texas Trip; LBJ: A Study in Character, Connections, and Cabals; LBJ and the Aftermath: Accessory After the Fact; The Requirements of Coups D'État; more.

342 Pages. 6x9 Paperback. $19.95 Code: LCKK

LEY LINE & EARTH ENERGIES
An Extraordinary Journey into the Earth's
Natural Energy System
by David Cowan & Chris Arnold

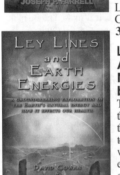

The mysterious standing stones, burial grounds and stone circles that lace Europe, the British Isles and other areas have intrigued scientists, writers, artists and travellers through the centuries. How do ley lines work? How did our ancestors use Earth energy to map their sacred sites and burial grounds? How do ghosts and poltergeists interact with Earth energy? How can Earth spirals and black spots affect our health? This exploration shows how natural forces affect our behavior, how they can be used to enhance our health and well being.

368 PAGES. 6x9 PAPERBACK. ILLUSTRATED. $18.95. CODE: LLEE

AXIS OF THE WORLD
The Search for the Oldest American Civilization
by Igor Witkowski

Witkowski's research reveals remnants of a high civilization that was able to exert its influence on almost the entire planet, and did so with full consciousness. Sites around South America show that this was not just one of the places influenced by this culture, but a place where they built their crowning achievements. Easter Island, in the southeastern Pacific, constitutes one of them. The Rongo-Rongo language that developed there points westward to the Indus Valley. Taken together, the facts presented by Witkowski provide a fresh, new proof that an antediluvian, great civilization flourished several millennia ago.

220 pages. 6x9 Paperback. Illustrated. References. $18.95. Code: AXOW

GRAVITATIONAL MANIPULATION OF DOMED CRAFT
UFO Propulsion Dynamics
by Paul E. Potter

Potter's precise and lavish illustrations allow the reader to enter directly into the realm of the advanced technological engineer and to understand, quite straightforwardly, the aliens' methods of energy manipulation: their methods of electrical power generation; how they purposely designed their craft to employ the kinds of energy dynamics that are exclusive to space (discoverable in our astrophysics) in order that their craft may generate both attractive and repulsive gravitational forces; their control over the mass-density matrix surrounding their craft enabling them to alter their physical dimensions and even manufacture their own frame of reference in respect to time. Includes a 16-page color insert.

624 pages. 7x10 Paperback. Illustrated. References. $24.00. Code: GMDC

TAPPING THE ZERO POINT ENERGY
Free Energy & Anti-Gravity in Today's Physics
by Moray B. King

King explains how free energy and anti-gravity are possible. The theories of the zero point energy maintain there are tremendous fluctuations of electrical field energy imbedded within the fabric of space. This book tells how, in the 1930s, inventor T. Henry Moray could produce a fifty kilowatt "free energy" machine; how an electrified plasma vortex creates anti-gravity; how the Pons/Fleischmann "cold fusion" experiment could produce tremendous heat without fusion; and how certain experiments might produce a gravitational anomaly.

180 PAGES. 5x8 PAPERBACK. ILLUSTRATED. $12.95. CODE: TAP

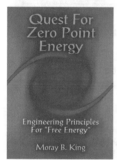

QUEST FOR ZERO-POINT ENERGY
Engineering Principles for "Free Energy"
by Moray B. King

King expands, with diagrams, on how free energy and anti-gravity are possible. The theories of zero point energy maintain there are tremendous fluctuations of electrical field energy embedded within the fabric of space. King explains the following topics: TFundamentals of a Zero-Point Energy Technology; Vacuum Energy Vortices; The Super Tube; Charge Clusters: The Basis of Zero-Point Energy Inventions; Vortex Filaments, Torsion Fields and the Zero-Point Energy; Transforming the Planet with a Zero-Point Energy Experiment; Dual Vortex Forms: The Key to a Large Zero-Point Energy Coherence. Packed with diagrams, patents and photos.

224 PAGES. 6x9 PAPERBACK. ILLUSTRATED. $14.95. CODE: QZPE

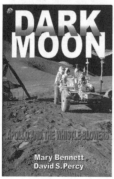

DARK MOON
Apollo and the Whistleblowers
by Mary Bennett and David Percy

Did you know a second craft was going to the Moon at the same time as Apollo 11? Do you know that potentially lethal radiation is prevalent throughout deep space? Do you know there are serious discrepancies in the account of the Apollo 13 'accident'? Did you know that 'live' color TV from the Moon was not actually live at all? Did you know that the Lunar Surface Camera had no viewfinder? Do you know that lighting was used in the Apollo photographs—yet no lighting equipment was taken to the Moon? All these questions, and more, are discussed in great detail by British researchers Bennett and Percy in Dark Moon, the definitive book (nearly 600 pages) on the possible faking of the Apollo Moon missions. Tons of NASA photos analyzed for possible deceptions.

568 PAGES. 6x9 PAPERBACK. ILLUSTRATED. BIBLIOGRAPHY. INDEX. $32.00. CODE: DMO

ROSWELL AND THE REICH
The Nazi Connection
By Joseph P. Farrell

Farrell has meticulously reviewed the best-known Roswell research from UFO-ET advocates and skeptics alike, as well as some little-known source material, and comes to a radically different scenario of what happened in Roswell, New Mexico in July 1947, and why the US military has continued to cover it up to this day. Farrell presents a fascinating case sure to disturb both ET believers and disbelievers, namely, that what crashed may have been representative of an independent postwar Nazi power—an extraterritorial Reich monitoring its old enemy, America, and the continuing development of the very technologies confiscated from Germany at the end of the War.

540 pages. 6x9 Paperback. Illustrated. $19.95. Code: RWR

SECRETS OF THE UNIFIED FIELD
The Philadelphia Experiment, the Nazi Bell, and the Discarded Theory
by Joseph P. Farrell

Farrell examines the now discarded Unified Field Theory. American and German wartime scientists and engineers determined that, while the theory was incomplete, it could nevertheless be engineered. Chapters include: The Meanings of "Torsion"; Wringing an Aluminum Can; The Mistake in Unified Field Theories and Their Discarding by Contemporary Physics; Three Routes to the Doomsday Weapon: Quantum Potential, Torsion, and Vortices; Tesla's Meeting with FDR; Arnold Sommerfeld and Electromagnetic Radar Stealth; Electromagnetic Phase Conjugations, Phase Conjugate Mirrors, and Templates; The Unified Field Theory, the Torsion Tensor, and Igor Witkowski's Idea of the Plasma Focus; tons more.

340 pages. 6x9 Paperback. Illustrated. $18.95. Code: SOUF

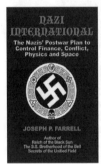

NAZI INTERNATIONAL
The Nazi's Postwar Plan to Control Finance, Conflict, Physics and Space
by Joseph P. Farrell

Beginning with prewar corporate partnerships in the USA, including some with the Bush family, he moves on to the surrender of Nazi Germany, and evacuation plans of the Germans. He then covers the vast, and still-little-known recreation of Nazi Germany in South America with help of Juan Peron, I.G. Farben and Martin Bormann. Farrell then covers Nazi Germany's penetration of the Muslim world including Wilhelm Voss and Otto Skorzeny in Gamel Abdul Nasser's Egypt before moving on to the development and control of new energy technologies including the Bariloche Fusion Project, Dr. Philo Farnsworth's Plasmator, and the work of Dr. Nikolai Kozyrev. Finally, Farrell discusses the Nazi desire to control space, and examines their connection with NASA, the esoteric meaning of NASA Mission Patches.

412 pages. 6x9 Paperback. Illustrated. $19.95. Code: NZIN

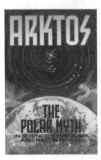

ARKTOS
The Polar Myth in Science, Symbolism & Nazi Survival
by Joscelyn Godwin

Explored are the many tales of an ancient race said to have lived in the Arctic regions, such as Thule and Hyperborea. Progressing onward, he looks at modern polar legends: including the survival of Hitler, German bases in Antarctica, UFOs, the hollow earth, and the hidden kingdoms of Agartha and Shambala. Chapters include: Prologue in Hyperborea; The Golden Age; The Northern Lights; The Arctic Homeland; The Aryan Myth; The Thule Society; The Black Order; The Hidden Lands; Agartha and the Polaires; Shambhala; The Hole at the Pole; Antarctica; more.

220 Pages. 6x9 Paperback. Illustrated. Bib. Index. $16.95. Code: ARK

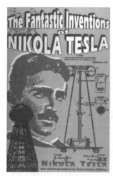

THE FANTASTIC INVENTIONS OF NIKOLA TESLA
by Nikola Tesla with David Hatcher Childress

This book is a readable compendium of patents, diagrams, photos and explanations of the many incredible inventions of the originator of the modern era of electrification. In Tesla's own words are such topics as wireless transmission of power, death rays, and radio-controlled airships. In addition, rare material on a secret city built at a remote jungle site in South America by one of Tesla's students, Guglielmo Marconi. Marconi's secret group claims to have built flying saucers in the 1940s and to have gone to Mars in the early 1950s! Incredible photos of these Tesla craft are included. •His plan to transmit free electricity into the atmosphere. •How electrical devices would work using only small antennas. •Why unlimited power could be utilized anywhere on earth.

342 PAGES. 6x9 PAPERBACK. ILLUSTRATED. $16.95. CODE: FINT

PRODIGAL GENIUS
The Life of Nikola Tesla
by John J. O'Neill

This special edition of O'Neill's book has many rare photographs of Tesla and his most advanced inventions. Tesla's eccentric personality gives his life story a strange romantic quality. He made his first million before he was forty, yet gave up his royalties in a gesture of friendship, and died almost in poverty. Tesla could see an invention in 3-D, from every angle, within his mind, before it was built; how he refused to accept the Nobel Prize; his friendships with Mark Twain, George Westinghouse and competition with Thomas Edison. Tesla is revealed as a figure of genius whose influence on the world reaches into the far future. Deluxe, illustrated edition.

408 pages. 6x9 Paperback. Illustrated. $18.95. Code: PRG

HAARP
The Ultimate Weapon of the Conspiracy
by Jerry Smith

The HAARP project in Alaska is one of the most controversial projects ever undertaken by the U.S. Government. At at worst, HAARP could be the most dangerous device ever created, a futuristic technology that is everything from super-beam weapon to world-wide mind control device. Topics include Over-the-Horizon Radar and HAARP, Mind Control, ELF and HAARP, The Telsa Connection, The Russian Woodpecker, GWEN & HAARP, Earth Penetrating Tomography, Weather Modification, Secret Science of the Conspiracy, more. Includes the complete 1987 Eastlund patent for his pulsed super-weapon that he claims was stolen by the HAARP Project.

256 pages. 6x9 Paperback. Illustrated. Bib. $14.95. Code: HARP

WEATHER WARFARE
The Military's Plan to Draft Mother Nature
by Jerry E. Smith

Weather modification in the form of cloud seeding to increase snow packs in the Sierras or suppress hail over Kansas is now an everyday affair. Underground nuclear tests in Nevada have set off earthquakes. A Russian company has been offering to sell typhoons (hurricanes) on demand since the 1990s. Scientists have been searching for ways to move hurricanes for over fifty years. In the same amount of time we went from the Wright Brothers to Neil Armstrong. Hundreds of environmental and weather modifying technologies have been patented in the United States alone – and hundreds more are being developed in civilian, academic, military and quasi-military laboratories around the world *at this moment!* Numerous ongoing military programs do inject aerosols at high altitude for communications and surveillance operations.

304 Pages. 6x9 Paperback. Illustrated. Bib. $18.95. Code: WWAR

ORDER FORM

**10% Discount
When You Order
3 or More Items!**

One Adventure Place
P.O. Box 74
Kempton, Illinois 60946
United States of America
Tel.: 815-253-6390 • Fax: 815-253-6300
Email: auphq@frontiernet.net
http://www.adventuresunlimitedpress.com

ORDERING INSTRUCTIONS

✓ Remit by USD$ Check, Money Order or Credit Card

✓ Visa, Master Card, Discover & AmEx Accepted

✓ Paypal Payments Can Be Made To:

    info@wexclub.com

✓ Prices May Change Without Notice

✓ 10% Discount for 3 or more Items

SHIPPING CHARGES

United States

✓ Postal Book Rate { $4.00 First Item
    50¢ Each Additional Item

✓ POSTAL BOOK RATE Cannot Be Tracked!

✓ Priority Mail { $5.00 First Item
    $2.00 Each Additional Item

✓ UPS { $6.00 First Item
    $1.50 Each Additional Item

    NOTE: UPS Delivery Available to Mainland USA Only

Canada

✓ Postal Air Mail { $10.00 First Item
    $2.50 Each Additional Item

✓ Personal Checks or Bank Drafts MUST BE

    US$ and Drawn on a US Bank

✓ Canadian Postal Money Orders OK

✓ Payment MUST BE US$

All Other Countries

✓ Sorry, No Surface Delivery!

✓ Postal Air Mail { $16.00 First Item
    $6.00 Each Additional Item

✓ Checks and Money Orders MUST BE US$
    and Drawn on a US Bank or branch.

✓ Paypal Payments Can Be Made in US$ To:
    info@wexclub.com

SPECIAL NOTES

✓ RETAILERS: Standard Discounts Available

✓ BACKORDERS: We Backorder all Out-of-
    Stock Items Unless Otherwise Requested

✓ PRO FORMA INVOICES: Available on Request

ORDER ONLINE AT: www.adventuresunlimitedpress.com

Please check: ✓

☐ This is my first order   ☐ I have ordered before

Name

Address

City

State/Province   Postal Code

Country

Phone day   Evening

Fax   Email

Item Code	Item Description	Qty	Total

Please check: ✓

    Subtotal ▶

    Less Discount-10% for 3 or more items ▶

☐ Postal-Surface   Balance ▶

☐ Postal-Air Mail   Illinois Residents 6.25% Sales Tax ▶
    (Priority in USA)   Previous Credit ▶

☐ UPS   Shipping ▶

    (Mainland USA only) Total (check/MO in USD$ only) ▶

☐ Visa/MasterCard/Discover/American Express

Card Number

Expiration Date

10% Discount When You Order 3 or More Items!